What people are saying about *Good Credit is Sexy* and the Credit Info Center website

Finally, a book that cuts through the credit fog! Kristy's straightforward, easy to understand approach to improving and protecting the credit you deserve is a *must have* in every household. -- *Don Upton*

I can't thank you enough for the information you have provided. Thanks to you, my credit is in better shape than I thought possible. -- *Eric Swanson*

Between the book and the website, I honestly have to say, "Kristy has changed my life." Words can't even begin to describe how wonderful it feels to have my credit back in order. I'm extremely grateful to Kristy for sharing her knowledge of credit, and for making my dreams a reality. -- *Kim Morrow*

Reading this book has changed my life. It taught me to treat your credit as you do your children, with respect and patience. I will be moving into my home soon and opening a business: helping others in Michigan to fix their credit and buy a home of their own, too! Thank you Kristy, my life has changed in so many ways. I will forever be grateful to you for getting this information out to us. -- *Dawn Florinchi*

Creditinfocenter.com has been a lifesaver for my family and myself. The information I learned from this site has been indispensable. Everyone should know his or her rights and this site teaches you. -- *Karen L. Perry*

Good Credit is Sexy has been a life altering experience for me, changing my entire thinking from a helpless victim to an empowered credit repair champion! -- *Yvonne Evans*

I first took a look at credit laws when I couldn't get a loan for a car because of bad credit bureau reports. By the time I educated myself properly on the law, that car had been paid for in full by those same bureaus and collection agencies. – *Chance Daniels, a reader who settled out of court with Equifax for $24,000*

Good Credit is
Sexy

HOW TO MAKE YOUR CREDIT AS ATTRACTIVE AS POSSIBLE

Second Edition

from the
CREDIT INFO CENTER
http://www.creditinfocenter.com

Published by:
   Techartist Publishing
   7904 East Chaparral Road
   Suite 110-604
   Scottsdale, Arizona 85250
   http://www.web-nation.com
   877-WE-DO-WEB (877-933-6932)

Cover design by:
   John Murdock
   http://www.murdockclark.com

ISBN 0-9712563-0-6

First Edition published October 2001
Second Edition published February 2004
Second Edition 2nd printing with revisions April 2005

Manufactured in the United States of America

This book contains material which has been reprinted with permission from *The Poor Man's Class Action Lawsuit to Use Against Your Creditors and the Credit Bureaus* © Copyright 2002, Kristy Welsh, ISBN 0-9712563-2-2 and *How to Settle Your Debts Yourself* © Copyright 2002, Kristy Welsh, ISBN 0-9712563-3-0.

To purchase *The Poor Man's Class Action Lawsuit to Use Against Your Creditors and the Credit Bureaus, How to Settle Your Debts Yourself,* or additional copies of *Good Credit is Sexy*, call 877-933-6932 or visit www.creditinfocenter.com.

For Reni:

My world is just not the same without you.

Disclaimer

The information contained in this book is true to the best of my understanding at the date of publication, but, alas, I am only human. I am not an attorney, a banker, a collection agency, or a credit card issuer. I seek to distribute useful information to the public in the most complete and accessible manner possible. But a word to the wise: Before you rely on any of the information here, check it out for yourself. Information varies around the country and changes over time.

This text relates to laws and customs in the United States and should not be taken as a guide to consumer credit in other nations. Also, it concerns itself primarily with federal law rather than state laws, which vary widely. But in every state you have at least the protections derived from federal laws that are noted here. I am always interested in state and local comparisons, but by design have omitted most state information from this book. It's long enough already!

In some cases, this book gives out website addresses as sources of supplemental information. Please be aware that these addresses may have changed by the time you read this book. We have no control over this, but we'll apologize for the inconvenience anyway!

Not that I would shamelessly plug my own website in this book (I am above that, really), but for the latest and greatest information about credit matters refer to http://www.creditinfocenter.com. It's free.

Acknowledgements

This book would be much less comprehensive if not for valuable input from readers and shared knowledge from the creditinfocenter.com discussion board. Over 15,000 emails have helped to enhance and expand this Second Edition. Two critical readers, editors John Dahlberg and Maureen Rooney, deserve credit for bringing it all together.

And in all fairness, I should also acknowledge the importance of one salesman in my past: the guy who recruited me to the mortgage world. If not for him, I wouldn't know the ins and outs of the loan process, the less-than-rosy world of the loan officer, or how to recognize and fix imperfect credit. Thank you.

CONTENTS

INTRODUCTION

Good credit is sexy.

"That's a bold statement," you may be thinking.

Perhaps the better statement would be, "Bad credit is a *major* turnoff." Don't believe it? Try these scenarios on for size:

SCENARIO 1

You have just finished a romantic dinner at home with that special lady you're desperately trying to impress. Everything is going great. You're just settling in to a comfortable cuddle on the couch when the phone rings.

You ignore it, but the answering machine doesn't and the volume is blasting: "Hello, Mr. X, this is Bob calling on behalf of Huge Risk Credit Services. Your account is seriously past due. The last time we spoke, you said I could expect payment two weeks ago..."

You lunge for the machine, but it's too late. Your date suddenly has a stomachache and is heading toward the door as Bob's voice fades.

SCENARIO 2

You're on a different romantic date (your last date still has her stomachache) at the latest chi-chi restaurant. This date is so impressed by you and your good taste that she practically coos. The bill arrives. You pull your triple platinum credit card smoothly from your wallet when the waiter arrives with the tab. The waiter bows tersely and retreats.

He returns momentarily with a snide smile. "Excuse me, Monsieur," he purrs a bit too politely, "but I have been told to confiscate your credit card. Do you have *another* form of payment?"

Your face turns purple as you sputter something about the profusion of computer errors these days and pull out another, less impressive, card. To your horror, it also is turned down. Avoiding further embarrassment, your date pulls her credit card from her purse and pays, then excuses herself to the ladies room. You watch the bathroom door, but she has slipped out the back window.

SCENARIO 3

You and the man of your dreams are engaged and have decided to purchase your dream home together. You gaze into each other's eyes so intently that the loan officer filling out your mortgage application feels like an intruder. "I'll be back," he says, "I'm going to go pull your credit files."

Returning ten minutes later, the loan officer seems confused. "Are you sure you've given me the right information, Ms. X? Your credit file seems to have a lot of problems."

Your fiancé is stunned. The interview is called to an abrupt end. The ride home is long and silent. Mr. Perfect is rethinking the situation.

Good credit is decidedly sexy. Scientific studies may prove it, but who needs proof? Good credit allows you to purchase that fabulous home, car, clothing, vacation, sporting event tickets—all the things that shout, "Sex appeal!"

Feeling good about your financial situation helps you feel good about yourself. Healthy finances ward off stress about paying the bills or being able to buy that new house. Stress not only kills; it can negatively impact your eating habits. If you start binging on junk food or drinking too much, your sexiness takes a serious dive. Financial worries can also hamper your ability to shine at work, costing you raises which could go a long way toward pampering your sexy self or your alluring loved one.

But I have great news. Good credit, a healthy financial situation, and sexiness are in your future.

One final comment before you read on: There is a lot of information in this book, and some of the most valuable information begins after the chapters end. Take a moment to see what's there before you start working with your creditors. Read and heed *The Importance of Documentation*, and document everything—every conversation, correspondence, every step you take—along the way. The importance of your documentation will prove itself in time, I promise.

SECTION I:
THE BASICS OF CREDIT

CHAPTER 1: HOW DOES CREDIT AFFECT YOU?

Joanne's Story

Joanne is a 45-year-old former homemaker who is recently divorced after 22 years of marriage. She and her ex-husband had always lived in apartments and paid cash for most of their belongings, including all of their cars, clothes, furniture, and supplies for their two children. Her ex, Bob, had always handled the money and Joanne has never even written out a check in her life. Joanne finds a full-time job in a daycare center to supplement her small alimony payments.

One of her girlfriends, Cindy, invites Joanne to a party where "There will be lots of handsome men." Excited that life just might get interesting again, Joanne's hopes are dashed as she stands before her closet. She hasn't bought a new outfit in five years, and money is tighter than last year's jeans. She goes clothes shopping at Today's Trends Clothing, where she has shopped for years. She selects three outfits, but has no cash and no credit card since the divorce. Confidently, she applies for the store's credit card, but is astonished when she is turned down. Listing off the credit cards she had with her ex only seems to bore the clerk.

Joanne has no credit in her own name.

Everyone Has a Credit History/Rating

Yes, everyone has one of these, even if you have never had a credit card or a loan. Your credit history is compiled in reports made by credit bureaus and provided to lenders, landlords, and utility companies at their request.

When you apply for a credit card, mortgage, or other loan, the fine print on the application gives the lender permission to check your credit history. The lender usually requests a credit report from one of the "Big Three" credit bureaus. In theory, the bureaus merely report the raw data of your credit history and don't assign you any kind of "credit rating." In reality though, credit companies do provide a credit rating in the form of a credit score. The lender looks at your credit score and decides whether to grant you the credit you are requesting. Of course, lenders also look at your total outstanding debts, your minimum monthly payments, even your credit limits to see how far into debt you could go if you max out your existing accounts. Primarily, though, they are concerned with your record of delinquencies, accounts paid unsatisfactorily, and anything else that suggests how much of a credit risk you might be, all of which is used to calculate your credit score.

Like Joanne, you may be surprised to know that part of what figures into your credit rating is a *lack* of credit history. If you have no credit history, you have no track record of payment and your rating is very low. Believe it or not, you're a bit of a credit risk.

Three Big Filing Cabinets—The Credit Bureaus

Most people think that credit bureaus are branches of the government. In actuality, credit bureaus are for-profit corporations that provide a service: storing and maintaining credit records. The three major bureaus, or Credit Reporting Agencies, (CRAs) are:

✧ Experian (formally TRW);
✧ Equifax; and
✧ TransUnion.

There also are local credit bureaus and reporting agencies, although their databases are not as extensive as those of the "Big Three." The local bureaus are, however, worth noting because they are used by some who may judge your credit worthiness. An example of a local agency is a Residential Mortgage Credit Reporting (RMCR) firm that provides a bureau-merged credit report. In addition, all of the "Big Three" send your disputes to what are known as "third party databases", to determine their validity. More about these in Chapter 25.

To report information to the credit bureaus, creditors must fill out an application and pay a fee to each bureau to which they wish to belong. Membership is completely voluntary. No creditor *has* to report anything to any bureau. The more "thrifty" creditors may expend the time, trouble, and money to report to only one credit bureau. Given the fact that each bureau has its own separate, private database and, because the credit bureaus generally don't pass information back and forth to each other, you actually may have up to three divergent credit histories.

So who subscribes to the credit bureaus for their services? Banks, finance companies, department stores, taxing authorities, landlords, and other "credit grantors" all subscribe to the CRAs. Once a creditor subscribes to a CRA's services, the creditor is allowed to report information on your account history. This information is stored by the CRA in a national database, and contains the following:

✧ Your payment history;
✧ Where you work and your employment history;
✧ Your age;
✧ Whether or not you've been divorced;

- ✧ Your address history; and
- ✧ In some cases, your salary.

Credit bureaus also search public records for:

- ✧ Bankruptcy information from the federal government; and
- ✧ Judgment and tax lien information from courts (district, circuit, justice, municipal, superior, magistrate, probate, and state), town clerks, and registers of deeds.

Just how current is the public records information? From Experian's website:

> *The currentness of data collected from courthouses depends on the size and/or location of each court. Data obtained from courthouses serving large metropolitan areas is updated frequently. In most cases, bankruptcies are collected on a daily basis. Almost all other courthouse data is collected monthly or weekly, with some information (usually from courthouses serving less-populated areas) collected quarterly.*

Experian also states that once it receives information, that information is added to its database within 24 hours. Records on tax liens, judgments, and bankruptcies are available nationwide.

Who Regulates the Credit Reporting Agencies (CRAs)?

CRAs are governed by the U.S. Fair Credit Reporting Act (FCRA) of 1971. The FCRA was amended in 1997, and again in December 2003, and includes protections for consumers by increasing the responsibility of credit bureaus to investigate consumer disputes. The Federal Trade Commission, an organization responsible for enforcing federal credit laws, also governs credit bureaus.

The complete FCRA is included in Appendix 1.

CHAPTER 2: HOW TO BUILD CREDIT IF YOU DON'T HAVE ANY

Steve's Story

Steve has a lifestyle most people would dream about. He owns and runs a successful electronic equipment repair and supply business out of his home. His business associates are willing to extend Steve unofficial credit for equipment he buys in bulk. He travels, owns lots of toys (boats, cars, expensive stereo equipment), and has paid cash for them all. Even his home is free and clear—this man has no debts. Now Steve is getting married, but his fiancée tells him there is no way she will move into his house with all of his equipment scattered throughout the living room and garage. Steve comes up with a plan to expand his business and lease or purchase a small warehouse to store his extensive inventory.

Steve is surprised and angry to discover that banks won't give him even a small loan to cover the minimal costs of moving his business. When he finally finds a small lending institution willing to help him out, he is furious when they insist on attaching his home to the loan and charging him a rate that is 5% above the rates the banks were advertising. Why? Although this man has always paid his business associates on time, and has absolutely no debt, Steve has no credit track record.

Believe it or not, Steve's story is not unusual. Some people may not have ever bothered to get credit after an initial attempt that was unsuccessful and embarrassing. It used to be fine to pay for everything with cash and live debt free. There's nothing wrong with this, and you may even sleep better at night. But the times, they are a changing. Nowadays, almost everything requires some kind of credit card—like renting a car, purchasing things over the phone or the Internet, and sometimes even writing a check.

No Credit is the Same as Bad Credit

As I mentioned in the last chapter, creditors regard a lack of credit history to be the same as a poor credit history, especially if you are not a young person. Why? Creditors want to see a history of how you handle debts. If there is no information upon which to judge you, you are deemed a risk. Not fair, but true.

Ironically, if you are a college student (even though you may not have a job), the creditors may be falling all over themselves to offer you credit because it is reasonable to expect that you haven't had time to build a credit history—just like having no dating history because you are still too young to date. Creditors want to hook you while you're in your formative years. It's true. If you are over 25, though, creditors are asking themselves: Why hasn't this person gotten credit? It's like the 50-year-old who has never married—people wonder what gives.

Situations Ripe for Building Credit

You go to the gym to build up your body and you feel sexier. You like the way you look in the mirror, and you develop a certain confident swagger. People of the opposite sex find you more appealing. It's the same with creditors—they love to see the power of your "credit muscles" (your repayment history). But sometimes, as in the following instances, you have not yet built your credit muscles:

- ✧ You're young and haven't used any credit yet; or
- ✧ Your old credit card spending habits got you into a lot of trouble and you cut up all your cards years ago. To avoid repeating your past mistakes, you pay for everything in cash and, consequently, your credit report is completely empty; or
- ✧ You think that debt is bad and have always paid for everything with cash. Many people think—erroneously—that being debt-free is a positive trait valued by lenders; or
- ✧ You're just out of a bankruptcy and you need to take those baby steps to rebuild your credit.

A certain amount of forgiveness is granted in these situations, but not forever. There must be some evidence of credit building. If you're a ninety-pound weakling all your life—credit wise—you'll have difficulty attracting that special someone willing to trust you with a loan.

Before You Apply Yourself...

When you want to look your very best, what do you do? You work out, start taking showers every day, even cleaning behind your ears and pulling up your socks, right? A little cologne, combing the hair. You don't leave the house until you have primped at least a little bit. Equally, you must first prep your credit report before using it to attract creditors.

Now I'm not talking about handing in a credit application laced with Old Spice, or sealed with a big pucker of lipstick; I'm talking about looking at your credit report just like you'd have a look in the mirror before stepping out of the house. Even if you have never gotten a credit card or a loan, it doesn't mean that your credit report may not have mistakes on it. Someone else's credit may have been placed erroneously on your credit report, for example. You must make sure that your credit report is as attractive as you can get it. Begin by obtaining a copy of your credit report and examining it thoroughly. Follow the guidelines in Chapter 4 for analyzing your credit report and Chapter 25 for getting rid of blemishes (errors or derogatory marks), then use Chapter 26 to lose that credit "spare tire" (excessive inquiries). Having your report in tip-top shape will help you immensely when you apply for new credit. Once your report looks almost as good as new, it is time to start adding positive credit.

Keep in mind, however, that building or re-building a credit report is not a quick-fix situation. It generally takes a year or two to complete. Don't fall for promises of a "glowing report in a matter of weeks" from so-called credit repair agencies. It just doesn't happen that way any more than you can flatten your stomach overnight. There are, however, a few things you can do to jumpstart the process.

Four Ways to Add Positive Credit to Your Credit Report

1. PIGGYBACK ON A FRIEND

If you know someone (a friend or parent) who has good credit, you can "borrow" that person's good credit listings. This friend must have credit card(s) and must trust you enough to allow you to become a "co-signer" on his card(s). Have your friend call the credit card company and request that you be placed on his card as co-signer. A copy of the card will be sent to you, but you never have to use it. (You can simply return it to your friend.) Your credit file should soon show an open account with all of the positive history that your friend has created over the years from that credit card. Remember, however, that when a new credit grantor reviews your file, he may insist that the balance on the card appear on your debt-to-income ratio balance sheet. So make certain that your friend doesn't have excessive debt, although this shouldn't disqualify you for credit if your income is sufficient and you don't have an excess of debt on your file.

2. GET A SECURED CREDIT CARD

Ask your local bank if it offers secured cards. Many national banks are starting to offer this service. Your past credit is less important when applying for a secured card, as you will be depositing funds into the bank to secure the credit line on the card. You can get this card even if you still have bad credit on your credit file. By putting $500 into a savings account, you will be allowed to charge up to $500 on the card. Some banks may give you a credit line that is two to three times the amount of your secured deposit.

Make sure that any credit card you get is not listed as a secured card to the credit bureaus, and that it also lists your credit limit. If your card does not have these characteristics, you could actually be damaging your credit by getting one.

3. SEEK EASY CREDIT

Many stores extend credit without tremendous regard for the credit standing of the applicant. These stores usually can be found in industries with small products or traditionally high mark-ups. Here is a list of creditors who often will extend credit to those without much credit history:

✧ Jewelry stores;
✧ Furniture stores;
✧ Tire stores;
✧ Appliance stores;
✧ Gas companies;
✧ Easy credit auto dealerships; and
✧ Credit Unions.

Make sure that these companies report to the credit bureaus, as not all of them do.

4. KEEP YOUR ACCOUNTS ACTIVE

Once you've successfully received new lines of credit, it is important to have activity on them each month. I don't suggest that you pile up large debt—maybe maintain a balance of $50 dollars or so. Pay the *minimum* when the bill arrives even though it will cost you a little in interest charges. **And pay it on time**. This is what future loan officers and other creditors want to see. (Inactive accounts with a zero balance aren't displaying a tendency to handle existing debts.)

You need to display at least one year of positive credit habits to be taken seriously, especially by a mortgage company. Start now, or you will always be a year or two from a good credit standing.

Credit Lines That Won't Help

There are certain forms of "debt" that won't help you build or re-establish your credit. These include:

✧ **Private loans from a relative or friend**. Private individuals are not qualified to report to the credit bureaus.
✧ **Loans for cars from small car lots**. If you are buying a car, your loan should be through a banking institution so that your timely payments will be reported. If you pay cash monthly to an office or individual, it will never be reported to the bureaus.
✧ **Rent**. Most apartment rental agencies do not have the time or money to report payments.
✧ **Utility payments**. Utility payments generally are not reported to the credit bureaus and are basically useless as a form of credit.

SECTION II:
YOUR CREDIT REPORT

CHAPTER 3: OBTAINING YOUR CREDIT REPORT

Susan's Story

After dating for a year, Susan and her boyfriend are considering moving in together. Her boyfriend, Greg, feels Susan has way too many credit cards and is concerned about her ability to afford the sumptuous apartment they want to rent together. Searching for answers, Susan sees an enticing advertisement on the Internet for a low-interest credit card that promotes the possibility of transferring the balances of her high-interest credit cards to this nifty new card. By transferring the card balances, Susan figures she will save $500 a month.

She applies online and, sure enough, within a week receives a letter from the credit card company. Ripping it open, she is surprised to find that she has been turned down for credit, especially since she considers herself to have excellent credit. Why has she been turned down? The letter informs her that she has too much available credit, making her a credit risk. Susan gets a copy of her credit report and, to her horror, discovers she not only has the nine accounts she uses regularly, but 20 other open credit card accounts she thought she had closed.

Why Would You Want to Obtain Your Credit Report?

Just like your body, to keep your credit as alluring as possible, you need to have annual check ups. Proactive sleuthing and repair of your credit history can save you a lot of headaches. If you know that you will be applying for a loan, employment, or an apartment, try to find out in advance which credit bureau your lender will be using. Then you can order just that one bureau's report, rather than buying all three of them, to see if your credit is attractive enough for a loan to be granted and to prevent unnecessary "inquiries" on your report. (See Chapter 26 for more information on inquiries.)

The Fair Credit Reporting Act (FCRA) was amended via the Fair and Accurate Credit Transactions Act (FACTA) and signed into law in December 2003. (A complete copy of the amended FCRA is included in Appendix 1.) The amendment allows everyone one free credit report a year from each of the three major credit bureaus—Equifax, Experian and TransUnion. Although the law went into effect January 1, 2004, it allowed the Federal Trade Commission six months to develop regulations for distributing free credit reports, and the credit bureaus had another six months to comply with the new rules. Access to free credit reports is being rolled out incrementally by region. The first free credit reports were distributed in the west in December of 2004. The last area of the country to have access to free credit reports is the east coast, which will come online in September of 2005. **Important to note:** even with the new law in effect, you will still have to pay (about $5.95) if you want to receive your credit score. To access your free credit report, the FTC set up the website annualcreditreport.com. Just follow the instructions and you can order your credit report from all three bureaus.

If you want more than one copy in a year's time, you must pay for it. You can obtain a copy of your credit report (for a small fee) by calling or writing to the credit bureau(s), or obtaining them online. Some states regulate the fees which can be charged for credit reports; some allow more than one free report a year.

TABLE 1—CREDIT BUREAU REPORT FEES (IF YOU'VE ALREADY RECEIVED YOUR FREE ANNUAL REPORT)

	Experian	**Equifax**	**TransUnion**
CO	$8.00	$8.00	$8.00
CT	$7.50 (plus $.45 tax)	$7.50	$7.50
GA	Free 2nd Report, $9.50 thereafter	Free 2nd Report, $9.50 thereafter	Free 2nd Report, $9.50 thereafter
HI	$9.50 (plus $.32 tax)	$9.50	$9.50
IL	$9.50 (plus $.48 tax for Chicago residents)	$9.50	$9.50
MA	$8.00	$8.00	$8.00
MD	$5.00	$5.00	$5.00
ME	$5.00	$5.00	$5.00
NJ	$8.00	$8.00	$8.00
NM	$9.50 (plus $.46 tax)	$9.50	$9.50
NY	$9.50 (plus $.66 tax)	$9.50	$9.50
PA	$9.50 (plus $.56 tax)	$9.50	$9.50
SC	$9.50 (plus $.32 tax)	$9.50	$9.50
SD	$9.50 (plus $.32 tax)	$9.50	$9.50
TX	$9.50 (plus $.66 tax)	$9.50	$9.50
DC	$9.50 (plus $.46 tax)	$9.50	$9.50
VT	$7.50	$7.50	$7.50
WV	$9.50 (plus $.48 tax)	$9.50	$9.50
Other States	$9.50	$9.50	$9.50

Note: Costs are subject to change without notice. Please see each credit bureau's website for more details.

Situations which entitle you to a free credit report

Okay, so you've already gotten your annual free report and you want to see your credit report again within the year. There are still some ways to get one free. If you are ever turned down for anything based (at least in part) on your credit report, the lender is required by law to tell you why you were turned down and give you the name and address of the credit bureau from which it pulled your credit information. This is true even if the credit report was only one factor in the decision. The same law instantly entitles you to receive a FREE copy of your credit report if you request it within 60 days after you were turned down. (It doesn't matter whether you have already received other free reports.)

Send a copy of your turndown letter to all three bureaus in question and ask for a free copy of your credit report. When you write to the credit bureau, state that you were denied credit, insurance, or employment based on your credit report from the bureau and that you are requesting a copy of it. Be specific about the name of the company denying you credit and the date on which it occurred. Hey, it's a $27 value, so don't look a gift horse in the mouth.

In addition to being turned down for credit, you are entitled to a free credit report:
- If you were charged higher rates and fees or deposits based on a credit report issued by a credit bureau, you have the right to get a free copy from that bureau
- If you certify in writing that either you are unemployed and plan to seek employment in the next 60 days
- If you are on welfare
- If you write to say you were a victim of fraud
- If you have experienced a negative change in your credit limit

Remember, these credit reports will not contain a credit score.

Contact Information for the Three Bureaus

REQUESTING YOUR REPORT VIA THE TELEPHONE

This information changes all of the time, so be sure to check before you call. You can call toll-free information at 800-555-1212 to check the number.

Experian: Call 888-397-3742. Fax: 972-390-3809. The voicemail system is available in Spanish or English. It will let you record your request if you were turned down for credit, employment, or insurance. If you weren't recently denied credit, it will quote a price and tell you how to write for a copy of your report.

Equifax: Call 888-873-5392. Fax: 888-664-4535 or 888-729-0083. The toll-free number has a voicemail system available in Spanish or English. It will let you record your request if you were turned down for credit, employment, or insurance.

TransUnion: Call 800-888-4213. Fax: 714-447-603 or 714-830-2449. The service is a recorded message available 24 hours a day. It asks you a few questions (available in English or Spanish) and your report is mailed within 72 hours via U.S. Postal Service (so allow 5 - 7 days for delivery). If you are faxing to TransUnion, please put "Attention: Consumer Relations" on the cover sheet.

Caution: If your phone request gets lost, you'll have to write anyway. If your letter is later than 60 days after you were denied credit, employment, or insurance, you might have to pay for the report. Equifax also requests that you follow up your phone order with a written request containing proof of address, your driver's license, name, date of birth, and Social Security Number.

REQUESTING YOUR REPORT VIA THE MAIL

Experian
P.O. Box 2002
Allen, TX 75013

Equifax
PO Box 105851
Atlanta, GA 30348

TransUnion
PO Box 1000
Chester PA 19022

REQUESTING YOUR REPORT VIA THE WORLD WIDE WEB

http://www.Experian.com
http://www.Equifax.com
http://www.TransUnion.com

Merged Credit Reports

You have probably seen advertisements for '3-in-1' credit reports. There are some credit reporting companies, not related to the credit bureaus, who have the ability to pull all the information from Equifax, Experian and TransUnion and put it into one report. Some people like this format, others don't as it can be confusing. Generally, though, the cost is more than if you had ordered the credit reports separately.

Companies who sell these merged credit reports do not have the ability to handle credit disputes nor correct any information, they merely repackage information from the credit bureaus into (what these companies say is) a more easily read format.

Other Credit Bureaus

Just when you thought your dance card was already full with the credit reporting agencies already mentioned, along comes a little bird to whisper to you that there's more to the credit bureaus than meets the eye. There are many other credit bureaus, both local companies handling local business for the "Big Three" and credit bureaus which the "Big Three" themselves use to verify information during credit disputes from consumers.

Why do you care about all these other bureaus? Let's say you had your eye on a hot dating prospect, but this person, unknown to you, has heard some unpleasant things about you that weren't true. It's hard to defend yourself when you don't know what's being said against you, isn't it? You may have heard of some of the following credit bureaus, especially Choicepoint and LexisNexis, in the light of the recent identity theft scandals when hackers were able to steal numerous personal information files. The rest are not as well known. You need to pull your credit report and keep the record straight! As per the FACT Act, you are allowed one free copy of your personal information file a year from any company which holds information [per FCRA §603(d)(1)] "bearing on a consumer's credit worthiness, credit standing, credit capacity, character, general reputation, personal characteristics, or mode of living which is used or expected to be used or collected in whole or in part for the purpose of serving as a factor in establishing the consumer's eligibility for" credit, insurance or employment purposes.

If you want to cover all of your bases to see what kind of information is being maintained on you, it's in your best interest to pull your file from the following companies.

Innovis

Innovis is a new credit bureau currently being developed by CBC Companies. The credit files it is keeping are not complete, as they have not yet wooed the majority of creditors to sign up with its system as have the other three bureaus.

Innovis Consumer Assistance
P.O. Box 1358
Columbus, OH 43216-1358
1-800-540-2505
FAX 877-261-7721

www.innovis.com

LexisNexis

This company serves as a repository for many public records and is used by the "Big Three" to verify consumer's public information. There are several divisions handling different types of data, but the two main ones are Banko and Hogan Information. For example, if you dispute a bankruptcy on your credit report, the credit bureau doesn't look up your records in the US Bankruptcy Court, it goes to a database service like LexisNexis. From the www.banko.com website:

> LexisNexis Public Records Data Services, Inc. is considered a Consumer Reporting Agency (CRA) and complies with the Fair Credit Reporting Act (FCRA). LexisNexis Public Records Data Services, Inc. collects public information (bankruptcies, deceased information, tax liens, judgments and other public court information), and sells this information to financial institutions (banks, credit lenders, etc.) other CRAs, law firms, collection agencies and others.

Since LexisNexis freely admits they fall under the FCRA, as stated previously, you can demand to see a copy of your file, as well as dispute items on it, much the same way you would dispute credit listings on your credit repair from, let's say, TransUnion. If you have a bankruptcy on your credit report, this is the first place you should start your dispute.

LexisNexis Group
Banko
100 South Fifth Street
Suite 300
Minneapolis, Minnesota 55402
800-533-8897
612-332-2427

www.hoganinfo.com

LexisNexis Public Records/Hogan
1900 N.W. Expressway
Suite 1600
Oklahoma City, OK 73118
(405) 302-6954
Fax (405) 302-6902

ChexSystems

Bet you didn't know there was a "credit bureau" just for checking accounts, did you? It's called ChexSystems, and if you ever have the honor of being listed with ChexSystems, you'll have a very tough time opening up a new checking account. If you're on their "blacklist," there are still a few banks which don't use ChexSystems. The list of banks which use and don't use ChexSystems fluctuates so frequently that it would be impractical to list these banks here. If you do a search on the Internet, you're going to find a lot of people who want to sell you the current list of banks. I recommend instead that you go to the following website, where some awfully nice folks have dedicated their free time to maintaining a free and current list:

www.chexvictims.com/AspNetForums/Default.aspx

ChexSystems regularly provides copies of credit reports to the public, as it is definitely a credit bureau and is regulated by the Fair Credit Reporting Act. You may also dispute listings with this credit bureau.

CHEXSYSTEMS
Attention: Customer Relations
12005 Ford Road, Suite 600
Dallas TX 75234
800-428-9623
www.chexhelp.com

Other banking/checking account information repositories

CheckRite
www.checkrite.com

Certegy
www.certegy.com

TeleCheck
www.telecheck.com

ChoicePoint

ChoicePoint is a consumer-reporting agency which keeps track of your auto claims and insurance history. Your ChoicePoint record, known as your CLUE® Report, report is often used to determine your overall risk as an insurance customer. This company and its data falls under the jurisdiction of the FCRA, so you may dispute anything on your CLUE report just as you would your Experian credit report.

You can order a copy of your report from them for free under FACTA. Instructions on how to order your report can be found on their website:

ChoicePoint's Consumer Disclosure
P.O. Box 105108
Atlanta, GA 30348-5108
http://www.choicetrust.com

The rules for obtaining free reports are the same as outlined for credit reports from the "Big Three" credit bureaus, as explained earlier.

Other data repositories which may contain your personal information

The Thomson Corporation - similar to LexisNexis
http://www.thomson.com/

CourthouseDirect.com

Mail: P. O. Box 70558
Houston, Texas 77270
Physical: 9800 Northwest Fwy, Suite 400
Houston, Texas 77092
Phone: (713) 683-0314 or (713) 683-0491
Fax: (713) 683-0493

Utilities

National Consumer Telecom & Utilities Exchange (NCTUE)
http://www.nctde.com/

Insurance

www.iso.com
Offers Auto and Home Insurance claim reporting. Because you receive one free
report per year, check Auto and Home Insurance claims yearly if you have filed
insurance claims within the last 5 years. If you have not filed a claim, check once
to verify that there is no derogatory information then check every 4-7 years
thereafter, primarily to alert yourself to ID Theft or the potential for inaccurate
information.

Tenant History Credit Bureaus

www.udregistry.com/tenant.htm
www.saferent.com (toll-free for consumers 888 333-2413)
www.ntnnet.com
These databases cover Alaska, Arizona, California, Florida, Georgia, Illinois,
Indiana, Iowa, Kansas, Kentucky, Massachusetts, New Jersey, New York, North
Carolina, Ohio, Oregon, Pennsylvania, Texas, Virginia, Washington .

Medical Information Bureau

The Medical Information Bureau (MIB) is a nationwide specialty consumer-
reporting agency that compiles and maintains records concerning individual life,
health, long-term care, and disability insurance. Generally, you will have an MIB
file only if you have applied for one of these insurance products within the last
seven years, and only if you've applied as an individual rather than as a member
of a group.

www.life-insurance-quotes-now.com/quote413.htm
www.mib.com Toll-free number for disclosure is (866) 692-6901

We are going to repeat ourselves here, but all of the above companies fall under
the regulation of the FCRA, so you may order a free copy of your report once a
year, and you may dispute items on a report just as you would with Experian.

CHAPTER 4: ANALYZING YOUR CREDIT REPORT

More of Susan's Story

Susan and her boyfriend Greg, whom you met in Chapter 3, settle onto her couch for a quiet evening together reviewing her credit report. A little Beethoven plays softly, and the lights are down low as they spread the pages out between them. The columns are neatly aligned, and they are able to identify her name, address, and a few of her credit cards. Unfortunately, the rest of it looks like Sanskrit.

Like any industry, credit has its own lingo. Even with the lights turned back on, they can make no sense of the pages.

What Does All That Information Mean?

As we saw in Chapter 1, your credit report contains a wealth of personal information about you: your name, address, Social Security number, and birth date. It also provides information about your open credit accounts, including balances and credit limits, whether or not you pay them on time, and whether any of them are or were turned over for collection. Any suits, judgments, or tax liens also are noted. It also may include the name of your employer and former employer, your position and income, your former address, and whether you rent or own your home. Your spouse's name, Social Security number, employer, and income also might be included. If you paid extra, you will also see your credit score. (Credit scoring is covered in depth in Chapter 5.)

When you first receive your credit report, you may be confused. The information on your report is coded in a way that is not immediately understandable by the layperson. Each credit report should arrive with a key that interprets the codes and indicators on the credit report. Study the credit report and the accompanying "decoder keys" until you understand what each number and code means. If it still looks like Sanskrit, you might ask a trusted friend to go over it with you. Someone in your personnel office at work, the dean of students office at your school, or at your bank might also be willing to help you (it's not their job to do this, so remember that you're asking a favor and you may be charged a fee). You also could call the agency that issued the report. The agency is required to explain it to you (but not to pay for any postage or phone bills you may incur). The following pages should help you figure out your report.

Each CRA Has Its Own Information and Layout

Please note that not all credit agencies will have the same information. This is because creditors do not necessarily report to the same agency and many do not report to all three major credit agencies. Therefore, *to do a complete job*, it is vital that you obtain credit reports from all three credit agencies.

Once you have obtained all of your credit reports, carefully note any records that you believe to be inaccurate, incorrect, erroneous, misleading, or outdated. Don't assume that because one bureau doesn't have a record of a late payment that they all will not.

Those Ugly Blemishes on Your Credit Complexion

If you have pulled your credit report expressly for the purpose of repairing your credit, you need to know how to identify all of the negative entries contained on the report. If a listing within your credit history contains one or more of the following indicators, it is considered a negative listing. If the listing contains none of these indicators, then the listing is positive.

Bankruptcies (BK)

If you have had a bankruptcy, the credit report will list the date you filed your BK and the date it was closed. It also can list the amount of debt that was discharged in your BK. See Chapter 23 for more details on this subject.

Foreclosures/Repossessions

A foreclosure and a repossession are essentially the same thing: your creditor takes back property you used to secure a loan because you didn't pay on time. A foreclosure describes only loans secured by real estate. All other types of seized property due to the defaulting of secured loans are called repossessions.

Tax Liens

If you owe state or federal taxes, these governmental agencies can put a lien on your home for the amount owed. Tax liens are public records, and they usually will find their way onto a credit report.

Judgments

If you've ever had a judgment filed against you, it means that you have been sued in court and a monetary award was given to the person or entity that sued you. Judgments are public records and easily find their way into your credit files. (Appendix 5 details state statutes of limitations on judgments; Chapter 29 explains how to get judgments vacated or dismissed.)

Profit and Loss Charge-offs

Profit and loss charge-offs are generally used only by credit card companies and usually are debts that a creditor considers uncollectable and does not bother to spend time or lawyer's fees to collect.

However, even if these companies aren't actively trying to collect from you, these debts are *still* owed by you to the company. If you refinance your house or apply for a loan, most mortgage companies will make you pay off these debts. The reason is that these debts can be turned into a lien against your property. Liens matter to a mortgage company for a couple of reasons:

- ✧ When you sell your home, the monies owed against a lien (plus interest) must be paid off to clear your title.
- ✧ Liens are in a higher position than a mortgage, meaning they get paid off before the mortgage company gets its money. If the mortgage company has to foreclose and you have lots of liens on your home plus a mortgage, the mortgage company potentially could lose thousands of dollars.
- ✧ Just because these debts are charged off doesn't mean that the creditor won't come after you later. Creditors have the right to sue you and win a judgment in court until the statute of limitations runs out.

Collections

If you have defaulted on a debt, your creditor most likely is first going to try collecting the money from you by using pressure tactics. After they give up on this approach, they hire professional hit, er ah, bill collectors—the collection agencies. Once your bill gets turned over to these oh-so-*not*-friendly people, your account is considered a collection account. Mortgage companies will also make you pay these items before the close of a loan. As with an original creditor and a charged-off account, collection agencies have the right to sue you over a collection account and win a judgment in court until the statute of limitations runs out, however unlikely they are to do so.

Late Pays

You will be reported as "late" to the credit bureaus for being more than 30 days late on a payment. If you are 0 - 30 days late on a loan or credit payment, you are not considered late paying a bill. I once asked a friend of mine who was applying for a loan, "Have you ever been late paying your loans?" to which she replied "Oh, all the time!" After saying this, I could tell she was concerned at this point that she had terrible credit. Further inquiry into the subject led me to discover that occasionally she'd been as much as a week (oh, horrors!) late on her credit card bills. After a chuckle, I assured her that her credit was probably perfect (it was).

Inquiries

Whenever you, or anyone else, request a copy of your credit report, the request is noted as an "inquiry" on your credit history. If you apply for lots of credit cards in a short time, this will produce a flurry of "inquiry" notes on your credit report, and will lower your credit score. The credit scoring models assume that a flurry of recent inquiries means you've applied for lots of credit, making you a greater credit risk, even though the inference is not strictly valid. For information on how to remove inquiries from your credit report, see Chapter 26.

Child Support

If you are delinquent in making your child support payments, it becomes public record and can show up on your credit report.

Specific Agency Indicators/Codes

As noted, each bureau has its own way of formatting and laying out the information on the pages of its standard report. They all look completely different, as a matter of fact. Here are some clues on how to identify what's BAD on a credit report:

EXPERIAN

- ✧ Any item marked with an asterisk; and
- ✧ Any inquiry.

EQUIFAX

- ✧ Any item preceded by a ">>>>" icon;
- ✧ Any item listed as "repossession," "foreclosure," "profit and loss write-off," "charge-off," "paid profit and loss write-off," "paid charge off," "settled," "settled for less than full balance," or "included in bankruptcy;"
- ✧ Any collection amount, whether paid or not;
- ✧ Any court account, including a lien, judgment, bankruptcy (Chapter 11, 7, or 13), divorce, satisfied lien, or satisfied judgment;
- ✧ Any item showing one or more 30-, 60-, or 90-day late payments in the column to the far right; and
- ✧ Any inquiry.

TRANSUNION

- ✧ An account closed by the credit grantor and not you;
- ✧ Any item listed as "repossession," "foreclosure," "profit and loss write-off," "charge-off," "paid profit and loss write-off," "paid charge off," "settled," "settled for less than full balance," or "included in bankruptcy;"
- ✧ Any collection amount, whether paid or not;
- ✧ Any court account, including a lien, judgment, bankruptcy (Chapter 11, 7, or 13), divorce, satisfied lien, or satisfied judgment;
- ✧ Any item showing one or more 30-, 60-, or 90-day late payments in the column to the far right; and
- ✧ Any inquiry.

How Long Do Negative Items Stay on Your Credit Report?

Accurate, negative information generally can be reported for seven years. Just like a broken heart, however, time heals all wounds. For example:

- ✧ **Delinquencies:** Payments made from 30 to 180 days after the due dates are considered delinquent. A record of this delinquency will remain on your credit report for seven years from the date of the missed payment. This is true even if you later bring your payments up to date.
- ✧ **Collection accounts:** If you fail to pay your bill for three to six months, the credit grantor may decide to turn the account over to a collection agency. These collection accounts remain on your credit report seven years from the date of the initial missed payment that led to the collection. When a collection account is paid in full, it will be marked "paid collection" on the credit report. It's important to remember that the collection account will remain on your report even if you later pay the account in full.
- ✧ **Charge-offs:** These accounts remain on your credit report for seven years from the date of the initial missed payment that led to the charge-off, even if payments are later made on the charged-off account.
- ✧ **Closed accounts:** Accounts no longer available for further use are considered closed. They may or may not have a zero balance. Closed accounts without a balance will remain on your credit report for seven years from the date they were reported closed, whether closed by the creditor or by you. Closed accounts with a balance will remain on your credit report for seven years after you make your final payment.
- ✧ **Lost credit cards:** When you report a lost credit card, the credit grantor will close your account. If there are no delinquencies, the account will continue to appear on your credit report for two years from the date the card was reported lost. If there were delinquencies before the card was lost, the account will continue to appear on your credit report for seven years from the delinquency.
- ✧ **Bankruptcies:** Chapters 7, 11, and 12 remain on your credit report for 10 years from the filing date. Chapter 13 remains seven years from the filing date. Accounts included in the bankruptcy will remain seven years from the date they were reported as included in the bankruptcy. These time frames apply even if the bankruptcy was dismissed or satisfied.
- ✧ **Child support judgments:** These remain on your credit report seven years from the date the judgment was filed.
- ✧ **Civil and small claim judgments:** These remain on your credit report seven years from the date the judgment was filed.
- ✧ **City, county, state, and federal tax liens:** These remain on your credit report seven years from the filing date of the lien.
- ✧ **Inquiries:** All inquiries remain on your credit report a minimum of one year from the date the inquiry was made.

Important Note: As indicated above, the length of time a negative mark can stay on your credit report *starts from the time you were late or the late payment went into collection, not from the last time you made a payment on the account.* Some collection agencies update their reporting status on you to keep the account active with the bureaus, to extend the time the account appears on your report. Very crafty and underhanded of them because most often the account is updated and the period of time the account was negative appears to be moved up. Challenge this using the information in Chapter 25.

In other words, paying a collection will *not* keep it on your credit report for a longer period of time.

For more information on the laws surrounding credit reporting time periods, refer to Section 605 of the Fair Credit Reporting Act contained in Appendix 1.

CHAPTER 5: CREDIT SCORING

John and Marie's Story

John and Marie, newlyweds, are applying for a loan to purchase their first house. Marie's friend, Jo, has advised her to make sure their credit is in order before applying for a loan. John and Marie follow the advice and obtain copies of their credit reports. Everything looks fine to them. Confidently, they apply for their loan.

But they are surprised and angry to find out that their loan application was turned down. "Your credit score is not high enough," the loan officer tells them. Marie presses for more information, pointing out to the loan officer that they have good credit. "We go by the credit score," the loan officer says, shrugging her shoulders. Marie tells her there was no credit score on the reports they had received. The loan officer replies that consumers must order their credit scores separately. She shows John and Marie their credit scores on the reports she just pulled. With a sigh, the loan officer tells her clients that she hates credit scoring, too, because "the scores change by the hour and no one really knows how they are calculated."

What is a Credit Score?

Imagine that you are walking down the beach in your bathing suit. Too scary? Okay, imagine someone else and a crowd is watching. The crowd holds up signs that read "10" or "6.5," depending on how attractive the person in the bathing suit is to them. Crass? Unfair? Subjective?

In the credit game, the crowd judging you is a company called "Fair Isaac" and the numbers range from 375 - 900. This is your credit score—your FICO score—which heavily determines your credit attractiveness to a large number of people (i.e., banks, insurance companies, loan companies).

It's unnerving enough just knowing you're being judged on *anything*. But how about being judged on things you have little control over, or not even knowing the criteria upon which you are being judged? It's like wearing a blue bikini and heels and not knowing that you should be wearing a red bikini and flip flops to score higher.

This is not an exaggeration. For the longest time, no one knew the criteria for credit scoring. Only after enormous public and government pressure, consumers are now allowed to get their credit scores, although the formula used to calculate your score is still as mysterious as the recipe for love.

Your credit score is derived from information accumulated in a credit bureau that issues your credit report. Your score is based on the number of credit accounts you have, your payment history, and your personal information, and is derived from a calculation so complex that there is no exact formula to print. But it is a statistical yardstick projecting whether or not you will default on future credit. Fair Isaac developed this statistical model (used by all three credit bureaus and most banking institutions), but will not reveal the exact recipe for the model. The company maintains that its model is a proprietary system, and keeping it a secret ensures its continued existence. If it gave away the product, how would Fair Isaac make money? What most people don't realize is that this credit scoring model is a product sold to lending institutions and, of course, credit bureaus.

This scoring model did not start out to be the industry standard, but since it was the most complete model available when the banking industry was interested in such information, it became an integral part of the credit granting process. The model took years to develop, and Fair Isaac has all kinds of empirical data to back up its accuracy. The lending industry considers this model to be fair and accurate. Since almost everyone uses it, it implies that *everyone* is measured by the same yardstick. Many (if not most) American and Canadian consumers are at the mercy of this statistical model.

At the credit scoring conference held by the FTC in July 1999, Fair Isaac gave the opening presentation and talked about some of the things used in calculating consumer credit scores. What I found out was that a lot of what goes into the score calculation is beyond the control of the consumer.

What Exactly Factors into Your Credit Score?

Below is a list of the factors used to score you, listed in order of importance. (Information marked with an asterisk [*] is obtained from information that you provided on an application and is not considered in a credit bureau score.)

- ✧ Major derogatory items on your report (i.e., bankruptcy, collections, foreclosure, slow-pays);
- ✧ Time at present job;
- ✧ Occupation (professionals are given heavy weight);[*]
- ✧ Time at present address;
- ✧ Ratio of balances to available credit lines (the lower the better);
- ✧ Whether or not you own your home (if you do, this is heavily weighted);[*]
- ✧ Number of recent inquiries;
- ✧ Age (50+ is the best);
- ✧ Number of credit lines on your report; and

✧ The number of years you have had credit in the credit bureau database.

Here are examples of some of the numbers used to calculate your credit score—these are not the actual numbers, but representative numbers to show you the weight of the various factors. In actuality, you receive a score on your credit report in addition to a score from your lender, the formulas of which both come from Fair Isaac. (To see the Fair Isaac presentation from which these numbers were pulled, go to: http://www.ftc.gov/bcp/creditscoring/ftc990722.ppt.)

TABLE 2—NUMERICAL FACTORS OF YOUR CREDIT SCORE

Consumer Trait	Consumer Status	Points Added/ Subtracted
Own/Rent:	Own	25
	Rent	15
	Other	10
	No Info	17
Years at Current Address:	<.5 Year	12
	.5-2.49 Years	10
	2.5-6.49 Years	15
	6.5-10.49 Years	19
	>10.49 Years	23
	No Info	13
Occupation:	Professional	50
	Semi-professional	44
	Manager	31
	Office	28
	Blue Collar	25
	Retired	31
	Other	22
	No Info	27
Years at Job:	<.5 Year	2
	.5-1.49 Years	8
	1.5-2.49 Years	19
	2.5-5.49 Years	25
	5.5-12.49 Years	30
	>12.5 Years	39
	Retired	43
	No Info	20

Consumer Trait	Consumer Status	Points Added/ Subtracted
Department Store/Major Credit Cards:	None	0
	Department Store	11
	Major Credit Card	16
	Both	27
	No Answer	10
	No Info	12
Bank Reference:*	Checking	5
	Savings	10
	Both	20
	Other	11
	No Info	9
Debt Ratios:**	<15%	22
	15-25%	15
	26-35%	12
	36-49%	5
	>50%	0
	No Info	13
Number of Inquiries:	0	3
	1	11
	2	3
	3-4	-7
	5-9	-20
	No Record	0
Years in File:***	<1 Year	0
	1-2 Years	5
	3-4 Years	15
	5-7 Years	30
	>8 Years	40
Number of Revolving Lines of Credit:	0	5
	1-2	12
	3-5	8
	>6	-4
Percentage of Balances Available:****	0-15%	15
	16-30%	5
	31-40%	-3
	41-50%	-10
	>50%	-18

Consumer Trait	Consumer Status	Points Added/ Subtracted
Derogatory Credit:	No Record	0
	Any Derogatory Credit	-29
	Any Slow Payment	-14
	One Satisfactory Line of Credit	17
	Two Satisfactory Lines of Credit	24
	Three Satisfactory Lines of Credit	29

Explanation of the Terms

BANK REFERENCE*

By this, they mean whether or not you have a savings and/or checking account. The only way that the Fair Isaac model would know your banking information is from the information you provided in filling out an application.

DEBT RATIOS**

Your debt ratio is the ratio of your monthly credit obligations (i.e., credit cards, mortgages, car loans—not food, insurance, or utilities) over your monthly gross (before taxes) income. For example, if your monthly credit obligations total $1,000/month and your monthly gross income is $4,000/month, your debt ratio would be 25%. How would the Fair Isaac model know about your income? You must have provided it when you filled out an application.

YEARS IN FILE***

This is the number of years that you have been in the credit bureau's files and, theoretically, the same amount of time you have had credit (though, of course, not necessarily).

PERCENTAGE OF BALANCES AVAILABLE****

This refers to the amount of available credit you have left on revolving credit (like credit cards). It is calculated by dividing your "total credit used" (over all of your cards) by the "total credit limits" (over all of your cards). For example, if you have a total credit card limit of $10,000 and you have used $2,000 worth of this available credit, you have used 20% of your available credit. Your balance available is 80%.

Profile of a High-scoring Consumer

According to the above scoring model, to get the highest score, you would have to (get ready for this):

- ✧ Be at your job for a long time;
- ✧ Be in a "professional" occupation (like lawyer, doctor, banker, corporate officer, etc.—does webmaster count?);

- ✧ Have lived in the same home (that you own, of course) for over 10 years;
- ✧ Have had credit and loans for many years;
- ✧ Be at least 50 years old;
- ✧ Have almost no debt, and not have applied for any new loans for the last two years; and
- ✧ Have no derogatory credit.

So is this fair? Have you noticed how few of the above items are entirely within your control?

Things You Can Do to Improve Your FICO Score

Keep in mind that changes in your FICO score take a long time to occur. But if you live by the following guidelines, your credit score will improve over time.

- ✧ Review your credit reports regularly for errors. You must check all three bureaus (Experian, TransUnion, and Equifax) to ensure that you will receive a fair evaluation the next time you apply for credit. Check a minimum of once a year, preferably every six months.
- ✧ Pay your bills on time. It seems almost too obvious, doesn't it? But hey, it works. Make sure you never pay a bill 28 days late or later. If you're cutting it close, make sure to count mail time when you send your bills.
- ✧ Pay down and close unneeded accounts. Over time, you should pay your higher interest accounts off then close them. An account that has been taken up to a high balance, brought down, and then closed is a good FICO builder. But don't close them all. You need at least three accounts open.
- ✧ On the flip side of this, don't apply for too much credit at the same time. A sure sign of desperation is someone who has applied for eight credit cards in the last 30 days.
- ✧ Don't allow prospective creditors to pull your credit report unless it is absolutely necessary.
- ✧ Keep all credit card balances low. If you carry a balance at all, make sure that you don't exceed one half (although 30% or less of the balance is optimal) of the credit card's limit. High credit balances can hurt even the most meticulous on-time bill payers.
- ✧ Delete negative credit listings (see Chapter 25), if possible.
- ✧ Delete inquiries (see Chapter 26), if possible.
- ✧ Pay down your credit card debt. Take money from an outside source, such as savings, a personal loan, or other credit cards, and apply that money to credit cards that are at or near their limit.
- ✧ Settle collections, judgments, or outstanding debts (see Chapter 25).

Okay, it's time to get out that bathing suit and try walking by Fair Isaac again!

Federal Government Publications

The Federal Reserve System publishes a series of pamphlets that describe your legal rights and offer advice on conducting your financial affairs. Most are free or cost less than a buck. You can get a free index of them from your nearest Federal Reserve Bank. (If you don't know where the nearest Federal Reserve Bank is, any bank can tell you.) Ask for the catalog titled *Public Information Materials*. Readers of this guide will be especially interested in the six pages of publications listed under the "Consumer Finance" section intended for the general public. There also are many publications on home equity loans and other home mortgages.

The Federal Financial Institutions Examination Council puts out a booklet called *Consumer Rights*. It lists federal laws that protect consumer rights and explains how to make complaints against financial institutions. You can pick up a copy in the literature rack at the Federal Reserve Bank or you can write to the Council at 1776 G Street NW, Suite 850B, Washington DC 20006. You might also ask for this at your local library.

For a complete list of publications by the Federal Trade Commission, write Best Sellers, Consumer Response Center, FTC, Washington, D.C. 20580, call 202-326-2222, or visit their website at http://www.FTC.gov.

The Use of Your Credit Score to Predict Other Kinds of Behavior

Currently, other organizations are using credit scoring for non-credit measures. In a large number of cases, the use of credit scoring has nothing to do with the extension of credit. Your score also is used by insurance companies, employers, apartment managers, utility companies, junk mail solicitors, and others for reasons that have nothing to do with credit. Your credit score is even being used to evaluate your likelihood of being a terrorist. The Computer Assisted Passenger Pre-Screening II program, better known as CAPPS II, is used by all commercial airlines to evaluate passenger risk for terrorism. It uses the credit bureaus as some of its data sources.

Most people would agree that a person's driving record and credit history are unrelated. Still, an increasing number of automobile insurers are using credit scores in the underwriting process. Insurance companies that use credit scoring often view the consumer's driving history as less important than his credit score. Exceptions are often made for consumers with one too many moving violations if they have high credit scores. Exceptions are *never* made for consumers with clean driving histories and low credit scores. There are an increasing number of cases in which people who have been with the same insurance company for years have had their premiums increased, or their policies not renewed, because of their credit scores.

SECTION III:
CREDIT CARDS

CHAPTER 6: CREDIT CARD TYPES

Wayne's Story

Wayne is in his first year of college and is discovering that not having a credit card is a major inconvenience when purchasing school supplies or participating in school activities. Wayne's parents are not willing to put their son on their credit cards, having read that this is a bad idea (they didn't tell him why it was a bad idea, though). His girlfriend, Susan, has been given a credit card by her parents for emergencies, a fact that Wayne frequently points out—to no avail—to his parents.

Then the big school-sponsored ski trip is announced. Susan loves skiing, so naturally, so does Wayne. The problem is that Wayne can't make their reservation without a credit card. Grabbing applications from the plethora of credit cards that are advertised all over campus, Wayne becomes overwhelmed and confused by all of his choices. Now the problem becomes, what kind of credit card should he apply for?

Which Card Should You Get?

With so many different cards advertised via every possible medium, and with all those *!@%& unsolicited credit card applications choking your mailbox, narrowing down your options may be a bit overwhelming. Should you get as many cards as you can so you can impress your friends, and that special someone, with your stack of plastic? Absolutely not! The more cards you have, the fatter your wallet is and the more cards you have to keep track of. If you have lots of cards, there is a good possibility that you can get yourself into trouble by running up lots of debt. As we saw in the last chapter, having too many cards lowers your credit score, even if most of your cards show a low or zero balance.

Some cards claim to be accepted "everywhere you want to be," while others smugly suggest that they could be the patron saint for your "priceless" memories. That's just great, really, but what exactly is the difference between one card and the next? They can't all be the same, right? Absolutely right.

Basic Credit Card Types

Your three basic credit card types are: bank cards, travel and entertainment (T&E) cards, and house cards. Automatic Teller Machine (ATM) cards and debit cards are linked to your existing bank accounts (checking and/or savings) and should not be confused with credit cards.

The best card for you is the one that is accepted where you shop and charges you the least amount of money for the services you actually use. For example, if you always pay off your balance each month, it is important to get a card with a grace period; the interest rate doesn't matter much.

Bank Cards

Bank cards are issued by, you guessed it, banks. Visa, MasterCard, and Discover are the most popular and widely accepted types of bank cards. Bank card rates are set independently by the banks issuing them, so don't make the mistake of thinking that all Visas or all MasterCards are alike. In fact, a given bank may offer several different rates and fee schedules on its bank card. Sometimes you can pick which one you want; other times, the bank will offer you a single set of terms with no option, even though it offers another customer a different set of terms. That's why it's worth shopping around rather than just applying for "a MasterCard" or "a Visa." (See Chapter 7 for help in evaluating these offers.) In addition to having to choose between banks to get the best rates, within the bank card category lies several credit card subcategories from which to choose: affinity cards, secured cards, and unsecured cards.

AFFINITY CARDS

An affinity card typically is a Visa or a MasterCard that carries the logo of an organization (such as Harley Davidson®, Yahoo!®, Disney®, etc.) in addition to the emblem of the card. You basically are getting a card with someone's logo on it. The organization solicits all of its members to get cards, with the idea of keeping its name in front of the card users and, hopefully, keeping card users loyal to it for future purchases, membership, and/or donations. There are some credit card companies that even offer a "design your own" card service, I guess so you can put the object of your affection on your credit card. (Wouldn't that impress him—talk about affinity!) If you've recently donated to any nonprofit organizations, belong to any clubs or fraternities, or if you're a university alumni, you've probably received applications for affinity cards.

Evaluate an affinity card as you would any other. If you would consider it a good deal in the open market, based on the way you use credit, then it's a good deal. Card users typically receive some benefit by using an affinity card (i.e., frequent flyer miles or points toward merchandise in a catalog). In addition to establishing loyalty, the organization receives a financial incentive (a fraction of the annual fee or the finance charge, some small amount per transaction, or a combination of the two) from the credit card company. But an expensive card doesn't become a good deal for you merely because a small fraction of the profits are turned back to your organization or a charity. Most of the profits go to the card issuer (the bank), and through the affiliated organization, the credit card company gets more of its cards into customers' hands. Unless the card is a good deal for you personally, it's a better idea to make a direct donation to your organization (and get a tax deduction, too, if it's a charity).

SECURED CARDS

Secured cards require you to make a bank deposit up front as security against charges on the card. The limit on the card usually is set by the amount of the deposit. Typically, the contract is written in such a way that the issuing bank maintains the right to take money from your "security" deposit if you don't pay your bill. Secured cards usually are sold to people who have credit problems and can't get a regular "unsecured" card but still need credit. But a secured card from a bank may be a good deal for anyone. You may want a secured card even if you can get an unsecured card. Why? Since a secured card represents less risk to the bank, interest rates may be lower than for an unsecured card. A secured MasterCard or Visa looks just like a regular one and the law ensures that it has all the same consumer protections.

When evaluating a secured card, use the same criteria as for any other card, and ask the bank some additional questions such as:

- ✧ What interest rate is paid on the deposit?
- ✧ Is there an annual fee?
- ✧ If I maintain a good credit record, will I be considered for an unsecured ("regular") card?
- ✧ Binding arbitration. If you sign something which agrees to settle all disputes with binding arbitration, you are basically waiving your right to have your day in court. Many credit card companies have taken unfair advantage of their customers by insisting on this practice.

Also, ask yourself if you might conceivably have a need for the deposited funds during the required term. If so, find out up front whether you can withdraw the deposit in case of financial emergency, and what it costs in interest and penalties to do that.

Call your own bank or check online for information about secured card offers. With all of the great information out there, you should be able to find lots o' good stuff and even apply on the spot! The Internet is an excellent source for finding the credit card to meet your needs.

UNSECURED CARDS

You probably won't hear the term "unsecured card" often because, in terms of credit cards, these are the norm. "Unsecured" means that the bank can't take specific assets of yours in the event that you don't pay your bill, but rather would have to sue you or force you into bankruptcy to collect. A "regular" card is unsecured.

Travel and Entertainment (T&E) Cards

American Express (AMEX), Diners Club, and their kin originally were aimed at the more upscale "travel and entertainment" market. They are accepted at many places, though not as many locations as Visa and MasterCard. Some places don't take MasterCard and Visa but do take AMEX or Diners Club.

Unlike bank cards, rates on T&E cards do not vary. One AMEX green card is like all other AMEX green cards in the country (although corporate AMEX card rates may vary from personal card rates).

Most "corporate cards" fall into this category, and typically are issued to certain employees of a company for the company's convenience in managing travel expenses. As the holder of a corporate card, there are a couple of possible concerns:

- ✧ You may be individually responsible for charges to the card, even though you use it only for business purposes. This can be a problem if your company is very slow to reimburse you for expenses.
- ✧ Corporate cards may not have the same buyer protections (like an extended warranty) that personal cards offer.

House Cards

House cards are good only at the stores of one chain. Sears is the biggest one, followed by the oil companies, the phone companies, and your local department stores. Like T&E cards, national house cards (like Sears) have the same terms and conditions wherever you apply.

ATM Cards and Debit Cards

ATM CARDS

An ATM Card is used to withdraw (or deposit) funds from your bank account by punching in your code number (PIN—personal identification number) at a cash machine. An ATM card looks nothing like a credit card and has no Visa or MasterCard logo on it.

DEBIT CARDS

A debit card looks very much like a credit card (with Visa or MasterCard logos), and is treated like a credit card by most merchants, but the charge is immediately deducted from your bank account. Therefore, as its name implies, a debit card is not a credit card. Instead of running up a bill that you pay at the end of the month, the debit card runs down your bank account the moment the sale is made. Merchants like these because they get instant payment without worrying about bad checks. Some consumers prefer them because they can only spend the money that is available in their accounts, avoiding the temptation to overspend on credit.

Debit cards are convenient but they do have drawbacks. It is a lot more painful to resolve a problem with a purchase if the money is gone from your account (as with a debit card) than if it's just numbers on a piece of paper (as with a credit card). But you can protect yourself by signing for your debit card purchases just as you do your credit card purchases. How?

After swiping your debit card, simply select "credit" on the PIN pad instead of "debit." The charge will still be debited from your checking account on the spot. But by choosing "credit," the charge gets processed through the Visa processing network, activating Visa's Zero Liability policy. The merchant will ask you to sign for the purchase instead of inputting your pin on the PIN pad.

When you choose "debit" and enter your pin number to complete a purchase, your liability is limited to $50 (as opposed to $0 when you choose "credit") *but only if* you notify the card issuer within two business days of the loss or theft of your debit card.

Be very careful with your debit card. If you lose it, your entire account can be emptied very quickly. Most banks limit the amount of cash that can be withdrawn in a single day to around $300, but the only limit to the amount of shopping a thief can do in a day is determined by the amount of money in your account. Report lost or stolen debit cards immediately and *never* write your PIN number where a thief can find it.

Consumers in the know don't like debit cards because they offer less protection than credit cards in the event of a billing dispute. (For more information about this, see Chapter 9.)

Note: Some banks now issue combined ATM/debit cards. Depending on your viewpoint, this gives you the advantages—or the disadvantages—of both.

Contacts for Credit Cards

A list of the best credit card deals can be found at http://www.bankrate.com/cic. This site truly is impressive in its in-depth evaluation of credit cards—secured and unsecured.

Here is where you can write for more specific credit information:

Visa
Director of Public Affairs
Visa USA, Inc.
P.O. Box 8999
San Francisco, CA 94128-8999

MasterCard
MasterCard International
888 Seventh Avenue
New York, NY 10106

Discover Card
2500 Lake Cook Road
Deerfield, IL 60015

American Express
200 Vesey Street
New York, NY 10285

CHAPTER 7: GOOD AND BAD DEALS IN CREDIT CARDS

More of Wayne's Story

Wayne, who you met in Chapter 6, after reviewing all of the possible credit card types and options, has decided that he wants to get both a Visa and a Master Card. That's a good start. But now what? The terminology on the applications is very confusing. A call to his parents didn't help one bit. The extent of their "technical advice" is, "The cards we have work for us."

Susan suggests they make a night of it—Chianti, candles, soft music, and a stack of credit card applications. Wayne arrives early, eager to begin.

Factors to Consider

There are three principal features to the card itself that determine whether or not you've found a good deal. These are the Interest Rate, Annual Fee, and Grace Period. By law, all three must be disclosed at the time you apply for the credit card. The United States Fair Credit and Charge Card Disclosure Act requires issuers of charge or credit cards (including retail stores) to reveal certain basic information in tabular form with the application or "pre-approved" solicitation. Disclosures also must be provided before annual renewal if the card issuer imposes an annual fee.

Other things to consider are Rebates, Discounts, and Miscellaneous Fees. Also important is the pattern of your shopping—a card that your favorite merchants don't honor won't be of much use for you.

Interest Rates

The interest rate is the rate charged on purchases and cash advances (generally, two different rates). It can be "fixed" or "floating." Fixed rates are not truly fixed because the banks will change them every year or so. Floating rates typically are a bit lower than fixed rates, but fluctuate every month according to the latest T-bill sale, the phase of the moon, or some other index (just kidding about the phase of the moon—sort of). By law, banks must apply floating interest rates according to a regulated index. Still, if you buy something you're expecting to pay off over many months, a floating interest rate will make it hard to guess how much finance charge you'll be paying. Some credit cards may refer to a "variable rate," which is the same as a floating rate.

ANNUAL PERCENTAGE RATE (APR)

Years ago, credit card issuers would quote an interest rate that was not directly comparable with other lenders' rates because the method of computation was not standard. The law now requires lenders to quote an annual percentage rate so that you might compare cards—a rate that includes the interest and all fees for a year (i.e., the total cost of the "loan" for the course of a year).

MAXIMUM INTEREST RATES

Interest rates are all over the map. There are limits, however, in most states on the maximum interest rates allowed. The laws concerning maximum interest rates are called "usury laws."

INTEREST RATE CALCULATIONS

To calculate the interest on your card each month, the lender multiplies the card's interest rate (the APR) times your card balance. This will give the interest for the entire year. The lender then will divide the interest calculated by the number of months in the year (12). The sticky part is determining the credit card balance. This is why it's important to choose a card with a grace period (see below). If you do have a balance on your card, there are three methods of calculating it:

- ✧ **Average Daily Balance (the most common method):** The issuer calculates the balance by taking the amount of debt you had in your account each day during the period covered by the billing statement and averaging it.
- ✧ **Previous Balance:** The issuer uses the balance outstanding at the end of the previous period—that is, the period prior to the one covered by the current billing statement.
- ✧ **Adjusted Balance Method:** The balance is derived by subtracting the payments you've made from the previous balance.

Annual Fees

The annual fee is, well, a fee that the card issuer bills to your account annually. Every year, on the anniversary of the date your account was opened, the fee for the upcoming year is billed to your account. Typical charges are $18 to $29 for regular bank cards (about $40 for gold bank cards) and anywhere from $35 on up for various flavors of T&E cards. House cards are typically free.

Many lenders waive the fee the first year to get you to sign up, then depend on you to forget a year later that you'll be charged an annual renewal fee. There's nothing shady about this as long as it's disclosed up front. Some lenders often have "secret" programs in effect where, if you ask them, they will waive the annual fee. Some do it only if you charge a certain amount per year; others have other criteria. It certainly can't hurt to call just before renewal time and ask to have the fee waived. (If you wait until after the fee is already on your statement, your chances aren't so good for getting it waived.)

Some banks will waive the annual fee if you tell them that you'll go elsewhere if you have to pay it. Others will not. You may want to ask (politely) to talk to a supervisor, since the front-line person may not care whether you cancel your card and may not have the authority to make concessions. Don't bluff on this unless you are confident you can get a card elsewhere.

Grace Periods

The grace period is the time after the billing date that you have to pay off the bill *without paying a finance charge*. Grace periods for cash advances are pretty rare, since the bank would lose money on them. T&E cards typically have generous grace periods; bank cards usually have 25 days, but a few have 30, and many have no grace period. In every case, the grace period runs from the date printed on the bill, not from the date you get the bill. For instance, suppose your bill is prepared on the 28th of every month and the grace period is 25 days. If you make a purchase on July 3, it will show up on the July 28 bill and you'll have until August 22 (July 28 plus 25 days) to pay it off without interest. If you don't pay the full balance, your August bill will show a finance charge, and so will every bill after that until you pay off your full balance.

Some banks give you a grace period only during those months when your previous balance is zero. Others (fewer of them all the time) give the stated grace period on all new purchases even if you have a balance from last month. The second method can save you big bucks; be sure to find out how your bank does it when you apply for the card.

Rebates, Discounts, and Other Kickbacks

Some cards, such as Discover, pay "rebates." Rebates are a percentage refund on your purchases, either by check or by a credit to your account. Discounts, on the other hand, actually reduce the price on the bill before you pay it. Discover offers rebates on all purchases. The Ameritech Complete MasterCard gives 10% rebates on credit card calls at the end of the year. Some things to keep in mind when looking for cards with rebates are:

- ✧ When will the rebate be issued? At the end of the month or at the end of the year? Typically, it's after the end of the year.
- ✧ How is the rebate calculated? Be sure to read the fine print. For example, let's say that Discover advertises "up to 1% rebate." That's true, but the fine print reveals that you get back 1% for every dollar you charge *after charging* $3,000 in a single year. The first $3,000 is rebated at rates between one-quarter and three-quarters of a percent.

Some cards offer other features like frequent-flyer miles and extended warranties on purchases. Is this a good thing? It may or may not be. Consider such questions as these to help you make this determination:

- ✧ Does the airline fly to places you really want to go?
- ✧ How many dollars must you charge to earn a free ticket? Is the airline likely to be around by then?
- ✧ Are you likely to spend more than you otherwise would, just to accumulate the miles?

Miscellaneous Fees

You have the right by law to know about all possible fees before your credit card application is processed.

APPLICATION FEES

Application fees are extremely rare with unsecured cards, but with secured cards they are very common. Though such fees are legal, look long and hard at the terms before you agree to pay an application fee, even if you are "guaranteed" acceptance. For an unsecured card, you can almost certainly do better elsewhere.

OVER-LIMIT FEES

Many cards assess an over-limit fee if you charge something that takes you over your credit limit. The creditor may or may not allow the charge if it assesses this fee. Common over-limit fees range from $20 to $29.

LATE PAYMENT FEES

Some cards charge a late payment fee in addition to the finance charges. Again, a fee of $20 to $29 is common.

CASH ADVANCE TRANSACTION FEE

Some cards charge a transaction fee for cash advances. This may be a flat amount (around $2), a percentage of the transaction dollar amount (1% to 2% is common), or a combination. These fees are in addition to the stated interest rate, which usually starts accruing as soon as you get the money.

Tips for Cutting Your Credit Card Expenses

1. PICK A CARD WITHOUT AN ANNUAL FEE

Some credit card companies can charge you as much as $50 a year. With all the choices out there, don't fall into this trap.

2. NEVER MAKE ONLY THE MINIMUM PAYMENT

Credit card companies make the majority of their money from you through interest on the unpaid balances on your credit cards. The minimum payment some credit cards ask you to make will not reduce the balance on your credit cards very quickly, if at all. For example, consider a $1,000 balance at 18% (a low rate by some cards issued today). If you make the minimum payment on the card (typically about 3% of the balance), it will take you six years and one month to pay off the balance, including an additional $559 in interest. That is, if you never purchase another thing with this credit card until after the balance is paid off.

3. PAY OFF THE FULL BALANCE

If you must carry a balance, always pay as much as you can afford every month.

4. PAY ON TIME

Mail your payment check early. Late credit card payments hurt you three ways: (1) Bad credit reports, which you already know about; (2) Late fees ranging from about $20 to $29; and (3) Bumped up interest rates—as few as one or two late payments during one year can put you into the penalty box (causing your interest rate to jump to a "penalty rate" of 24% or more). Make sure you send in your payment a little extra early – some companies are known to be "slow" about getting your payment from their mail room to the processing center, which can result in a late fee, even if the payment itself was received on time. Try to allow one week for your payment to arrive.

5. BEWARE OF CREDIT LINE INCREASES

If you make timely payments, your bank will automatically raise your credit limit without asking you, and other banks will send you offers for more "pre-approved" cards. This could be good or bad. If you have a tendency to push the limits on your credit cards, they could entice you to go more into debt with this additional available credit. On the other hand, such credit line increases could give you a better debt-to-available-credit standing—but only if you keep the balances where they are —thus, actually increasing your credit score because you have all these high available credit amounts (which means you can be trusted) yet you keep low balances (which means you handle money well).

6. AVOID CASH ADVANCES

Don't use your credit card like an ATM card for cash withdrawals. The interest rate on cash advances is at least 2% higher than on purchases and the interest begins to accrue immediately.

Students Beware!

College students are special to the credit card companies. Our friend Wayne, for example, could likely score plenty of credit cards (and potentially get himself into deep trouble) even if he has no income. Why? Because he has the *potential* of earning a good income once he graduates.

Believe it or not, if you're in college, credit card companies want your business so badly they're offering much more than trinkets and soda. They'll let you apply for credit cards without a job or income! You can apply for credit cards with a blank credit report, even without getting a co-signer! No other consumers can get cards this way. They want to get you hooked early—like giving cigarettes to kids in junior high.

CHAPTER 8: MAKING PURCHASES WITH CREDIT CARDS

William's Story

William's first wedding anniversary is coming up and he wants to get something special for his wife, Marcia. He decides to buy a piece of jewelry over the Internet from a site that received good reviews in a national consumer products review magazine. He is leery about using his credit card on the Internet and decides to send in a check to the company after placing his order on the company's website.

Although Wayne orders the item two months in advance, and even pays extra to have the item next-day delivered, the jewelry he purchased does not arrive. William watches for his check to clear, and when it does he immediately calls the Internet jewelry company to inquire about his order. To his horror, the company claims to have no record of his purchase or his payment. William mails them a copy of the cancelled check and calls them back, only to find out that this Internet company has just gone belly up, leaving him out $500 with no anniversary present for his wife. He calls his friend Eric, a paralegal, to see what can be done to get his money back. Eric has the unhappy job of telling his friend that there is no recourse in this matter. Eric advises William to pay with a credit card next time, as there are many protections obtained under the law when using a credit card. Too little knowledge too late.

Credit Cards vs. Debit Cards

Generally, it's better to use a credit card than a check or a debit card. We know this flies in the face of good stay-out-of-debt strategies. However, when you pay by credit card, the United States Fair Credit Billing Act (included in Appendix 2) offers protections. These safeguards don't apply if you pay by check or by debit card. However, be aware that credit card debt is about the most expensive legal kind of debt there is. With banks paying as low as 2% on savings accounts while charging 19% or more on credit card balances, it makes sense never to carry a balance past your grace period.

It might be worth your while to do a quick review of Chapter 6 for tips on how to get the same protections as a credit card when using your debit card.

If Asked for Additional Information when Making a Credit Card Purchase

There is no federal law regarding whether or not a merchant may request an address and telephone number when accepting a charge. The laws of CA, DE, GA, MD, MN, NJ, NV, and NY prohibit recording personal information in connection with credit card transactions. Note the word "recording." Strictly interpreted, this means they can ask you to show a driver's license but can't write anything down from it.

According to Visa and MasterCard, merchants are not allowed to refuse a sale solely because the customer refuses to provide additional personal information. The same is true when you use your AMEX card, but not when you use Discover.

If merchants have "sufficient" reason to suspect you are not the authorized cardholder, they may ask for further ID. This exception rarely comes up in real life, and even if it does they must not write the information on the AMEX, Visa, or MasterCard charge slip.

Many merchants don't know the rules. They may think (wrongly) that getting extra information from you will protect them in some way. The truth is that if they follow the procedures of the credit card company, they will get paid. Period.

On the other hand, some merchants deliberately flout the rules and depend on you to acquiesce. Why? Because they can sell your address or phone number, or add you to their in-house list of sales prospects.

Don't accept the old line about "in case there's a problem." If the merchant follows proper procedures at the time of sale, there won't be a problem. If you leave your card behind, for example, they can send it to the card issuer, who will return it to you.

The most effective response, when additional personal information is requested, is to simply ignore the request. When they say, "I need your signature and phone," simply sign in the proper place and hand them the charge slip without your phone number. Don't comment on the request in any way. More often than not, they won't follow up.

If they do notice that you didn't put down the personal information, and ask you again, simply say, "I don't give that out." Almost every time, the clerk writes down something like "refused" and that's the end of it. If they still insist, you have to decide how important it is to you to make a point. If you don't much care, give them what they want so you can get on your way. Depending on your mood, you could even try flirting with them!

If you're a privacy fanatic, you can do one of several things:

✧ Point out that Visa and MasterCard rules don't allow them to require this information and wait to see what they do. Typically, the clerk calls the manager to "authorize" the sale, which she does right away.
✧ Tell them your phone number is unlisted. They usually accept that without question.
✧ Make up a phone number. Please use one beginning with 555 so that some television character receives all the nasty calls. If you happen to know the phone number of the store, it's always a nice touch to give them that.

Be firm, but pleasant, through it all. Don't raise your voice. But if this is important to you, don't let yourself be bullied either. After all, this is America and you can almost always get equivalent merchandise from another store.

Using a Credit Card as a Check Guarantee

In CA, DE, FL, GA, IA, IL, KS, MD, MN, ND, NJ, NV, NY, OH, VA, and WA, it's illegal for merchants even to write your credit card number on your check, so don't let them do it. In IL, the merchant can request a look at your card, but can't write the number on your check. The merchant *can* write the type of card and expiration date.

In states other than those listed above, the merchant has the legal right to refuse the sale and payment with a check if you refuse to give requested credit card information. However, Visa, MasterCard, and AMEX all forbid merchants to charge a credit card account to cover a bounced check or to use card numbers to locate a customer whose check bounces. Since the merchant can't do anything legitimate with the card number, and since providing it makes you a possible victim of fraud, you should politely decline. One possible compromise, if you're at an impasse, would be to show the card with your name on it, but to cover up all or part of the card number and to insist that no part of the number be written down. The situation may be different if your credit card also is a check guarantee card. See the preceding section for further cautions.

Nearly 90% of bounced checks are due to consumers' math errors in balancing their checkbooks. Despite this, the law in some states dictates that if you bounce a check it is assumed to be deliberate unless you can prove otherwise. And deliberately bouncing a check is a crime in every state.

It's better never to get into this hassle than to deal with it after the fact. If you have credit cards, why pay by check at all (as we discussed earlier)? If you do pay by check, don't give a credit card number. And if you bounce a check, don't make the merchant come to you but go to the merchant immediately to make things right. Give the merchant a good check (probably a cashier's check) or cash for the amount of the purchase, and expect to pay a reasonable fee to the merchant in addition to your bank's fee.

Surcharges

If merchants go about it the right way, they may charge credit card users more than cash customers **for the same item**. This is called a "surcharge." The Federal Truth in Lending Act prohibited surcharges on credit card purchases until 1984; since then, there has been no federal law on the subject (other provisions of the law are still in force). The states of CA, CO, CT, FL, KS, MA, ME, NY, OK, and TX have laws against surcharges.

Discover allows surcharges on credit card purchases, except in the above states. Visa and MasterCard prohibit them. AMEX discourages them in general, and specifically prohibits them by merchants that also take MasterCard or Visa because AMEX doesn't allow merchants to discriminate against it.

There is a loophole: Merchants are allowed to give cash discounts. This means in practice that merchants can't charge you more than the labeled price if you pay by credit card, but they can charge you *less* if you pay cash. Some companies announce (usually in tiny print in the catalog) that all prices "reflect cash discount of *X*%" so credit card users must pay *X*% more than the stated price. This may be legal, but it certainly violates the spirit of the law or the regulations.

There is another loophole: Certain government agencies are not allowed (by law) to pay "discount fees" which are the processing fees the bank charges merchants for handling credit card slips. Since banks won't handle these for free, you may well have to pay a surcharge for the privilege if your state lets you pay license fees by credit card. However, there are no exceptions for retail merchants.

Charge Minimums

Have you ever tried to charge a $10 item only to have the merchant point to a sign that states "Minimum charge: $20"? You may be wondering about the validity of such a practice. After some research, I found that this sort of practice is *never* kosher with Visa or MasterCard, and that generally goes for AMEX as well. However, Discover allows the merchant to set a minimum purchase amount.

MasterCard and Visa rules dictate that a merchant may not require any minimum purchase amount. This is the merchant's agreement with Visa or MasterCard, not federal law. On the other hand, if you insist on charging a 79-cent ballpoint pen, I hope you get four flat tires on the way home.

According to AMEX, if a merchant takes AMEX and also Visa or MasterCard, AMEX doesn't let the merchant impose a minimum purchase on AMEX users because that would discriminate against them. Merchants who take AMEX but neither Visa nor MasterCard may impose minimum charges, but AMEX officially discourages the practice.

Reservation Guarantees

Most hotels and motels (but not all) subscribe to the "Lodging Services Addendum" in their merchant agreement with Visa. If the hotel is one that participates, and they have no room for you when you arrive with a guaranteed reservation, their agreement with Visa requires them to:

✧ Provide you with at least comparable accommodations for one night at another establishment;
✧ Provide transportation for you to that establishment;
✧ If requested, allow you to make a three-minute local or long distance call; and
✧ If requested, forward all messages and calls for you to the alternate establishment.

However, your unsupported word is not exactly proof that you had a reservation. Always write down the date and time that you placed the reservation, the rate you were quoted, which credit card you used for the guarantee, and the confirmation number (you may have to ask for a confirmation number). You will need this information if there's a problem with your reservation, or if your plans change and you have to cancel.

Some state laws may protect you when you have a guaranteed reservation, whether you guaranteed it by a deposit or by credit card.

Shipping and Payment

According to Visa USA, "a merchant is not permitted to bill ahead of time" (i.e., prior to shipping) except in the case of a deposit or down payment that the customer agrees to have billed in advance.

MasterCard dictates that a merchant can charge you before shipment only if he tells you and you agree to "the terms and conditions of the sale" at the time of purchase.

AMEX dictates that the merchant can charge your card as soon as you relinquish your account number, but if you receive the bill before the merchandise, call AMEX customer service and you won't have to pay while they investigate.

Billing Due Dates

When making payments on a credit card, you may wonder whether the payment must reach the lender by the "due date" on the bill or if it is enough if the payment is mailed by the due date. The answer to this question varies. The Uniform Commercial Code reads that a bill is considered paid on the postmark date of the payment, but many states have different laws. Even in states where the bill is considered legally paid on the postmark date, you may find that lenders will consider it paid on the date they process it. Avoid hassles by always mailing your payment a reasonable time before the due date. The few extra days of "float time" are not worth the aggravation of fighting with the lender over this point.

Payments Via Automatic Withdrawal

Generally, you may obtain a Visa or MasterCard from the same bank at which you have a checking or savings account. In these cases, the bank often provides the option to set up your checking account for automatic withdrawal on the due date to pay the credit card. If you tend to forget to pay your bills on time, this arrangement can save you late charges or finance charges. On the other hand, if you forget to enter the automatic withdrawal into your checkbook, you may find you're overdrawn and start bouncing checks.

Some consumers have reported problems with disputed charges being paid automatically, or the bank disregarding special requests to alter a scheduled payment. However, the Fair Credit Billing Act does not let them take any collection action at all if you have properly notified them of a dispute (as we discuss in Chapter 9).

Another consideration is that the bank can probably freeze your account or take money from it if you miss a payment on your credit card bill. You should check your cardholder agreement. The typical agreement gives the bank the right to take the money from any accounts you have with them if you are delinquent on your bill. Even if there's no such provision in your cardholder agreement, it's probably buried somewhere in the fine print that governs your deposit account. You should carefully weigh the promised benefits against the additional loss of control over your checking account.

What to Do When Merchants Aren't Following the Law

If you find that a merchant is not following the law, politely mention it to the merchant and explain why. If this fails to impress him, you can report the merchant to your state's or city's consumer protection office or attorney general. If the merchant violates any rules of AMEX, the company would like to know about it. Report violations of Visa or MasterCard rules to the bank that issued your card. If the sale was completed, you can also send a letter with a copy of the charge slip to the Visa or MasterCard address at the end of Chapter 6.

CHAPTER 9: BILLING ERRORS AND OVERCHARGES

Mischa's Story

Mischa recently took her boyfriend on a fabulously romantic vacation to Hawaii to celebrate his becoming a full partner in his architecture firm. She originally booked a room at a hotel a colleague had recommended, but the dates her boyfriend could travel changed and the first hotel could not accommodate them on the new travel dates. Mischa received a cancellation number and made new reservations at a hotel offering equal accommodations for the new dates.

When Mischa received her bill the following month, she was annoyed to find that the hotel that held her cancelled reservation had billed her credit card for the first night anyway. She immediately called and was further angered when they could find no record of her cancellation, even after she gave them the cancellation number.

The United States Fair Credit Billing Act

The United States Fair Credit Billing Act (see Appendix 2) protects you from honest errors and outright fraud by merchants when you make the purchase through a bank credit card. This includes protection from:

- ✧ Billing errors;
- ✧ Charges for goods ordered but never shipped;
- ✧ Charges higher than agreed;
- ✧ Charges for goods not shipped as ordered;
- ✧ Charges for products that don't work as represented; and
- ✧ Charges for unsatisfactory services and similar kinds of problems.

This protection is extended under the Fair Credit Billing Act if:

- ✧ The purchase was made with a credit card. If the purchase was made with a debit card, the money is already gone from your account and the bank won't get involved.
- ✧ The amount charged is more than $50. The amount in dispute could be less; for example, if you bought a lamp for $90 but were billed $100—the amount in dispute is $10.

✧ You made the purchase somewhere in your home state, or within 100 miles of your mailing address. I am not an attorney, but my understanding is this: if you are having goods shipped to you by mail or phone order, the place of purchase is the address they are shipped to.

If some of the above are not true, you are still protected if the credit card company owns or operates the merchant, or if the credit card company mailed you the advertisement for what you bought. In that case, your purchase is covered by the above rules no matter where you bought the product or how much you paid.

Additionally, you may successfully protest charges outside of these parameters, but there is no legal requirement for the credit card company to correct the problem.

Act Quickly to Dispute Billing Errors and Overcharges

When dealing with billing errors and overcharges on your credit card statements, you should first notify the credit card issuer. The issuer must receive your claim within 60 days of the billing date before it can start an investigation. Next, notify the merchant. Under the law, you must try "in good faith" to resolve the problem directly with the seller. The credit card issuer will not get involved at this point. However, it's a good idea to start a parallel effort.

"In good faith" is not defined in the law, but in practice it means that you behave like a reasonable person. The merchant is expected to act reasonably, too. At a minimum, you should talk to the merchant's customer service department and send a follow-up letter. You have to allow the merchant a reasonable time to respond. What's reasonable? It depends on the circumstances, but usually is enough time for mail to go both ways, plus a couple of working days.

"In good faith" also means that you act promptly. Don't wait three months after the charge shows up on your bill from that lingerie store to complain that you never got what you ordered.

Back orders are a frequent problem. If the merchant tells you the stuff is back ordered, you have the right to cancel the order. If it's a mail order, the merchant is supposed to give you a postage-paid reply card indicating that the merchandise is on back order. Then you can tell the merchant you don't want to wait and ask for the charge to be canceled. This may not happen the same day, but it should be reasonably prompt. Wait a few days and call the bank to see if the credit has come through yet.

Remember that the person you are talking to is probably not the person who caused the problem. Don't yell. Don't run on at great length. Don't sound crazy or make threats. Plenty of good people work for bad companies. Lots work for good companies that make an occasional mistake. Remember the Japanese proverb: "The first man to raise his fist or voice has lost the argument."

Tips to Remember When Disputing Errors

Keep the following points in mind when disputing any and all errors:

✧ Be prepared with specific information before you call the merchant.
✧ Have all of the pertinent paperwork in hand.
✧ Make sure you can give the order date, what you ordered (the item number and price), when you were promised the item(s), your credit card number, and how much you were charged.
✧ Be clear about what you want—a refund, a replacement, shipment by a certain date, repair, etc.
✧ Most people (not all) respond best if you tell them clearly, calmly, and reasonably what you want.
✧ Keep notes of your conversation.

If you are not able to resolve the issue and the error/overcharge persists, instructions on how to proceed are printed on your bill, probably on the back. Just follow them. The rules are simple: If you report a problem to the lender in writing within 60 days of the billing date, the bank *must* investigate it and respond to you within 30 days. While they are investigating, you don't have to pay the disputed amount or any finance charges on it. However, if their investigation shows that the item was correct, they can restore finance charges retroactively and you will have to pay them.

If you've tried "in good faith" to resolve the problem with the merchant, by law the bank must help. All banks know this and most will be very helpful. Don't expect a fight.

The Next Step—Asking for a Credit in Writing

Most credit card issuers require that you make a formal request for a credit to your account (called a chargeback) to make up for the billing error/overcharge. When writing to the credit card issuer, make certain that you give these important facts in the letter and use the same address as required for errors on your bill:

✧ The date you are writing the letter;
✧ Your name and address, as they appear on your bill;
✧ Your account number and the statement date on the bill;
✧ Start with "I am writing about a problem with (company name). The transaction date was (mm/dd), the posting date was (mm/dd), and the transaction amount was $(amount);"
✧ Then explain, clearly and briefly, what's wrong;
✧ State that you tried "in good faith" to resolve the problem directly with the merchant, but you were not successful. List the date(s) that you made phone calls and what you were told by the merchant. Enclose photocopies of your letters to the merchant and the merchant's response,

if any. Don't overload the bank with information. You're only proving that you acted in good faith—you're not writing a romance novel;

✧ Keep copies for your records; and

✧ Always, always, always send your letter certified or registered mail.

When you request a chargeback, the bank will credit your account and charge the amount back to the merchant. If you have done everything you were supposed to, this must happen within one billing cycle. If the merchant doesn't respond, the amount is gone from your bill forever. If the merchant disputes the chargeback, the bank has to decide who is telling the truth. And if you don't like the decision, you can always take it to court.

If You Happened to Pay Your Bill in Full Before Noticing an Error

If you do this, you may run into problems. Strictly speaking, the Fair Credit Billing Act (see Appendix 2) states that you may not have to pay "the remaining amount due," which by this time is already too late.

My advice (and remember I am not a lawyer) is to follow the standard procedures for disputing a charge and don't simply bring up the issue of whether you've already paid part or all of it. Odds are, your bank won't raise that issue either.

Of course, it's always a good practice to examine bills carefully before you pay them. If you question a charge 58 days after the date of the infraction or a month or more after you've already paid the bill, the bank may wonder if you're really acting "in good faith."

Unauthorized Charges

If you find that someone else (perhaps an ex-spouse?) has used your credit card number, write to the card issuer and specify that an "unauthorized charge" was made. If you don't use those words, the issuer most likely will treat the incident as a "billing error."

There's a big difference between an unauthorized charge and a billing error. While a billing error must be reported within 60 days, there are no time limits for reporting unauthorized charges. Most people don't get this straight. In fact, a brochure prepared by the Federal Trade Commission (FTC) and a pamphlet prepared by AMEX incorrectly states that cardholders should report unauthorized transactions as billing errors, and that they have only 60 days to do so. A spokeswoman for AMEX stated that its information came from the FTC; a lawyer for the FTC stated that the agency is now aware of the mistake.

"The most a cardholder will be liable for if someone used their card is $50," the FTC lawyer said. "If the card is not used in the transaction, the cardholder won't have to pay any of it."

That last bit, about "if the card is not used," seems to refer to phone or Internet charges, where the person helping themselves to your account doesn't need the actual card to complete the purchase.

SECTION IV: MORTGAGES

CHAPTER 10: YOUR CREDIT AND THE MORTGAGE APPROVAL PROCESS

More of Joanne's Story

Time has passed and Joanne, who we met in Chapter 1, has been busy building her credit. With a new credit card in hand, new clothes in her closet, a student loan and a college class under her belt, *and* a new boyfriend, Joanne is contemplating homeownership. She considers this prospect more seriously one Saturday morning while browsing the personal ads in her local newspaper. (Just for kicks, mind you.) She notices that one of the oft-mentioned items men put in their ads is that they are "homeowners." Does this mean that they are *sexier*? Men seem to think so and thousands of lovelorn men just can't be wrong.

Homeownership by a woman is also alluring. These days, it's a bold statement of independence for a women to set up shop on her own, something most men (at least publicly) say they want in a woman.

Not everyone, as you know, can qualify for a mortgage. But you might be surprised by how little it really takes to get one…

Qualifying—A Sure Sign of Sex Appeal

Good credit goes a long way toward qualifying for a loan. However, even if you don't have good credit, you're still in the ballgame. There are a great variety of loan programs to suit individual needs. If one doesn't land you those house keys, perhaps another program would. Don't give up too easily if you are really serious about homeownership.

After the credit score, underwriters (the people in charge of deciding who gets a loan) just want to see a general pattern in your past that suggests you'll pay on time. They do take into account circumstances truly beyond your control. These circumstances just can't be along the lines of "the dog ate my bills." Banks want to give you a loan—it's how they make money. Although each bank has its own set of rules to decide whether or not to give a person a loan, the criteria provided below is a general guideline of what attracts them. Of course, you've already primped for your credit exam, as we discussed in Chapter 2.

Putting Your Best Bikini Forward

Remember the bikini test in Chapter 5? Now is the time to be buffed and to slip on that special sort of bikini that only loan officers get excited about—a good credit report. Remember that by this time you have already received a copy of your credit reports and groomed them as much as possible. Let the judging begin!

An "A" type loan means a loan for a person with excellent credit, good stability, and sufficient income to make the payments comfortably. I will discuss the loan criteria for "A" loans first. Loans for people who don't fit these requirements will be discussed further along in the chapter.

These days, the first thing a loan officer or underwriter looks at when he runs your credit report is your credit score, also known as your FICO score. FICO scores range from 375 - 900 points—the higher the score the better. If you are applying for a home loan, though, you will not be expected to maintain a 900-point FICO score. In fact, a score of over 650 generally is worthy of an "A" paper loan. If your score is below 650 but above 620, you'll be required to produce more documentation but still will probably receive "A" rates on the loan. If your score is below 620, you typically will be relegated to the higher risk and higher cost financing of "B" through "D" loans.

If your credit score is attractive enough, the underwriter usually will *not* take a closer look at the specifics of your credit history. However, if your credit score is not up to snuff, he may try and qualify you on what is contained in your credit report and ignore the score.

Basically, a good credit record means that you have a history of paying your rent and other bills on time and will be able to prove that through a credit report or through compiling a nontraditional credit history. A good credit history tells the lender that you use credit wisely—important information for a lender to know when you want a mortgage loan.

Although lender credit standards may vary, being late on a payment or having gone over your credit limit once or twice doesn't necessarily mean that you don't have good credit, particularly if you can reasonably explain why. But if you show a repeated pattern of not paying accounts as agreed, it will negatively impact your credit history.

In the "A" credit requirements below, a late payment means a payment that is more than 30 days yet less than 60 days late from the due date. There are four types of credit items on your report: mortgages/rent, auto loans, credit card and other non-secured loans, and collections/judgments.

- ✧ **Mortgages/Rent:** Mortgages are secured loans, in other words, a loan secured by some real property. If you don't have a mortgage, most likely you are paying rent, and you will be substituting your rent payment history for your mortgage payment history. Therefore, when you are applying for a mortgage, the lender needs to be sure that paying your mortgage or rent payments is important to you. You should not have any "late pays" in the last two years.

✧ **Auto Loans:** Lenders consider your payment history on auto loans almost as important as mortgages, as most people need their homes and their cars above all else. You should not have any late payments in the last two years.

✧ **Credit Cards and Other Unsecured Debt:** When it comes to these loans, lenders are much more forgiving. If you were late on making one of these payments (more than 30 days late, but less than 60 days late) you should still be okay. If you have a lot of credit lines showing up on your credit report, and you have two late payments, you should still be all right.

✧ **Judgments and Collections:** Judgments usually result in an automatic loan denial unless you have a really good explanation, and proof, to back it up. Collections are generally regarded the same way, unless it is a medical collection. Mortgage companies are extremely sympathetic about medical collections. They know that the medical profession often turns over unpaid accounts to a collection agency immediately, and often without notifying you.

What Income Can You Count?

Just like potential mates, lenders care about your income and what you do for a living. Lenders, however, are less subtle about wanting to know the specifics of this information. Imagine a date handing you an income application!

Income is one of the most important variables a lender will examine because it is used to repay the loan. Income is reviewed for the type of work, length of employment, educational training required, and opportunity for advancement. You must be able to prove your income through such documents as tax returns, bank statements, and pay stubs. An underwriter will look at the source of income and the likelihood of its continuance to arrive at a gross monthly figure.

✧ **Salary and Hourly Wages:** Calculated on a gross monthly basis, prior to income tax deductions.

✧ **Commission, Bonus, and Overtime Income:** Can only be used if received for two previous years. An employer must verify that it is likely to continue. A 24-month average figure is used.

✧ **Part-time and Second-job Income:** Not usually considered unless it is in place for 12 to 24 straight months. Lenders view part-time income as a strong compensating factor.

✧ **Self-employment Income:** Although being self-employed may make you appear independent and attractive to the opposite sex, lenders think otherwise. They review self-employed borrowers very carefully. Two year's minimum business ownership is necessary because two years is considered a representative sample. Lenders use a two-year average monthly income figure from the adjusted gross income on the tax returns. A lender also may add back additional income for depreciation and one-time capital expenses. Self-employed borrowers often have difficulty qualifying for a mortgage due to large expense write-offs. A good solution to this challenge is something called the "No Income Verification Loan" that any loan officer can discuss with you.

✧ **Alimony and Child Support:** Must have been be received for the 12 previous months and continue for the next 36 months. Lenders will require a divorce decree and a court printout to verify on-time payments.

✧ **Automobile Allowance and Expense Account Reimbursements:** Must be verified with two year's tax returns and reduced by actual expenses listed on the income tax return Schedule C.

✧ **Education Expense Reimbursements:** Not considered income. Only viewed as a slight compensating factor.

✧ **Notes Receivable, Interest, Dividend, and Trust Income:** Proof of consistently receiving these funds for the 12 previous months is required. Documentation showing income due for three more years also is necessary.

✧ **Rental Income:** *Cannot* come from a primary residence roommate. The only acceptable source is from an investment property. A lender will use *75% of the monthly rent* and subtract ownership expenses. The Schedule E of a tax return is used to verify the figures. If a home rented recently, a copy of a current month-to-month lease is acceptable.

✧ **Retirement and Social Security Income:** Must continue for at least three years into the future to be considered. If it is tax free, it can be grossed up to an equivalent gross monthly figure (multiply the net amount by 120%).

What Debts Count Against You?

Ok, let's say you have a new Mercedes, a sleek 52-foot yacht, and the trendiest of clothes. Is your date going to be overly impressed by these extravagances if you can't even buy her a glass of wine because all of your money goes toward payments on your toys?

In the same way, a lender wants to know that you have enough income for your next new toy—a house—after you make payments on your other obligations. When applying for a mortgage, your liabilities are reviewed for cash flow. The following factors come into play:

✧ All loans, leases, and credit cards are counted. (Minimum payments required each month are considered.) Utilities, insurance, food, clothing, schooling, etc. are not part of the equation.

✧ If a loan will be paid off in less than 10 months, a lender will usually disregard it.

⟡ An applicant who co-borrowed for a friend or relative is accountable for the payment. If the applicant can show 6 to 12 months of on-time canceled checks from the co-borrower, the debt will not count.

⟡ Loans can be paid off to qualify for a mortgage, but credit cards sometimes cannot (varies by lender). The reasoning is that if the credit card is paid off, the credit line still exists and the borrower can run up debt after the mortgage is closed. Your best bet is to pay off credit cards and close the accounts.

⟡ A borrower with fewer liabilities is thought to demonstrate superior cash management skills.

The Dreaded Debt-to-income Ratio

Ugh, math.

Once an underwriter calculates a potential borrower's income and debts, he figures out how much of the money the borrower brings in each month is consumed by existing debts. The underwriter wants to see if there is enough money left over for the borrower to comfortably make his payments.

Please note: the debt ratios below are examples and your loan's debt ratios may be different.

Now that we know what counts as income and what counts as a debt, the underwriter wants to see one of two things:

⟡ Either your total monthly mortgage payment (including principal, taxes, insurance and interest) is 29% or less of your gross monthly income (your pay before taxes are taken out); or

⟡ Your total payments per month (not including personal insurance, utilities, and food) are less than 40% of your gross monthly income.

A Mortgage Debt Ratio Example

An applicant has $4,500 gross monthly income. At a maximum debt ratio of 29%, the maximum mortgage payment is:

$4,500 X .29 = $1,305

A Total Debt Ratio Example

This same applicant has other debts totaling:

$500	Car
$ 20	Visa (minimum payment)
$ 30	Sears (minimum payment)
$ 75	MasterCard (minimum payment)
$625	per month

Remember the total debts (mortgage plus other debts) must be less than or equal to 40% of the gross monthly income.

$$\$4,500 \times .40 = \$1,800$$

$1,620 is the maximum debt the borrower can have—debts and mortgage payments combined. In this case, the borrower, since he has high debts, must adjust the maximum mortgage payment downward:

$ 625   Debts
+$1,305   Mortgage
$1,930 (which is more than the $1,800 [40% of gross debt] we calculated above)

The maximum mortgage payment is therefore:

$$\$1,800 - \$625 \text{ (monthly debt)} = \$1,175.$$

Of course, the applicant could also pay down his debts, reducing those monthly payments and bringing down the debt ratios as well.

Financial Stability

Although credit and income are the two biggest deciding factors regarding whether or not to give someone a loan, stability plays a part. Good stability means:

✧ You have been in the same line of work and/or job for two or more years.
✧ You have lived in the same house or apartment for more than two years.

Cash in Savings

Most loan programs require a minimum borrower contribution, called the down payment. Typically, you need to have saved up an amount equal to 5% of the price of the home (at the minimum) to qualify. AND you can't have gotten this money by way of a gift from Mom and Dad. The lender wants to see that you are capable of saving the money on your own.

Lenders evaluate savings for a couple of reasons:

✧ Most loan programs require a down payment. Lenders want to know that you have invested your own money into the house, making it less likely that you will walk away from your life's savings should times get tough. Savings documentation is analyzed to insure that you did not borrow the funds or receive a gift.

✧ They know that the more money a borrower has left in savings after closing, the greater the probability of on-time payments.

✧ Lenders want you to be able to maintain the house in good shape, which requires cash. (It's their house, after all, until you pay the loan off.)

Lenders look at the following types of accounts and assets for down payment funds:

✧ **Checking and Savings:** 90 days "seasoning" in a bank account is required for these funds.

✧ **Gifts and Grants:** After a borrower's minimum contribution, a gift or grant is permitted.

✧ **IRA, 401K, Keogh, and SEP:** Any amount that can be accessed is an acceptable source of funds.

✧ **Sale of Assets:** Personal property can be sold for the required contribution. The property should be appraised and a bill of sale is required. Also, a copy of the received check and a deposit slip are needed.

✧ **Sale of a Previous Home:** Must close prior to purchasing the new home for the funds to be used. A lender will ask for a listing contract, sales contract, or a HUD 1 closing statement.

✧ **Secured Loans:** A loan secured by property also is an acceptable source of closing funds.

✧ **Sweat Equity and Cash-on-hand:** Generally not acceptable. FHA programs allow it in special circumstances.

Qualifying When Your Application is a Tad Tarnished

The decision to approve a loan is not dependent on any one of the above factors alone, but upon all of them together. For instance, if you have excellent credit, but no verifiable income, no one will give you an "A" type loan on a new home. You may still be able to get a loan with less than "A" credit, but the application process will be harder and the interest rate (and points) probably will be higher.

Below are several "classifications" of credit, all of which are below an "A" credit loan rating. These classifications are extremely general (keep in mind that lenders have a vast array of loan programs with an equal array of standards). Use them only as a guideline to assess your situation.

"A-MINUS" CREDIT

Acceptable blemishes within the last two years: Charge-offs or collection accounts of minor amounts (e.g., less than $500 in all) are acceptable. Medical bills, including hospitalization and clinic visits, are usually disregarded by the lender. As for payment habits, the borrower can have no more than two 30-days late payments, or one 60-days late payment on revolving (credit cards) or installment (car loan) credit.

"B" CREDIT

Acceptable blemishes within the last 18 months: Up to four 30-days late, or up to two 60-days late payments are allowed on revolving and installment debt. If the credit ding is an isolated incident, a 90-days late payment is allowed within the last 12 months. Charge-offs or collection accounts which are isolated, insignificant, and less than $1,000 in all, are acceptable. However, outstanding collection accounts less than four years old must be paid. A bankruptcy or foreclosure that has been discharged or settled prior to the 18-month time frame is allowed.

"C" CREDIT

Acceptable blemishes within the last 12 months: No more than six 30-days late payments, three 60-days late payments, or two 90-days late payments are allowed on revolving or installment credit. Open collection accounts and charge-offs may not exceed $4,000 and must be paid in full. A bankruptcy or foreclosure that has been discharged or settled prior to the last 12 months is acceptable.

"D" CREDIT

A disregard for timely payment or credit standing categories: Open collection accounts, charge-offs, and judgments must be paid off—if you are purchasing a home, these must be paid off before the loan is funded; if you are refinancing, you may be able to use some of the loan monies to pay these off. Either way, these must be paid off. The borrower who had filed bankruptcy and had it discharged prior to the last six months is acceptable, as well as the ex-homeowner who had his previous home foreclosed and settled prior to the last six months. However, mortgage payments cannot be longer than 90 days past due.

If You've Had a Bankruptcy

Even if you have had a bankruptcy in the last three to four years, you may be able to get an "A" credit loan. You may be considered to have "A" credit, even with a bankruptcy if:

- ✧ You have a good explanation for why you filed bankruptcy;
- ✧ You have reestablished at least three new lines of credit since the dismissal of bankruptcy; and
- ✧ Your bankruptcy was at least three—preferably four—years ago and you have perfect credit since the discharge of bankruptcy. (No exceptions!)

CHAPTER 11: BANKERS VERSUS MORTGAGE BROKERS—WHICH TO USE?

Josh's Story

Josh is a brilliant engineer and has recently landed a great job with a new, promising company. With the signing bonus and the salary he negotiated, he feels as though he can afford the home he deems important to attract the traditional stay-at-home kind of wife he wants to meet and marry. Most of the girls he has dated have been unimpressed with the apartments he rented in the past, no matter how nice they were. Despite the fact that his friends tell him that he doesn't want a woman who is impressed with a nice house, he really feels handicapped without a luxurious house to call his own. He too has read all the personal ads where the guys mention they are homeowners, and he's listened to women friends who tout the attractiveness of homeownership.

He interviews several realtors and decides to go with Ed, a nice conservative man who seems to know just what Josh wants. Happily, Ed finds a home for Josh right away and the contract on it is accepted. Although Josh has been pre-qualified by a loan officer Ed has used often in the past, Josh wants to look around for one himself. He is offered all kinds of advice, both solicited and unsolicited: "Use my bank, they have pretty good deals." "Have you tried the company's loan program, they throw in closing costs free." "My uncle John used some guy a couple of years ago that he liked, maybe I can get the number for you."

Although Josh is a pretty bright guy, and he spends some time researching the subject, he can't decide which is the better deal—going to his bank or using a mortgage broker "who has a huge variety of products to chose from." The information Josh collects just doesn't fit on a spreadsheet.

Who Has the Better Deal?

There are always two sides to a coin. Choosing between using a banker or a mortgage broker to help secure your loan is strictly a personal preference. Read on, do your homework, then go with your gut.

Bankers

A bank usually, although not always, has its own money to lend and makes a profit by collecting loan fees and the interest the customer pays on the loan, called "servicing fees." However, most banks package up loans in packets of $1,000,000 or more and sell them to the secondary mortgage market, making a commission on the sale. Why? Consider today's low interest rates of 7 - 8%, while stocks and mutual funds are averaging 10% returns or more. Why have millions of dollars tied up in low return investments?

No matter what people tell you, your best deal will usually be found at a bank—yes, that same building where you have your checking and savings accounts. This is because there aren't a lot of add-on fees and middlemen who touch your loan and get paid for it. Plus, these guys do a volume business and, therefore, can cut corners on costs. The employees generally don't get a commission, just an hourly rate, so they aren't looking for ways to charge you extra. Again, banks may be lending their own cash and making money through the servicing of a loan so they don't need to charge origination fees.

Another reason a bank might be cheaper is that banks don't give out loans to anyone without "A" credit, good job stability, long-time residence, and good income. If you fit their criteria, getting a loan is practically automatic and follows the same procedure every single time, without extra work or effort on the part of the bank.

Banks make money by processing a cookie-cutter type of loan. If you don't fit the "A" profile in job, credit, and income, forget it—your loan application will get pitched into the reject pile. Why should the loan officer do any extra work if he won't be paid for it? It's not that you're not a good loan risk, but look at it from the loan officer's point of view…

Consider that in banks that do pay commission, a loan officer may receive a flat $100 commission for every loan. Therefore, why would a loan officer work on a more "complex" loan that takes the time of two easy loans? It's just common sense for him to pitch out a difficult loan.

What about banks that don't pay commission? Are you kidding? Why deal with the stress if you can just stamp "reject" on the file? And those rejected files? That's where mortgage brokers come into play; they take the bank-rejected loans and try to put together a loan package.

Thus, a bank is your best option if:

✧ You have top-notch credit;
✧ You have a steady job/work history;
✧ You have a low debt load; and
✧ You are self-employed, but your last two years of income tax returns easily prove your income.

Brokers

A broker "buys" loans from a variety of mortgage lenders at a wholesale cost and sells the loans to their customers—you and me—receiving a commission on the sale. In the mortgage broker world, you usually pay a higher fee/interest rate for getting your loan accepted, although this is not always the case. The sharp loan officer can take a look at your application and know in advance how much effort will be required to get your loan through the system. Not every broker handles difficult loans, most prefer handling "A" clients. Again, like the guys working in banks, they'd rather make a lower commission for less hassle and go for volume.

So why would an "A" client go to a broker? The reasons are numerous: Some people never think of the bank for mortgages; the broker actually has a better deal (it happens) either in interest or fees; or a realtor recommends the broker. Usually the broker, if he is good and has been in the business a while, has a regular clientele consisting of real estate agents or referrals by past satisfied customers.

Buying a house is very stressful. A competent, hand-holding professional may be a service worth paying for. Generally, your bank will not offer you the same level of comfort and attention.

Loan Officer

There are a lot of loan officers who have been around for a while, but the turnover rate is high in this profession. The typical loan officer working for a mortgage broker:

✧ Has no college degree and may never have finished high school.
✧ Makes about $1,500/month income (about $500/loan) for which they typically work like dogs.
✧ Spends the day getting rejected while looking for business by visiting real estate offices, cold calling customers, going to banks looking for rejected loans, and sending out mailers.
✧ Gets viciously yelled at by borrowers, title companies, realtors, builders, underwriters, and his boss (for not bringing in enough business)—all part of the day, no matter how good a loan officer is.

Loan officers are heavily involved in one of the biggest purchases a person makes in a lifetime, and everything about the deal looms large and frightening for the borrower. Mild-mannered people turn into screaming monsters if anything goes wrong, and there are so many things that can hold up a loan. It's not a fun business; it's stressful, hard work, and it's a good day if no one gets upset with the loan officer. Have some compassion for these folks. Also realize that most of them don't respond well to yelling, hysterics, or threats. It's nothing new to them and will only get you an increase in loan fees as compensation for your abuse, or earn you terrible service. Loan officers are people, too.

If you have less-than-perfect credit, you will most likely qualify for a "non-conforming loan" (those "tarnished" loan packages mentioned in the previous chapter). Know that it will cost you more for a variety of reasons. The loan officer specializing in these "non-conforming loans" knows he or she will work harder for this deal and will either charge you more money in closing costs or hope that you will be impressed enough to send many referrals in the future. How much extra they may charge really is their call (and yours—you can always walk away). However, overcharging isn't the norm. Loan officers with clients who feel they've been overcharged don't get repeat business—the real money in this industry. Unfortunately, you still need to be careful. Desperate people can get taken because they'll do anything to get a loan.

If you think you're being overcharged, shop around. Most brokers have access to the same products (meaning they can usually find and buy the same loans as other brokers), so call around and compare interest rates and fees, especially if you're not an "A" loan. Don't believe the loan officer who tells you that you won't get a loan anywhere else. By shopping around, you usually can discover who's trying to gouge you. Once you find the interest rate and fees you can live with, fill out an application at the broker's office, and lock the terms of the loan.

A broker (or loan officer) is your best option when:

- ✧ You have less than perfect credit;
- ✧ You are self-employed (and can't prove your income);
- ✧ You just switched professions; and/or
- ✧ You have a high debt load.

Mortgage brokers can get you a loan when the banks just aren't interested in the hassle. But if you are a non-conforming borrower, you will pay more in both fees and interest rates for your loan.

Keep in mind that a broker may have competitive rates/fees as compared to a bank, so don't necessarily rule out a broker even if you'd qualify for a bank loan.

The bottom line is that you need to shop around. You probably didn't buy the first house you "sort of" liked. Don't go for the first mortgage program you "sort of" like, either. One is no less of a commitment than the other.

CHAPTER 12: MORTGAGE COSTS

Don and Ann's Story

Don's company offers him a promotion with a relocation to a city that just happens to be near his in-laws. Don knows Ann wants to be closer to her family, and remembers that Ann moved away from them to support his career. He would also like to build his relationship with his in-laws, which has always been on shaky ground. So it's decided. They fly to the new city, find the perfect home, and even have a few moments left over to visit Ann's parents.

Because their credit is slightly rocky, Don and Ann decide to go through a local mortgage broker in their new city. They expect to have to settle for less than an "A" loan and are pleasantly surprised when their loan officer, Jordan, tells them that she has a special program for them that will allow them to qualify at the interest rate for "A" loans. Everything is falling wonderfully into place, and they return to their apartment to pack.

Sure enough, after sending in the loan paperwork, they receive a Truth In Lending (TIL) notice confirming the interest rate and fees that Jordan had promised them. And before long, they get a call from Jordan telling them that their loan is ready to close. She also tells them the amount of the cashier's check they need to bring to cover closing costs and the down payment. Excitedly, Don and Ann pack all of their belongings into a huge rental van and drive to their new city.

While signing the papers for their new home at the title company, Don and Ann discover that, although the interest rate is fine, the closing costs are $3,000 more than they had been told, and the extra fees are cutting into their down payment. The title agent places a call to Jordan, who speaks to her clients. She explains that they were turned down for the loan with the interest rate they wanted and she had to switch loan programs to qualify them. The extra $3,000 is to buy down the interest rate to the rate they had wanted. If they don't want the loan, she continues, they could try someplace else, but this is the best they can get.

Ann, tears in her eyes, asks the title agent what they can do. All the title agent can offer is simply that it is their decision about whether they want the loan and, consequently, the house. Knowing that all of their worldly possessions are parked outside, Don swallows hard and convinces Ann they should sign.

Money for Closing Costs and, O Yeah, a Down Payment

Yep, loans cost you more than just interest. It seems amazing how many people have their hands out when it comes time to make a loan: the loan officer, the title company, the state, and the appraiser. On top of that, you still have to come up with a down payment. The amount of the minimum down payment required varies depending on your credit and how much the property is worth. For example, if you have less-than-perfect credit, you will be required to put more money down when purchasing a home than someone with a stellar credit rating.

The Real Estate Settlement Procedures Act (RESPA) contains information on the settlement or closing costs you are likely to face. The act also requires lenders to give you an information booklet, titled **Settlement Costs and You**, written by the U.S. Department of Housing and Urban Development. This booklet discusses how to negotiate a sales contract, how to work with various professionals (i.e., attorneys, real estate agents, lenders), and your rights and responsibilities as a homebuyer.

The Costs of a Loan

Okay, you've chosen your loan officer, and you've been approved for a loan. Now you need to know how to negotiate the costs of securing that loan. We'll give you an idea of the costs to expect, then discuss how the mortgage broker makes his money from a deal.

Upfront Fees

When you are ready to start your loan, the loan officer will ask you for money upfront to pay for:

- ✧ **An Appraisal:** Appraisals are conducted because lenders want to be sure that the property is worth at least as much as the mortgage. Professional property appraisers will compare the value of the house to that of similar properties in the community.
- ✧ **A Credit Report:** Lenders require a special kind of credit report, you won't be able to bring one in and have them use it. It is basically a "merged" credit report containing information from all three credit bureaus.

These fees are non-refundable; the mortgage company has to pay for these services whether or not the loan goes through.

Other Fees You Likely Will Be Charged for a Loan

There are an enormous amount of fees associated with a mortgage loan. The following fees are a part of every loan. The loan officer and mortgage company have no control over them. They include:

Fees Due to Inspections, Insurance, or Searches Required by the Mortgage Bank Making the Loan

- ✧ **Title Search Costs:** Usually your attorney or title company will do or arrange for a title search on your property to make sure there are no problems (i.e., liens, lawsuits) attached to the home.
- ✧ **Lender's Title Insurance:** Even though there is a title search for any obstacle (i.e., liens, lawsuits), many lenders require insurance just the same. In the event a problem does arise, they can recover their mortgage investment. This is a one-time insurance premium, usually paid at closing. It is insurance for the lender only, not for you as a purchaser.
- ✧ **Inspections Required by the Lender (termite, water tests):** If you apply for an FHA or VA mortgage, the lender will require a termite inspection. In many rural areas, lenders will require a water test to make sure that the well and water system will maintain an adequate supply of water to the house (this usually is a test for quantity, not a test for water quality).
- ✧ **Land Survey:** Many lenders require that the property be surveyed to make sure that no one has encroached on it and to verify the buildings and improvements to the property.

Other Fees Charged by the Mortgage Bank Giving You the Loan

- ✧ **Lender's Attorney's Fees:** Lenders may have their attorney draw up documents, check to see that the title is clear, and represent them at the closing. This will be in place of the document preparation fee.
- ✧ **Document Preparation Fees:** You will see an amazing array of papers, ranging from the application to the acceptance to the closing documents. Lenders may charge for these, or they may be included in the application and/or attorney's fees.
- ✧ **Preparation of Amortization Schedule:** Some lenders will prepare a detailed amortization schedule showing the monthly breakdown of principal and interest over the full term of your mortgage. They are more likely to do this for fixed mortgages than for adjustable mortgages.
- ✧ **Lender's Mortgage Insurance:** If your down payment is less than 20% or 25%, many lenders will require that you purchase private mortgage insurance (PMI) for the amount of the loan. This way, if you default on the loan, the lender will recover his money. These insurance premiums will continue until your equity in the property equals 20% or 25% of the selling price, but they may continue for the life of the loan. The premiums usually are added to any amount you must escrow for taxes and homeowner's insurance.

Fees Possibly Due to the Purchase Agreement Between the Buyer and Seller During the Sale of a Property

Typically, this includes inspection fees (i.e., structural, water quality tests, radon tests). In addition to inspections required by the lender, you may make (and probably should if you are buying a resale home) the purchase offer contingent on satisfactory completion of a home inspection. You and the seller will need to negotiate these fees.

Title Company Fees

✧ **Owner's Title Insurance:** You may want to purchase title insurance for yourself so that if problems arise, you are not left owing a mortgage on a property you no longer own. A thorough title search (going back to 1900, if necessary) is often assurance enough of a clear title.
✧ **Recording Fees for Deed:** Recording fees pay for the county clerk to record the deed and mortgage and change the property tax billing.
✧ **Other State and Local Fees:** Can include mortgage taxes levied by states as well as other local fees.

Fees That Create Your Escrow Account at the Title Company

Your mortgage loan is secured by your property, and the lender wants to do everything possible to make sure that if you default on the home, they can get the property back in good (saleable) condition.

You can lose your house if you don't pay your property taxes, and lenders, of course, know this. If your house burns down and you have no homeowner's insurance, the property won't be worth the amount of the mortgage. The lender is going to *insist* that you pay a portion of your annual property taxes and hazard insurance as part of your mortgage payment to them. In turn, the mortgage company takes this money each month and gives it to the escrow or title company, who then pays your property tax and insurance bills for you when they come due.

✧ **Prepaid Interest:** Your first regular mortgage payment usually is due about six to eight weeks after you close (for example, if you close in August, your first regular payment will be in October covering the cost of borrowing money for the month of September). Interest costs, however, start as soon as you close. The lender will calculate how much interest you owe for the fraction of the month in which you close (for example, if you close on August 25, you would owe interest for the remaining six days of August). In some cases, this is due at closing.
✧ **Prorated Property Taxes:** Pro-rated property taxes (such as school taxes and municipal taxes) may have to be split between you and the seller because they are due at different times of the year. For example, if taxes are due in October and you close in August, you would owe taxes for two months while the seller would owe taxes for the other 10 months. Prorated taxes usually are paid based on the number of days (not months) of ownership. Some lenders may require you to set up an escrow account to cover these bills, as mentioned previously. If your lender does not require an escrow account, you may want to set up a special account on your own to make sure you have money set aside for these important—and large—bills.

❖ **Homeowner's Insurance:** Most lenders require that you prepay the first year's premium for homeowner's insurance (sometimes called hazard insurance), and bring proof of payment to the closing. This insures that their investment will be secured, even if the house is destroyed.

Fees Profiting the Mortgage Company

The following fees determine the profit on the loan for the loan officer and the mortgage company, and are completely under their control. There is no standard for these fees, so watch very carefully for them. While these fees may be necessary to get you a loan if your credit is shaky, an unscrupulous loan officer could try to make as much as possible from you with the addition of these fees.

❖ **Application Fees:** Application fees are non-refundable and 100% pure profit for the mortgage broker. Walk out if they ask for an application fee up front. The only exception to this rule is if you have tough credit. In this case, the loan officer will have to do a lot of work before he can tell if your loan will go through. Time is money and he will want to be paid for this effort. If your loan gets denied without an application fee up front, the loan officer has put in a lot of hours for nothing.

❖ **Origination Fees:** These are fees for processing the mortgage application and may be a flat fee or a percentage of the mortgage. They usually are equal to one point. In fact, they are just a point called by a fancy name so the loan officer can charge more for the loan.

❖ **Points:** A point is equal to 1% of the amount borrowed. For example, one point on a loan amount of $50,000 is $500 dollars. Points can be payable when the loan is approved (before closing) or at closing. For FHA and VA mortgages, the seller—not the buyer—must pay the points. Even if you are not using an FHA or VA mortgage, you may want to negotiate points in the purchase offer. Some lenders will let you finance points, adding this cost to the mortgage, which will increase your interest costs. If you pay the points up front, they are deductible from your income taxes in the year they are paid. Different deductibility rules apply to second homes.

❖ **Points "On the Back":** These are fees and commissions earned by the mortgage broker by selling you a loan whose interest rate is above the going rate. More about this momentarily.

The Role of the Loan Officer

Now that you know which fees a loan officer or mortgage broker charges to make a profit, let's examine the role of the loan officer in the making of a loan. This is important so you will know how to recognize a shady loan officer if you meet one.

Most loan officers are *not* paid a salary; they are paid a commission for every loan they originate that closes. Loan officers typically split the profits on each loan (usually 50/50) with the company they work for. Therefore, every dollar they can squeeze out of you is 50 cents into their pocket. To originate a loan, the loan officer merely gets a client to fill out a loan application. A good loan officer also should:

- ✧ Collect all of the documentation the bank will need to approve the loan;
- ✧ Collect fees for the credit report;
- ✧ Take the time to explain everything you need to know;
- ✧ Be available to take your phone calls, should you have questions;
- ✧ Report to you once a week via the phone on the status of your loan (even if there is no real status); and
- ✧ Be creative about finding solutions to any problems that may arise.

If they do all of this, they deserve their commissions. However, they will still get paid even if they only do the minimum.

The "normal fees" in the industry are an origination fee (1 "point") plus one additional point. Some brokers have a limit on how much a loan officer can charge in fees—the loan application fee, the origination fee, and the points—but not all. Since most mortgage broker companies split the profit earned from every loan with the loan officer, can you see how it is in the interest of a mortgage broker not to enforce a maximum fee policy on its loan officers?

Getting Points on the Back

We mentioned this before as one of the ways a loan officer makes more funds available to the total loan "kitty." It is essentially a "kick-back" from the mortgage bank the loan officer is buying the loan from, earned by selling a customer a loan at an interest rate that is above the going rate.

Each day, loan officers receive rates from banks for all of their loan programs. Listed for each program is the "par interest rate." The par interest rate is the rate at which the broker does not have to pay a fee to "buy" the loan and then sell it to you, nor does he receive a commission for selling you the loan. You might say that the par rate is "loan equilibrium." Table 3 on the next page shows an example of the types of rates a bank might publish to their subscribing mortgage companies every day. The "par rate" is indicated by 0.00.

Table 3—Example Rate Sheet on a 30-Year Loan

	6.5	6.75	7.0	7.25	7.5
15-day Lock	.50	.25	0.00	(.5)	(1.5)
30-day Lock	.75	.50	.25	0.00	(.25)
45-day Lock	1.50	.75	.50	.25	0.00
60-day Lock	2.50	1.00	.75	.50	.25

In the above example, the "par" value for a 15-day lock is 7.0%. (I will explain locking later in the chapter). The numbers in parentheses are the points returned to the loan proceeds as additional funds to offset the costs of the loan (or as a commission for loan officer). Why would anyone knowingly pay this higher rate? To get a "no-cost loan."

For example, if you wanted a $150,000 loan, but didn't have enough to cover the loan costs, you could bump up your interest rate to 7.5%, giving you: $150,000 x 1.5% / 100 = $2,250. This money will be credited to the loan proceeds at closing. What does this mean? It means that if your closing costs are $2,250, you won't have to lay out a dime for closing costs. (Keep in mind, though, that you can't just up the interest rate to cover your down payment requirement. You must have your own money for down payment.)

And if you didn't know that the rate you were getting was higher than the par rate (meaning that you paid full loan costs and a higher interest rate, too)? The loan officer gets that $2,250. Do some loan officers "forget" to tell you about this little loan surplus? Unfortunately, some do. It is one of the most profitable methods used by loan officers to boost their commissions.

No-cost Loans

You've heard of those no-cost refinance loans? Forget it. **There is no such thing**. A broker must make money on *every* loan. Many well-intentioned loan officers honestly believe they are giving you a loan for free, but this simply is not the case.

In the example above, you saw how you could get a loan at an interest rate above the par rate and get points on the back. The points on the back translate to extra funds available to pay the cost of the loan *plus* pay the loan officer a commission. So what's wrong with this? Nothing. But it is not "no cost." You are financing the costs of the loan (paying interest on them) over the term of the loan (usually 30 years), which can double or triple the closing costs by the time you are done paying them. A "no cost" loan *may* be the right choice for you, but consider the real costs carefully.

Is Your Loan Officer Jacking Up Your Interest Rate?

It bears repeating that it is the loan officer who picks the interest rate he is going to sell you and, consequently, the commissions he will earn on the loan. If he is competing with another loan company to get your loan, he may not be greedy and not jack up the rate. But if you don't shop around, don't trust him to be honest. Some loan officers are completely up-front with you, but some aren't. *Always* shop around, especially if you have "A" credit. Some loan officers will charge you less if they know your loan will be a piece of cake to process.

Take extra caution if you have less than stellar credit and must get a non-conforming loan, as these are typically the biggest target of shady loan officers. Desperate people have been known to swallow higher interest rates and 5 points in fees. This definitely is gouging.

Watch mortgage rates offered by other lenders. They're published in your local newspaper. Ask your loan officer if this is the best rate you can get. If you're not satisfied with the answer, look elsewhere for your loan.

You can always figure out how much "extra" money your loan officer received by looking at your closing statement. Your title officer will gladly point it out. However, at this stage of the game, you're usually signing loan documents and it's too late to do anything about it short of canceling the deal. (That's why it is important to try to review your Uniform Settlement Statement ahead of time, if possible. We'll talk more about the Uniform Settlement Statement shortly.) If you notice that your mortgage company is getting three points on the back (meaning the interest rate you're getting is much higher than the par rate), you can always walk out on the deal. Some loan officers count on the fact that the moving van containing all of your worldly possessions (like our friends Don and Ann) is parked outside and you won't do that.

Locking Down Your Interest Rate

> *"Ya just gotta ask yourself one question: Do I feel lucky? Well, do ya, punk?"*
> - Clint Eastwood as *Dirty Harry*

In Table 3, you may have noticed the 15-, 30-, 45-, and 60-day lock rates. Market interest rates fluctuate not just every day but *every hour*. The rate sheets are only good at the moment they are issued. Locks are offered to alleviate confusion, and to allow brokers to offer a rate that will remain steady for a certain period of time. To do this, the broker can tell the mortgage company that he wants it to hold a loan at a certain interest rate for a certain period of time. This is called "locking a loan." You may have noticed that the longer the lock, the more expensive (points-wise) the loan. This is because the bank is taking a gamble that the rates will remain steady for the period the broker wants. If the market rates shoot up, the bank will still have to honor the locked rate at the lower interest rate.

Locking down your interest rate is *always* a good idea. If you're worried that the rates may go down further while your loan is being processed, ask yourself, "Am I a risk-taker?" Yes, the interest rate may go down, but it also may go up, no matter what the loan officer or anyone else may say. I've seen it happen lots of times—everyone says the rates are going down and they go up, sometimes way up. If the rates go up, you may have to pay as much as an extra point to get your original rate if you didn't lock it down.

Remember also that when you say you want to lock the rate, the loan officer sends in the paperwork to the banker selling the loans and the banker gives him a commitment.

What if the rate does go down? It's not fair to ask the loan officer to break his commitment to the bank where he's buying his loans and re-lock you at a lower rate. Doing this a lot can dry up future supplies of loans if the loan officer gets a bad reputation. After all, if the rates go up, don't you expect the bank to keep its commitment and give you the lower rate?

Buying Down the Interest Rate

The reverse situation to "getting points on the backside" is paying extra points for a lower interest rate. This is called "buying down the interest rate." For instance, the par rate for a 15-day lock back in Table 3 is 7.0%. But if you look to the left of the table, you'll see that you could "buy down" the rate to 6.5% by paying .50 points at closing. Give it some thought. It might suit you to pay a bit more up front to get a lower interest rate, and lower monthly payments, over the life of the loan.

Truth in Lending

All mortgage lenders are required to give you a Truth in Lending (TIL) statement containing information on the annual percentage rate, the finance charge, the amount financed, and the total payments required. Federal law requires this to be sent to you within three days of the time you apply for the mortgage. This *estimate* should give you a good idea of how much cash you will need at closing to cover pro-rated taxes, first month's interest, and other settlement costs. Note the emphasis on the word "estimate." This is not a guarantee of anything but, rather, a "best guess" at the moment.

The TIL statement also may contain information on security interest, late charges, prepayment provisions, and whether the mortgage is assumable. If you have an adjustable rate loan, it may outline the limits on the adjustments (annual and lifetime caps) and give an example of what your next year's payment might be, depending on interest rates.

You should note a couple of things about this document. **It is the most misunderstood of all the paperwork and generates the most panic calls to the loan officer**.

✧ **The APR listed on the paperwork is not the rate you applied for**. The APR calculates the interest rate in some complicated formula which takes into account your closing costs and fees, and is generally much higher than the agreed-upon interest rate. Ignore this number. The actual loan interest rate should also be listed on the TIL and clearly marked. Most people don't get this far because the APR is the first number they see.

✧ **This TIL doesn't mean a thing**. It is not an agreement between you and the broker. The mortgage company or loan officer is bound in no way, shape, or form to the terms or fees listed in the TIL. The bank can change the interest rate and terms at any time, should you not meet its requirements or documentation. The TIL just indicates the initial estimate by the loan officer. If you want to guarantee your interest rate, see the above section on "Locking Down Your Interest Rate."

The Uniform Settlement Statement

Unlike the TIL, the Uniform Settlement Statement (USS) *is* the document that deserves your close attention. This document *does* accurately reflect your true interest rates and costs and is the final settlement statement. If the loan officer "neglected" to tell you a few things (like the fact that you are not getting a par interest rate), it will show up on the USS.

Unfortunately, and of necessity, this statement is not available for your review until one business day before you close (because the final figures are not calculated, the title company or attorney is busy and hasn't gotten to it yet, etc.). You are entitled to see a copy of the Uniform Settlement Statement with your figures on it so you will know just how much the final costs will be. Most attorneys and title companies will go through it with you line by line. If at all possible, have the title company fax a copy to you as soon as it is available so you can review it at your leisure *before* going in to sign.

CHAPTER 13: SECOND MORTGAGES

Norma's Story

Norma admits to going a little crazy on her credit cards after her husband of 20 years divorced her. She hired a personal trainer, bought all new clothes, and traveled every chance she got. She felt and looked great, and met lots of interesting new people—many of them fascinating men who wondered where she'd been hiding all these years. Being single again was an absolute blast, until she realized how much it was costing her.

Norma knew she was in big trouble when the checks she wrote to pay her credit card bills ate up a third of her take home pay, and that barely covered minimum payments. Confiding her troubles to the new man in her life over coffee, she was relieved to find a sympathetic ear. He confessed to being in the same boat not long ago, and had paid off his credit cards by taking a second mortgage on his house. Her house was nearly paid off, wasn't it?

What is a Second Mortgage?

A second mortgage is a loan secured by real estate that already has a primary or first mortgage on it. The maximum amount of the second mortgage is determined by the equity in the home. The equity is the difference between what is owed on the home and value of the home:

Value of home - Total amount of loans = Equity

Types of Second Mortgages

Home Equity Line of Credit: This type of mortgage typically is an Adjustable Rate Mortgage (ARM). The interest rate on this loan will be fixed for a stated period of time and will then become adjustable for the remainder of the loan. This adjustment is based on changes in a pre-selected index, and will take place according to a pre-defined schedule (generally once a year). Your interest rate and monthly payment will fluctuate based on changes in your index. The most common indices are the Treasury Bill, a Certificate of Deposit (CD), the London Inter-Bank Offered Rate (LIBOR), and the Cost of Funds Index (COFI).

A line of credit is much like a credit card: you have a maximum limit, and you are able to take out any amount of money up to the amount of the maximum over the life of the loan. You also may pay off the entire amount ahead of schedule, and keep the line open for future withdrawals. Unlike a credit card, though, the line of credit has a fixed life, or length of time to withdraw from and pay off the debt. When the life of the loan ends, you must pay off the entire balance or refinance it.

Fixed-rate Mortgages: These are second mortgages that have a fixed interest rate and a fixed term for the loan. Typical lengths of second mortgages are 15 and 30 years.

Why Would You Want a Second Mortgage?

Many people use a second mortgage to pay off credit card debts or other kinds of debts, seeking to lower their total monthly payments. Some people say this also is a way to save money, as the interest from a second mortgage is deductible, where credit card interest is not. If you are making the minimum monthly payments on your credit cards, you'll be paying on them for about 30 years anyway, so the low interest on second mortgages may be a good deal for you. (Don't think you'll be paying on your credit cards for 30 years if you only pay the minimums? See the discussion of credit cards in Chapter 7.)

Other reasons people take out second mortgages include home improvements, business loans, college expenses, etc.

Are Second Mortgages a Good Idea?

Second mortgages can be dangerous, actually hurting you in the long run. Do you really want to pay for that romantic dinner you had last month for 15 years with interest? That's essentially what happens when you use the proceeds from a second mortgage to pay off your credit card bills. If you have had a tough time controlling your credit card spending in the past, think carefully about what is going to happen when you suddenly find yourself with zero balances on your credit cards. Sadly, many people find themselves in the position of first paying off their credit cards with a second mortgage, only to find the cards maxed out again in a year's time or less.

What Kind of Credit Do You Need?

As in first mortgages, there are a wide variety of programs to fit most every credit need. If you have perfect credit, there are many programs out there that will loan you up to 125% of your equity. Yes, this means that even if you have no equity, you can get a second mortgage.

However, just as with first mortgages: the worse your credit is, the higher the interest rates will be, and the less you will be able to borrow against your equity.

For instance, if you have less-than-perfect credit, a lender may only be willing to loan you up to 80% Loan-to-Value (LTV).

Let's say you have a $200,000 house, can get a loan at 80% LTV, and you still owe $125,000 on the house:

$200,000 x 80%/100 = $160,000

$160,000 (80% LTV)
-125,000 (owed on house)
$ 35,000

Since you owe $125,000 on the home, you will be able to get a second mortgage for $35,000. (Of course, your interest rate may be 11%, but hey, that's beside the point!)

SECTION V:
OTHER TYPES OF LOANS

CHAPTER 14: AUTOMOBILES

Martin's Story

Martin, single and just out of college, is looking for the ultimate "chick magnet" on wheels. Through his college years, he managed to save all of about $1.75 while accumulating $22,000 in student loans. But no worry. He just landed a job as a computer programmer, so fat paychecks are in his future.

What is of utmost importance to Martin at the moment is the little red Spyder convertible he just took for a test drive. He's seen women swoon over this car and it's time that some of that swooning included him.

Nearly panting as he sits in the sales office with his salesman, Bernie, it's clear that Martin wants this car at any price. Bernie is blissful, too, sensing that this one commission will finance the diamond engagement ring that will make his girlfriend so happy.

Rule #1

Be cool. Try not to let your excitement show. If Martin panted this obviously over a prospective date, he'd probably find himself going to the movies alone. Do your homework before you start shopping and keep your wits about you.

If you are susceptible to sales tactics, consider bringing someone with you when you visit the dealership. And although it sounds totally uncool, if you are young like our friend Martin, think about bringing a parent to help with negotiations. The embarrassment of a chaperone for one afternoon can save you from making a rash decision in the heat of the moment (and years of regret as you make overpriced payments month after month).

The Variables

Most people finance their vehicles these days. We've all heard horror stories about the car sales guys. But what about the finance people? Keep in mind that there are three ways for an auto dealership to make money on you:

✧ **The price of the vehicle**. Even if you pay the dealer's "invoice price," there is a 2% profit margin built into this price. There also may be kickbacks from the carmaker that are not revealed to the consumer. If you want to see the exact manufacturer's invoice price, you can look it up with the information published twice a year by Edmunds, either from their books titled *Edmunds Used Cars and Truck Prices and Ratings* and *Edmunds New Cars Prices and Reviews*, or at their website at http://www.edmunds.com. Before you step foot onto the lot, make sure you are armed with information about the invoice price of the vehicle you have selected.

✧ **Trade-in value of the car**. The folks at the dealership are naturally going to offer you as little money for your trade-in as possible. A common tactic is to combine the two transactions of your car deal and your trade-in by coming up with the total amount of cash you need to get into your new car. This is an attempt to distract you from the money (or lack of it) you are getting for your trade-in. (It also works to distract you from the price of the car.) A salesman will always ask you if you are considering trading in your car. Tell him that you don't know yet, and proceed to negotiate the price of the new car. Only after you have agreed on the price of your purchase should you begin discussions on the value of your trade-in. And yes, you guessed it—the best place to find the value of your trade-in is Edmunds or the *Kelly Blue Book* (http://www.kbb.com). Both of these online references have current data on the value of most used car models.

✧ **Financing**. Be very wary of obtaining financing at an auto dealer. True, you can get some good deals at an auto dealership. (Remember the 1% financing that was going on in the early 90s?) We'll discuss this financing option in more detail shortly.

If you are getting a good deal on one of the above three areas, most likely the folks at the dealership are trying as hard as possible to make money on one of the other aspects of the deal. We all have better things to do with our evenings, but it really does pay to do your homework before visiting your friendly car dealership. Do your research and bring your notes with you.

Most sales pitches will start along the lines of "How much do you want your payment to be?" This is an attempt to distract you from the best overall deal. After all, you could have a monthly payment of $50 if you financed your $20,000 car over 40 years. When they ask you this question, tell them you want your payment to be $0 (well, isn't it true?), and then start negotiating things one item at a time.

Financing Options

Typically, you have three options when it comes to financing:

✧ Conventional auto loan;
✧ Lease; and
✧ Payment shaver loan.

Conventional Auto Loan

A conventional auto loan is very similar to a mortgage loan in that you must qualify for the loan based on your credit and income. Most banks and auto dealerships carry loan products for people with less-than-perfect credit.

For "A" credit, your interest rate should be close to the interest rates you can get for an "A" credit mortgage loan. For fair credit, you should be able to get a loan for two to three percentage points above the "A" credit rates. If you think you are being charged too much for a loan, you probably are. Shop around. There are a number of options when it comes to financing your auto loan:

✧ **Finance Companies:** A finance company that is owned by an auto manufacturer, such as Ford Motor Credit or General Motors Acceptance Corporation, is called a "captive finance company." Captive finance companies account for approximately 20% of new car loans. Finance companies buy a loan wholesale, mark it up, and sell it retail. It may be easier to get credit through a finance company than through a bank, but it usually is at the cost of a higher interest rate.

✧ **Dealers:** As in mortgage lending, the auto dealership typically has a large variety of loan products to offer you. Naturally, they will try to sign you up for a loan with the highest profit for the dealership. The larger the interest rate they charge you, the larger the commission given to the dealership. Some loan companies have a limit on how much they will allow an auto dealership to "gouge" you in extra interest percentage points, but some do not. It usually is best to arrange your own financing for the auto before you walk onto the car lot. As in the negotiations for your trade-in, treat financing as a completely separate transaction from the other two—talk only about one thing at a time.

✧ **Banks:** Banks are the most common source for financing, accounting for about 40% of new car loans. You may be able to negotiate better terms, such as a lower interest rate, if you have a longstanding relationship with a bank. But you don't need to have an existing account at a bank to acquire a loan from them, so check with several banks in your area for the best interest rate. Some banks offer a pre-approved loan, which allows you some flexibility in shopping.

✧ **Credit Unions:** You must be a member of a credit union to obtain a loan from them. They account for approximately 25% of new car loans. Credit unions offer the best loan rates—typically, one half to one percentage point lower interest than bank car loans. Further, credit unions typically charge simple interest, saving you additional money.

✧ **Online:** The Internet allows you to compare rates nationwide, any time of day or night. There are several "e-loans" available exclusively online, and many sites also have built-in calculators to help you determine the cost of financing your vehicle.

✧ **Home Equity Loans:** The positive difference between what you paid for your property and its current value is called the "equity." This equity can be used as collateral on a loan, which you could use to purchase a car. You can obtain a home equity loan at a bank or credit union. In effect, this is a second mortgage on your home (as we discussed in Chapter 13) and is, therefore, tax deductible. If you have an approved line of credit and don't have to pay any new origination fees, this is an especially good deal. But consider this type of loan carefully. You are using your home as collateral to secure your car loan and could potentially lose your house if you default on your auto payments.

Prepayment Penalties

Some loans have a prepayment penalty to insure the highest profitability possible. You need to be sure to ask your loan officer if the program he is offering you has a prepayment penalty attached to the loan.

Rule of 78s

Sometimes a loan has a prepayment penalty built into it that doesn't appear to be one. This is called the "Rule of 78s." Suppose you want to pay off your loan early. You have your amortization schedule and calculate the payoff based on it. You call and tell your bank that you intend to pay off the loan two years early, and they throw out a payoff number much higher than your amortization schedule indicated. What gives?

When lenders use the Rule of 78s, they distribute the total finance charge over all payments but charge more interest early in the loan term and less later, compared with other methods. The Rule of 78s, also called "the sum of digits method," gets its name because the sum of digits 1 through 12, the months in a one-year loan, equals 78.

Here's how the Rule of 78s works for a 12-month loan: You pay 12/78 of the total finance charge the first month, 11/78 the second month, 10/78 the third month, and so on. The rule of 78s applies the same way for long-term loans. For example, a 24-month loan—where the sum of the digits for months 1 through 24 is 300—would have a first month's interest of 24/300, second month's interest of 23/300, and so on. Interest on a 36-month loan would be broken into 666 parts.

Not sure if your loan uses the Rule of 78s? Look at your Truth in Lending disclosure. If you see a phrase like "you will not be entitled to any rebate of part of the finance charge if you prepay," ask the lender if it computes interest using the Rule of 78s.

Leases

If Martin wanted a car with extra sex appeal, he could afford a much more expensive one – if he went with a lease program. When the price of the average car increased to $15,000 - $20,000 in the 1990s, auto dealerships had to come up with a way for average people to afford their products. They came up with the leasing idea, which allows people to get more car for their monthly car payment. A lease is essentially a long-term rental of a brand-new car. A customer signs a contract to rent the car for a period of two to three years, making monthly rental payments. The customer agrees to keep the car in good shape and drive it only a certain number of miles a year. At the end of the lease term, the customer can purchase the vehicle for a predetermined cash amount. This value is called the residual value.

Leases can be a good option for people who:

- ✧ Have good credit;
- ✧ Buy a new car every two to three years;
- ✧ Don't put a lot of mileage on their vehicles;
- ✧ Are going to have a payment no matter what;
- ✧ Keep their cars in immaculate condition; and
- ✧ Are writing off the car payments through a business expense.

Beware of Dealer Tactics

Most people don't understand how leases work, so it's pretty easy for dealers to rip them off. Like a magician who distracts you with some meaningless hand movement to disguise the way the trick really works, the dealer keeps you focused on the monthly payment.

Cap Cost

Even if you think you have negotiated a price, known as the "cap cost," the dealer can inflate the price on your paperwork, and often they succeed. The cap cost is important because it is the price on which the lease payments are based. If you do catch a dishonest dealer in the lie of raising the cap cost, he may tell you that it represents finance costs (baloney), or that your lease payments are not based on this cost (blatant lie). The bottom line: Read your paperwork and take your time about getting questions answered.

Comparison Pricing

Dealers also try to sell you on leases by doing a comparison between the payments for a lease and the payments for the same car on a conventional loan. Invariably, the comparisons show the lease payment to be the winner. Check the payment calculations—are they based on the same number of year's payment calculations? Most lease payments in these comparisons are based on a five-year payment schedule. Conventional loan payments are often calculated on a three-year schedule, so the dealer is giving you a comparison of apples and oranges.

Inflated "Interest Rate"

Since you are just "renting" the car, and technically are not getting a loan, the leasing company isn't required by law to tell you the interest rate on which they are calculating the lease payments. In fact, the "interest rate" a lessor is charging you is not an interest rate at all (since again, you are not getting a loan) and is called the "money factor." The money factor is a fractional number, such as 0.0042, to calculate the lease fee or charge. The monthly payment combines the resulting fee with the depreciation charge. Neither the money factor nor the lease charge is an interest rate in the traditional sense; both are part of a formula devised by lessors to determine their profit. Yep, profit. The reason lease companies are in business.

Will dealers tell you the money factor? Yes, but only if you ask. The formula for converting the money factor to an APR is also not required to be given to the consumer by law—like credit score calculations, it is somewhat of a mystery.

Down Payments

You are not buying the car, so there is no such thing as a down payment in a lease. What you are doing is making payments in advance. Say you put $2,000 down to make a $400 payment over 24 months drop to $350. Sound like a good deal? Let's look a little closer. This may prove more expensive in the long run.

Let's say, for example, that you have a two-year lease—you will pay $400 x 24 = $9,600. But if you slap down the $2,000 up front, you're actually paying $800 more for the vehicle:

$$\begin{aligned} \$350 \text{ x } 24 &= \$8,400 \\ + \ &\underline{\$2,000} \\ &\$10,400 \end{aligned}$$

How a Lease Payment is Calculated

To calculate a lease payment, you must know what the car will be worth at the end of the lease—the "residual value." The difference between the cap cost and the residual value is the figure that the lease payments are calculated on.

So if you have a car with a cap cost of $18,940, and a residual value of $7,125, the payment amount is calculated on $11,815. With a money factor of 0.00166 (an APR of 4%), the payments are $329.

Other Things to Be Wary of with Leases

Watch out for these additional factors when considering a lease:

- ✧ Some leases involve all kinds of up-front fees, many of which are non-refundable.
- ✧ Most leases only allow a maximum of 12,000 - 15,000 miles a years, after which you are charged between 10 - 25 cents a mile.
- ✧ In addition, when you turn in your vehicle, it is inspected with a fine-tooth comb, and you can expect to pay high fees for every scratch, nick, or dent.

Should You Purchase Your Vehicle at the End of the Lease?

Suppose your residual value is several thousand dollars *below* the retail value, as given in the *Kelly Blue Book* (http://www.kbb.com). After paying lease payments for two years, you may feel that you should "get something out of it" by purchasing the car.

You also can trade in your leased car as if you owned the car with another dealership. Some benefits to selling the car out of the lease are that you will get the full security deposit back, you won't pay a lease disposition fee, you don't have to worry about excess wear and tear charges, and you don't have to worry about how much tread is left on the car's tires. But before you start counting your profits, make sure that your lease agreement allows you to trade or sell the car before the end of your lease term.

The Bottom Line

In the end, you must pay attention to every aspect of the deal:

- ✧ Always calculate your own lease payments and be ready to challenge the dealer.
- ✧ Look over your paperwork carefully; don't allow dealers to pressure you into signing until you are ready.
- ✧ Ask to have the money factor (and its corresponding APR) given to you in writing.

Payment Shaver Loans

As lease payments are getting more and more expensive these days, some credit unions are offering a type of loan called a Payment Shaver Loan. This loan combines the low payments (up to 30%) found with a lease with the equity-building payments of a regular conventional loan. In addition, there are no up-front fees and no "disposal fee" often charged at the end of a lease.

At the end of a Payment Shaver Loan, the borrower has four options:

    ✧   Return the car to the credit union and the balance will be paid off.
    ✧   Sell the car and pay off the loan balance.
    ✧   Trade the car in and pay off the loan balance.
    ✧   Keep the car and pay off or refinance the balance.

Other nifty features of a Payment Shaver Loan include:

    ✧   You don't have to worry about a down payment or a security deposit.
    ✧   It offers a mileage allowance of as much as 18,000 miles a year, with a penalty of eight cents for each additional mile.
    ✧   Other than excess mileage, you have little to worry about at the end of a Payment Shaver Loan. The car will be examined for insurable physical damage, including damage to the windows, grille, or headlights, and missing or stolen items. But that's it. You won't be charged for a nick in a door or a small stain on a seat.

Financing Wisdom

The single most important thing you can do to ensure that you get the best financing deal for your new car is to ask questions. Lots of questions. And don't sign anything until you are satisfied with the answers.

CHAPTER 15: STUDENT LOANS

Esteban's Story

Esteban is an above-average senior in high school who wants to pursue a college degree in business. His schooling is important to him, but so is his girlfriend Sarah. They want to attend the same college so they can continue to spend as much time together as possible. Both apply to their state university.

Sarah's acceptance letter, to her delight, includes notification that she will receive a full scholarship. Esteban's includes a pile of information on financial aid. For the next three weeks, they put their heads together investigating potential grants and loans, and filling out all the paperwork to apply.

By the time school rolls around in the fall, Esteban has received two grants and taken out a student loan to pay for his tuition and books. Along with a part-time job waiting tables at the local hamburger joint, and the small savings his parents are contributing to his college costs, he is set financially to begin school. And be with his girl.

Types of Student Loans

Like any other loan, student loans are borrowed money that must be repaid with interest. Both undergraduate and graduate students may borrow money. Parents also may borrow to pay education expenses for dependent undergraduate students. Maximum loan amounts increase with each year of completed study. Some of the different loan types include:

- ✧ **Federal Stafford Loans**, which include two loan programs:
    - ◆ **Direct Loan Program:** Participating schools allow their students to borrow directly from the federal government.
    - ◆ **Federal Family Education Loan Program:** Private lenders provide the funds.
- ✧ **Perkins Loans** are offered by some schools to provide the neediest students with low-interest loans.
- ✧ **Federal Plus Loans** are made to qualifying parents of dependent undergraduate students.

Some of the requirements to receive aid from the federal student financial aid programs are that you must:

- ✧ Be a U.S. citizen or an eligible non-citizen of the United States with a valid Social Security Number;
- ✧ Have a high school diploma or a General Education Development (GED) certificate, or pass an approved "ability to benefit" test;
- ✧ Enroll in an eligible program as a regular student seeking a degree or certificate; and
- ✧ Register (or have registered) for Selective Service, if you are a male between the ages of 18 and 25.

Applying for Student Loans

To apply for a student loan, follow these steps:

1. Complete the FAFSA (Free Application for Federal Student Aid). The FAFSA lists deadlines for federal and state aid. Check the deadlines! Schools and states may have their own deadlines for aid. You must fill out a new FAFSA for each year you plan to be enrolled in school. The best time to apply for aid is between January 1 and March 1, since most schools award aid on a first-come, first-serve basis. About six weeks after you submit your FAFSA, you will receive a student aid report that will give you an opportunity to correct previously reported "incorrect information" before the form goes from the Department of Education to your school.

   You may obtain a FAFSA from:

   - ◆ A high school guidance office;
   - ◆ A college financial aid office;
   - ◆ A local public library;
   - ◆ The Federal Student Aid Information Center at 1-800-4-FED-AID (1-800-433-3243); or
   - ◆ You can apply for financial aid online at: http://www.fafsa.ed.gov/.

2. One to four weeks after you submit your FAFSA, you will receive a Student Aid Report (SAR). The report confirms the information reported on your application and will tell you your Expected Family Contribution (an amount you and your family are expected to contribute toward your education, although this amount may not exactly match the amount you and your family end up contributing).

3. Contact the school(s) you're interested in attending and talk with the school's financial aid administrator. They will review your SAR and prepare a letter outlining the amount of aid (from all sources) that their school will offer you.

4. Figure out what other forms you need to complete:

    ♦ Some colleges have their own institutional forms, in addition to the FAFSA.
    ♦ Some colleges require the CSS/Financial Aid PROFILE® to apply for non-federal aid. You can apply online and learn more at http://www.collegeboard.com

Even if You Don't Think You Qualify, Fill out the FAFSA Anyway

Even if you don't think you're eligible for federal assistance, definitely fill out the form because the FAFSA is used by many non-government aid programs to determine your eligibility for the scholarships, loans, and other programs they offer.

Here are the items you need to help you fill out the application:

✧ Your Social Security card and driver's license;
✧ Your W-2 Forms or other records of earned-income along with your federal income tax return (and your spouse's, if you are married); you'll need IRS Form 1040, 1040A, or 1040EZ, and any 1099 forms you received;
✧ Your parent's federal income tax return (unless you are filing as independent); records of other untaxed income you received, including AFDC or ADC, child support, welfare benefits, Social Security benefits, TANF, veteran's benefits, and military or clergy allowances;
✧ Your current bank statements, mortgage information, and records of stocks, bonds, and other investments;
✧ Medical and dental expenses for the past year that weren't covered by health insurance;
✧ Your business or farm records, if applicable; and
✧ Your alien registration card (if you are not a U.S. citizen).

Expected Family Contribution

The EFC is a measure of your family's ability to pay for college based on student and parent income and asset information, your state of residence, household size, and number of household members in college. You can get a free copy of the EFC formula by calling 1-800-4FED-AID and requesting the current *SFA Handbook*.

Since you probably don't have a copy of the *SFA Handbook* in your hands yet, a brief explanation of the EFC might be helpful. The EFC is the sum of the student contribution and the parent contribution. Some schools (mostly private) expect both natural parents to contribute to their children's educational expenses, regardless of a divorce or any court orders to the contrary. In cases of divorce where the custodial parent remarries, the financial information for both the custodial parent and the stepparent must be included on the FAFSA as well as any child support and/or alimony received from the non-custodial parent.

The calculation of the expected student contribution generally is 35% of the student's assets and 50% of the student's prior year (including summer) earnings. The federal calculation is 50% of the net earnings above $2,200 and 35% of the student's reported assets.

A few things to note about the needs assessment formula: (1) student assets are assessed more heavily than parent assets; (2) student income is assessed more heavily than parent income; and (3) in most cases, the EFC will go down when the number of family members in school goes up.

The school you attend will establish a Cost of Attendance (COA). The school's COA will include tuition, fees, room and board, books and supplies, travel, and personal and incidental expenses. In many cases, there is a standard fixed budget amount for some of these categories. But the budget amount for travel may vary depending on the student's home state. Likewise, room and board expenses may be reduced and travel expenses increased for commuter students.

When Your Parent's Income/Assets Are Not Counted in the EFC

If you are classified as an independent student, only your (and your spouse's) income and assets are considered. To qualify as an independent student, you must meet at least one of the following criteria:

- ✧ Be at least 24 years old;
- ✧ Be an orphan;
- ✧ Have a dependent other than a spouse;
- ✧ Be a graduate or professional student;
- ✧ Be a veteran of the Armed Forces;
- ✧ Be married; or
- ✧ Be a ward of the court.

Eligibility for Student Loans

As you can see, the COA and the EFC may be different for every school. However, once these are calculated, every school uses the same formula to determine how much federal financial aid to award to students:

COA - EFC = Financial Need

To receive need-based aid, your COA must be greater than your EFC.

As you probably have guessed, most schools have money to help out only the most needy of students. The financial aid office at your school will use the need-based resources it has available to try to meet your financial need.

Here are Esteban's calculations for financial aid:

Esteban filed his FAFSA online in January. He received his Student Aid Report (SAR) a few weeks later, which had calculated his EFC to be $800. Esteban and Sarah, with the help of the university financial aid office, figured the COA for the university to be $15,000.

Therefore, Esteban figured his financial need to be:

$15,000 - $800 = $14,200

Because of his relatively high financial needs, Esteban was able to get two grants through the university:

✧ A $1,000 Institutional Grant; and
✧ A $1,550 Federal Pell Grant.

He also was able to get approved for two student loan programs:

✧ A $1,000 Federal Perkins Loan; and
✧ A $4,500 Federal Subsidized Stafford Loan.

Thus, his total financial aid came to be: $8,050. That job at the hamburger joint will help to come up with the rest.

Defaulted Student Loan Information

Unfortunately, many students find themselves in the terrible position of defaulting on their student loans. Sometimes, that high-paying job just doesn't materialize as fast as they expected. As a result, student loan borrowers in default now have more options than ever to repay their student loans.

When is a student loan considered to be in default? In a nutshell, when you're not making payments.

For student loans authorized under Section 435(i) Title IV of the Higher Education Act, default occurs on a FFEL loan after a default has persisted for 270 days in the case of a loan repayable in monthly installments or 330 days in the case of a loan repayable in less frequent installments. The change is effective for loans for which the first date of delinquency occurred on or after October 7, 1998. During the delinquency period, the lender must exercise "due diligence" in attempting to collect the loan; that is, the lender must make repeated efforts to locate and contact you about repayment. If the lender's efforts are unsuccessful, it usually will take steps to place the loan in default and turn the loan over to the guaranty agency in your state. Lenders may "accelerate" a defaulted loan, which means that the entire balance of the loan (principal and interest) becomes due in a single payment.

If the loan is placed in default, the loan is then turned over to the U.S. Department of Education (ED).

The following are the consequences for defaulting on the various loans. If you are not sure what type of loan you have, check your promissory note. If your loan is not one of the loans listed below, the information listed does not apply to you.

Federal Family Education Loans (FFEL)

These include Federal Stafford and Federal PLUS loans. When placed in default, these loans are first assigned to a guaranty agency (an organization that administers the FFEL Program for your state) for collection. Periodically, guaranty agencies assign loans to ED for collection.

Direct Loans

Federal Stafford and PLUS loans are also offered through the William D. Ford Direct Loan Program. When placed in default, these loans are assigned to the ED's Debt Collection Service.

Federal Perkins Loans

When placed in default, Perkins Loans may remain with the school or be assigned to ED for collection.

Repaying Student Loans Held by the U.S. Department of Education

If you default on your student loan, the maturity date of each promissory note is accelerated, making payment in full immediately due, and you are no longer eligible for any type of deferment or forbearance. However, all guaranty agencies and the ED will accept regular monthly payments that are both reasonable to the agency and affordable to you.

If your defaulted student loan is held by ED, you should establish a repayment arrangement with the debt collection service or the collection agency currently administering your account on behalf of ED. Failure to repay the loan may lead to several negative consequences for you, such as:

- ✧ The U.S. Treasury may withhold your tax refunds toward repayment of your loan;
- ✧ You may have to pay additional collection costs;
- ✧ You may be subject to administrative wage garnishment, whereby the government will require your employer to forward 10% to 15% of your disposable pay toward repayment of your loan;

✧ Federal employees face the possibility of having 15% of their disposable pay offset by the government toward repayment of their loan through the Federal Employee Salary Offset Program;
✧ The government may take legal action to force you to repay the loan; and
✧ Credit bureaus may be notified, and your credit rating will suffer.

In addition, you may not receive any additional Title IV Federal student aid if you are in default in any Title IV student loan.

Statute of Limitations

By virtue of section 484A(a) of the Higher Education Act, there are now limits to the ED's or the guaranty agency's ability to file suit, enforce judgments, initiate offsets, or take other actions to collect a defaulted student loan. However, regardless of the age of the debt, statutes of limitation are no longer valid defenses against repayment of a student loan. There is no statute of limitations.

Online Information

To obtain more information and to download student loan default forms, go to the website: http://www.ed.gov/.

SECTION VI:
PROTECTING YOUR CREDIT

CHAPTER 16: WHAT YOU CAN DO TO PROTECT YOURSELF

Jennifer's Story

Jennifer has a good job and always pays her bills on time. One day, she receives her Visa bill and finds that someone has charged $1,100 in merchandise at an online store to her, putting her over her credit limit. She's always been very cautious about her personal information, but somehow, someone, somewhere got hold of her credit card number...

Calling her credit card company immediately, the customer service representative tells her not to worry, then patiently walks her through the process of filing a dispute. The rep cancels her credit card account and opens a new one for her. That's the good news. The bad?

Jennifer's grand plan to take Ray on a romantic weekend to celebrate their first anniversary just went up in smoke. The Visa is the only credit card she has, and her new one won't arrive for a few weeks. Without a credit card for the hotel room, the anniversary getaway won't happen.

Why Should You Protect Your Credit?

First, let me say that Jennifer offers a good example of why it is a good idea to have more than one credit card. No matter how careful you are, things can happen, and it does take time to set them right again. You don't realize how much you rely on your credit card until you find yourself unexpectedly without it.

Credit, second only to your family and your time, is the most important asset you possess. The difference between having credit or not can be the difference between freedom and oppression, between opportunity taken and opportunity denied. Just ask Jennifer how she feels about missing out on that romantic weekend with Ray.

Credit card companies continually upgrade and revise fraud protections on their cards, but they haven't managed to stop it yet. They have whole departments that deal with it on a daily basis. But you can take simple measures to protect yourself.

How You Can Protect Your Credit

The most important things you can do to safeguard your credit are:

WHEN TRAVELING

- ✧ Don't leave the car rental agreement inside the car where thieves can get it.
- ✧ Shred travel itineraries and ticket receipts issued by airlines and travel agents.

WHEN AT SHOPS AND RESTAURANTS

- ✧ Refuse to write your address and phone number on credit slips, or credit card account numbers on checks. (See "If Asked for Additional Information when Making a Credit Card Purchase" in Chapter 8.)
- ✧ Don't let a clerk write your driver's license number on your check if it's the same as your Social Security Number.

WHEN USING A CALLING CARD

- ✧ Don't use a personal identification number (PIN) that's obvious, such as a birth date, work extension, or consecutive numbers.
- ✧ Block the view of the phone with your body to prevent anyone from seeing what you dial; if you must tell an operator your account number, assume people are eavesdropping.

WHEN AT HOME

- ✧ Don't just throw "junk mail" in the trash unopened. Destroy all pre-approved credit card applications, or anything that contains personal information.
- ✧ When cleaning out files, shred old statements, pay stubs, and checks.
- ✧ Don't give your credit card numbers to callers who say you've won a prize.
- ✧ If a monthly statement doesn't arrive on time, call the issuer immediately.

OVER THE INTERNET

- ✧ Make sure you are buying from a vendor that uses secure information transmission methods. In plain English, you need to make sure that the page on which you are giving your information is secure. You can tell if it is secure by noting a picture of a yellow padlock in the bottom margin of your browser (below the web page area).

- ✧ Read the security information posted on the website. Don't use your credit card unless you are convinced by the information posted that it is safe to do so.

✧ Check out the company if you have not heard of them before. You can do this through the usual methods: the state attorney general's office or the Better Business Bureau (BBB). It's easy to check the company's status online at the BBB's site: http://www.bbb.org.

✧ You should delete your browser cookies after shopping online. Websites sometimes store sensitive information in these cookies which are a single line of text stored on your computer. You may lose saved passwords/settings on frequently traveled sites when you do this, but you will also cut down on your vulnerability. You will also stop some sites from getting your email address and spamming you.

✧ Find out the return policy on the site. Is it clear? Will they give you a refund? How long do you have to return the merchandise?

Buy a Shredder

Shredders are inexpensive these days; about $25 in most office supply stores. Buy one. Use it religiously. It is the cheapest and easiest way to protect your privacy. Some of the newer models feature cross-cutting and even CD shredding. For a few dollars more than a "regular" version, it's definitely worth the investment.

Shred any paperwork containing personal information before it hits the trashcan. Dumpster-diving, the practice of looking through trash for personal information, is the most common method that identity thieves use to get personal information. Therefore, shred:

✧ Those credit card applications you receive in the mail;
✧ Credit card receipts;
✧ Pay stubs;
✧ Bank statements and deposit receipts;
✧ Utility bill stubs;
✧ Old tax returns; and
✧ Anything containing your Social Security Number.

Review Your Credit Card Statements

Like Jennifer, you can catch any unauthorized use of your accounts early by simply reviewing your statements when they arrive. The sooner you notify the credit card companies, the easier it is to correct any problems. If you just can't take the time when the bill arrives, be sure to review your bill before sending a payment.

Pull Your Credit Report at Least Once Every 6 Months

I used to recommend pulling your credit report once a year, but with rapidly escalating identity theft, I am now recommending every 6 months. As stated in Chapter 3, all consumers will be able to request and receive one free copy each year once the free annual report system is rolled out. There is currently only a minimal cost to pull your credit report more than once a year. And depending on which state you live it, it may cost nothing. Make it a habit.

There are lots of "credit monitoring" companies out there who will charge you $60 a year for their services. It may be a convenient service, but you can save a few bucks by pulling your own reports (for $27 or less).

If you find indications of theft on your credit reports, don't panic. Use the credit repair methods in Section VIII to challenge accounts you know aren't yours; it could just be a mistake. Check the following closely:

◇ Are all of the credit lines on the report yours? Make note of each one.
◇ Were there excessive inquiries made on your report? Can you account for all of them? Excessive inquiries could mean that someone is trying to get credit in your name.

New laws will require creditors to notify you if they add negative information to your credit file

The new identity theft section of the FCRA (scheduled to kick in December 1, 2004) requires creditors to notify you in writing when any negative information about you is reported to the credit bureaus. Banks will also be required to notify you in writing if they grant you credit at less favorable terms than those received by most other consumers. If you've been paying your bills on time, this should be a red flag that you may be a victim of identity theft.

Secure Your Mail

Why would someone steal your mail? Mail thieves want your bank statements and credit card bills so they can create counterfeit checks or fake IDs with your account information. They also look for your personal checks, which they "wash" clean of handwriting, then fill in nice large amounts payable to themselves. They are a clever bunch! The US Postal Service recommends the following precautions:

◇ Place mail for pick-up in a blue collection box, or drop it at your local post office. Don't put it in your mailbox and raise the little red flag that tells thieves, "Yoo hoo! Come and get me!"
◇ Pick up your mail promptly after delivery. Don't leave it in your mailbox overnight.
◇ Tell your post office when you'll be out of town, so they can hold your mail until you return. Or ask a trusted neighbor to collect it for you.
◇ Don't send cash in the mail.
◇ Ask your bank for "secure" checks that can't be altered.

If your mail is compromised, report it to your postal inspector immediately. Call 1-800-ASK-USPS to find the number for your local inspector.

Secure Your Paperwork, Especially if You Have Roommates

The saddest tales of all are when people you know steal your identity. You don't think this happens? You would be surprised.

How do you secure your paperwork? Buy a filing cabinet and *lock* it or rent a safe deposit box. Obviously, a safe deposit box is not as convenient as a filing cabinet, but if you don't trust the people around you, it is a great option. (Of course, if you don't trust the people you live with you might want to consider moving…)

What kind of paperwork should you lock away from prying eyes?

- ✧ Any credit card receipts with your number on them;
- ✧ Pay stubs;
- ✧ Bank statements and deposit receipts;
- ✧ Utility bill stubs;
- ✧ Old tax returns; and
- ✧ Anything containing your Social Security Number.

Take Your Name Off Mailing Lists

Isn't it annoying to get all that junk mail from companies trying to get you to apply for their credit cards? Not only does it kill baby trees, it fills up your trash bin, and tempts you unnecessarily. Perhaps more importantly, you run the real risk of having someone steal your discarded mail and apply for the card for you, essentially hijacking your identity. This is not a pleasant experience.

Protect yourself by taking your name off of the credit bureaus' mailing lists. Some of the agencies and the addresses of companies used by the credit bureau Experian are given below. To remove your name from their lists, write a letter giving your complete name, any name variations, and mailing address to:

Mail Preference Service
Direct Marketing Association
P.O. Box 9008
Farmingdale, NY 11735

Make a call to:

Opt Out
888-567-8688 or
800-353-0809

One call to the Opt Out Request Line is all it takes to remove your name from any marketing lists that the four credit reporting agencies supply to direct marketers. You do not need to call each one. You will be given the choice to "opt out" for a two-year period, renewing your request at any time in the future, or to "opt out" permanently.

To remove your name from many telephone solicitation lists, send your complete name, address, and phone number with area code to:

Telephone Preference Service
Direct Marketing Association
P.O. Box 9014
Farmingdale, NY 11735

Once you write, you'll remain on the Direct Mailing Association opt-out list for five years. It may take up to three months before you notice a significant reduction in the amount of direct mail and phone calls you receive.

To be removed from the mailing lists of the major data compilers, call or write to these firms. (Note: These companies also subscribe to the DMA's Mail Preference Service.):

R. L. Polk & Co.
List Compilation
26955 Northwestern Highway
Southfield, MI 48034
810-728-7000

First Data Info-Source Donnelley Marketing, Inc.
Data Base Operations
1235 "N" Avenue
Nevada, IA 50201
888-633-4402 or 515-382-8321

Metromail Corp.
List Maintenance
901 West Bond
Lincoln, NE 68521
800-426-8901

Database America
Compilation Dept.
100 Paragon Dr.
Montvale, NJ 07645
201-476-2000 or 800-223-7777

Online resources for reducing junk mail include:

- ✧ The Junkbusters (http://junkbusters.com/) website offers a number of free services to help you get rid of unwanted snail-mail and email.
- ✧ Outpost Network (http://www.outpost.net/) is another online service that helps you cut down on junk mail (a fee is charged).

✧ The Computer Professionals for Social Responsibility site offers tips for reducing junk mail (http://www.cpsr.org/cpsr/privacy/junkmail.html).

Other online resources include:

✧ Consumer Research Inst.: http://www.stopjunk.com/environment.html.
✧ Obviously Implementations Corp.: http://www.obviously.com/junkmail.
✧ Ecofuture: http://www.ecofuture.org/ecofuture/jnkmail.html.

Take Your Name Off Call Lists

While you are doing away with those mountains of junk mail, why not stop those disruptive sales calls, too? Although it does not protect your credit rating in any way (unless you are susceptible to saying "yes" to whatever the salesperson du jour is selling), adding your phone number to the Do Not Call list will protect your privacy and prevent unwanted interruptions during romantic moments at home.

Thanks to recent legislation, you can now register your home and mobile phone numbers with the National Do Not Call Registry and stop most unsolicited sales calls. (It won't stop calls from companies you do business with, charities, political organizations, or telephone surveyors.) It takes three months from the date you register to take effect and will remain in effect for five years.

To register online:
1. Go to **https://www.donotcall.gov/default.aspx**. Submit your phone number(s) and email address for registration.
2. You will receive email verification from Register@donotcall.gov. To complete your registration, open the email and click on the link provided within 72 hours. Your registration is not complete until you do this.
3. After you click on the link, print the web page and keep it for your records. You will need it in order to file a complaint in the future.

You can also register by calling toll-free at 1-888-382-1222, but you must call from the phone you want registered.

Now you will have a legitimate place to complain if a telemarketer calls just as you are getting ready to relax in the hot tub with that gorgeous guy. You'll need to provide the date of the call and either the name *or* telephone number of the company that called you. To register a complaint, visit www.donotcall.gov.

CHAPTER 17: IF YOU ARE A VICTIM OF IDENTITY THEFT

Michael's Story

Michael, 52, runs a small family dry cleaning business with his wife, Sally. He has been in business for 20 years and keeps meticulous books. His credit—both personal and business—is perfect. Perfect, that is, until he was turned down for a credit card that offered great frequent flier miles.

Michael took advantage of the law requiring the credit bureau to provide a free credit report after denying him credit. Like everything he does, Michael studied his report carefully and used the instructions provided by the bureau to understand it. He found four accounts on his credit report that did not belong to him—all seriously delinquent.

He called one of credit card companies. They verified his name and Social Security Number, but the address did not match his own. When they read him some of the charges on the latest statement, Michael realized they were all made in another town—the town where his son, Michael, Jr., lives. He called another of the credit card companies with the same result. His next call was to Michael, Jr.

Michael, Jr., 23, admits to using his dad's Social Security Number to apply for a number of credit cards since he couldn't get approved on his own. He apologizes to his dad, naturally. But that doesn't help much. Michael Sr. is angry and a bit bewildered. And now he faces a dilemma: how to resolve this problem without sending his son to jail, something Sally is vehemently against.

Michael, Sr. could pay off the cards and close the accounts, but this would not erase the bad credit on his report. To clear his damaged credit, he must file an affidavit with the credit card companies explaining the situation. The credit card companies would subsequently press charges against Michael, Jr. and turn the matter over to local authorities. Michael, Jr. has no money to pay off the credit card debt he has accumulated.

Is Michael, Sr. in trouble? It depends on what course of action he takes. Michael, Jr.? Big trouble, no matter which way his father decides to go. Fraud is a felony offense, even if the "victim" is your own family.

What to Do if You Are a Victim of Identity Theft

Michael, Sr.'s situation is tragic but, unfortunately, it is not all that unusual. According to the Federal Trade Commission, there were 9.9 million victims of identity theft in 2002 and those victims spent a total of *297 million hours* resolving the problems that resulted.

Michael, Jr. had an easy time opening fraudulent accounts because his name is so similar to his father's, however, complete strangers can also heist your identity and open an account in your name. It's pretty easy. All they need is your name and Social Security Number.

We said it in the last chapter, but it is so important that we will say it again: shred all of those unsolicited credit card applications you receive in the mail and destroy all records containing personal information before you place them into the trash. It's amazing the sensitive information people place in public places (trash bins) for all the world to see and use.

If you suspect that you are a victim of identity fraud, it is important that you act quickly. In addition to reporting your identity theft to the proper authorities, you should start a log of your efforts to protect yourself. This information could prove invaluable later in proving you are not responsible for false debts or even crimes. Thus:

- ✧ Record all conversations with your creditors, the authorities, etc.
- ✧ Send correspondence by certified or registered mail.
- ✧ Keep copies of all letters and documents.
- ✧ In cases where you may actually collect damages in a lawsuit, you might also want to jot down the lengths of time you spent and any money you spent clearing your identity.

Follow these steps if you discover, or suspect, you are a victim of identity theft:

1. CONTACT THE AUTHORITIES

Under the new credit laws scheduled to be enacted December 1, 2004, identity theft victims that file police reports will be able to block fraudulent information from appearing on their credit reports.

Report the crime to all police and sheriff's departments with jurisdiction in your case. Until the new laws take place, credit card companies and banks may require you to show them the police report to convince them of your innocence. If you are not able to convince these institutions of your innocence, they may hold you responsible for bounced checks, charges made in your name, etc.

Give the police/sheriff's department as much documented evidence as possible, and get a copy of your police report. Make sure to take note of your detective's (or the official taking the report/handling your case) direct phone number. This bit of information will make it easier for creditors/banks to carry out their own investigation. Some police departments have been known to refuse to write reports on such crimes. If you can't get them to take a report, at least document your call and who you spoke with.

2. PULL YOUR CREDIT REPORT!

In most cases, it is difficult to obtain a mortgage or car loan using someone else's identity; typically, the thieves go for credit cards. Pull your credit report immediately to make sure no one has opened up new accounts in your name. Be aware, though, that new accounts may not show up for quite awhile (six months or more), so be sure and check frequently for the first year. It is definitely worth the small inconvenience of pulling your credit report.

If accounts have been opened in your name, contact the creditors immediately.

3. PUT A FRAUD ALERT ON YOUR CREDIT REPORT

Under the new laws scheduled to be enacted on December 1, 2004, identity theft victims can put fraud alerts on their credit files after they learn impostors are ringing up charges in their names.

Under the new law, once a credit bureau receives a fraud alert, it must take steps to ensure that the consumer and not the thief will be granted credit in the future. This extra step could be something as simple as calling the phone number listed in a consumer fraud alert whenever a new application for credit pops up.

To do this, immediately call the credit reporting agencies (CRAs). Fraud reporting hotlines for all three are listed below, but calling one will automatically share your information with the others. They will:
- ✧ Flag your account with a fraud alert;
- ✧ Remove you from prescreened offers of credit (the same thing that happens when you call them to "opt out" of mailings);
- ✧ Report the fraud to the other agencies; and
- ✧ Mail you complimentary copies of credit reports from all three agencies.

Typically, fraud alerts remain on your credit report for two years, and will prevent anyone (including yourself) from opening new accounts without additional verification.

Toll-free "Report Fraud" Hotlines:
Experian:	888-EXPERIAN, 888-397-3742
Equifax:	800-525-6285
TransUnion:	800-680-7289

In the meantime, if your credit report has already been damaged (i.e., inquiries you did not make, accounts you did not open are on your report), go through the normal credit repair procedures (explained in Section VIII) to have these items removed. Mention to all concerned that you have already placed a fraud alert on your report, to strengthen your case. For items you cannot immediately remove, you may want to ask the credit bureaus to change the status of disputed accounts to "disputed."

4. IF YOUR CREDIT CARDS WERE STOLEN, CALL YOUR CREDITORS!

In addition to the other identity theft measures which will be enacted under the new FCRA laws, consumers will soon have the right to demand copies of records from creditors when identity thieves fraudulently open accounts in their name.

It's important that you act quickly to limit your responsibility for fraudulent charges. Call your creditors and follow up your call with the facts in writing. Most creditors will issue replacement cards with new account numbers for accounts that have been used fraudulently with no trouble, if you act immediately. If fraudulent charges have been made to your accounts, at the very most you will be responsible for no more than $50.

Important Note: Ask that old accounts be processed as "account closed at consumer's request." This is better than "card lost or stolen" because when this statement is reported to credit bureaus, it can be interpreted as blaming you for the loss. It is rumored that your credit score takes a hit with a lost or stolen status.

Finally, carefully monitor your mail and credit card bills for evidence of new fraudulent activity, in case your thief comes back to haunt you.

5. IF YOUR CHECKS WERE STOLEN, NOTIFY YOUR BANKS!

If you've had checks stolen or bank accounts set up fraudulently, close your accounts immediately. It is also important to report the fraud to any of the following check verification companies your bank uses. Don't rely on your bank to do this.

CheckRite: 800-766-2748
ChexSystems: 800-428-9623 (closed checking accounts)
National Processing Co. (NPC): 800-526-5380
SCAN: 800-262-7771
TeleCheck: 800-710-9898

We talked about ChexSystems in Chapter 3. Most banks use ChexSystems, and you may want to have an in-depth conversation with your bank about anything it may have reported to ChexSystems. Any negative items reported to ChexSystems will prevent you from opening a checking account anywhere else for five years. Really. If your bank has reported anything to ChexSystems as a result of your identity fraud, insist that it remove the listing immediately. (A sample letter to ChexSystems is included in Appendix 7.)

As a further stop gap measure, put stop payments on any outstanding checks that you are unsure of, although this can cost you a pretty penny ($15/check or more). Give the bank a secret password for your account (other than your mother's maiden name; this is an easy piece of information for a thief to obtain).

6. IF YOUR ATM CARD(S) WAS STOLEN, ORDER A NEW ONE!

Again, time is of the essence. If your ATM or debit card has been stolen or compromised, report it immediately. When you open new accounts, insist on password-only access. Cancel the card and get another with a new PIN. Do not use your old password. When creating a password, don't use common numbers like the last four digits of your Social Security Number or your birth date.

7. NOTIFY THE PASSPORT OFFICE

If you have a passport, notify the passport office in writing to be on the lookout for anyone ordering a passport (http://travel.state.gov/passport_services.html).

If Someone Fraudulently Changes Your Address

Why would anyone do this? Revenge (to cause you inconvenience) could be one reason. I actually saw this idea posted on a website as a way to get back at an ex-lover. However, some identity thieves use this tactic to grab your mail and use the sensitive, personal information it contains. You don't need to show anyone ID at the post office to enter a forwarding address.

Notify the local Postal Inspector if you suspect an identity thief has filed a change of your address with the post office or has used the mail to commit credit or bank fraud. Find out where fraudulent credit cards were sent. Notify the local Postmaster of that address with instructions to forward all mail in your name to your own address. You may also need to talk with the mail carrier (http://www.usps.gov/websites/depart/inspect).

If Your Social Security Number Has Been Misused

Call the Social Security Administration (SSA) to report fraudulent use of your Social Security Number. As a last resort, you might want to try to change your number. Because of the many people trying to escape their bad credit by getting a new SSN, the SSA will only change your number if you fit their fraud victim criteria.

You also may be facing the possibility that someone is using your SSN for employment to avoid paying taxes. To ensure this is not happening, you may order a copy of your Earnings and Benefits Statement and check it for accuracy (http://www.ssa.gov or 800-772-1213).

If Someone Is Making Phone Calls in Your Name

If your long distance calling card has been stolen or you discover fraudulent charges on your bill, cancel the account and open a new one. Provide a password that must be used any time the account is changed.

If Your Driver's License Number Has Been Misused

You may need to change your driver's license number if someone is using yours as identification on bad checks. Call the state office of the Department of Motor Vehicles (DMV) to see if another license was issued in your name. Put a fraud alert on your license. Go to your local DMV to request a new number. Also, fill out the DMV's complaint form to begin the fraud investigation process. Send supporting documents with the completed form to the nearest DMV investigation office.

Other Identity Theft Resources

Further identity theft resources include:

- ✧ http://www.privacyrights.org/
- ✧ US Government Consumer Information on Identity Theft (http://www.consumer.gov/idtheft/)

CHAPTER 18: DIVORCE AND YOUR CREDIT

Jack's Story

Jack, 42, is an aircraft mechanic who went through a divorce from Susan three years ago. The divorce was amicable. It was easy for them to come to an agreement on splitting their assets and their accumulated bills. Susan retained custody of their two children because her work-from-home business allowed her to cut down on daycare expenses. She wanted to keep the house, both for the children and for her business, and there was enough cash and retirement funds between them for Susan to buy out Jack's half of the equity. Jack signed over his interest in the home to Susan via a "quit claim deed." Susan had just started her business and could not qualify for a home loan on her own so the original mortgage (obtained jointly) was left in place.

The divorce decree issued by the court clearly stated Susan's financial responsibility. She would make the home mortgage payments, her own car payments, and cover half of their outstanding credit card bills.

Now Jack has remarried and he and his bride, Angela, want to buy a home in a beautiful new housing division that borders a national forest. The development appeals to their mutual appreciation of nature, and the newlyweds have even enjoyed a romantic picnic lunch on a lot Angela hopes to make their own.

Jack has always prided himself on paying his bills before they came due and keeping current with his child support payments. He has saved money for a down payment and managed to accumulate minimal credit card debt. Angela's credit is outstanding. Sure they will have no problem getting a loan, Jack is astounded by his credit report. The mortgage on his former home shows 60-day late payments. His ex-wife's car loan is still showing on his report and it, too, has been late several times. He has a copy of the divorce decree that spells out Susan's responsibility for those debts, but his loan officer can only express his sympathy.

Is Jack in trouble? Unfortunately, yes. **A divorce decree does not relieve one spouse of mutually-contracted debt obligations**. Those payments are Jack's responsibility as much as Susan's, and the creditors can legally report Jack late to the credit bureaus. Susan is heartbroken to hear that her financial trouble has ruined her ex-husband's credit rating. And Angela? She is understandably upset, though she knows her new husband was just being a nice guy.

A Divorce Decree Does Not Relieve Joint Debt

Divorce lawyers may tell you that your creditors will accept the divorce decree and relieve you of your ex's debt. *Don't believe them.* When two people jointly apply for credit, they sign a legal agreement to the creditor to pay back the debt. If one can't pay, the other is responsible. A court cannot overturn contracts between individuals unless they are fraudulent or not lawful. A divorce does not fit either of these definitions, so the contract remains in tact until the contract ends (when the debt is paid off).

Myths About Divorce Decrees

MYTH 1#: A DIVORCE DECREE CAN RELIEVE A SPOUSE FROM FINANCIAL OBLIGATIONS OF DEBTS

Fact: Debts that were obtained in the name of both spouses before a divorce (meaning both the husband and wife signed a document or application saying that they were both responsible for the debt) remain the obligation of both parties after a divorce, no matter what a divorce decree says.

Why? Because *both of you* signed a legally binding contract with the creditor, and the divorce decree does not amend this contract. Amendment of any contract requires agreement by all parties (including the creditor). Proof of the amendment requires the signature of all parties. During a divorce, the creditors are not even consulted, let alone a part of the divorce courts, and therefore the original agreements/contracts stand. Consequently, if your ex-spouse does not pay a debt that he was assigned in a divorce decree, then *you* are responsible for it.

MYTH 2#: A DIVORCE DECREE PROTECTS MY CREDIT IF MY EX-SPOUSE DOESN'T PAY THE DEBTS HE WAS ASSIGNED IN THE DIVORCE

Fact: If you have a joint financial obligation with your ex-spouse, and your divorce decree states that your ex-spouse is responsible, and your ex-spouse is delinquent on paying, your credit as well as his is affected. As stated above, your legal responsibility for a debt does not go away because a divorce decree assigns responsibility for a debt to your ex-spouse. Along with a legal responsibility to pay comes the right of the creditor to report a debt delinquent on your credit report if it is not paid as agreed in the original contract. Period.

Especially tragic are situations where one ex-spouse files bankruptcy and includes many joint debts in the BK. The spouse not filing bankruptcy is left holding the bag for these joint debts, and many times is not notified of the ex-spouse's filing until months or years down the road when it is too late to correct the situation. So not only is the spouse who didn't file BK responsible for the unpaid debts (and can be legally sued for them), but the non-filing BK spouse's credit also is ruined—something that cannot be corrected—because the credit bureaus have the right to report them delinquent.

What Could Jack Have Done Differently?

Jack and Susan could have, and should have, paid off their mutual debt at the time of their divorce. If the house had to be sold to do that, so be it. It would have meant an adjustment for the kids and some new letterhead for Susan's business, but these are relatively minor changes in the scheme of things. Their joint credit cards should have been paid off and the accounts closed. Both Jack and Susan should have opened new credit card accounts as individuals, making each responsible for their own future debt. If Susan really was determined to keep the house, she might have been able to obtain her own mortgage with the help of a family member co-signing the loan.

In cases where the divorce is less amicable than Jack and Susan's, especially in community property states, a spouse usually can force the sale of mutual assets, using the proceeds to pay off any outstanding debt and splitting the proceeds down the middle.

How to Protect Your Credit During a Divorce

The purpose of divorce is to split off emotionally, and financially, from your ex-spouse. If you aren't careful, your spouse's handling of your once-joint accounts can haunt you for years. If you had joint debts that existed before your divorce, and these accounts are not both paid off and closed, you are asking for trouble.

Also, although some divorcing couples definitely are out to get each other, most problems with joint accounts prior to divorce are caused by *ignorance*, not malicious intent. Don't think that just because your split is amicable problems can't occur. Taking precautions can protect *both* of you.

Here are the typical joint accounts which many married couples share and what you need to do with each *before* you get divorced.

YOUR HOME/MORTGAGE

This should be your first priority. It is vital to *not* walk away from a divorce with the mortgage in both of your names. Here are possible ways to cope with joint home ownership, listed from most preferable to least:

- ✧ **Sell the home.** Make sure the sale occurs *before* the divorce, especially if your ex is living in the house during the divorce proceedings. If you have an agreement to sell (the house has not yet sold) at the time of your final divorce, and your spouse is secretly opposed to selling it, he can make it very difficult for a realtor to show or list the home, dragging out the sale indefinitely. In the meantime, you are responsible for the payments and your credit is in jeopardy. It's actually best to have the house empty during the sale of the home; if possible, both of you should be out of the house before it goes up for sale.

✧ **Have one spouse refinance the home in his own name.** If one spouse is to keep the house after the divorce, insist that your soon-to-be-ex obtain new financing in his own name. You can't just call up the mortgage company and say, "Hey, I'm getting divorced, can you take my spouse off the loan?" Your lender is going to insist on having your ex go through the formal loan process to qualify. Do not let the final gavel sound on your divorce papers before the house has been through the refinancing process. Having your spouse show you loan approval papers is not enough; last minute glitches that prevent loans from closing occur every day.

✧ **If selling or refinancing isn't an option.** This is the worst possible option. Try to avoid it at all cost. If moving out of your joint home is going to cause hardship to your ex (and/or your kids), and he is unable to refinance the home on his own, here are some things you can do to protect yourself:

♦ Don't take your name off the title. If you take your name off of title (using a quit claim deed), you *are* removing ownership but *not* loan responsibility, a very dangerous situation. This also means that you will not be able to split the equity in the home at the present time.

♦ Place a limit on how long your ex can stay in the house before it will be sold or refinanced.

♦ Notify the mortgage company of your change of address and have all statements and coupon booklets sent to your new address (also, see if you can get your ex to mail the payments to you). At the very least, inform the lender that you wish to be notified if the payments get in arrears. In this way, if your ex is late on payments, you will be notified and have the chance to make up the payments.

Car/Car Loans

This is the second most important item in need of your attention, because car loans are the second most important kind of financing on your credit report after your mortgage. As you will notice, my suggestions for handling joint car loans are very similar to those for a joint mortgage. Here are possible ways to cope with joint car ownership, listed from most preferable to least:

✧ **Sell the car.** Make sure the sale occurs *before* the divorce. If you just have an agreement to sell (the car has not yet sold), you are responsible for the payments and your credit is in jeopardy. If the car is upside down (meaning you owe more than it is worth), it's still better to sell the car at a loss than to risk your credit. The difference between good and bad credit can be worth thousands of dollars in interest and fees per year on future financing.

✧ **Have one spouse refinance the car in his own name.** If one spouse is to keep the car after the divorce, before you get divorced, insist that your soon-to-be-ex obtain new financing in his own name. As with a mortgage, your lender is going to insist on having your ex go through the formal loan process to qualify. Do not let the divorce process complete before the car loan has been completely through the refinancing process.

✧ **If selling or refinancing isn't an option.** This is the worst possible option. Try to avoid it at all cost. If selling the car is going to cause hardship to your ex (and/or your kids), and he is unable to refinance car on his own, here are some things you can do to protect yourself:

♦ Don't take your name off the title. If you take your name off of the title, you are removing ownership but not loan responsibility, a precarious situation to be in.

♦ Place a limit on how long your ex can have possession of the car before it will be sold or refinanced.

♦ Notify the car finance company of your change of address and have all statements sent to your new address (also, see if you can get your ex to mail the payments to you). At the very least, inform the lender that you wish to be notified if your ex isn't making the payments.

Joint Credit Card Debt

Most people think that "closing out" joint credit card accounts is the end of the headache. Unfortunately, they forget that the account is not really closed out until any balances are paid off. Even worse, it's very easy to reopen accounts if the accounts are being paid on time—credit card companies encourage this. If you cannot pay off and close the balances immediately (it may be difficult to legally divide up debts that have not been paid off, check with your lawyer), here are some solutions for getting rid of it, listed from best option to worst:

✧ Sell a joint asset (perhaps your home—kill two birds with one stone) and pay off the debt, then close the account.

✧ Apply for a separate credit card for each of you and have agreed-upon amounts transferred into these sole and separate accounts from the joint debt accounts.

✧ If your spouse can't qualify for credit on his own, get one of his relatives to co-sign on a new card, then transfer the balances.

Note: If you have debts that don't fit into the above categories, use this simple rule of thumb: *After a divorce, all of the joint debts you had should be closed and paid off; all of the assets you owned jointly should be sold. No exceptions.* We know you still have some love for her, that she is the mother of your beautiful children. We understand. Really we do. But things can happen. Don't let them. Learn from Jack and Susan.

SECTION VII:
OVER YOUR HEAD IN DEBT

CHAPTER 19: COLLECTION AGENCIES

Carl's Story

Carl, 55 and divorced, recently took early retirement with a nice severance package. Driving around one day, he spots a mint 1970 SS Chevy Malibu in a local used-car lot. Carl always wanted one in college but could never afford it. With his pension and settlement, he knows he is now able to purchase it with ease. Carl is equally tickled since he shares an interest in old muscle cars with his new girlfriend, Amy, and he'd love to impress her while treating himself in the process. He trades in his old truck for the Chevy and pays the difference in cash.

Three days after Carl buys the Malibu, the used-car lot folds before they paid off Carl's loan on his old truck. The bank holding his old car loan starts calling him asking him why he has stopped making payments on the loan. Carl naturally is very upset. He contacts a lawyer, hoping to resolve the matter. In the meantime, he refuses to make the payments. Soon, the bank turns the account over to a collection agency that subjects Carl to all kinds of fun tactics, including an attempt to repossess the truck that Carl, of course, doesn't have. The collection agency calls so often that he stops inviting Amy over, for fear that she will hear his heated conversations with the collectors. Finally, several thousand dollars later, his lawyer is able to get him out from under the situation.

Your Rights When Dealing with a Collection Agency

If your credit problems have progressed to the point where your creditors have turned your case over to collection agencies, it is important to know your legal rights. (More about how to take legal action against them in Chapter 30.) Collection agencies are *not* allowed to:

- ✧ Call your office;
- ✧ Call your home before 8 a.m. or after 9 p.m.;
- ✧ Address you in an abusive manner;
- ✧ Call family or friends in an attempt to collect your debt;
- ✧ Harass you;
- ✧ Make false or misleading statements; or
- ✧ Add unauthorized charges.

If any of the above is happening to you, tell the collection agency to stop harassing you. If it continues, ask for its name and address and report it to the Better Business Bureau, the Federal Trade Commission, or your state's attorney general's office. These telephone numbers can be found in your telephone book or by calling directory assistance.

The federal Fair Debt Collection Practices Act (FDCPA, see Appendix 3) also states that you can demand that the collection agency stop contacting you, except to tell you that collection efforts have ended or that the creditor or collection agency will sue you. You must put your request in writing.

Please note, however, that the FDCPA applies only to bill collectors who work for collection agencies. While many states have laws prohibiting all debt collectors (including those working for the collection departments of creditors) from harassing, abusing, or threatening you, these laws don't give you the right to demand that the collector stop contacting you. There is one exception: Only residents of New York City have a local consumer protection law that allows them to write to *any* bill collector and say "Stop!"

If a bill collector violates the FDCPA, try to get the collector back on the phone and repeat whatever you said the first time that caused the collector to make the illegal statement(s). Have a witness listen in on an extension or tape the conversation. Taping is permitted without the collector's knowledge in all states except CA, CT, DE, FL, IL, MD, MA, MI, MT, NH, PA, and WA.

Then file a complaint—in writing. You can even file a complaint if you don't have a witness, but a witness helps. File your complaint with:

Federal Trade Commission
6th Street & Pennsylvania Avenue NW
Washington, DC 20850
202-326-2222
http://www.ftc.gov

Next, complain to your state consumer protection agency. Then send a copy of your complaint to the creditor who hired the collection agency. If the violations are severe enough, the creditor may stop the collection efforts.

If the violations are ongoing, you can sue the collection agency, and the creditor that hired the agency, for up to $1,000 in small claims court for violating the FTC regulations. If the violations are outrageous, you can sue the collection agency and creditor in regular civil court. (More about this in Chapter 30.)

Common Collections Tactics and Rebuttals

Some collection agencies do employ collection methods involving the use of false and misleading statements. A common tactic is to insist that you wire the money that you owe through Western Union. They might tell you that if they do not receive the funds immediately, interest might be added to your debt.

Tell them "Nice try" (in other words, "No.") It's only going to add more money to your debt in Western Union fees if you did do it. Many collectors, especially when a debt is more than 90-days past due, will suggest several "urgency payment" options, including:

✧ Sending money by express or overnight mail. This will add at least $10 to your bill. A first class stamp is fine.
✧ Wiring money through Western Union's Quick Collect or American Express' Moneygram. This is another $10 waste.
✧ Putting your payment on a credit card not charged to its maximum. You'll never get out of debt if you do this.
✧ Provide your checking account number so that they can access your funds immediately over the telephone (or they will "post date" the check for when you know that the funds will be in your account). Are you crazy? NEVER give out your checking account and check routing numbers.

While the FDCPA allows a collector to add interest if your original agreement calls for the addition of interest during collection proceedings, or the addition of such interest is allowed under state law, it is not necessary to spend the money or risk your checking account for an "urgent" payment. The three or four days it may take to mail a payment with a first class stamp, if they *do* decide to come after you for interest, won't break the bank.

The "urgent payment" scam aside, however, it is generally in your best interest to settle your debts as quickly as possible. Before obtaining a court judgment, a bill collector generally has only one way of getting paid: Demand payment by calling you and sending you threatening letters. If you refuse, the collector can't do much else short of suing you. Once the collector (or creditor) does sue and gets a judgment, however, you can expect more aggressive collection actions:

✧ If you have a job, the collector will try to garnish up to 25% of your net wages.
✧ The collector also may try to seize any bank or other deposit accounts you have.
✧ If you own real property (real estate), the collector will probably record a lien, which will have to be paid when you sell or refinance your property.

Some collection agencies will agree to settle with you for far less than you owe and then turn around and hire another collection agency to collect the difference. However, in many states this is illegal. Once a creditor deposits or cashes a full payment check, even if she strikes out the words "payment in full," or writes "I don't agree" on the check, she can't come after you for the balance. The states in which this law is enforced include:

Arkansas	Colorado	Connecticut	Georgia
Kansas	Louisiana	Maine	Michigan
Nebraska	New Jersey	North Carolina	Oregon
Pennsylvania	Texas	Utah	Vermont
Virginia	Washington	Wyoming	

Some states have modified this rule. In the following states, if a creditor cashes a full payment check and explicitly retains his right to sue you by writing "under protest or without prejudice" with his endorsement, then he can come after you for the balance. But those exact words must be used. If he writes "without recourse," communicates with you separately, notifies you verbally, or writes on the check that it is partial payment, it is not enough.

Alabama	Delaware	Massachusetts	Minnesota
Missouri	New Hampshire	New York	Ohio
Rhode Island	South Carolina	South Dakota	West Virginia
Wisconsin			

CHAPTER 20: OVERWHELMED WITH DEBT

Jane's Story

Jane, 28, comes from a poor neighborhood of a large Midwest city. Determined to overcome her roots, she studied hard and graduated at the head of her class with an MBA from an Ivy League school. Pursued by several investment firms right out of college, she selected a Fortune 500 company. A star achiever from the get-go, Jane soon commanded a six-figure income with attractive bonuses and stock options.

Still feeling the sting of her deprived background, Jane's motto was to "Buy only the best." She purchased a home right away and contracted the services of a housekeeper, a gardener, and a pool maintenance company. The home association fees were high (it was the best area, after all). She bought a great sports car with high insurance premiums and payments. She bought expensive suits and eveningwear at the most exclusive retailers.

Her clientele and profits continued to grow at an increasing pace, but so did her credit card bills and expenses. To pay them off, she sold her lucrative stock options, borrowed against her 401K, and eventually had to take out a second mortgage to further consolidate her debt payments. Along the way, she stopped contributing to her 401K since it was eating into her disposable income. The second mortgage had paid off all of her credit card debt, but she was already in the process of charging them up again.

Jane knew she was in financial trouble and told her boyfriend, Greg, that she couldn't afford the extended European vacation they had been planning for months. It had become the source of arguments lately. Greg felt betrayed by what he saw as Jane's unreliability in keeping commitments.

One evening after another heated discussion about the upcoming trip, Greg (a general contractor with his own business) offered a solution. They'd look over her finances, see where she might do a little cost-cutting, and Jane could go as planned.

This is what they found:

Monthly Net (after taxes) Income:	$6,533

Expenses:

Mortgage:	$1,943
Homeowner's Fees:	250
Second Mortgage:	550
Car Loan:	660
Car Insurance:	235
401K Loan:	540
Credit Card Bills:	850
minimum monthly payments	

Totals:	$5,028

Jane has a little over $1,500/month left for utilities, food, gas, and emergencies.

Greg looked at the available balance on Jane's credit cards. Of the $40,000 in available credit from all of her credit cards combined, she had used up $15,000. If she used them all to their limit, Greg calculated that her minimum monthly payment would balloon to $1,650, leaving her with only $700 each month for living expenses.

Was Jane in trouble? Obviously, yes. If her car needed repairs she would probably charge them. Ditto for the expenses of schmoozing important clients or bailing her ailing mother out of unplanned medical expenses not covered by insurance.

The biggest danger was that Jane could afford to pay only the minimum payment on her credit card debt. If she made only the minimum payment on her credit card debt, she would never pay it off. Why? The minimum payment almost never covers the interest accumulated each month on a credit card balance. The difference between the interest due and the minimum payment is added to the balance each month, causing it to slowly but surely increase over time.

Greg made half as much as Jane, yet he was able to afford a trip to Europe, dinners out, and a recent model SUV. He had investments, savings, and little credit card debt, and was shocked at Jane's financial situation. Need I say it? He found Jane *less* alluring after finding out how poorly she handled her finances.

What could Jane have done differently to avoid this situation? For those of you playing along at home, it seems pretty simple. Jane should have lived within her means! Admittedly, we're all human and want to live the best lifestyle possible. Yet, even at the first signs of trouble, Jane got into bigger trouble by going deeper into debt—taking out a second mortgage on her home and borrowing against her 401K. And even then, she continued to charge up her credit cards.

Perhaps if Jane had figured a budget (similar to the one Greg did with her) at the first sign of trouble, she could have adjusted her spending, saved herself further financial strife, and been happily on her way to Europe with her relationship intact.

You're Not Alone

Going into debt is reaching epidemic proportions. In 1990, the national consumer debt was $789 billion and grew to $1.6 trillion dollars in 2001, more than doubling in just 11 years (source: Wall Street Journal). Why are consumers going into more debt? It's partly technology (with nearly everyone accepting credit cards these days instead of checks) and partially the credit card industry. Credit card companies spent $3.4 billion dollars mailing out credit card applications in 2001 (source: Wall Street Journal).

Of course, if you're over your head in debt, you don't really care how you got there. But you should, as learning how to budget will not only get you out of debt now, but also prevent you from finding yourself in a similar circumstance in the future. (We will talk more about budgeting in Chapter 24.)

Things You Can Do if You Are Overwhelmed With Debt

Before you get to work on settling any unpaid debts, it is important to first get an accurate understanding of the true risks and realities of overdue debts. The severity of an overdue debt most often lies in the nature of the debt. Second, before you even attempt to settle a debt, check the statute of limitations (see Appendix 4)—it may already have expired. The next thing you should do is negotiate your credit rating with your creditor and make payment arrangements. Some people have expressed skepticism that you can actually negotiate with creditors using my strategy or other creative methods of reducing their debts, but the methods outlined in this chapter have already proven to be highly successful.

You have many options when it comes to dealing with high debt loads. I've listed the options in the best to worst preference.

1. STOP SPENDING SO MUCH MONEY!

It seems simple, doesn't it? But most people get into debt by simply refusing to accept the limitations of their incomes. You may impress lots of people with your Rolex, but in the end, no one is really fooled. Allow me to pontificate for a moment. In today's American culture, things that really are just a "want" have been confused with things you actually *need*. Some people refuse to accept this fact at the expense of their credit and blood pressure. Take that cutie pie at the office on a nice hike with a $10 bottle of wine instead of spending $200 on dinner just to impress her. You'll have much more time to get to know each other while communing with nature than you will at some loud snooty restaurant anyway.

2. TAKE OUT AN EQUITY LOAN AND PAY OFF YOUR DEBTS

It sounds really good, getting a cheaper second mortgage to pay off high cost credit cards. However, you must be careful about doing this. The pros and cons of taking out a second mortgage were given in Chapter 13, but it is well worth repeating. Read carefully!

Taking out a second mortgage can be a great source for financing things like home improvements that will be appreciated for the entire time you remain in your home. Spending money on a new kitchen or adding closet space can be a good investment, adding to the value of the home.

Consolidating your credit card debt is another matter. Many people throw in their credit card debt during a refinance so they can deduct the interest on their taxes. It's true—credit card interest is not a tax deduction; mortgage interest is. But think about what people charge on credit cards the most—dinner out, clothes, vacations. Do you really want to pay for that steak dinner for the next 30 years? Think how much interest a $30 dinner racks up over 30 years at 10% a year. The money you save with interest deductions will be more than spent on additional mortgage interest over the life of the loan. Rolling your bills into your mortgage will lower your total monthly expense for two reasons: Because the interest rate is lower (a good thing) and because the payments are spread out over a much longer period (not such a good thing).

If you are in dire straits and a second mortgage will let you better afford your monthly bills and keep your credit intact, it might not be a bad idea. For heaven's sake, though, please don't charge up your credit cards again or you will find yourself right back in the same trouble.

3. BORROW AGAINST YOUR 401K

On the surface, borrowing from your 401K seems like a good idea. You pay yourself back the money with interest and incur no penalties by accessing your money. But even though you are being charged a reasonable rate to borrow, you may be short-changing yourself. Your account might earn more if you leave it invested than if you remove it from your account—even if you're paying your account interest. For example, if you had borrowed money from your account during the past five or ten years when the stock market was averaging more than a 15% return and you were paying back your account at 8% or 9% interest, you would have missed out on that additional growth.

In addition, most plans have a five-year window for repaying loans. If you leave your company (even if it's not your choice to leave), most plans require you to repay the outstanding balance within 30 to 90 days. If you cannot repay the money, your loan will be considered in default and the outstanding balance would be treated as a taxable withdrawal. You would owe income taxes on the outstanding balance and, if you are under age 59 1/2, you may also owe an early withdrawal penalty.

4. NEGOTIATE WITH YOUR CREDITORS

Why not? You have nothing to lose by trying to get your creditors to settle for lower amounts. Most lenders would rather get something than nothing. If your circumstances have changed abruptly (if you've lost your job or encounter major health problems for yourself or your family), it's best to visit your creditors before your accounts are past due. Explain the situation directly, let them know that you do intend to pay the debts but need to work out reduced payments, then make those payments on time. You may also want to place a statement in your file to explain a period of delinquency caused by some unexpected hardship, such as serious illness, a catastrophe, or unemployment, which cut off or drastically reduced your income. The strategies for doing this are covered in the next chapter.

If you seem to be honestly trying to pay what you owe and if you have communicated with your creditors, they may be willing to be patient rather than turn your account over for collection.

5. GO THROUGH A DEBT RELIEF ORGANIZATION

There are many debt relief/credit counseling organizations to choose from, the most prominent being Consumer Credit Counseling Services (CCCS). We will discuss them in depth in the next chapter.

If you're really over your head in debt and are considering bankruptcy, it may be very helpful to talk to a credit counseling service. But be sure to read the small print before signing with such a service. "Bad credit? We can help," is often a claim made in advertisements by credit repair companies who state that they can erase negative information on your credit report. Know that only time, not miracle cures or exorbitant fees, can heal bad credit.

6. DON'T PAY YOUR BILLS

Most consumers overestimate the risk involved with overdue debts. They worry about possible repercussions such as wage garnishment and property seizure by their creditors. When the debt relates to a secured property, such as an automobile or a home, the possibility of repossession is quite serious. In the case of unsecured debts (such as credit cards) the dangers are much less serious.

It is important to remember, however, that the creditor would be within his rights to get a judgment, allowing him to garnish your wages and/or seize your property, even for a small debt. There is a risk of financial reprisals when any debt goes unpaid. But the fact remains that very few creditors will push all the way to a judgment on a relatively small unsecured debt. Getting a judgment and subsequent garnishment and seizure are a creditor's most terrifying weapons in collecting past due debt, but they are expensive and time-consuming. Even if the creditor went all the way to recover the small debt, he probably wouldn't be able to recover enough to offset the collection costs. Therefore, there is very little risk of a creditor taking an unsecured debt farther than simple collections.

7. FILE BANKRUPTCY

Many consumers fold under the perceived strain of unpaid debts. Hundreds of bankruptcies take place each week for incredibly small amounts. These consumers are so intimidated by creditors that they flee to bankruptcy, even though bankruptcy can bring financial hardship if you don't do all the right things for the next ten years. If these same consumers had simply waited and ignored the threatening letters and telephone calls, they would have realized that their creditors were all bark and no bite.

The risks of judgments, garnishments, and property seizures must be properly balanced against the likelihood that such drastic collection measures will ever happen. The risk, and the decision to take that risk, is entirely yours. Bankruptcy is the best option for some consumers, but it is much overused and should not be undertaken lightly. (Bankruptcies are covered in Chapter 23.)

CHAPTER 21: NEGOTIATING YOUR DEBTS FOR LESS THAN YOU OWE

John's Story

John is in dire straits, credit wise. He graduated from college four years ago and landed a decent job—not the best job, but one he knew he'd move up from if he just kept plugging away. The credit cards he scored so easily in college were used to furnish his apartment and buy new clothes—an elegance to which he has grown quite accustomed. Always a bit of a talker, he let his new girlfriend, Deb, believe that he makes more than he truly does.

John continues juggling the credit cards to pay for more fancy dates and a weekend in Las Vegas, until every one of his credit cards is maxed out. He encourages more nights at home with Deb, who seems to like the new romantic John. He does the numbers and figures out that if he can just hang in there and pay the minimum balances on his credit cards until his normally hefty annual raise kicks in two months hence, he can pay the extra income toward the balances and everything should be fine.

The plan goes bust when he is laid off. It gets worse as the weeks pass and the bill collectors call much more frequently than the job prospects. Although Deb remains loyal to him, she is not at all impressed when he confesses that he was living beyond his means to impress her.

Finally, he lands a new job but for less money. With the past due amounts compiling, and the late fees and the over-the-credit-line fees stacking up, there is no way he can get caught up. He considers bankruptcy until his friend, Ray, suggests he negotiate with his creditors to pay off his balances, but for less than he owes, and with a cessation of all additional fees.

NOTE: This chapter focuses primarily on dealing with the original creditor, although the philosophy and strategy can be used in countering the tactics of collection agencies. When negotiating any debt, especially if you are dealing with a collection agency, demand a "debt validation," which we discuss in Chapter 28.

Which Debts Are Negotiable?

Most Unsecured Debts Can Be Settled

As mentioned before–probably numerous times–an unsecured debt is a debt where there is no collateral. Unsecured debts include medical bills, credit cards, department store cards, personal loans, collection accounts, student loans, amounts remaining after foreclosure or repossession, and bounced checks. There are a few creditors who will not compromise (utility companies rarely settle for less than the full balance), but most creditors will take a less-than-full payment as "settlement-in-full" to close a troublesome account.

Secured, Collateralized Debts Are an Entirely Different Story

It is unlikely that you will be able to negotiate a settlement on any kind of secured loan. A secured loan is a loan which, upon default, has a piece of property which is repossessed by the loan company in order to recoup the costs of making the loan and the money lent. You will never find yourself looking at a charged off mortgage–your home will have been repossessed. The same is true for auto loans.

If you have one of these types of loans, you can ask the creditor to rewrite the loan for the balance owed including all past due amounts with extended terms to accommodate a lower payment. You should also request that the new loan be at a reduced interest rate. (It doesn't hurt to ask.) In any case, once re-written, the past due account will be paid-off and the new loan will begin a new reporting history.

If the creditor will not agree to lower payments, they may consider at least rewriting a new loan with payments equal to the old loan. The lender would then take the new loan proceeds and pay off the old loan balance. This may not help in lowering your payment, but it will provide you with a fresh start, with the account reflecting a current status. These options are not always available with all creditors but should be taken into consideration and presented to the creditor (they won't always offer) when trying to get your credit in order.

Repossessed Loans

The one exception to "no settlements on mortgage and auto loans rule" is if a piece of property is repossessed to satisfy a secured loan balance, and the sale of the property fails to cover the full loan amount. Then you may find yourself with a collection account for the remainder of the unpaid loan. In this case, you can usually negotiate a settlement on the balance.

Student Loans

Student loans are a completely different kind of loan animal. In rare cases, fees and penalties might be waived in order to help a student rehabilitate a loan, but that is usually the limit. An excellent source of information on student loans and settlement programs can be found at http://www.ed.gov/. (For more information on student loans, refer to Chapter 15.)

Do everything possible to prevent your debts from going to a collection agency

Simply put, it is usually easier to negotiate with the original creditor. Avoid having an account turned over to a collection agency at any cost.

It varies from creditor to creditor, but most credit card companies allow 180 days to 210 days before an account is charged off. After a debt is charged off, typically, the account is turned over to collections.

While the account is considered a "past due" account and may be approaching the charge-off stage, it is often possible to prevent the charge-off by starting to make the normal monthly payment. This holds the account from going further past due. Once the normal payment is being paid regularly, even though the account may remain past due, regular monthly payments may prevent further delinquency and prevent charge-off. If possible, pay the normal monthly payment plus a little more in order to begin to catch up the past due payments. Extra payments will eventually bring the account current.

Many creditors will allow you to keep your accounts open or even to reopen closed accounts if you bring your accounts current. They also have programs where you can make three payments that are larger than the minimum in order to catch up and bring your account current. You may want to consider these options.

Statute of Limitations

Before you begin settlement negotiations, take a good look at the statute of limitations on older debts. Every day, consumers pay off collection accounts and charge-offs that they do not have to pay off because the statute of limitations has expired for the open account. Consumers pay off these accounts because they still appear on their credit reports. **The Statute of Limitations begins to run from the day the debt, or payment on an open-ended account, was due.** This information can be a powerful weapon in unburdening yourself of old debts, because creditors have a limited time in which to sue you.

The first thing you should do is determine if the statute of limitations for collecting a debt in your state has passed. (See Appendix 4 for state-specific information.) In most cases, a debt will disappear from your credit report after seven years. If the debt is older than the statute of limitations, you should tell the bill collectors they are wasting their time by harassing you for an uncollectable debt, as the original creditor or the assigned collection agency cannot take you to court to get a judgment. Trying to collect on a debt is also a violation of the FDCPA. Your credit report will tell you the date of the last activity on your account (the last time that you made a payment). If necessary, send the collector a copy of your credit report with the date of last activity circled, along with a certified letter stating that the statute of limitations has expired.

Please note that the amount of time a late payment can appear on your credit report has nothing to do with the statute of limitations. **This is a very important distinction**. Even though a debt may no longer legally appear on your credit report after seven years, you could still be sued for the debt if the statute of limitations in your state is longer than seven years.

Also, depending on which state you live in, if you make a partial payment you could be postponing the statute of limitations taking effect on your collection account or charge-off. A collector might call you one day and say you waived your rights when you made a deal with the collection agency. Do not take anything a collector tells you for granted. Make them prove it to you, in or out of court. For about half the population, the statute of limitations started ticking the day the last payment was made on their account.

If the debt is gone from your credit report *and* the statute of limitations is up on this debt, you're home free! If your debt meets both of these conditions, it is considered uncollectable and cannot appear on your credit report.

Sometimes consumers will pay off these accounts when they are *not* on their credit reports. In these cases, even though an account was removed from the credit file, a collector was monitoring the credit report for *any* activity. When the collector spotted activity, he assumed that the consumer was in a position to pay off old, expired debts and called the consumer for payment. All the consumer needed to say to the collector was, "I have an absolute defense, the statute of limitations has expired."

If you cannot wait for the statute of limitations to pass on a debt, you may consider trying to settle your debts yourself. Settling your debts is a time-consuming ordeal that many people find intimidating. As a result, they leave it to Consumer Credit Counseling Services to tackle. (More about Consumer Credit Counseling Services in the next chapter.) But you can do it yourself and will most likely get a better deal if you do. Consumer Credit Counseling Services' main goal is a worthy one, but they often do not negotiate on how the account will be reported, which could leave you debt free, but with a ruined credit report.

You really have two goals when settling debt:
1) Paying off the debt; and
2) Negotiating how the debt will be reported to the credit bureaus, so you are left with a clean credit report when it is all said and done.

It is possible, but not guaranteed, of course, that the average consumer can settle a debt for about 50-75 cents on the dollar. However, if your credit report reflects the fact that you didn't pay as agreed, future creditors will be more reluctant to grant you credit.

The Effect on Your Credit

As your mother, father, or teacher has probably told you (no doubt numerous times in your life): "There's no such thing as a free lunch." Sometimes you can negotiate for an untarnished credit rating with a debt settlement, but this is getting increasingly tough to do. In most cases, when you settle with a creditor, your credit report will say "settled" next to the account for which the settlement took place. This has a negative affect on your credit score.

You should weigh the fact that even if you have 90- or 120-day late payments, these may have less effect on your credit score than having a "settled" account notation. (Refer back to Chapter 5 for credit scoring factors.) Don't believe what any collector tells you about the effect something will have on your credit. They are generally minimum wage, short-term employees who don't have a clue. (I helped a friend to settle her debts and I talked to a representative of a major credit card company and she had no idea how anything would be reported on a credit report. She told me that negative entries would fall off after 2 years, which is absolutely not true. I quoted Section 605 of the Fair Credit Reporting Act. There was a long silence, and then an embarrassed, "Oh.")

Getting Ready to Negotiate

Ok, you've decided that you want to go ahead and settle your debts.

If you haven't already done so, refer back to Chapter 3 and get copies of your credit reports from all three agencies. There's no point in dealing with the one creditor who is harassing you with phone calls at dinnertime if there are others out there who'll be calling you next month.

Once you have your credit reports in hand, identify the debts that you are interested in settling. Look for accounts notated with:

1) Account turned over for collections;
2) Account sold;
3) Account charged off; or
4) Will say nothing at all, but give late payment dates.

Who Do You Contact?

It really depends on who is holding the "strings" to your debt. Obviously, if an account has been "turned over for collections," you will need to contact the collection agency. (Before you try to settle collection accounts, though, try using the debt validation techniques described in Chapter 28.)

If your account listing falls under numbers 2 or 3 above, or says nothing at all but includes late payment dates, call the original creditor to determine the status of the account.

The method of contact varies by the situation and whom you are working with.

Collection agencies

Never contact a collection agency by phone. *Never!* Collection agents are not trained to settle with you. They are paid to collect money, and they will say anything to get you to pay. You are opening yourself up to possible abuse, which though it is illegal, is extremely common. If you say the wrong thing to a collector in the heat of the moment, it could ruin your chances for a good settlement in the future.

Letters are the best way to contact a collection agency. Send the letter certified, signature required, so you have a paper trail to follow during the settlement procedures. Believe me, you might need it. Some collection agencies are starting to refuse certified mail if they think the letters might be part of your gaining the legal upper hand. There is a sneaky way around this, though. Write "payment enclosed" on the envelope. This is sure to get them to accept and open the mail!

If you know the fax number, you can also fax your settlement offer to the collection agency. There are many services available which offer a "certified" delivery of the fax receipt, which is almost as good as the certified letter receipt.

Original creditor

While contacting a collection agency is *not* recommended, you should initiate contact with the original creditor by phone. If you still have your credit card, the 1-800 number should be listed on the back. Otherwise, look on an old statement or call the toll free information directory at 1-800-555-1212.

One thing to remember as you speak with a representative: they are taking notes and these notes become part of your permanent account information. Keep your conversation simple and straightforward. Don't lose your temper. It's pointless, and it definitely won't help your efforts.

Ask for the customer service department. When the agent gets on the phone, ask for the status of the account. If the account is in collections, you may also find that you will be transferred to the collection department of the company. Don't panic, this is all normal.

When you have the right customer rep on the line, ask them if they would be interested in considering an offer to settle the account, or if you have to go through the collection agency currently handling the account.

If the answer to the question "will you consider an offer to settle" is yes, don't be surprised if you are made an offer on the spot. If you like the offer, tell them you will be following up with a letter and a fax. Ask them where the paperwork should be sent. *Keep in mind, though, that you can usually get a better deal than the first offer.* Ask for the representative's first and last name, and direct telephone number. Never give them the money at this time, though they will try to get you to pay on the spot with a check by phone or a credit card. You absolutely need a written agreement between you and the creditor *before* you send them a cent. If you don't like the offer, tell them you will think about it and get back to them.

If they don't make you an offer or say that they won't consider an offer (this rarely happens), thank them and ask for mailing and fax information. The rep may not be aware of settlement programs or might simply be wrong.

What if the creditor contacts me first and makes an offer?

Sometimes the creditor may contact you by phone or mail, and make you an offer to settle the account. When this happens, you can be sure that you can get a better deal than the one offered. If this contact is by phone, listen carefully, get the rep's name and direct telephone number and the company address to which you will be sending your settlement.

After you get off the phone, or review the letter, use the sample letter *Counter Offer* in Appendix 7 to prepare an offer of your own.

If you have been getting a series of letters from the credit card company and the offer keeps getting better, you may be wondering at what point you should accept. Keep this basic rule in mind: *most creditors will not go below 30%-50% of the original balance.* If the offer approaches these figures, consider accepting. Use the sample letters *Acceptance of Written Offer* and *Agreement to Settle a Debt* in Appendix 7 to get your settlement agreement in writing.

Other places to get address and fax numbers

If you've been unable to get the address and/or fax number for the creditor, some online resources may help:

- ✧ The Better Business Bureau – http://www.bbb.org
- ✧ Links to all 50 United States government Corporation Commission websites - http://www.residentagentinfo.com

You could also try your secretary of state or your state corporation commission who maintains a list of all businesses in the state and their contact information.

How long does the debt settlement process take?

If you are making a lump sum payment to settle your debts, the process can take as little as one month. That is, of course, if negotiations between you and the creditor don't drag out. Obviously, if you are making payments to settle the debt, it could take as long as four years to settle your debts.

What Makes a Creditor Say 'Yes' to a Debt Settlement?

Creditors will agree to a plan when they feel it is their only chance to get money from you. Their thinking is that some money is better than nothing. You can help this impression along by hinting that your only other option is declaring bankruptcy. However, no matter what you may hint or flat out state to them, creditors have their own ways of determining if you are teetering on the brink of bankruptcy.

What would make you appear as a candidate for bankruptcy?

- ✧ If you haven't been making payments on any of a significant portion of your debts, especially credit cards.
- ✧ If you don't have anything to lose in a bankruptcy, like a home or car.
- ✧ If you are out of work, or show no probable future increases in pay.

You may think to yourself, "Ok then, I'm going to tell them that I haven't been making payments on my other accounts, I'm out of work and I don't own anything." Be careful about this, as many creditors have invested large sums of money in high technology information-gathering systems. In talking to a representative for a major auto-loan company, I learned that they have software that obtains the following information just by entering your phone number:

- ✧ Where you bank
- ✧ Your credit rating
- ✧ Your criminal records
- ✧ Your payment history on all of your accounts
- ✧ Where you work
- ✧ How much you make
- ✧ Whether or not you own a home, a car, boat, etc.

Where is their software getting this information? From your credit report, from the credit application you originally gave them, public records, motor vehicle division, Social Security Administration, you name it – if records are public, you can bet they are being accessed. Public records not only contain any court records, but also recording of deeds of trust and other property transactions.

Get the picture? Creditors have "tools" to help them assess the situation.

What Makes a Creditor Say 'No' to a Debt Settlement?

You are current on all of your payments to this creditor and every other one on your credit report

What if you are an honest person who wants to warn a creditor that you may not be able to make payments in the immediate future because of a job layoff or medical emergency? It's counterintuitive, but some creditors are only willing to deal with you when there is a significant problem. It's possible you will get them to work with you if you provide convincing documentation, however this is going to be a tough road. If they see you are in good standing on all of your accounts on your credit report, it's going to take some pretty fancy talking to convince them this kind of payment history isn't going to continue.

You have recent activity (charges and payments) on your account

In one case that I know of, recent charge activity on the account made the creditor insist on 65% of the balance due over a lower 50% settlement amount. And can you blame the creditor? Obviously, the debtor believes he has money to spend.

You offer a very low settlement and want to make payments over an extended period of time

You've got to give somewhere, and most creditors are not going to go for a 30% settlement offer payable over five years. They will be wondering what is going to prevent you from missing your payments again.

However, if you are going to make a full payment settlement offer, they might be willing to take a chance on an extended period.

They think they can sue you and recover the money

If they think (or know) that you are making big bucks and/or have a lot of assets, why settle? They won't if they can simply take you to court and garnish your wages to recover the full debt. It's a better return for them, even considering legal fees, than accepting a settlement offer from you.

How Much Should I Offer?

This is the number one question asked when someone begins the debt negotiation process. How much should I offer to settle the debt?

Each creditor is different

Like any other industry, each company in the credit card industry has its own debt settlement policies. You may be able to settle with one company for 30 cents on the dollar, while another won't accept less than 75 cents on the dollar, even though the amounts of the debt and the terms of the repayment plan are identical.

Don't get stuck on this point. If a creditor is immovable in their settlement policies, it's because of internal policies written in stone from the dawn of time. Accept the offer, move on, and spend your time on a creditor who is more willing to work with you.

Lump sum offerings

Obviously, if you are going to give your creditors cash, they will be much more interested in working with you. You will always get a better deal when offering cash. As a matter of fact, you may not get ANY deal if your offer includes a payment plan. However, if you have cash, you can usually get 30-50% reductions in the balances of the debt you owe, sometimes even lower. Again, we are in no way guaranteeing that you will get this kind of reduction.

Payment Plans

If you don't have all of the cash that you need to pay off your agreed upon debt settlement, you have two options: a short-term payment plan or going on one of their "hardship programs."

If you choose the payment plan option (usually because you don't have another option), don't hold that information back while negotiating the settlement plan. It may completely torpedo the whole deal if you agree on a certain figure, then ask: "Can I make my payments over the next five years?"

Short-term: Some creditors will still agree to a sizeable debt reduction if you can pay off the whole amount in three to six months.

Hardship program: Credit card companies are used to dealing with the many debt reduction companies out in the world, and to save time by coming up with a custom plan for each one, they usually have a specific program for people who want to pay their debts but need one to four years to do it. One note here: Discover allows a maximum of one year on their hardship program.

What If I Can't Make the Payments on the Plan I Negotiated?

You're kidding, right? If you have any reason to believe that you will not be able to make the payments on a plan you have negotiated, don't agree to it. Keep negotiating the payment schedule until you are confident it fits into your family's budget. No one can predict the future, especially in today's economy where layoffs are so common, but by making too optimistic a payment plan, you are hurting your future chances of working with this company.

If you find yourself in a situation where you absolutely can't afford your payments and you need to file bankruptcy, all the money you paid towards settling your debt is lost. Why? If you had filed a bankruptcy before going through the debt settlement process, you would be discharging the entire amount, not the amount remaining after making the payments. Bankruptcy wipes out all credit card debt. Are we encouraging you to file a bankruptcy? Absolutely not. We are just trying to cover all of the bases here.

Repayment Plans

As we already mentioned, you will get the best terms if you can make a lump sum payment. But if you can't afford a lump sum settlement, keep the payment period as short as possible. If you need to stretch things out to six months, you will have less clout but still be in a strong negotiating position. As mentioned before, many credit card companies have a hardship program that may work for you.

Sometimes, your only option is to stretch out the payment period. There are some downsides to doing this:

⋄ Payment plans may come at an interest rate as high as 20%. Obviously, the longer you take to pay off your debt, the more money you will pay. Keep in mind that your debt payment plan *doesn't have to include interest*. This is one more thing for you to put on the negotiation table.
⋄ At some point you will want to begin rebuilding your credit. This process cannot begin until all of your old debts have been settled.

Working out the payment plan

Just like buying a car from a dealership, the salesman (or creditor) tries to keep you focused on your monthly payment instead of the full price of the car (debt settlement). If you haven't run the numbers yourself, you may find yourself paying unseen interest or fees. Pay attention to all facets of the settlement: time period, interest rate, and penalties.

Negotiating the interest rate on the payment plan

If your repayment period is six months or less, you can probably avoid paying any additional interest on the balance. Even if your payment plan exceeds six months, try to push for no additional interest on the balance during the repayment process.

Compounded interest adds up quickly. Let's say that you agree to pay off $2,000 over two years at $100/month with 12% interest, compounded monthly:

First year:
Month 1: ($2000.00 - $100) x 1% = $1900.00 + $19.00 = $1919.00
Month 2: ($1919.00 - $100) x 1% = $1819.00 + $18.19 = $1837.19
Month 3: ($1837.19 - $100) x 1% = $1737.19 + $17.37 = $1754.56
Month 4: ($1754.56 - $100) x 1% = $1654.56 + $17.55 = $1672.11
Month 5: ($1672.11 - $100) x 1% = $1572.11 + $16.72 = $1586.83
Month 6: ($1586.83 - $100) x 1% = $1486.83 + $15.86 = $1502.69
Month 7: ($1502.69 - $100) x 1% = $1402.69 + $15.02 = $1417.71
Month 8: ($1417.71 - $100) x 1% = $1317.71 + $14.17 = $1331.88
Month 9: ($1331.88 - $100) x 1% = $1231.88 + $13.31 = $1245.19

Month 10: ($1245.19 - $100) x 1% = $1145.19 + $12.45 = $1157.64
Month 11: ($1157.64 - $100) x 1% = $1057.64 + $11.57 = $1069.21
Month 12: ($1069.21 - $100) x 1% = $969.21 + $10.69 = $979.90

At the end of the first year of payments, your balance with compounded interest would be $979.90. If you had negotiated an interest-free payment plan, your balance would be $800. Big difference. That $179.90 could pay for a romantic dinner at home, complete with wine and flowers, and still leave plenty to make an additional payment.

You may find that the companies have a set program and will not negotiate the interest. But it never hurts to ask, does it?

If I had the money to settle my debts, I would have paid them. What do I do?

Well, you may have to make some hard choices to resolve your problems. You may have assets and cash that you hadn't thought to use for debt payments. Think about these ideas:

Tap into the Olde' Savings Account, Money Market Account, CD's

What's 2% interest, when you can save 50%? In addition to saving this money, (and potentially saving your credit rating if you get them to report you as "Paid As Agreed") you'll avoid high interest charges, late fees and other related charges.

Increase Your Income

Ever consider getting a second job? You can earn some extra money *and* meet new people! Stash this extra income into a special savings account until you have enough to negotiate a lump sum payment with your creditor.

Decrease Your Expenses

You've probably already thought of this, but just in case you haven't—it's an obvious place to start. How about learning to budget more carefully? (Budgeting is covered in Chapter 24.) If you learn to spend less, and put the savings into a special savings account, you'll have the cash to negotiate that lump sum payment. (And once you no longer have HBO to entertain you at home, you may even get out of the house more. Those beautiful babes don't usually just appear on the doorstep...)

Yes, It's Time to Tap into Stocks, Bonds, Mutual Funds or Other Investments

Even if you are making 10% on your money in these accounts, you are getting a better deal by negotiating a lump sum payment with a potential reduction of 50% or more. Getting a 10% return on an investment is often considered great, especially these days. But the piece of mind and peaceful-looking credit report you'll get by settling your debts is well worth some delay in building your retirement.

Borrow from Family, Friends, or Relatives

Don't be afraid to ask those who love you to help. You'll be surprised how often family members and friends are willing to step up to the plate and render assistance, especially if this is the first time you've gotten into trouble.

Retirement Funds

Although the experts warn against borrowing against your 401K, it's still better than defaulting on your debts. And if you have an IRA, SEP account, annuity, trust fund, or other forms of retirement funds, the tax penalties may still be less than the money you will save on a debt settlement. It's not a step to take lightly, so you are smart to consider all your options carefully.

Borrow from Whole Life Insurance Policy

If you have cash value in a life insurance policy, you can typically borrow from these funds at a very low interest rate. Best of all, you need not repay the loan. As a consequence of this, however, your life insurance benefit will be reduced by the amount you borrow and any accrued interest. But, being debt free, the reduced stress may add years to your life!

Sell Assets

Come on, now. It's time to be practical! You may have valuable assets that can be sold to raise the money you need for debt settlements, things that really are luxuries—like that extra car, recreational vehicles, jewelry you never wear, family heirlooms, gun collections or even your home. Remember, if you are unable to resolve your financial hardship through debt settlement, it's possible that the creditor will sue you for the cash.

Home Equity Loan, Second Mortgage, Home Refinancing, Reverse Mortgage

This method should ONLY be used when it results in significant savings, and the effect of it resolves your financial hardship. You must be reasonably certain that you will never default on the obligation. Otherwise, it is neither practical nor financially sound to convert unsecured debt to secured debt and risk losing your home in the future.

Automatic Deposits into a Savings Account

Talk to your bank about setting up an automatic transfer from your checking account or other regular account. Although we are not recommending it, sometimes you can simply stop paying your unsecured bills and transfer this money into savings until you have enough to start negotiating. (Remember, creditors are much more likely to settle for less money when you pay in a lump sum, and also when you are not current on the account.) Once you have the cash, begin negotiations to settle the account which is most troublesome and which will result in the greatest savings first. One by one, continue the process in this fashion until all debts have been settled in full.

Other Negotiation Tips

Time is on your side. As time passes, calls from creditors will eventually stop and the debt will be filed away for future attention. The longer the debt remains uncollected, the better your chances will be of getting a good settlement. Eventually, the creditor will consider the bad debt a loss in order to receive a corporate tax write-off. This does not necessarily mean that they won't pursue you for the debt. The corporation has options. They may then collect on the debt themselves, sell or assign the debt to a collection agency, press for a judgment and garnishment, or temporarily ignore it.

If you're contacted by more than one collection agency for the same debt, it means that the original creditor has hired a secondary or even tertiary collection agency. This indicates that the original creditor and even the first collection agency have given up on you. A collection agency that agrees to take your debt at this time will insist the original creditor pay a generous fee (usually 50%-60% of what is owed). Many secondary and tertiary agencies will take 33-55 cents on the dollar. If the agency hasn't been able to reach you by phone, but knows that you are receiving its letters, it may be willing to take even less.

Never look too eager to settle. Just like dating, sometimes it is better to play hard to get! Take plenty of time to reach an agreement. Don't accept the first, or even second, settlement offer. Let them call you to move the deal forward. You cannot expect to reach an affordable settlement if the creditor thinks he has the upper hand. If, for example, you tell a creditor that you really need to get this debt settled to get into your dream home, you can forget any kind of settlement. The creditor will insist on the full balance.

Remind the creditor that the statute of limitations is approaching on the debt and they only have a limited time to deal with you. Have the facts ready and be prepared to give the creditor the time line.

Use the threat of bankruptcy. It will be in your best interest if the creditor believes that you have very little money and you are teetering on the edge of bankruptcy. You should approach each creditor as though this is their last chance to compromise, and get something out of your debt, before you declare bankruptcy and they get nothing. Be careful when doing this, however. If you accumulate any more debt after stating this to a creditor (they do record all of your correspondence and phone calls, remember?), you may not be able to discharge this debt if you do declare bankruptcy.

Keep good records! Keeping good records during your debt settlement process is crucial to your success. Records can make the difference between a good and bad settlement.

✧ Send all correspondence via registered mail (about $2/letter). If you send a fax, get a fax confirmation, and follow up with a hard copy in the mail.

✧ Keep a copy of every letter you send.
✧ Include a self-addressed, stamped envelope with every letter. (Make it as easy as possible for them to contact you.)
✧ If you call, keep a log of when you spoke to the agencies, and who. Ask for the name of the supervisor of the person you spoke to, as the turnover rate at collection agencies is high.
✧ Follow up all phone correspondence with a letter (registered, of course) and/or fax confirmation.

Negotiate Your Credit Rating

You should always push for a Perfect Pay Rating. Your final goal in negotiating your debt settlement is to get the creditor to list your account after the settlement as "Paid as Agreed" or "Account Closed - Paid as Agreed." Anything other than this listing will have a negative effect on your credit report.

If you are dealing with a collection account, you want a complete removal (a deletion) from your credit report, however, NOT a "Paid As Agreed." Any notation on your credit report from a collection agency is considered negative, so even if the listing read, "this person has the best paying record we've ever seen," it would still hurt your score. Much like a well-built blonde in form-hugging jeans: if he returns your admiring gaze with a smile but his front tooth is missing, it completely ruins the overall attractiveness.

Reasons why a creditor would agree to change a listing

Some creditors will tell you that it is illegal to change a listing on your credit report. Hogwash. A creditor can agree to change your listing based on a new contract (the one you will negotiate with them to settle your debts) and if you pay per this new contract, isn't this "paying as agreed?" Remind them of this point.

Creditors make their profits by collecting from their customers, not by reporting negative credit information. Because creditors recognize this, they will often agree to delete any negative listing upon settlement of the debt. You have to realize that creditors won't try to ruin your credit rating as a personal vendetta. It's strictly business. If it pays them to collect from you and restore your rating to perfect, they will do this. Talk to them in terms of money, not principals or morals. Something along the line of "I know you would love to receive the $3,000 I owe you, but it will not help my credit report if you can't change my rating to 'Paid as Agreed'. All I have is $3,000 and I will pay it to other creditors who will agree in writing to change my credit rating."

One note here: It is getting tougher and tougher to get credit card companies to change negative history to positive history. Many, these days, will agree to do this only if you pay your entire balance in full, including all interest and penalties.

For the advanced and ultra-smooth negotiators

If you are dealing with an account that has been placed in collections, you now have two negative listings (in most cases) appearing on your credit report – the collection and the original creditor. If the original creditor refuses to deal with you and sends you to the collection agency, it's very difficult to get the original creditor to remove the negative mark. But impossible? No. You need to get the collection agency to agree to remove their listing entirely from your report and have the original creditor change the rating to "Paid As Agreed." At the very minimum, you are within your legal rights to demand the removal of the collection account from your report.

Some collection agencies will tell you they have no power over what the original creditor will do regarding your credit. To some extent, this is true. However, both the collection agency and the creditor want their money. If the collection agency gets paid, it is likely that the creditor will, too, therefore it is to their advantage to cooperate. And baloney if they tell you they don't know how to get in touch with the original creditor. Did the account magically appear on the collector's desk? No. The collection agency was hired. Explain to the collection agency that you will pay them their money if they can get a written agreement from the creditor. Otherwise you will pay a more cooperative creditor with the only money you have left, and they will get nothing.

Remember, though, not all collections result from credit cards. Doctor's bills cannot appear on your report, but collections resulting from these accounts can.

If You Must Accept an Imperfect Credit Listing as Part of Your Settlement

You may find that some of your creditors are willing to hold out longer than you are before agreeing to delete the negative listing from your file. It may seem that they are unwilling to delete the negative listing under any circumstance. Once again, let it be said that sometimes creditors will eventually give you what you want if you speak to the right person, are patient and persistent, and make the right offer. But if you are on a time-line, you have a couple of other options:

List the account as "Unrated." Many times, a creditor will agree to list the account as "unrated." What does this mean? It means just that, the account is not listed as good or bad. As far as we can tell at the time of this writing, an "unrated" notation for an account does not negatively impact your score. However, if the listing is unrated, make sure that any lates on the account are removed, as these lates WILL have a negative affect, even if the account is unrated.

List the account as "Paid" only. You may counter-offer for the creditor to list the account as "Paid" rather than delete it altogether. This is a true indication of the status of the account and many creditors will concede and agree to this wording. A "Paid" status is still very negative for a collection account or an account that will show "Paid Charge-off" or "Paid Repossession." You should insist that the account show "Paid" *only* and that all other negative notations (such as "Charge-off," "Repossession," late notations, or "Collection") are deleted at the same time. A simple "Paid" notation on a regular trade line is neutral and should not hurt your credit.

List the account as "Settled" only. You may counter-offer that the creditor simply lists the account as "Settled" rather than delete it altogether. "Settled" is an inherently negative listing but not as negative as "Paid Charge-off." Don't agree to a "Settled" listing until you have exhausted all other possibilities. "Settled" will still trigger a credit denial. You should only agree that the account show "Settled" if all other negative notations (such as "Charge-off," "Repossession," late notations, and "Collection") are deleted at the same time. If you agree to a "Settled" notation, you must continue to work hard to delete the notation through the credit bureau dispute process.

List the account as "Paid Charge-off" or "Paid Collection" or "Paid was 30-, 60-, or 90-days late." This will be the creditor's first choice, and your last choice, of what to place on your credit report once you have paid. These notations are almost as damaging as showing the same debt unpaid. It is very common, though, for an account to be deleted (through credit bureau disputes) once it has been paid. The creditor now has no compelling reason to keep the negative listing on your report. For this reason, it is still usually a good idea to settle even if the creditor won't budge on deleting or positively modifying the negative listing.

Writing the Offer

In many cases, once you've agreed to a verbal offer with the credit card company, they will send you the paperwork to clinch the deal. However, it always pays to be proactive, as you don't know exactly when you will be hearing from them.

Confirmation of acceptance of verbal offer

OK, if you've gotten a verbal offer on the phone and wish to accept it, follow up with both a fax and a certified letter. (You can use the *Acceptance of Verbal Offer* and *Agreement to Settle a Debt* sample letters in Appendix 7.)

Counteroffer to an offer

If you have received an offer, either by phone or by mail, you don't have to accept it. You can also counteroffer with a lesser amount and see what they say. In the next chapter, we cover the "typical" debt settlement amounts many lenders seem willing to accept. Use the *Counter Offer* and *Agreement to Settle a Debt* sample letters in Appendix 7. Send them by fax and by certified mail.

Unsolicited offers

An unsolicited offer is one you make to a creditor without discussing the specific offer on the phone. Sometimes this is the only way to get an offer before a creditor. Obviously, in order for these offers to even be read, it is very important that you have the correct address and fax number.

A good example of an unsolicited offer is included in Appendix 7: *Unsolicited Offer to Creditor*. Also use the *Agreement to Settle a Debt* letter.

Tips on Payment

Once you have reached an agreement on a settlement amount, be careful about the way you make the payment.

Never disclose where you work or bank.
If you are asked, simply say "no comment." Why? Just in case your settlement falls through and the creditor gets a judgment against you. Knowing where you work or bank makes it easy for them to collect the judgment.

Make sure you get the cashier's check from a bank other than your own

The form of payment is very important, as it protects you from other creditors learning about your financial status and bank account numbers. For this reason, *never send a personal check.* Get a cashier's check or money order. And don't get it from your own bank. Get it from a different bank, the post office, or a store.

Make sure you keep a copy of your money order or cashier's check! (We can't say it enough: good record keeping is vital.)

Never pay your settlement with "Check By Phone"

"Check By Phone" is an electronic transaction. You give your creditor your checking account number and they deduct an amount from your account. This is the very worst thing you can do. It gives your creditors full access to your checking account (and we've heard more than one horror story where more than the agreed amount was removed from a checking account.)

Some Legalities

Can I be sued for the balance once a debt has been settled?

Yes, depending on the state you live in and how you handled your payment. Some collection agencies will agree to settle with you for far less than you owe, then turn around and hire another collection agency to collect the difference.

However, this is illegal in many states. Once a creditor deposits or cashes a full payment check, even if she strikes out the words "payment in full" or writes "I don't agree" on the check, she can't come after you for the balance. The states in which this law is enforced are:

Arkansas   New Jersey
Colorado   North Carolina
Connecticut   Oregon
Georgia   Pennsylvania
Kansas   Texas
Louisiana   Utah
Maine   Vermont
Michigan   Virginia
Nebraska   Washington

Some states have modified this rule. In the following states, if a creditor cashes a full payment check and explicitly retains his right to sue you by writing "under protest or without prejudice" with his endorsement, he can come after you for the balance. But those exact words must be used. It is not enough that he writes, "without recourse," communicates with you separately, notifies you verbally or writes on the check that it is partial payment. These states are:

Alabama   Ohio
Delaware   Rhode Island
Massachusetts   South Carolina
Minnesota   South Dakota
Missouri   West Virginia
New Hampshire   Wisconsin
New York

Can debt settlement stop creditor lawsuits the way a bankruptcy filing can?

No. Sometimes, though, they may choose to drop a lawsuit against you.

Tax Consequences of Debt Settlement

So you've been successful at settling your debts with a creditor, and you think the nightmare is over. Well, not quite. Most people don't know this, but the IRS regards debt forgiveness (paying less than you owe on a debt) as income.

If you are dealing with the original creditor, and you work out a settlement for less than you owe, the creditor may send you a 1099-C at the end of the tax year for the difference. You are required to report the amount listed on the 1099-C as income.

So how bad is this? Well, it depends on your tax bracket. Income tax is beyond the scope of this book, but briefly, your tax bracket depends on how much income you report, after deductions to the IRS.

Just as an example, and we **are not using real numbers** here, let's say:

1. If you are below the poverty line, you don't pay any taxes.
2. If you make over $35,000, you pay 20% taxes
3. If you make over $50,000, you pay 35% taxes
4. If you make over $70,000, you pay 39% taxes

Let's also say that you get a $5,000 break in your debt settlement. The creditor sends you a 1099-C for $5,000 at the end of the year.

You would pay:

1. no extra taxes if your income is below the poverty line
2. $1,000 in additional taxes if you are in the 20% bracket (hey, you are still saving $4,000 overall by negotiating)
3. $1,750 in additional taxes if you are in the 35% bracket
4. $1,950 in additional taxes if you are in the 39% bracket

Consider tax consequences when negotiating a debt.

CHAPTER 22: NONPROFIT CREDIT COUNSELING SERVICES

Rachel's Story

Rachel, 45, attractive and divorced, is a machinist with two grown daughters. She has been with her manufacturing company for 15 years. When the plant announces plans to reduce its workforce, she decides to take the generous severance package they offer as inducement. Jobs are plentiful and she figures she won't be out of work long. She will use the severance money to pay off her bills and take her daughters on the cruise they have always talked about.

Rachel is as good as her word. She pays off her credit cards, and has great fun shopping for the perfect cruise with her daughters. The trip is terrific—time spent together that they will not soon forget.

Fresh from the cruise, Rachel begins her job hunt, only to find that jobs for her skill set are not as plentiful as she expected. It takes four months longer than she planned to land a good job. Though she's been thrifty, she finds herself $10,000 in debt by the time her first paycheck arrives. (Cash advances and her Visa got her through those four rough months.)

Rachel decides to call her credit card companies and work out a payment plan that will let her catch up on her bills. One rep suggests that she call Consumer Credit Counseling Services (CCCS), a free service by a national network of nonprofit agencies. When Rachel calls, they assure her they can get the creditors to agree to a payment plan, bringing Rachel out of debt in about a year. Rachel agrees to the program and begins making one payment to CCCS for all of her monthly debt.

A year passes. Rachel completes the CCCS program, paying off all her debts on schedule. With a raise in her new job and fond memories of the cruise with her daughters, Rachel is thinking about another—a single's cruise this time. She applies for a new credit card that advertises free vacation points that can go toward singles cruises. To her amazement, she is turned down! The rejection letter informs Rachel that she is entitled to a free credit report, and she wastes no time requesting one. When it arrives, it is filled with late payment notations.

Is Rachel in trouble? Yes, unfortunately she is. CCCS, while they mean well and do get your debts paid off, tends to ruin your credit in the process.

Consumer Credit Counseling Services

What Consumer Credit Counseling Services (CCCS) does is negotiate your debts and payments with your creditors, reducing some of them and getting creditors to lower the minimum monthly payment in other cases. CCCS generally is not recommended unless you are deeply in debt. Although CCCS may be helpful in pulling you out of debt as painlessly as possible, it can have the bad side effect of ruining your credit.

Here's how CCCS works:

- ✧ Consumer Credit Counseling Services talks to you to determine how much you can afford to pay each month.
- ✧ They negotiate with your creditors, getting them to accept lower monthly payments until all your debts are paid.
- ✧ You must sign an agreement to not obtain any new debt until the current debt is paid off.
- ✧ You make a single monthly payment to CCCS who pays your creditors.

Sounds easy, right? The problem with this service, as Rachel discovered too late, is that many of your creditors, even though they agree to accept a lower payment, still report you as late to the credit reporting agencies. Why? Because you are not making the minimum payment as defined in your original agreement with the creditor. If you pay less than the minimum payment, a creditor has the right to report you late, because you didn't make the full payment on time.

CCCS usually does not get the creditor to agree to report you as paying on time, and even if they do, they do not get this agreement in enforceable form (in writing). If your creditors report you late, your credit report may show 30-day, 60-day, and 90-day+ lates, essentially ruining your credit. Although you will have a good reason why your credit rating looks this way, it will fall on deaf ears. Prospective creditors don't care *why* your credit looks bad; they only care that *it is* bad. Your future ability to get another loan will be impaired to a certain degree.

Read on for alternatives to CCCS. Once your eyes are wide open, you may decide that CCCS is still the best solution for you. If you do, you will find their local office in the phone book. They have offices in almost every city in America.

More information is available at their national website: http://www.nfcc.org.

Alternatives to CCCS

Rachel could have contacted each of her creditors and tried to negotiate a reduced payment schedule (or even reduce the debt by waiving interest and penalties as we discussed in the last chapter). As long as she gets the agreement in writing, including a clause where the creditor agreed to accept partial payments as on-time payments and report them as such, she would be doing well. Admittedly, not all creditors will negotiate with individual consumers. CCCS has considerably more clout with negotiations.

At any rate, it's not the end of the world. If Rachel opens new credit accounts and maintains good credit, her credit will recover within two or three years.

There are nonprofit organizations in every state that counsel consumers in debt. Counselors try to arrange repayment plans that are acceptable to you and your creditors, or they may coach you on how to talk to your creditors directly. And perhaps more important for your future credit health, they can also help you set up a realistic budget.

Most will suggest that you not take on any new debt. (One we've heard of suggests that you cut up all but one credit card, and store that one in your freezer, frozen in a block of ice, to prevent any impulse buying!) These counseling services (not the same as the "loan consolidation services" that are actually for-profit finance companies) are offered at little or no cost to consumers. Here is a partial list of suggestions:

- ✧ Credit unions often offer workshops that help their members use credit wisely. If you are a member, give them a call.
- ✧ Neighborhood Housing Services and other NeighborWorks® organizations across the country offer financial literacy workshops at little or no cost and credit counseling for prospective homebuyers at a minimal fee. They do not offer debt consolidation loans. Visit http://www.nw.org to find the affiliate near you.
- ✧ http://www.HUD.gov lists approved counseling agencies that help homeowners in financial trouble.
- ✧ Universities, military bases, and housing authorities sometimes operate counseling programs.
- ✧ Check with your local bank or consumer protection office to see if it has a list of reputable financial counseling services available.

Beware of the Wolf in Sheep's Clothing!

Nonprofit debt consolidation companies are not always what they seem. There are numerous nonprofit organizations that seem to offer an instant solution to your debt problems. They advertise on TV, the radio, and they are ALL OVER the Internet. Be very wary of these companies.

Many of them, though they tout their nonprofit status, still find ways to make money from their customers. Let us provide a few examples:

> There used to be a nonprofit company called Genus who funneled $74 million dollars or so of their $134 million revenue through a for-profit company called Amerix by allowing Amerix to process customer payments. The founders of both companies happened to be the same person.

> Ameridebt, a nonprofit organization (which is still in business) used to steer consumers to a debt consolidation loan company called Infinity Resources. The consumers were persuaded to get loans from this company at 14-15% interest. You guessed it, a member of Ameridebt's Board of Directors owned Infinity Resources. The attorney general's office in Washington, DC filed suit against Infinity. Ameridebt is no longer allowed to direct customers to Infinity.

> You should also be aware that lawsuits have been filed recently (Fall of 2003) against Ameridebt by the FTC, states of Missouri and Illinois.

Debt consolidation companies do not address the typical cause of consumer debt: poor budgeting. None of these companies has an office where a consumer can receive one-on-one counseling; all contact is via the Internet, fax, phone and mail.

"Nonprofit" Doesn't Mean No One Makes Money

To be a not-for-profit organization, you usually are a corporation that doesn't show a profit at the end of the year. A company doesn't show a profit if its expenses equal or exceed its income. What counts as an expense? Oh, trivial little things like corporate salaries. The presidents of the companies mentioned above reported salaries of $350 million dollars for the 2000 calendar year! There's no limit to how much you can pay officers of nonprofit organizations.

What does it take to start a nonprofit corporation? Paperwork and legal fees. You also have to be a church, recreational organization, a charity, or have the intent to help your fellow man. Many local social clubs, such as hiking or ski clubs, are nonprofit organizations. Doesn't a debt organization sound charitable?

Many of these debt-relief organizations rake in lots of cash. How do we know? For one thing, they can afford to pay lots of money for the advertising mentioned above. It costs tens of millions of dollars to advertise the way they do.

Smell a rat? You should.

Debt Relief Companies

Similar to Consumer Credit Counseling Services, debt relief companies offer a counselor's analysis of your bills and your income, and figure out a payment plan for you. They negotiate with your creditors for lower interest rates and payments. Some may collect a small fee from you up front. They call these fees "donations."

As with a CCCS payment plan, you make one payment a month to the debt-relief corporation. One method some debt counseling services use to collect "donations" is to keep the first month's payment as a fee. So, your first payment is swallowed whole by the company, and you missed your first month's payment on your new plan. Also, when you make your second payment, the debt-relief agency may not forward your money on to your creditors for up to 90 days. What happens in the meanwhile? Your creditors are harassing you at an ever-increasing pace, and your credit, if it wasn't in good shape before, is now completely trashed.

Debt Settlement/Debt Negotiation Companies

These companies will tell you that they are different than debt consolidation companies. They are mostly wrong and a little bit right. How they are right: debt consolidation companies tell you that you are making a donation to the company so they can "help" others out. The debt settlement/debt negotiation companies are up front about the fees they charge for their services and are not nonprofits. But they are wrong in that you will get taken for a ride with either type of company.

The main scheme used by debt settlement/debt negotiation companies:

1. You will be paying your monthly minimum payments to the debt negotiation company, but they will not be paying your creditors, just putting the money into some kind of an "account."
2. When the time is right (meaning your account is about to be charged off by the original creditor), they will take the money you have built up in your account and negotiate with the creditor to settle for this amount.
3. In this way, they tell you, you will have paid off your account in six months or less and your credit will be fixed.

Sound good to you? Run for the hills, I say. There are some problems here.

First of all, what if the credit card company won't deal? What if the total of your minimum payments for an account is less than 10% of what you owe? Some credit card companies would rather take the tax write off then take so little money. In this case, the debt negotiation company takes their fee (remember, they are NOT nonprofit), your credit rating is ruined, your account is charged off and possibly in collections, and you have received no value for your money. What a deal!

Avoid debt consolidation, debt settlement and debt negotiation organizations at all costs. You can get the same service, for less money and less hassle, at your local CCCS. CCCS is a member of the National Foundation for Credit Counseling, offers person-to-person counseling, and includes important budget counseling that will help prevent future problems. Their website:

http://www.nfcc.org

CHAPTER 23: BANKRUPTCY

Declaring bankruptcy is a drastic option, but it's not the end of the world...

Elaine's Story

Elaine, 30, is a single mom with two small children. She is an administrative assistant at a small New England company. With day care and other expenses, Elaine and her kids live on a modest budget; but she is doing fine and takes pride in her ability to provide for herself and her children.

Disaster strikes. She is involved in a car accident that shatters her right leg and keeps her in traction at the local hospital for four months. Corrective surgery and two months of physical therapy are required before she can return to work part-time. To survive in the meantime, she has run up her credit card bills to a point where she can no longer afford the minimum payments. Full-time wages would not even do it.

Compounding her problems, the insurance provided by her employer is severely inadequate, and the hospital is looking to her for the extra $53,000 that her insurance company doesn't even want to hear about. She crashed alone on an icy road, so there is no other vehicle insurance to tap.

After a long depressing meeting with her lawyer, she agrees that her only course of action is bankruptcy. She files for Chapter 7. Over the next few years, Elaine fully recovers from her accident and enjoys success at her job—raises and promotions. Determined never to get into financial trouble again, she saves earnestly and pays cash for everything.

She meets and marries a wonderful man who adores her children. Elaine tells her new husband of her past financial trouble and he assures her that enough time has passed since her bankruptcy discharge for her to be able to qualify for their new home. They find out differently when they apply for the loan together. When they ask why the loan was turned down, they are told it's because Elaine has no *re*established credit. Elaine is angry. She believes she has acted like a model citizen since her bankruptcy—saving until she could afford to pay cash for purchases and accumulating no debt.

Is Elaine in trouble? Sadly, yes. She was a woman with bad credit. Now she is a woman with *no* credit.

What Elaine Could Have Done Differently

It's difficult to imagine that anything short of a fairy godmother (perhaps in the form of better disability insurance, better auto insurance, or better health insurance) could have saved Elaine from bankruptcy. As part of her recovery, she followed her best instincts and avoided future credit problems by avoiding credit altogether. Many people feel this way, but it is actually the wrong way to proceed. As soon as you have recovered from a big credit upset like a bankruptcy, you should work to reestablish credit *immediately*. (Methods for establishing credit are given in Chapter 2.)

Can YOU Avoid Bankruptcy?

You should consider your alternatives long and hard before embracing bankruptcy as a solution to your credit woes. Remember that **there is no easy way to get out of debt**—despite what those slick ads might suggest. If you have already carefully considered settling your debts with your creditors (covered in Chapters 20 and 21) and using a credit counseling agency (as discussed in the previous chapter), and none of these strategies will work for you, you may be a candidate for bankruptcy.

After arming yourself with the following facts, talk to a lawyer who is familiar with the bankruptcy law in your state.

Chapter 7 Bankruptcy

Chapter 7 bankruptcy is a liquidation proceeding. The debtor turns over all non-exempt property to the bankruptcy trustee who then converts it to cash for distribution to the creditors. The debtor receives a discharge of all dischargeable debts. The most common reasons for consumer bankruptcy are:

- ✦ Unemployment;
- ✦ Excessive medical expenses;
- ✦ Seriously over-extended credit;
- ✦ Marital problems; and
- ✦ Other large unexpected expenses.

Chapter 7 Eligibility

To qualify for a Chapter 7 bankruptcy, you must:

- ✦ Reside or have a domicile, a place of business, or property in the United States or a municipality;
- ✦ You must *not* have been granted a Chapter 7 discharge within the last six years or completed a Chapter 13 plan; and
- ✦ You must *not* have had a bankruptcy filing dismissed for cause within the last 180 days. It must not be a "substantial abuse" of Chapter 7 to grant the debtor relief. Generally speaking, if after you pay the monthly

expenses for necessities there is not enough money to pay the remaining monthly debts, then granting a discharge would not be an abuse of Chapter 7.

How it Works

The underlying policy of bankruptcy law is that the honest debtor who is in debt beyond his ability to repay should be given a fresh start through the discharge of debts in a bankruptcy proceeding. Not all debts are dischargeable. Generally speaking, the following debts will **not be discharged**:

- ✦ Taxes;
- ✦ Spousal and child support;
- ✦ Debts arising out of willful misconduct and or malicious misconduct by the debtor;
- ✦ Liability for injury or death from driving while intoxicated;
- ✦ Non-dischargeable debts from a prior bankruptcy;
- ✦ Student loans; and
- ✦ Criminal fines, penalties, and forfeitures.

Secured debts will be discharged. However, expect the creditor to take the necessary legal steps to repossess the property. In most cases, if the debtor's equity interest in the property is exempt, the debtor may retain the property by redemption or reaffirmation.

You can file for bankruptcy yourself, but it is wise to use an attorney. There are a multitude of forms to fill out—as many as 30 to 60 pages in your petition, schedule, and other papers. You must follow local and federal bankruptcy court rules in completing the forms, which requires an understanding of both bankruptcy law and local state law to enter the information correctly and accurately. The forms have to be typed, and a certain number of copies must be included with the filing. Today, most attorneys use a computer system to prepare these forms because of their complexity and voluminous nature.

About 30 to 40 days after you file the bankruptcy, you will have to attend a hearing presided over by the bankruptcy trustee. This hearing is called the "First Meeting of Creditors." At this hearing, the trustee will ask you questions under oath regarding the content of your bankruptcy papers, assets, debts, and other matters. After the trustee is finished, your creditors will be permitted to question you. Not to worry. (You decided to use an attorney, right?) Your attorney will help you prepare for the hearing and will be there to represent you.

When you discuss your situation with your attorney, you will need to be prepared to discuss all areas of your case. This includes each and every debt you owe and creditor you have. It is very important to list all your creditors in your bankruptcy. Sometimes, after your hearing is over, various creditors will approach you to discuss the status of secured property or your desire to retain a credit card. Your attorney will negotiate with them, with your knowledge and approval.

If you forget to list a creditor on your bankruptcy papers, you are permitted to file an amendment to your schedules up to a certain time before discharge (this is a hassle after the fact, so be thorough and list everything when you prepare your schedules). If the amendment is filed in a timely manner, the omitted creditor is added to the bankruptcy. It is perjury to intentionally omit a creditor. However, if you do not know that a creditor exists and there are no assets to pay your creditors, the debt will be discharged anyway.

You normally will not need to return to court after the First Meeting of Creditors. However, if a creditor files a motion or an adversary action, you may have to return to court. This is the exception and only your attorney can determine if this is likely to happen. After you file your bankruptcy, the court will automatically issue the discharge 60 to 75 days after the First Meeting of Creditors.

In the unfortunate event that you should need to file bankruptcy again, you must wait at least six years to re-file. If your bankruptcy was dismissed, you usually must wait 180 days to re-file.

What Chapter 7 Will and Will Not Do

Chapter 7 bankruptcy *will* **stop a wage attachment and most civil judgments**.

Chapter 7 bankruptcy *will* **stop bill collectors from calling**. Debt collection efforts and foreclosure is halted. Once a creditor or bill collector becomes aware that you have filed for bankruptcy protection, all efforts to collect the debt must stop. After your bankruptcy is filed, the court mails a notice to all creditors listed in your schedules. This usually takes a couple of weeks. If this is not soon enough, ask your representative to inform the creditor immediately. If a creditor continues to use collection tactics after having been dutifully informed of your bankruptcy, the creditor may be liable for court sanctions and attorney fees for this conduct.

Chapter 7 bankruptcy *will* **stop a foreclosure**. However, a home is an asset usually secured by a deed of trust. The lender is entitled to apply to the court for relief from the automatic stay (the order preventing creditor action by virtue of the bankruptcy). Depending upon several factors, you may be able to prolong a foreclosure until you have received your discharge from bankruptcy. You usually have to make a deal with the lender to keep a home that is in foreclosure.

Chapter 7 bankruptcy *will* **stop an eviction or "unlawful detainer" action**. However, this will only delay the inevitable. The owner is entitled to possession of his property. At best you will be able to remain in the property until you have received your discharge from bankruptcy or the landlord obtains an order from the bankruptcy court. If the only reason you filed the bankruptcy is to stop an eviction, this may be considered an abuse of Chapter 7. If the bankruptcy court finds that this is true, the court can immediately dismiss the bankruptcy and impose other legal and monetary sanctions on you. Also, in California, laws have been passed favoring the landlords. Apparently, landlords in California can evict even when a tenant files a bankruptcy.

Chapter 7 bankruptcy *will* **remove a lien**. Under some circumstances, a special motion can be filed to remove certain liens once the bankruptcy proceedings have started. It will take a bankruptcy court order to remove them. This is a complicated area of the bankruptcy law and an attorney should be consulted. However, the following are guidelines for removing tax liens. You can discharge (wipe out) debts for federal income taxes in Chapter 7 bankruptcy only if all five of these conditions are true:

1. The IRS has not recorded a tax lien against your property. If all other conditions are met, the taxes may be discharged, but even after your bankruptcy, the lien remains against all property you own, effectively giving the IRS a way to collect.
2. You didn't file a fraudulent return or try to evade paying taxes.
3. The liability is for a tax return actually filed at least two years before you filed for bankruptcy.
4. The tax return was due at least three years ago.
5. The taxes were assessed (you received a notice of assessment of federal taxes from the IRS) at least 240 days (eight months) before you filed for bankruptcy (11 USC. §§523(a)(1) and (7)).

Chapter 7 bankruptcy *will* **remove dischargeable community debts** if you are divorced. However, you should discuss this with your family law attorney to understand the other implications of the filing of a bankruptcy during the pendency of a dissolution action (divorce case).

Also, remember that if you are discharged from community debts, your spouse becomes responsible for the entire balance owing on the debt. Put another way, the debt does not go away; it simply shifts from you to your ex spouse. Mmmm…revenge?

Chapter 7 bankruptcy *will not* **require your spouse to file bankruptcy**. In some cases where only one spouse has debts, or one spouse has debts that are not dischargeable, it might be advisable to have only one spouse file.

Chapter 7 bankruptcy *will not* **cause you to lose your job**. Bankruptcy laws prohibit discrimination based upon a debtor filing for protection under the bankruptcy laws. Also, under normal circumstances, unless your employer is a creditor, your employer will not know.

Chapter 7 bankruptcy *will not* **cause you to go to jail**. There are no debtor's prisons in the United States.

How Chapter 7 Affects Personal Property, Real Property, and Other Assets

All property of the debtor at the time of the bankruptcy filing (and certain other property to be received in the future) becomes the property of the bankruptcy estate once bankruptcy is filed. This means that the bankruptcy trustee will take control of this property for purposes of satisfying the creditors. However, there is certain property that is either excluded or exempt that the debtor will be able to keep. Property or asset exemptions are determined based upon your situation, income, and the laws of your state. The best way to determine which property you may keep requires a detailed analysis of your situation. You need a good lawyer.

As for **real property** (including your **house**, if you own it), in many states you may exempt up to $100,000 in equity dependent upon which exemption scheme is selected and your circumstances. When calculating your equity, you should use a value that is based upon a forced liquidation as opposed to the best selling conditions to arrive at a value for your home. Once you know the value, subtract the amount owed, plus selling and transfer costs, from the value of the property to calculate the equity. In depressed markets, liquidated properties often are valued at less than you think the property is worth.

In California, you are permitted exemptions for a variety of **personal property**. This includes automobiles, household furnishings and personal effects, jewelry, tools of the trade, retirement plans, unmatured life insurance, personal injury awards, earnings, animals, and other miscellaneous property.

Again, state laws vary. In other states, depending upon which exemption scheme is selected, you may keep your **automobile** if your equity is equal to or less than the allowed exemption. Generally speaking, you may exempt as little as $1,200 or as much as $9,100. Using the *Kelly Blue Book* or a comparable guide to calculate your equity, subtract the amount still owing from your *Kelly Blue Book* value to determine the amount of equity.

Most courts understand that you need a car to earn the money that will get you back on your feet after bankruptcy. Apply rules of common sense here. If you own vintage cars that are free and clear and worth thousands of dollars, you probably are not going to be able to keep them. If, on the other hand, you have a car worth $10,000 and you owe $8,000 on it, you most likely will keep it. Again, the need to talk to a good lawyer should be evident. Most leased vehicles have no equity and, therefore, are entirely exempt. If you owe money on your car, or if it is leased, you must still make the payments. In those instances, you will have to redeem or reaffirm the property to keep it. And in some circumstances, your representative can re-negotiate the loan or the lease to get a more favorable deal for you.

Under some circumstances, you may even keep your **credit cards**. Many factors must be considered including the credit card balance at the time of the bankruptcy, what the credit card company is willing to do, and your ability to pay the present and future credit card debt.

How Chapter 7 Affects Your Credit

How is your credit rating after a Chapter 7 bankruptcy? It sucks, plain and simple.

The bankruptcy is a judgment and will be listed on your credit report for a period of up to 10 years after the discharge.

However, you can reestablish credit and be back in "A" credit two to four years after the discharge of bankruptcy. For a while though, expect to pay through the nose in interest and fees. There is a whole new mortgage industry springing into action, loaning to people with less-than perfect (or even rotten) credit.

Getting new credit cards and good car loans will be a lot tougher after a bankruptcy. If you open up new lines of credit after the bankruptcy (it is recommended that you obtain secured credit cards) and maintain *perfect* credit for two to three years you'll be back to "A" rates on mortgages (especially FHA loans).

It will be easier to get a loan on a home then on a credit card. Why? The creditor gets the home if you default on a mortgage while the issuer of a credit card can wind up with nothing (even if you don't or can't file a bankruptcy).

You basically can't get a regular loan for three years. (It takes between six months to a year to file and have your debts officially dismissed by the courts, plus two more years to reestablish your credit.) It may be tough to get an equity loan on your house until the bankruptcy is off your credit report.

Chapter 13 Bankruptcy

Chapter 13 is a section of the Bankruptcy Code that helps qualified individuals, or small proprietary business owners, who desire to repay their creditors but are in financial difficulty. It is often referred to as a "mini Chapter 11" because you usually repay something to your creditors while you retain your property and make payments under a plan.

The main purpose of a Chapter 13, as opposed to a Chapter 7, is to enable a debtor to retain certain assets that otherwise would be liquidated by a Chapter 7 trustee. In most cases, you can keep your home and your car under either plan (provided your equity does not exceed certain limits). However, under Chapter 7, you wouldn't be able to keep your rental properties, those antique guns, etc. (The goal of most Chapter 7 bankruptcies is to discharge your existing debts and allow you a "fresh start" on your finances; in other words, once your discharge is granted, you no longer need to repay the debts that were incurred before you filed your bankruptcy). Under a Chapter 13, however, you repay most or all of your debts before your slate, so to speak, is wiped clean. Because you repay your debts, you gain certain advantages over a Chapter 7. These include keeping all of your property and a better credit situation after completing the process.

Chapter 13 Eligibility

Only an individual with regular income who owes, on the date the petition is filed, less than $250,000 in unsecured debt and $750,000 in secured debt can qualify for Chapter 13 bankruptcy. These debts must also be non-contingent and liquidated, meaning that they must be for a certain, fixed amount and not subject to any conditions.

How it Works

Chapter 13 protects individuals from the collection efforts of creditors, permits individuals to keep their real estate and personal property, and provides individuals the opportunity to repay their debts through reduced payments. Another benefit is that your Chapter 13 bankruptcy remains on your credit report for a shorter period of time (7 years) than a Chapter 7 (10 years), so it takes less time to rebuild your credit. You also may be able to discharge debts in a Chapter 13 that would be non-dischargeable under other Chapters (for example, fraud judgments).

The size of your monthly plan payments is determined by the amount you can afford to pay after paying necessary living expenses (i.e., insurance, mortgage payments). Typically, the plan payments last for 36 months, unless additional time is requested, but in no event will they last more than 60 months. Therefore, if your payment analysis shows, for example, that you can afford to pay $200 per month (above and beyond your normal living expenses), you would pay that each month to the Chapter 13 trustee, who would disperse it pro rata among your creditors. At the end of 36 months, you are discharged from all dischargeable unsecured debts, regardless of how much your creditors have received. Be conscientious with your payments, though, because if you miss any payments *at all* that are due under your plan, the court will dismiss your case.

In addition to your plan payments, you must stay current with any ongoing obligations that you have to secured creditors, such as your mortgage. Chapter 13 (or any bankruptcy chapter for that matter) only affects debts that you owe on or before you filed the bankruptcy. Therefore, for mortgages and other secured debts, your plan payment goes to pay any arrearages that exist on the date you file. You can repay that arrearage over the life of the plan, but you must stay current from the filing date forward with any mortgage payments, etc.

Secured debts (your mortgages) must be repaid in full, but Chapter 13 enables you to cure the defaults (reinstate the loans) over 36 months (or up to 60 months with creditor consent and court approval). You also have the ability to eliminate junior liens from your real property (your mortgages) under certain circumstances and restructure mortgage and other payments.

How Chapter 13 Affects Your Credit

A Chapter 13 bankruptcy will appear on your credit report for seven years after you file. (The credit bureaus can technically report a Chapter 13 for 10 years, but currently it is their policy to only report it for 7 years). This means that when all is said and done, and you've completed the three years of bankruptcy, it will appear on your credit report for only four more years. This is a *big* advantage over a Chapter 7. Your credit will definitely be less damaged than had you completed a Chapter 7.

The usual limitations will apply until the bankruptcy disappears from your report. You will not get as high a credit limit as you once had, nor will you be able to borrow a large sum of money. But getting some credit (such as a secured credit card) shouldn't be that difficult and you will be able to rebuild your credit over time. What you will probably face is higher interest rates, required higher down payments, more points, etc., but you will be treated more leniently than a person with a Chapter 7. For instance, mortgage lenders will give you the benefit of the doubt, giving you preferred credit status over those filing Chapter 7.

New Bankruptcy Laws

In April 2005, new bankruptcy legislation was signed into law. The provisions of the law will come into being approximately October 2005. The changes are sweeping, though some of the details will no doubt continue to be hammered out in the legal community as the laws take effect. Some of the major changes:

✧ Means tests to identify debtors who have the financial capacity to pay some money to their creditors. The test process will work as follows:

> TEST # 1:
> Is the family earning above the average income for their state?
> 1997 US average for a family of one = $18,762;
> 1997 US average for a family of two = $39,343;
> 1997 US average for a family of three = $47,115;
> 1997 US average for a family of four = $53,165.
> If the answer is "No" Chapter 7 can be filed!

> TEST # 2:
> If the answer is "Yes" to TEST # 1
> ■ Do you have excess monthly income of more than $166/month income to pay $10,000 of debt over 5 years?
> If the answer is "No" you must answer another question; if "Yes" Chapter 7 cannot be filed but Chapter 13 may be filed!

> TEST # 3:
> If the answer is "No" to TEST # 2

- Do you have excess income to pay $100/month over the next 60 months at least 25% of your unsecured debt?

If the answer is "No" you can file Chapter 7; if "Yes" Chapter 7 cannot be filed but Chapter 13 may be filed!

✧ Proof of Income:
Debtors filing Chapter 7 or Chapter 13 bankruptcy must provide to the trustee, at least seven days prior to the 341 meeting, a copy of a tax return or transcript of a tax return, for the period for which the return was most recently due.

✧ State Exemptions:
You cannot use the exemptions in your state of residence unless you have lived there at least 2 years.

✧ Vehicles:
If there is security (put in place within 3 years) over your vehicle, you must pay the full amount owed or lose the vehicle. Current bankruptcy laws allow you to get the loan stripped down to the value of the vehicle and you make payments at that rate.

✧ Counseling:
You must have finished financial counseling within the last 6 months before you can file. Critics say this requirement, in addition to adding costs, ignores Senate investigations that suggest the counseling industry is rife with excessive fees, pressure tactics and poor service. Moreover, no approved list of counselors exists. The legislation charges the U.S. Trustees office with creating such a list.

I've stated my reservations about these companies in Chapter 22.

✧ Child Support and Alimony:
These debts would go from a priority of 7th to 1st.

✧ Homesteads:
The exemption is limited to $125,000 if the property was acquired within the previous 1215 day (3.3 years). The cap is not applicable to any interest transferred from a debtor's previous principal residence (which was acquired prior to the beginning of such 1215-day period).

✧ Tithing:
Up to 15% of your income can be given to charity. This is seen by some as a loophole allowing people who may be just over the threshold of having to file Chapter 13 to drop down low enough to file Chapter 7.

CHAPTER 24 - HOW TO BUDGET

Randy and Val's Story

Randy has always admired the fact that his parents raised four kids and helped three of them through college on a single teacher's salary. They always seemed to be able to work miracles with a dollar. Although Randy's first job out of college didn't bring the big paycheck he had hoped for, he was still able to pay off his student loans in less than four years by following his parent's advice and example.

Now Randy has fallen madly in love with Valerie and they are planning to be married in the fall. During the last few months, though, Randy has noticed Val's seemingly out-of-control spending habits. She's not too happy when he mentions that her weekly shopping trips with her girlfriends seem a bit extravagant to him. Val insists that money is no problem for her.

Things come to a head when the perfect little house comes up for sale and their offer is accepted. On the loan application, it is difficult to hide the fact that while Randy has no debt, a retirement account and a nice bit of savings; Valerie has a small 401K and $25,000 worth of credit card debt. On the positive side, though, her credit rating is perfect.

After some gentle encouragement from Randy to talk more openly about her financial situation, Val admits that sometimes she is afraid to open her credit card statements when they come in the mail. In truth, Valerie doesn't want to look cheap with her friends, and the idea of a budget seems so old-fashioned and confining.

Randy asks Val if he seems cheap to her, and she answers with all honesty that he has never seemed anything but generous. She knows she can learn something from him that will help their soon-to-be-joint finances. So she calls to cancel her shopping trip with the girls, asks for his indulgence in one last extravagance, then runs out to purchase a good bottle of champagne. An hour later Val settles on the loveseat next to the man in her life, toasts to "our future," and asks him to share his secret to managing money so effortlessly and effectively.

So What's the Secret?

From the people we have met in preceding chapters, you might think the secret is a closely guarded one. But it's not. One way to improve your life in general is to learn better money management skills, and budgeting is the first step.

We're not talking about reusing plastic sandwich bags or driving a 15-year old car. Not at all! We're talking about some very simple things you can do in your everyday life that can add up to huge savings over the course of a month.

The "B" Word – Budget

Are you one of those people who need to learn how to manage your money better? Here are some questions you can ask yourself:

- ✧ Do you feel really strapped for money all of the time, just barely covering your living expenses?
- ✧ Do you see your credit cards as the only way to finance a vacation, buy Christmas presents, or purchase clothes for you or your family
- ✧ Would an unexpected layoff mean you couldn't pay next month's rent?

If you answered yes to any of the above, budgeting can help relieve some stress in your life.

Track your expenses

You would be amazed at the number of people who have no idea how much money goes in and out of their bank accounts on a regular basis. This is called cash flow. You don't need to know your cash flow to the penny, but we bet those millionaires do! Be as thorough as possible when tracking your expenses.

Tools you can use:

- ✧ Microsoft Money or Quicken.
- ✧ A spreadsheet program like Excel or Lotus.
- ✧ A pencil and a simple piece of notebook paper.

Carry a small notebook with you to note expenses or an envelope to collect *all* those little receipts (debit slips, credit charges, checks, cash receipts). If you buy a can of soda at the gas station when you fill your tank, write down how much you spent for "gas" and how much you spent on "meals eaten out." (I know. A can of soda doesn't sound like a meal… Create categories that make sense to you.)

Track everything. Use the sample Budget Worksheet in Appendix 10 to set up your own system. Tally all your expenses with the tool of your choice and include all sources of income you receive on your spreadsheet, too. You'll want to track your expenses for three months, then average the amount spent in each category. This will provide a good picture of your spending habits.

Prioritize

Once you have established your expense categories (and you can't really do this until you've tracked yourself for a few months), put them in some kind of priority order with the most important at the top.

Now above your highest priority, add a line for savings and investments. Already there? GOOD! You're learning. Hopefully, the categories you have at the bottom of your list will be things like movie rentals, dining out, tattoos, etc.

Examine what you've spent each month on each category

You may be surprised at how much you've spent on items you thought were insignificant. (When I did this exercise, my Starbucks expenditures were scary!)

Figure out what you'd like to spend next month on each category

Most people can't stick to a budget because the one they make for themselves is too complicated, is not fully supported by a spouse, does not plan for the unexpected, or is just plain unrealistic.

Here are some tips to help you come up with a winning formula:

- ✧ **REALITY** - If you're spending $80/month on gas, don't think you'll be able to cut that amount in half. Unless you are changing jobs so you're closer to home, or thinking about biking to work, gasoline is a pretty static cost. The same goes with groceries and utility bills. These are fairly fixed costs. Don't short yourself here or you will find yourself scrambling to find enough each month to pay basic living expenses.
- ✧ **UNITY** – Is there a particular goal you are working toward? Maybe the goal is for Mom to be able to stay home with the kids, or for the family to pay off all credit cards and get out of debt. Budgets work best when everyone in the family understands and agrees on the end goal.
- ✧ **CONSISTENCY** - An exercise program won't work if you don't stick with it. Neither will a budget. You have to be consistent, not on-again-off-again. If you spend more than you should one month, it's not the end of the world. Just buckle down and commit to doing better next month.
- ✧ **FLEXIBILITY** - It takes time and experimentation to find a system that works for you. Also, remember that things will happen that you didn't plan for. Do you have a little breathing room in your budget?
- ✧ **GOALS** –If your goal is to take a singles cruise next summer, make sure you add a "savings for cruise" line to your budget. (You may need to cut spending on low-priority categories in future months in order to reach your goal.) If little Junior's college education is already a goal, add a savings line into your budget now. (Even if you can't afford to start

saving now, it will be there when your next raise comes through.) And in many cases, one look at your actual expenses will help you set some new goals. If your "rent" total is more than you know your friend is spending on their mortgage payment, perhaps home buying should be a goal.

With these tips in mind, you are ready to write down what you would like to spend next month. Put it right next to your actual expenses for each category.

Congratulations! You have a budget.

Finding Extra Dollars in Your Current Income

Hopefully, the income line in your budget exceeds your expenses. But if you do have a negative number in the "Cash Over/Short" line, don't worry. It may take a few tries. Revisit your lower-priority categories. If you've cut everywhere you can, and still come up "Cash Short," it's time to get creative. Read on…

Save energy. Deregulation in some states has allowed electric and natural gas suppliers to compete for your business. Shop around for better deals. A more energy-efficient home can also help. There are some services, both on line and in person, which can give you an analysis of your home and make suggestions.

How about doing the simple things:
- Turn the thermostat up a few degrees in summer; down a few in winter.
- Shut down the computer when not in use.
- Turn off the lights when you leave the room.
- Turn off the TV if no one is watching it.

Mortgage. Are mortgage rates so favorable right now that you could refinance and get a lower payment? How about getting rid of PMI (mortgage insurance)? Mortgage insurance is very expensive, but you can usually stop paying it once you have 20% equity in your home. If the value of your home has increased, contact your bank to learn how to stop paying this insurance.

Lower your long-distance bill. Examine your phone bills to see what you're paying for local, long-distance and wireless service. There are so many plans now to choose from, you are bound to find a better deal. Also, many people are choosing to use their cell phone free long-distance minutes rather than more expensive land-line calls.

Coupons. We all hate 'em, but they do help to save you money. Do a little homework: can cutting coupons make a difference in your grocery bills?

Use your local library. Do you really need things like cable TV? How about borrowing movies from the library rather than renting them. And while we're talking about the library, how about borrowing books rather than buying them?

Computer games? Many libraries offer them free. Music? My library has a vast selection of CDs. Free Internet? You guessed it. Most libraries offer it.

Go on a Wi-Fi hunt. If you have a laptop with a Wi-Fi card (wireless Internet capabilities), why not make a date out of finding all the "hotspots" with the cute-looking geek at the office? Free wireless high-speed Internet access locations are becoming more and more common, especially in large urban areas.

Cut down on the use of your car. Car expenses include more than just gas. There's the wear and tear on your car, parking, and maybe even parking tickets. Can you use public transportation, walk or bike to work, carpool? Not only are these great ways to save money, but you'll meet new people *and* be in better physical shape to boot!

Pack your own lunch. Most people spend $5 to $9 each time they go out to lunch while at work. Most packed lunches of an apple, cookies or chips and a sandwich cost about $2 to make. Many micro-wavable lunches cost $1.50 to $2.50. You do the math. Unless you have an expense account, it may be worth your time.

Convenience foods are expensive. Have you heard the one about the frozen peanut butter and jelly sandwiches or the frozen micro-wavable baked potatoes? It's not a rumor. A little extra effort in the kitchen can save you large dollars. Cooking with your sweetie can be highly romantic!

Avoid buying coffee in coffee houses. If you stop for coffee each morning on your way to work you're probably spending between $1 and $3 a day. Bringing a thermos of coffee from home to work could save you $5 to $15 per week.

Free checking. Another no-brainer way to pare expenses is by finding a checking account that's right for you. Don't let bank fees steal your money. Many programs offer reduced or no-fee accounts if you keep an account balance above a certain limit. If you have a credit union available to you, look into joining. They generally offer no-fee accounts.

Avoid recreational shopping. For some people, shopping at the mall is a way to unwind and relax. Some couples actually go shopping on dates! This can get very expensive if you're buying things you don't need. Mall magic can make the most useless junk seem like a "must have." Find another outlet for yourself that doesn't involve the mall.

Pay your bills on time to save on fees and penalties. Credit card companies charge errant customers hefty fees for minor infractions. Pay your bill a day late and you could get slapped with a $29 fee. If the fee pushes you over your credit limit, bang, another $29 can hit your account. That's $58, for nada.

For other tips on saving money, we like the http://www.stretcher.com website.

Comparison to the Average Person's Expenditures

It may help you to figure out if your spending habits are out of line by comparing them to the average person's expenditures in 2000. The average income for the people who participated in this study was $45,000.

Food: According to the Bureau of Labor Statistics 2000 Consumer Expenditure Report the average consumer unit (that's 2.5 people) spent $5,158 on food in year 2000. That's $2,063.20 per person if you split it up among everyone in the average home.

Transportation: The average person spent $2,966.80 getting from one place to another in the year 2000.

Clothing: The average person spent about $742.40 on apparel in the year 2000.

Entertainment: The average person spent about $745 on entertainment in the year 2000. That's about 5% of the total average expenditure for that year.

Housing: By far the largest expenditure, the average person spent $4,927.60 in order to have a place to live in 2000. With the average household being 2.5 persons that would be $12,319.

Dining Out: Consumers spent $854.80 eating out in 2000. (That would pay for 1/3 of the food they ate at home that year!)

Pensions and Social Security: The average person spent $1,186.40 on pensions and Social Security.

And the Money Left Over?

Now that you've found some ways to cut expenses, and have a reasonable budget to live by, what will you do with the "Cash Over" you came up with?

Bonus points are awarded for the following answers:
- ✧ I'll accelerate payments on my high-interest credit card balances.
- ✧ I set myself a goal to buy a new car in two years and added a "savings for car" line to my budget so I'll have a good down payment. (Singles cruise savings qualify for bonus points, too! You name it. It's your goal.)
- ✧ I'll invest some of my paycheck in the company's retirement plan (with the added bonus of a pre-tax deduction that cuts my income tax bill.)

Budgeting may not seem like fun at first, but the process is certainly creative. Make it your own. Those girlfriends you normally go to the mall with every Saturday? Invite them to spend next Saturday at your house for a budgeting brunch. Before long, you'll be able to go shopping for that sexy lingerie *without* going into debt.

Other Online Resources

www.americasaves.org: Includes savings strategies and tips, and links to local chapters that can help you gain financial planning skills.

www.consumeralert.org: Consumer tips and a downloadable budget planner.

www.asec.org/toolshm.htm: The American Savings Education Council offers financial planning calculators.

www.choosetosave.org: More than 100 financial planning calculators.

SECTION VIII: REPAIRING AND REBUILDING YOUR CREDIT

CHAPTER 25: REPAIRING YOUR CREDIT

Eduardo's Story

Eduardo's car, a hand-me-down from his father, is ready to give up the ghost. His girlfriend, Charisse, suggests he try to buy a newer car, though he is reluctant to spend the money. Although Eduardo makes a great living, his credit is in terrible shape due to a large number of unpaid medical bills from a recent accident. Eduardo has seen advertisements in the local paper for credit repair services, and wonders how easy (and how expensive) it would be to "fix" his credit.

Charisse makes a few calls to credit repair agencies for Eduardo, and is suspicious of their claims. It's one of the reasons that Eduardo was attracted to her in the first place—she is so street wise! With the credit repair company ruled out as an option, Charisse offers an alternative. She once successfully disputed a late payment on her credit report. Perhaps Eduardo can do the same. They decide to see what they can do on their own to fix Eduardo's credit.

Can You Really Fix Your Credit?

First of all, the phrase "Credit Repair" is a misnomer. You cannot simply repair your credit like fixing a flat tire. It takes time and patience to repair your credit, as we have said numerous times already.

Everything that a credit repair clinic can do for you legally, you can do for yourself at little or no cost. The information in this chapter helps you fix errors on your credit report and clean up those "questionable" items. While you may not be able to remove accurate, negative information from a credit report, the law does allow you to request a reinvestigation of information that you dispute as inaccurate or incomplete. There is no charge for this. Also, if the credit bureaus cannot verify information on your credit report, they must remove it. For instance, if a credit bureau cannot contact a collection agency that reports a collection on your report, it cannot verify the information and it must delete the entry.

Basic Strategy

There are 10 easy steps to repairing your credit, but you must have patience and persistence. The credit bureaus are not always greatly cooperative, or fast moving.

1. GET YOUR CREDIT REPORT.

For directions on how to obtain copies of your credit report, see Chapter 3. Request them from all three of the credit reporting agencies—Equifax, Experian and TransUnion.

2. ANALYZE YOUR CREDIT REPORT.

Analyze your credit as outlined in Chapter 4.

3. DECIDE WHICH ITEMS YOU WILL TARGET FIRST.

Chapter 4 discusses how to identify items—positive and negative—on your credit report. Make a list of all negative information you find. Once you develop this list, rank each item according to the amount of damage it is doing to your overall credit picture. Rank the most damaging information first, followed by the next most damaging information, and so on. As we discussed in Chapter 4, these are:
- Bankruptcy;
- Foreclosure;
- Repossession;
- Loan default;
- Court judgments;
- Collections;
- Past due payments (less than 30 days late);
- Late payments (30+ days late);
- Credit rejections; and
- Credit inquiries.

You will want to get rid of the most damaging items first, so ranking them will help you form your plan of attack. Do this for each credit report, as they may not all contain the same information. If two bureaus duplicate the same bad information, you will need to write to each credit agency individually.

4. REQUEST CORRECTIONS AND DISPUTE QUESTIONABLE NOTATIONS.

What to challenge

Always shoot for a complete deletion of any bad information. Just like a permanently stained dress is not sexy no matter how low the neckline, a blemished notation on your credit report is still a blemish. Thus, don't bother challenging the information *within* a collection listing, charge-off, court record, repossession, foreclosure, or settled account. Since the basic nature of these listings is negative, changing the information within the listing will yield no improvement. Severely negative listings must be disputed on the basis of complete deletion or not be disputed at all.

Don't forget to dispute personal information

As a matter of policy, we generally advise disputing everything on your credit report that is not current, including previous addresses, employers and maiden names. As identity theft is becoming so rampant, you don't want to have anything on your credit report possibly causing mix-ups with other people's information. I know of several instances where a consumer's prior address allowed the poor credit information of another person to creep on to the consumer's report. Be sure all variations of your personal information are completely removed from your credit report. Make it your goal to show only one entry for each of the following: your employer, your legal name (no extra nicknames or maiden names), your current address and your social security number.

The possibility of identity theft is one good reason to remove as much personal information as possible. Another is that they may not be able to verify information without an old address or maiden name, earning you an instant deletion.

Address each item individually

It is very important that each questionable item is dealt with individually. If you attempt to have the credit reporting agency correct several items (or even all items) at once, it will be easier for the agency to claim that your request is frivolous or irrelevant. This doesn't mean you can't challenge several items in the same letter, just that you must give separate, complete information for each item. A sample letter is included in Appendix 7, *Requesting the Removal of Inaccurate Information,* as an example.

If the information a credit bureau is reporting is inaccurate, incorrect, erroneous, misleading, or outdated, it has to be removed upon investigation. The specific law on disputes is found in United States Code, Title 15, Chapter 41, Subchapter III, Section 1681i, titled *"Procedure in case of disputed accuracy."* (See Appendix 1.)

Write a letter to each credit reporting agency

The Fair Credit Reporting Act (FCRA) states that if a bureau corrects a mistake on your report, it is required to share this information with other bureaus, but this doesn't mean that the other bureaus have to do anything with this information. And since the law doesn't require agencies to update their information in their databases based on other bureau's actions, they don't.

What to say in your dispute letter

You don't have to be fancy or technical in your dispute letters to the bureaus. The most important thing is to be clear about what you are disputing and why you are disputing it. Here are some tips to keep in mind when writing your letter:

✧ **Always provide a reason for your dispute.** Always indicate exactly what you are disputing (i.e., "not mine," "not late," or the accuracy of the information contained within the listing). The credit bureau must know if you are disputing the *existence* of the listing or the *information* within the listing. The bureau cannot begin an investigation unless it knows whether you believe the listing doesn't belong on your report or if you believe the information on the listing should be changed. If you are unclear in your dispute letter about the nature of your dispute, the credit bureau will promptly return your letter. If you dispute a listing on the basis that you were "not late," and if the credit bureau fails to verify the listing, then the listing will be changed and appear as a positive listing. If you dispute a listing on the basis that it is "not mine," and if the credit bureau fails to verify whether or not the information is indeed yours, you're out of luck. Keep in mind that without a clear statement that the accuracy or completeness of specific information is "disputed" or "challenged," your letter might *not* be construed as an exercise of rights under the Fair Credit Reporting Act. Sample letters are included in Appendix 7.

✧ **You can still dispute a negative listing even if you were late paying on the account.** You have the right to dispute your credit report so long as you have reason to believe that it is unverifiable, inaccurate, or obsolete. To dispute information that is technically accurate, but should still be investigated and deleted on the basis of verifiability, you must invent other means of disputing the listing besides claiming that it is "not mine" or "was never late." In this case, make a clear statement that the accuracy or completeness of specific information is "disputed" or "challenged."

✧ **Always tell the credit bureau your desired outcome of the investigation.** You must always include in your dispute letter what you would like done with the listing. There are two options—a correction to the listing or an entire deletion. I've seen positive listings deleted when only a correction was wanted because the outcome was not indicated.

✧ **Don't sound like you work for a credit repair agency.** The credit bureaus receive over 10,000 disputes a day and your dispute should look much like any other one they receive—not polished and professional. Always include indicators of authenticity in your dispute. Don't forget that the job of the checker is to reject irrelevant disputes and to investigate bona fide disputes. You may ensure that your disputes sound authentic by including things that only a true, frustrated consumer would write, such as "My son's a banker, and he mentioned that I could write to you and you would clear up these mistakes." Original indicators of authenticity cannot be listed here or they would cease to be effective, but you must get creative and always include sentences or phrases that will convince the credit bureau that you're for real. Handwriting your dispute letters is recommended.

✧ **Remember that the bureaus don't care about the "unfairness" of your situation.** The bureaus are not going to take your word or delete information because you've been caught in an "unfair" situation. Even if your situation is not your fault, or you've been robbed or cheated, this will make no difference in disputing your credit. Clearly defined disputes—stating your rights and why the information on your report is not correct—get results.

✧ **Include any documentation you have that substantiates your dispute.** If you have any documentation that backs up your dispute, like a bank letter stating that the information is false, include it with your dispute letter. (Note: If you decide to contact the original creditor as outlined in Chapter 9, it's great insider information to know that the credit bureaus are legally required to pass on all information supplied by consumers to the original creditor during a dispute.)

✧ **Don't use the credit bureau-supplied forms to dispute your listings.** With each copy of your credit report, you should also receive the credit bureau's form for disputing credit listings. You should *not* use these forms for your dispute letters. Since the form often forces you to address things within their perimeters, you may not be able to cover all your points by using the form. Interestingly, the forms are not very specific and often are not taken as seriously by the credit bureau checkers as a personal letter. Prepare your disputes on your personal stationary, perhaps even handwritten.

Order of dispute reasons

Most likely, your listing will come back as "verified," for reasons we will be discussing a little later in the chapter. But you're not done yet. You will need to change the reason for the investigation so the credit bureau will have something new to investigate. The order of the reasons should be:

✧ Not mine
✧ Wrong amount
✧ Wrong account number
✧ Wrong original creditor
✧ Wrong Charge-off Date
✧ Wrong Date of Last Activity
✧ Wrong Balance
✧ Wrong Credit limit
✧ Wrong Status (there are about 20)
✧ Wrong High Credit (the highest amount you used)
✧ I didn't pay late that month

For example, the first time you challenge a listing, you would say the account is "not mine." The second time through, you would say "never late."

5. DOCUMENT YOUR CREDIT REPAIR EFFORTS.

Documenting your efforts is such an important part of the process, that an entire section has been dedicated to it. See *The Importance of Documentation,* which follows the last chapter.

As soon as you have ordered your credit reports and photocopied your credit report order letters and checks, you must create a precise organizational system to track your correspondences with the credit bureaus and your creditors. Why? Unfortunately, credit items you have worked so hard to remove can mysteriously reappear. If this happens, it is usually easy to have the items deleted again if you show your complete records on the first removal. Why take a chance? As you proceed through these steps, keep copies and records of all correspondence you send and receive, in addition to notes on all telephone conversations! Also, if you should encounter any special difficulty and would like help in repairing your credit, you will need these records to proceed.

Every time you have a telephone conversation with a creditor, you must document the conversation by recording the name of the person to whom you spoke, his position, the date and time of the conversation, what was said in the conversation, and what was agreed upon.

6. WAIT FOR THE CREDIT BUREAU TO FINISH INVESTIGATING.

Once the credit reporting agency receives your dispute letter, it is obligated to investigate. The obligation is not contingent upon you having been denied credit. According to the Fair Credit Reporting Act (see Appendix 1), the credit bureaus must take the following steps:

◇ The credit reporting agencies must resolve consumer disputes within 30 days.
◇ If a consumer complains that documentation in support of a dispute was disregarded, the credit bureaus have to consider and transmit to the furnisher all relevant evidence submitted by the consumer the first time.
◇ Consumers must receive written notice of the results of the investigation within five days of its completion, including a copy of the amended credit file if it was changed based on the dispute.
◇ Once information is deleted from a credit file, the credit bureaus cannot reinsert it unless the entity supplying the information certifies that the item is complete and accurate and the credit bureau notifies the consumer within five days.

The Federal Trade Commission notes that inaccurate credit reports are the number one source of consumer complaints, and that it is quite common for problems to take six or more months to be resolved. All of the big three agencies are working on making sure that all disputes are handled within 30 days.

If the new investigation reveals an error, you may ask that a corrected version of the report be sent to anyone who received your report within the past six months. Job applicants can have corrected reports sent to anyone who received a report for employment purposes during the past two years. However, this is unlikely to repair any damage done when your credit report was first pulled, so don't waste your time or energy on this approach.

7. EVALUATE THE RESULTS OF YOUR REPAIR EFFORTS.

Okay, so you saved the original credit reports you ordered, *didn't you*? And each item you challenged? Good, you will need them to evaluate how well you did. It's all part of Step 5 above—documenting your efforts.

When you get your "repaired" credit report back from the credit bureaus, the bureau will summarize what changed on your credit report due to your challenges. You can compare this list to your own notes or to the previous credit report.

Each item will have been resolved in one of three ways:

1. If the listing is **not mentioned in the results list**, check to make sure that you included it in your dispute. If you did include it, was your request sufficiently clear? You will need to dispute the item again in your next dispute letter.
2. The bureau will tell you **the disputed item was investigated but verified**. If the item is not removed, the credit bureaus will probably give you a cryptic reason, like "item verified." The creditor may have responded to the credit bureau's request for re-verification. They may have simply stated that the listing was correct and, in this case, the bureau will take their word for it. Now it is up to you to prove to the bureau that the item is not correct. The law requires that the bureaus accept any proof you may submit, as well as pass any documentation you provide on to your creditor for consideration. Be sure to send any documentation you have if you didn't do it the first time.
3. The bureau indicates that **the item was unverifiable**. The disputed listing was investigated as to the correctness of the information within the listing (such as late pay notations) and the listing was found to be inaccurate or unverifiable. In this case, the negative listing will now show up as a positive listing, or it will be deleted from your report altogether. Be careful not to have positive items deleted, especially if you don't have many to begin with. As mentioned previously, this happens on occasion if you are not clear in your dispute. Credit repair agencies are notorious for disputing *everything* and having positive entries deleted.

IF THE CREDIT BUREAU SENDS YOU A LETTER BEFORE THE INVESTIGATION IS COMPLETED.

Sometimes consumers get letters in the mail after submitting a credit dispute asking for more information on your "credit repair agency." Many people panic over this, but it seems to be an automatic response, especially from TransUnion.

Why do they do this? Two reasons: to discourage the use of credit repair agencies (a good thing) and to try and trick you into submitting more information about your disputer (a sneaky underhanded thing). Why it is sneaky? Under the FCRA, if you provide more information about your dispute, even if you only write back to tell them you are not using a credit repair agency, this gives them 15 more days to investigate your dispute, which is definitely not to your advantage. Don't send ANYTHING back until your 30 days are up.

8. IF A DISPUTED ITEM COMES BACK AS "VERIFIED," REQUEST THE METHOD OF VERIFICATION.

If you get a notice from your the credit bureaus telling you the information you disputed has been verified as accurate, you can request the method of verification, which is your right under the FCRA section 611 (a) (7). The credit bureau must give you this information within 15 days of the request.

This is an extremely important tool, as most credit bureaus these days are not doing a thorough job of investigating disputes.

Each credit reporting agency has a different process for handling these disputes, but all three use a similar system. The three bureaus collaborated through their trade organization to automate the entire reinvestigation process using an online computer program, E-Oscar.

All disputes received by the credit bureaus are done via written letter, the telephone or the credit bureaus online dispute service. Even if the credit bureau receives a written dispute highly detailed and with documentation, each dispute is reduced to a two-digit code – the best guess of a minimum wage employee.

Under the FCRA, the credit bureaus are required to send the information on to the furnisher of the consumer's account (in other words, the original creditor), but all they receive is the two-digit code.

According to testimony from Leonard A. Bennett: [1]

> The employees of all three CRAs operate under a quota system whereby each employee is expected to process all of the disputes of an individual consumer in less than four minutes. Worse still, the "codes" used by both the CRAs and their subscribers (the furnishers) are limited in number and rarely describe the actual basis for the consumer's dispute.

---

[1] Testimony Before Subcommittee on Financial Institutions and Consumer Credit of the Committee on Financial Services Regarding *"Fair Credit Reporting Act: How it Functions for Consumers and the Economy,"* June 4, 2003, Leonard A. Bennett P.C. on behalf of the National Association of Consumer Advocates (http://www.naca.net)

For example, in two of my recent cases, both identical, consumers <names omitted> wrote dispute letters to all three bureaus. The disputes were conveyed in great detail and explained that the consumers were not responsible for the disputed accounts and that any signatures claimed to be theirs were forgeries. Each consumer dispute letter also enclosed copies of handwriting exemplars such as signatures on driver's license, military IDs and other credit cards. <Name omitted> had also obtained a copy of the forged note and included it in his dispute letter. When Equifax and TransUnion received the letters, their employees simplified the disputes to a code and the description "not his/hers." The [two-digit code indicating "not mine"] was all the furnishers received. In a deposition taken in a Pennsylvania case, TransUnion's responsible employee explained the CRA's "investigation procedure."

Q. [T]he dispute investigator looks at the consumer's written dispute and then reduces that to a code that gets transmitted to the furnisher?
A. Yes.

Q. Does the furnisher ever see the consumer's written dispute?
A. No.

Q. Are there any instances in which the dispute investigator would call the consumer to find out more about the dispute?
A. No.

This is consistent with CRA testimony in every other case of which I am aware. The Bureaus do not convey the full dispute or forward any of the documents to the furnishers.

As an expected result, nearly all consumer disputes are verified against the consumers.

So write to request the method of validation. (See Appendix 7 for sample letters.)

9. CALL OR WRITE THE ORIGINAL CREDITOR AND ASK FOR PROOF THAT YOU WERE LATE, OR THE TRADELINE IS NOT YOURS, ETC.

It is up the creditor, such as a credit card company, auto or mortgage loan company to report information about your accounts accurately. If they are unable to provide you with proof of the negative listing, and you insist that the information they are reporting is inaccurate, then they could be in violation of the FCRA, section 623. As explained previously, DO NOT contact the original creditor if you have not first disputed the negative item with the credit bureaus.

For a long while it was difficult to sue the original creditor for providing inaccurate information, and therefore consumers did not have much luck trying to force creditors to do any research. Per the new provisions in the FCRA, you are now allowed to take the original creditors to court to force them to either prove negative information or remove it from your credit report. [FCRA § 623 (a)(8)] For a list of potential creditor violations, see Chapter 30 *How to Fight Back in Court Against Your Creditors.*

10. DID YOU RECEIVE A NOTICE FROM THE CREDITOR THAT THEY POSTED NEGATIVE INFORMATION ON YOUR CREDIT REPORT?

The new version of the FCRA requires that any creditor reporting negative information to a credit bureau must notify the consumer in writing within 30 days of the insertion of negative information. [FCRA § 623 (a)(7)] This is an important bargaining tool! If you did not receive a notification from the creditor, they are in violation of the FCRA and you can certainly remind them of this.

11. REPEAT THE STEPS ABOVE IF YOU ARE NOT GETTING THE DESIRED RESULTS FROM THE CREDIT BUREAUS.

As explained above, the possibility that your claim was misunderstood, overlooked, or mishandled is good. Fixing your credit takes time, and there is nothing you can do to expedite the process. However, you can always resubmit your claims. Here are some tips for doing so:

 ✧ **Be persistent.** Become more insistent with each dispute. As you submit one dispute after another, it may become increasingly difficult to get the checker to initiate an investigation. Your first one or two disputes should be friendly and polite. Just like any other consumer, you can become frustrated as time passes. You may threaten to hire an attorney; you may threaten to complain to the FTC and your state's attorney general, etc. (A sample follow-up letter is included in Appendix 7.)
 ✧ **Be creative.** Create and utilize other techniques that help further the idea that the dispute letter is from a truly wronged and disadvantaged consumer. The checker is only interested in investigating disputes that truly are erroneous and damaging. Again, because the agencies are flooded with requests, they tend to give priority to those that seem most urgent.
 ✧ **Do not bombard credit bureaus with disputes.** Sending one dispute right after another is wasteful and counterproductive. You may wind up alienating the credit agency so that it holds up your progress. Remember they cannot legally stop you from restoring accurate information, but the people who run the agencies—like anyone else—probably do not respond well to harassment. Also remember, that credit repair is a time-consuming operation requiring great patience. The rule of thumb is to wait 60 days between disputes.

If a Removed Item Comes Back onto Your Credit Report

Okay, you've removed a listing and are breathing a deep sigh of relief. Then you get a letter in the mail from a credit bureau telling you the item has been added back on. What happened?

This actually is becoming more commonplace since new credit laws require that bureaus investigate and resolve disputes within 30 days. The bureaus sometimes will remove the negative information temporarily until the information is verified as true. Then the bureau will reinstate any information verified to be true and notify you of this. By law, they can do this, but they have to notify you in writing within 5 days of putting the item back on your report. If they don't do this, it's a violation of the FCRA and you could potentially sue them for $1,000. For more details, see Chapter 30. One of our Creditinfocenter discussion board readers settled with Equifax for $24,000 out of court for continually reinserting a listing without notification.

Specialized Credit Repair Techniques

Depending on the type of listing, you may also want to try these separate techniques:

COLLECTIONS.   You should always try to use the debt validation technique on collections. This should be in addition to your credit repair efforts with the credit bureaus. The debt validation technique is given in Chapter 28.

CHARGE-OFFS. Try disputing the information within the listing, like the date the account was opened, the high balance, the amount owed, etc. If any of the information is incorrect, you have a good chance of getting the whole thing deleted off of your report.

JUDGMENTS. If you were never served for a judgment, you may have a chance of getting it vacated (dismissed) as we discuss in Chapter 29. Call your county courthouse for information on judgment serving requirements in your state and how to file a motion to vacate.

LEGAL ACTION. If you feel that a credit bureau is not taking you seriously enough or that they are flat out refusing to perform the necessary investigations to handle your dispute, you can sue them in small claims court. Potentially, you can win a settlement against them and get the listings removed. (See Chapter 30 for details.)

Federal Government Information Sources

Copies of three free FTC brochures for consumers titled *Credit Repair Scams, A New Credit Identity: A New Credit Repair Scam*, and *How to Dispute Credit Report Errors*, are available from the FTC:

FTC Public Reference Branch
Room 130
6th Street and Pennsylvania Avenue, NW
Washington, D.C. 20580
202-326-2222; TTY for the hearing impaired 202-326-2502.

E-resources:

- ✧ Federal Trade Commission: http://www.ftc.gov
- ✧ Fair Isaac Credit Scoring: http://www.fairisaac.com
- ✧ An online guide to consumer affairs (US): http://www.pueblo.gsa.gov

CHAPTER 26: ERASING CREDIT INQUIRIES

Simon's Story

Simon has an interesting hobby. He loves test-driving new cars. At least once a month for the past several years, he has gone to different dealers to test-drive their latest models.

One day, he decides to pitch his Ford Pinto and get some wheels that will attract the ladies. (The Pinto, although it has an awful lot of character, is a strong repellent.) He's driven them all so has no problem choosing the model he wants. After one last test drive, Simon applies for a car loan. To his surprise, he is turned down. The reason? "Excessive inquiries" on his account. He is angry to learn that every time he drove a car off the lot, they had pulled his credit. Now he has more than 30 credit inquiries over a 24-month period on his otherwise good credit report. He was completely unaware that his credit was being pulled.

When Is It Worthwhile to Get Inquiries Removed?

As we've noted, every time you apply for credit and the credit grantor checks your credit report, a credit inquiry is placed on your file. If you have too many inquires on your report, this can have a negative impact on your credit. To attract potential creditors, you don't want to appear too used and abused in your previous credit "relationships." Lots of inquiries can give the wrong impression.

Further, some merchants and credit granters are oh-so-sneaky, pulling your credit without your knowledge. The legality of this practice is a little fuzzy, with lots of loopholes credit grantors can use. Why would credit grantors pull your credit without you knowing it? Most of the time it's because they think they have something to sell to you.

Credit inquiries generally do not destroy an otherwise perfect credit report. They can turn your credit report from good to marginal or marginal to bad, however. (If your credit is utterly trashed, don't bother removing inquiries; concentrate on rebuilding your credit or repairing existing credit.)

If you have been turned down for credit because of excessive inquiries, however, it's time to get them off of your report. It is hard to tell how much impact inquiries have on your credit score, but readers tell me they have noticed a marked increase in their score with the removal of inquiries.

Permissible Purpose

Under the FCRA, there are only five reasons why someone is allowed to pull your credit:

- ✧ Firm offer of credit (from a creditor with whom you applied for a loan or credit card)
- ✧ Firm offer of insurance
- ✧ Employment
- ✧ As directed by a court order
- ✧ The government can pull your information under the new Uniting and Strengthening America by Providing Appropriate Tools Required to Intercept and Obstruct Terrorism (USA PATRIOT) Act of 2001 for counterintelligence and counterterrorism purposes.

If you have a creditor who is pulling your credit for any reason other than the above, they are in violation of the FCRA. And yes, you can sue them. You might mention this in the letter you write asking that they be removed.

Basic Strategy

Many of your inquiring creditors may simply agree to delete the inquiry as a courtesy, or because they cannot (or will not) verify your authorization. It is not likely that you will need all of your credit inquiries removed—just enough of them to keep you from being denied credit.

There are four basic steps:

1. GET AND REVIEW YOUR CREDIT REPORT

See Chapter 3 for information on obtaining your credit reports. Request them from all three credit reporting agencies—Equifax, Experian and TransUnion. If you have recently been denied credit, like our friend Simon, the reports will be free.

2. ANALYZE YOUR REPORT FOR INQUIRIES

When your credit reports arrive, look toward the end of the report to find the inquiries. Identify only the inquiries that are shown to credit grantors:

- ✧ Inquiries that will count against you are ones that actually occurred because you applied for credit. Your credit report will indicate that this is the case next to such inquiries. All other inquiries don't count and you can ignore them.

✧ You should recognize some of these as places where you applied for credit, but others may be a complete mystery to you. The ones that are a mystery are the ones you should really pay attention to, making them the prime target of your credit inquiry removal process.

✧ Find the addresses for each credit inquirer. Your Experian credit report will list addresses for each. Your TransUnion and Equifax reports will not include addresses. Match your Experian with your TransUnion and Equifax reports. You should be able to use the same addresses for the inquirers that are listed on Experian. If some of the inquirers don't show up on Experian, but do show up on either TransUnion or Equifax, you will have to call the credit bureau to get the address. (Use the 800 number listed at the top of the report.) If you have an inquirer on your TransUnion credit report and you can't reach TransUnion by telephone, you might try calling the toll free directory (1-800-555-1212) and request the toll free number for the inquiring creditor.

Once you have found all of the addresses for each inquiring creditor on each credit report, you are ready for step three.

3. WRITE TO THE CREDITOR TO DISPUTE THE INQUIRY

Prepare letters to each inquiring creditor asking them to remove their inquiry. The Fair Credit Reporting Act (see Appendix 1) allows only authorized inquiries to appear on the consumer credit report. You must challenge whether or not the inquiring creditor had proper authorization to pull your credit file.

What to do if the creditor sends you documentation stating you authorized your credit to be pulled

Some creditors may provide documentation that you authorized a credit inquiry. Read the authorization that you signed very carefully. If there is any ambiguity, you can write back and argue that the inquirer's authorization form was too complicated and not easily understood by the layman. Simon's letter might say something like, "I had no idea I was authorizing a credit check, and your salesman certainly never mentioned it." You can threaten to contact the State Banking Commission and complain about a deceptive and unclear authorization form if they don't remove your inquiry.

Some creditors will try to ignore your challenge

Be sure to send each letter "certified mail, return receipt requested" and keep close track of the date you sent the letter. If the inquiring creditor doesn't respond within 30 days, you will have ample grounds to call the inquiring creditor and demand some action. At that point, it's almost irrelevant whether or not you authorized the inquiry. Now the issue becomes the creditor's lack of response to a consumer dispute. Stand your ground. Demand that the inquiry be removed immediately or you will complain to the State Banking Commission or similar authorities.

4. SEND PROOF TO THE BUREAUS

If the creditor sends you a letter agreeing to remove the inquiry, don't take their word for it. Send a copy of this letter to each of the credit bureaus that includes the negative inquiry.

CHAPTER 27: CREDIT REPAIR AGENCIES

Marlena's Story

Marlena admits to being careless with her credit in the past. Although she's much more responsible these days, she's afraid of what her new husband will think of her absolutely horrible credit history. Nick has been hinting that it's time to buy a house, and she knows the truth will soon come out. Her sister, Rose, tells Marlena that she's heard of a place that can completely clean up her credit for only $400. Marlena decides to check it out.

Do Credit Repair Agencies Work?

You see the advertisements in newspapers, on television, and on the Internet. You hear them on the radio. You've been spammed to death with these offers. You may even get calls from telemarketers offering credit repair services. They all make the same claims:

- ✧ "Credit problems? No problem!"
- ✧ "We can erase your bad credit—100% guaranteed."
- ✧ "Create a new credit identity—legally."
- ✧ "We can remove bankruptcies, judgments, liens, and bad loans from your credit file forever!"

Do yourself, and your wallet, a favor. *Don't believe it.* Only time, a conscious effort, and a personal debt repayment plan will truly improve your credit report—and this generally is something you can tackle on your own. (See Chapter 25, *Repairing Your Credit.*) A typical credit repair agency disputes any unfavorable items on your credit report, whether or not they are true. The agency doesn't have to give reasons, just a mechanical "I dispute this" starts the process.

But if you decide to respond to a credit repair offer, beware of companies that:

- ✧ Want payment for credit repair services before any services are provided. Before paying them any money, make certain that you know exactly what they intend to do and get any guarantees they make in writing. Thanks to the new Telemarketing Sales Rule, it's also a crime for telemarketers who offer credit repair services to require you to pay until six months after they've delivered the services.

✧ Do not tell you your legal rights and what you can do (yourself) for free.

Credit Segregation—Is It Legal and What is It?

The FTC has officially ruled that credit segregation is illegal.

If someone offers you a credit repair plan that will segregate your credit history by applying for an Employer Identification Number (EIN), *beware*. The claim will be that an EIN (pretty much indistinguishable from a SSN) can then be used to establish a new credit history. If you never default on your bills, you might just get away with it. But there are HUGE caveats to this:

✧ Even if you could pull it off, you would have a new identity but no credit history. As noted in the beginning of this book, no credit is equivalent to bad credit.

✧ If you default and your creditor discovers that you had bad credit under another SSN, the creditor may decide to prosecute you for felony fraud.

We advise you to personally dispute all information in your credit report, and never take any action that seems illegal, such as creating a new credit identity. If you follow illegal advice and commit fraud, you may be subject to prosecution. You could be charged and prosecuted for mail or wire fraud if you use the mail or telephone to apply for credit and provide false information. It's a federal crime to make false statements on a loan or credit application, to misrepresent your Social Security Number, and to obtain an Employer Identification Number from the Internal Revenue Service under false pretenses.

How Do They Do It?

Unscrupulous firms often rely on a portion of the Federal Fair Credit Reporting Act that requires a credit bureau to omit some information on a credit report during the time when an investigation is being conducted after a challenge has been filed by a consumer. As a result, credit repair firms will flood credit bureaus with multiple, frivolous disputes. Fees paid by consumers who are desperate for clean credit can range from a few dollars to thousands of dollars, but the legitimate negative information is not always permanently erased from a credit file by the paperwork generated by a credit repair firm.

Credit reporting company officials estimate that about 30 percent of their workday is wasted on credit repair companies that intentionally abuse laws and policies established to protect consumers.

Consumers Beware

Know the following facts:

- ✧ Virtually every service that a credit repair firm provides legally can be done by consumers themselves for free or at minimum cost.
- ✧ No one can legally remove accurate information from a credit report. Only time can wipe out bad credit.
- ✧ Any consumer can dispute inaccurate information at no charge. Inaccurate information will be changed or deleted free of charge.
- ✧ There are no miracle cures for bad credit.
- ✧ Lenders are in business to lend money and want to say "yes." However, their livelihood depends on extending credit only to consumers who repay their debts.

Problems With a Credit Repair Agency?

If you have used a credit repair agency and have had problems, feel free to take whatever legal action is allowable by law. Many states have laws strictly regulating credit repair companies and may be helpful if you've lost money to credit repair scams. If you've had a problem with a credit repair company, don't be embarrassed to report the company. Contact your local Consumer Affairs Office or your State Attorney General. Many State Attorney Generals have toll-free consumer hotlines which you can find in your phone book or by visiting http://www.naag.org.

You also may wish to contact the FTC. Although the Commission cannot resolve individual credit problems for consumers, it can act against a company if it sees a pattern of possible law violations. If you believe a company has engaged in credit fraud, send your complaints to Correspondence Branch, Federal Trade Commission, Washington, DC, 20580.

The National Fraud Information Center (NFIC) also accepts consumer complaints. You can reach NFIC at 800-876-7060, 9:00 a.m. - 5:30 p.m. EST, Monday - Friday, or at http://www.fraud.org. NFIC is a private, nonprofit organization that operates a consumer assistance phone line to provide services and to help in filing complaints. NFIC also forwards appropriate complaints to the FTC for entry on its telemarketing fraud database.

Marlena's Solution

After talking to a few credit repair agencies, Marlena wisely decided to stay clear of them. She took three steps herself to make things right. She put herself on a budget; made an effort to clean up her credit report herself; and admitted her problems to Nick.

And Nick? He gave her hugs and kisses for her honesty and promised to help her with her future finances. They agreed to postpone house hunting while Marlena cleaned up her credit. And Nick gave her another huge hug for not taking her sister's advice to use a credit repair agency. (Some of the very worst advice you will ever get is from your well-meaning relatives!)

CHAPTER 28: DEBT VALIDATION

Judy's Story

Judy decided that being a 43-year-old woman living with her parents, although economical, was seriously cramping her dating lifestyle. She decided to go ahead and buy a condo. After talking it over with some co-workers, she decided that in preparation for her bold new purchase she should pull her credit report. In reviewing it, Judy found several collections on her credit report that she did not recognize. She called the collection agencies to inquire about them. Surprise, surprise, the woman Judy spoke to at the collection agency couldn't even determine who the original creditors were. But she demanded immediate payment.

On further advice from her friends at the office, Judy, did not pay up. Instead she disputed the collection accounts on her credit report. She sent a dispute letter to Experian, Equifax, and TransUnion. Equifax deleted two of the collections, but the other two agencies did not remove any of them.

Judy was very upset because she knew the collections were not hers, and she felt powerless to remove them. Then she ran across an article on a debt validation method to use with collection agencies and decided to give it a try. To her delight, the collection agencies were unable to validate the collections, and she was able to use this information to get the Credit Reporting Agencies to remove the listings from her credit report.

Debt Validation—The Ultimate Secret Weapon

If you have lots of collection accounts on your credit report, there is a great new secret weapon to use against your creditors—all legal and pretty and everything. A little something called "debt validation." This is particularly handy if you are dealing with a collection agency. Under the FDCPA (see Appendix 3), if a collection agency opens an account with the intention of collecting a debt from you, it is required to notify you in writing, using specific language and information. You, the consumer, have 30 days to dispute the debt and question its validity. However, even if the 30 days has passed, it's unlikely that they have proof that you received a letter from them. Technically, you can request debt validation from a collection agency at any time.

In addition, the FDCPA specifically spells out the course of action required by a "creditor." If they don't follow these precise steps, they must stop all efforts to contact and collect monies from you.

The specific section of the FDCPA (Section 809, Validation of debts [15 USC 1692g]) stipulates:

> (b) If the consumer notifies the debt collector in writing within the 30-day period described in subsection (a) that the debt, or any portion thereof, is disputed, or that the consumer requests the name and address of the original creditor, the debt collector shall cease collection of the debt, or any disputed portion thereof, until the debt collector obtains verification of the debt or any copy of a judgment, or the name and address of the original creditor, and a copy of such verification or judgment, or name and address of the original creditor, is mailed to the consumer by the debt collector.

What kind of information will provide adequate validation? A computer printout listing the bill is not sufficient to validate a debt. (FTC opinion letter Levre-Wollman. A copy of this letter is included in Appendix 9.)

The agency must validate the debt to your satisfaction. The following pieces of information must be provided to you in order for the collection agency to validate your debt:

⬦ Agreement with your client that grants you the authority to collect on this alleged debt.
⬦ Agreement bearing the signature of the alleged debtor wherein he agreed to pay the creditor.
⬦ The complete payment history (starting with the original creditor) on the account so that the exact amount of the debt may be determined.

So, if a creditor can't verify a debt:

⬦ They are not allowed to collect the debt;
⬦ They are not allowed to contact you about the debt; and
⬦ They are also not allowed to report it under the Fair Credit Reporting Act (FCRA). Doing so is a violation of the FCRA, and the FDCPA states that you can sue for $1,000 in damages for any violation of the act. The FDCPA also states that you can sue in federal or state court. So if you have them on five violations, then you have damages of $5,000. Small claims court, anyone? (See Chapter 30 on how to sue your creditors.)

The opinion letter from the FTC (Levre - Cass) which clearly spells out that a collection agency CANNOT report a debt to the credit bureaus which has not been validated is included in Appendix 9.

Original Creditor vs. Collection Agency

The FDCPA does not cover collection tactics employed by the original creditor, meaning the bank that issued you the credit card or the loan company who gave you an auto loan. It was written to protect the consumer from collection agencies. Let's look at the definition of a "collector" as defined by the FDCPA:

> The term "debt collector" means any person who uses any instrumentality of interstate commerce or the mails in any business the principal purpose of which is the collection of any debts, or who regularly collects or attempts to collect, directly or indirectly, debts owed or due or asserted to be owed or due another.

Important Note: As indicated in numerous examples of case law, any attorney who acts on the behalf of an original creditor is also a collection agency and is subject to the laws of the FDCPA.

Step-by-Step Process

Follow these steps in seeking a debt validation:

1. Send a letter requesting validation to the collection agency. (Sample letters are included in Appendix 7.) If you don't know the address, here are some online resources to help you find it:
   a) www.residentagentinfo.com
   b) www.bbb.org
2. Wait 30 days.
3. If they haven't sent you satisfactory proof, as outlined above, send a copy of the receipt for your registered mail, a copy of the first letter you sent and a statement that they have not complied with the FDCPA and are now in violation of the act. (Use the follow up letter in Appendix 7 as a template.) Tell them they need to immediately remove the collection listing from your credit report or you are going to file a lawsuit because they are in violation of the FDCPA, section 809 (b).
4. Wait 15-20 days. They will either remove it or not respond.
5. If they do provide complete debt validation per the requirements stated above, check to see if licensing is required in your state. (See state-specific information in Appendix 6 for licensing requirements.) If you believe they are not licensed and licensing is required in your state, write them another letter and tell them they are in violation of your state's collection laws and are subject to prosecution and fines. (You'll have to cite your state's fines and procedures here. This is a last ditch effort, but has worked in some cases.)
6. Typically, your work will stop here, as most collection agencies will bow down to your demands and send you a letter agreeing to remove the listing. Now all you need to do is send a copy of the letter to all three credit reporting agencies.

If the collection agency did not agree to remove the listing, then you need to move on to the next steps:

1. File a lawsuit in small claims court against the collection agency on the basis of violating the FDCPA.
2. Have the papers served to the collection agency. (You can find a paper server on the Internet for about $25. Here is a good link: http://www.guaranteedsubpoena.com/rules.htm.)

In the meantime, in a parallel effort with your lawsuit against the collection agency:

1. Dispute the collection if it appears on your credit report.
2. If the credit bureaus come back to you and say the collection is "verified," you have just been provided proof of a violation by the collection agency. Since they are not allowed to pursue collection activities after you request debt validation, they cannot report the collection on your credit report. In the opinion of the Federal Trade Commission, reporting a collection on a credit report is collection activity. Continue on with your dispute with the credit bureau as outlined in Chapter 25, by requesting method of verification of the credit investigation, etc.
3. If the credit bureaus are refusing to work with you, then it's time to sue them as well. File a small claim suit in court on the credit bureaus, on the basis of defamation of character, violations of the FDCPA or FCRA. (Refer to Chapter 30 to see if you can find anything they have done wrong.) Credit bureaus are usually eager to stay out of court, so if you have them on anything, they will usually call to settle with you.

I have had readers work wonders on their credit reports using debt validation. One reader went so far as to actually file suit against Equifax, Experian, and TransUnion. Though he never went to court, he obtained the desired results—his credit report was completely cleaned up.

CHAPTER 29: VACATING A JUDGMENT

Marianne's Story

When the mailman asked Marianne to sign for a certified letter, she suspected it wouldn't be good news. And when she opened the envelope to find a court ordered judgment to pay a collection bill she had been trying to resolve for a year, she was irate. Eddie, arriving to pick her up for their movie date, saw a new side of his girlfriend. He had no idea that mild-mannered, soft-spoken Marianne had such a colorful vocabulary!

They decided to forego the movie and deal with their very own real-life drama. Marianne (still simmering but rational now thanks to Eddie's soothing ways) can't understand how this went to court without her knowledge. She has copies of her unanswered requests for debt validation and the signed post office receipts that show her letters were received by the collection agency. This can't be right...

Can a Judgment Be Overturned?

Filing a motion to dismiss a judgment is like filing an appeal on the outcome of a jury trial. If the outcome was not fair, and you have good reason why the court should overturn its prior ruling, you should file a motion. Don't be intimidated by the thought that you are challenging a court ruling. It happens all the time.

As with many collection agencies, many people who file lawsuits to collect money from you in court didn't follow the law. You may be asking yourself why the judge didn't know about this improper deviation. As in most professions, judges tend to specialize in one type of case. For the same reason that you can't expect a heart surgeon to know the best psychiatric medications to prescribe to a patient with schizophrenia, a judge doing small claims or injury lawsuits may not be intimately familiar with consumer law. Sure they know the basics, but one person can't know everything. Before deciding on a case, most judges need to look up and study existing statutes and case rulings. In addition, if the person who sues says they followed the correct procedure and the defendant or his lawyer does not dispute it, it's a sure bet they were given the benefit of the doubt.

Another thing to look out for: even if the person suing you followed all the right court procedures, you can still win on technicalities. The two biggest reasons a judgment is "won" are: A) the defendant failed to respond to the court summons with the proper paperwork in the allowed period of time, and B) the defendant failed to appear for their court date. This is called winning by default.

If you receive a judgment or a writ of restitution and you believe you had a good reason for not responding to the eviction summons or appearing at the "show cause" hearing, there still may be grounds for asking the court to vacate the judgment. If the court agrees that you may have had good reasons for not responding or appearing, the court may decide to set a hearing on your motion to vacate the judgment.

Some Definitions

A **judgment** is the actual court decision stating that the person suing is in the right. It issues the method to "right the wrong," such as fines, the actions you need to take to correct the violation, or the amount of money you need to pay the plaintiff.

A **writ of restitution** is generally used only by landlords. It is basically a court order, in writing, that would be given to a sheriff to evict you if your landlord was trying to get you to move based on non-payment. You don't need to worry about this document if you are not being sued by your landlord.

Vacate basically means dismiss.

The **plaintiff** is the person suing you.

The **defendant** is the person being sued (you).

Prepare Your Motion and Declaration to Vacate

You must prepare a Motion and Declaration to Vacate Judgment and an Order to Show Cause. A sample document is included in Appendix 8 which you can use as a template to write up your motion. This document tells the court why the judgment against you should be vacated. First, you need to identify the case by name and court reference number and all the persons involved in the judgment.

Next, explain your reasons for bringing the motion. State your "procedural defenses," that is, the good reason(s) why you did not respond to the summons and complaint on time or appear at a "show cause" hearing. For example:

⟡ I was not served with a summons and complaint – you need to check your state laws here. Some states say that a non-certified letter delivered by the US Postal service is all that is required to properly serve a complaint. Most states, however, require that you be served in person or at least get your summons sent certified, return requested mail. Here is a good link to double check your state and county procedures:

http://www.findlaw.com/10fedgov/judicial/district_courts.html

✧ I responded to the summons and complaint in time, but a judgment was issued anyway without a hearing.

✧ I was not able to answer the summons and complaint or appear at the show cause hearing because…

In the same space, also tell the court about your defense to the judgment (why the case would have been dismissed had you shown up in the first place). For example:

✧ The collection agency never responded to my request for validation, therefore never providing proof that the debt was mine under the FDCPA.

✧ The amount of the debt exceeded the state's usury interest limits.

Please note that the court will only respond to violations of existing laws. They won't accept reasons like: "My insurance company was supposed to pay this debt and never did, therefore I shouldn't have to pay this medical bill."

File the Paperwork

Most likely, you will have to file your motion at the same court which granted the judgment in the first place. This means that if the judgment was granted in Anchorage, Alaska, and you now live in Miami, Florida, you will have to fly to Alaska to both file the paperwork and to attend the court trial. However, this is not true in all cases. One reader was able to file the motion to vacate out of state. She included a sworn statement stating that the judgment holder and the judgment holder's attorney had been notified of the motion to vacate, all through the mail. Call the court in which the judgment was granted and find out if this is an option for you.

Go to the courthouse with your typed document and tell the court clerk that you are filing a motion to vacate a judgment. There may be additional forms to fill out at the courthouse, and there will probably be a nominal filing fee. The clerk should know exactly what needs to be done with your paperwork, and can answer all of your questions and even help you fill out the forms.

Once your paperwork is in order, the court will notify you of the upcoming court date. The original plaintiff in the lawsuit (now the defendant in your motion to dismiss – are you confused yet?) will typically have 35 days to respond.

You must follow your state and county rules of court procedure

Following the court rules of procedure is vital. Rules of procedure include things like which forms to file, what kinds of disclosures you must make, how long you have to serve the person or company you are suing and what kinds of things must be covered in your basis of lawsuit.

If you don't follow these procedures, you could lose your case on a technicality. Fortunately, everything is posted on the internet these days and you can look it up fairly easily. Here's a good resource:

http://www.law.cornell.edu/topics/state_statutes.html#civil_procedure

Notify the Plaintiff

In some cases, once the paperwork is filed the court will notify the plaintiff and/or plaintiff's attorney. Be sure to ask if the court will serve notice or if you need to, as serving the notice of summons is crucial to winning your case. If it is your responsibility to serve notice, you can hire a third-party professional service company for a nominal fee (typically around $35). Here's a good link to find a service company: http://www.guaranteedsubpoena.com/rules.htm.

What If They Offer to Settle Out of Court?

Very often the original plaintiff in your lawsuit will come back to you and offer to vacate the judgment, especially if they blatantly flouted the laws in winning the case in the first place and have no proof, say that you were properly served, or that they violated the FDCPA, etc.

If they offer to settle out of court, you should demand that they themselves file paperwork to dismiss the lawsuit. Also demand that they notify any collection agencies they may have hired to collect money *and* notify the credit bureaus of the "mistake." It is also crucial before accepting any settlement offer (in writing, naturally) that they send you copies of any paperwork received from the courts about the judgment vacation or dismissal.

What Happens at Court?

In the best of all possible scenarios, the original plaintiff will not show up for the hearing to dismiss and you will win by default. If this happens, you shouldn't have to present anything to the court and should receive your dismissal automatically, especially if the original plaintiff never responded in writing to the summons.

In the second best of all possible worlds, they will show up for the hearing but be unable to disprove your reason for requesting the dismissal:

- They are unable to show proper documentation that you were properly served.
- They are unable to show that the debt was legal in the first place (unable to show what the correct debt amount should be, if a contract existed in the first place, etc.)

This means, of course, that *you* should have good documentation on the case and have it available to present in court. See Chapter 30, *Suing your Creditors*, for court tips.

What Happens When You Win?

You should receive a court document showing that the case was dismissed. Send copies of this document to any collection agency that's contacted you about the case and to the credit bureaus so they will remove any mention of the judgment from your credit report. Even though you demanded that the defendant do this, it only takes a few stamps and a few minutes of your time to insure that your credit history gets corrected promptly.

CHAPTER 30 – SUING CREDITORS, COLLECTION AGENCIES AND CREDIT BUREAUS WHO VIOLATE YOUR RIGHTS

Shirley's Story

Shirley has come a long way on her credit journey. Over the past year, she has completely cleaned up her credit report except for one last item, a collection from the ACME collection agency. Though she has sent a cease and desist letter as well as a debt validation letter, the collectors continue to call her on a weekly basis and have even called her at work, though she has informed them in writing that she is not allowed to receive phone calls at her place of employment.

Naturally, Shirley wants to buy a house, and the mortgage company who approved her loan has made the loan conditional on paying off this final collection. Shirley is mad as hell; her rights have been blatantly ignored, and she feels that she shouldn't have to cough up $2,000 for a collection that the agency has made no attempt to prove is even hers in the first place.

Shirley's significant other, Gary, thinks she should just drop it and pay the collection so the loan can close. He is anxious to move into the home, which Shirley and he are buying together. After receiving a phone call from ACME at 9:30 PM one night, Shirley has had it. A little research provides her with a lawsuit template, and Shirley uses it to create a two-page document, clearly outlining the chain of events, the laws that have been broken and the monetary damages she wants. Shirley decides that the collection agency has violated both the FDCPA and the FCRA five times, so she is asking for $5,000, plus the deletion of the collection from her credit report.

After asking the advice of a friendly court clerk at the local small claims courthouse, who explains the procedure and helps her fill out the additional forms, she hands over her basis of lawsuit and the filing fee of $37. She then hires an agency to serve the paperwork to ACME, notifying ACME that they are being sued and the court date.

The court date arrives and so does Shirley. She comes armed with proof of the letters she has sent, a certified statement from a co-worker stating that she indeed received phone calls from ACME at work, highlighted copies of the FDCPA and the FCRA, and a log book in which she has recorded every phone call from ACME including notes of any abuse she received and the date and time of every call. The lawyer for ACME is stunned when the judge finds in Shirley's favor, though clearly Shirley was in the right.

On the way home, Shirley giggles in delight at the thought of hiring her own collection agency to collect the judgment she has just won from ACME!

Will This Really Work?

Absolutely. It's the law. If you can prove any violations, it is pretty cut and dried that you will win. The amount of the fines and your right to them is spelled out explicitly. Most collection agencies—and certainly the credit bureaus—are unprepared for such attacks, and will usually settle with you to avoid court.

You know the old sayings, "Money talks" and "Vote with your dollars"? Well, most companies, the credit bureaus and creditors included, are not going to change their ways unless it is in their best interest to do so. All of these companies have stockholders to report to, so if one of their practices is costing them a better bottom line, you better believe they will act to change their ways. One of these ways is for you, the consumer, to take legal action against these companies when your rights have been violated.

I'm Pretty Intimidated by the Court System

In the majority of cases, you can take your case to small claims court, which is designed to serve the consumer. In many states and counties, lawyers aren't even allowed to represent clients in small claims. Filing a small claims suit is fairly easy, and the filing fee ranges between $20 and $60. You don't need to know fancy lawyer speak, just be able to present the facts backed up by documentation and a little knowledge of the law.

The table that follows lists all of the most common offenses committed by the credit bureaus and collection agencies. If you go into court armed with documentation, a copy of the FCRA, the FDCPA and copies of the right court ruling and FTC opinion letters, you will most likely win.

So Who Can You Sue and What Can You Sue For?

Who	Why	Precedent/Law	Fine
Creditors if they report your credit history inaccurately	Defamation, financial injury	US Court of Appeals, Ninth Circuit, No. 00-15946, Nelson vs. Chase Manhattan, **FCRA** Section 623 (a) (8)	Extent of damages incurred by the wronged party as deemed by the courts
Creditors if they pull your credit file without permissible purpose	Injury to your credit report and credit score	**FCRA** Section 604 (A)(3)	$1,000
Credit bureaus if they refuse to correct information after being provided proof	Defamation, willful injury	**FCRA** Section 623 CUSHMAN v. TRANSUNION CORPORATION US Court of Appeals for the Third Circuit Court Case 115 F.3d 220 June 9, 1997, Filed (D.C. No. 95-cv-01743).	Extent of damages incurred by the wronged party, as deemed by the courts
Credit bureaus if they reinsert a removed item from your credit report without notifying you in writing within 5 business days.	Consumer protection afforded by the FCRA	**FCRA** SECTION 611 Part (A)(5)(B)(ii)	$1,000

Who	Why	Precedent/Law	Fine
Credit bureaus if they fail to respond to your written disputes within 30 days (a 15 day extension may be granted if they receive information from the creditor within the first 30 days)	Consumer protection afforded by the FCRA	**FCRA** Section 611 Part (A)(1)	$1,000
Creditors or collection agencies, and credit bureaus if they try and "Re-age" your account by updating the date of last activity on your credit report in the hopes of keeping negative information on your account longer	Consumer protection afforded by the FCRA	**FCRA** Section 605 (c) Running of the reporting period	$1,000
Creditor, if they fail to notify you in writing within 30 days of inserting negative information into your report	Consumer protection afforded by the FCRA (new FACTA rules)	**FCRA** Section 623 (a) (7) Negative Information	$1,000
Collection agencies if they do not validate your debt yet continue to pursue collection activity (i.e., file for judgments, call or write you)	Consumer protection afforded by the FDCPA	**FDCPA** Section 809 (b), FTC opinion letter *Cass from LeFevre* (See Appendix 9).	$1,000
Collection agencies if you have sent them a cease and desist letter and they still call you	Consumer protection afforded by the FDCPA	**FDCPA** Section 805 (c)	$1,000

Who	Why	Precedent/Law	Fine
Collection agencies if they have not validated your debt and they still continue to report to the credit bureaus	Consumer protection afforded by the FDCPA	Section 809 (b), FTC opinion letter ***Cass from LeFevre*** (See Appendix 9), BOATLEY vs. DIEM CORP. and DENCEK No. CIV 03-0762 PHX-SMM US District Court for AZ	$1000
Collection agencies if they: - Cash a post-dated check before the date on the check - Cost you money by making you accept collect calls or COD mail - Take or threaten to take any personal property without a judgment	Consumer protection afforded by the FDCPA	**FDCPA** Section 808	$1,000
Calls you after 9 PM at night or before 8 AM	Consumer protection afforded by the FDCPA	**FDCPA** Section 805. (a)(1)	$1,000
Calls you at your place of employment if the debt collector knows or has reason to know that your employer prohibits the consumer from receiving such communication.	Consumer protection afforded by the FDCPA	**FDCPA** Section 805. (a)(3)	$1,000
The collection agency can not use any kind of harassment or abuse*	Consumer protection afforded by the FDCPA	FDCPA Section 806	$1,000

Who	Why	Precedent/Law	Fine
Calls any third party about your debt (i.e., friends, neighbors, relatives, etc.) However they can contact your attorney, a consumer reporting agency, the creditor, the attorney of the creditor, or the attorney of the debt collector.	Consumer protection afforded by the FDCPA	**FDCPA** Section 805. (b)	$1,000
Collector cannot claim to garnish your wages, seize property or have you arrested **	Consumer protection afforded by the FDCPA	FDCPA Section 807	$1,000
Collector must bring action against you in the county in which you lived when you signed the original contract for the debt or where you live at the time when they file the lawsuit	Consumer protection afforded by the FDCPA	FDCPA Section 811 (a) (2)	$1,000 Also a good grounds for getting a judgment vacated
Collection agency tries to collect after the statute of limitations for the debt has passed. (Threat to take any action that cannot legally be taken or that is not intended to be taken.)	Consumer protection afforded by the FDCPA	FDCPA Section 811 (5)	$1,000

* (1) The use or threat of use of violence or other criminal means to harm the physical person, reputation, or property of any person. (2) The use of obscene or profane language or language the natural consequence of which is to abuse the hearer or reader. (3) The publication of a list of consumers who allegedly refuse to pay debts, except to a consumer reporting agency. (4) The advertisement for sale

of any debt to coerce payment of the debt. (5) Causing a telephone to ring or engaging any person in telephone conversation repeatedly or continuously with intent to annoy, abuse, or harass any person at the called number. (6) Placement of telephone calls without meaningful disclosure of the caller's identity.

** If the collection agency gets a judgment against you, then they will be able to garnish your wages and seize property, but until that time, no.

How Do You Prove Harassment?

Harassment by a collection agency is a tough thing to prove, as most collectors do this by phone and there is no written documentation. If a bill collector violates the FDCPA, try and see if you can get the illegal behavior on tape.

Taping phone conversations

There are important questions of law that must be addressed when considering whether or not to record a phone conversation with anyone. There are both federal and state statutes governing the use of electronic recording equipment. The unlawful use of such equipment can give rise not only to a civil suit by the "injured" party, but criminal prosecution. You should carefully review the following paragraphs before attempting to tape a phone call.

A majority of the states and territories have adopted wiretapping statutes based on the federal law. Thirty-eight states and the District of Columbia permit an individual to record a conversation to which they are a party without informing the other party that they are doing so. These laws are referred to as "one-party consent" statutes, and as long as you are a party to the conversation, it is legal for you to record it. In this case, the laws generally referring to electronic recording of a conversation, but in the majority of the cases, also cover eavesdropping.

Twelve states require, under most circumstances, the consent of all parties to a conversation. Those jurisdictions are California, Connecticut, Delaware, Florida, Illinois, Maryland, Massachusetts, Michigan, Montana, New Hampshire, Pennsylvania, and Washington. These laws are sometimes referred to as "two-party consent" laws, which is a bit misleading: if there are more than two people involved in the conversation, *all* must consent to the taping.

Just in case you're trying to be a supersleuth and can videotape your encounters with collection agencies or creditors, you should also be aware of the laws governing video recording. Twelve states have laws outlawing the use of hidden cameras in private places: Alabama, California, Delaware, Georgia, Hawaii, Kansas, Maine, Michigan, Minnesota, New Hampshire, South Dakota, and Utah.

If you live in a state which forbids "secret" phone taping

A logbook with notes on all conversations with your creditors usually impresses judges. Make a note of each time you call or are called by a creditor. Note the phone number, date, time of day, the people you talked to, the company called and brief notes on the conversation. Make special notes of any harassments, threats and demands that you think are in violation of your rights. Exact quotes are highly beneficial.

In addition to impressing the court, this will also help you keep your own sanity! Trying to keep track of multiple creditors is extremely difficult!

Filing Suit

Statute of Limitations on filing

Under the FCRA § 618. [15 U.S.C. § 1681p], you have 2 years from the date of discovery of the violation, or 5 years from the date the violation occurred, whichever is longer. This is important! If the violation occurred outside of this time frame, you are out of luck.

Small claims court is quick and easy

Most states allow you to recover between $3,000 and $7,000 in damages in small claims court. Some states allow larger sums. (For example, Tennessee allows up to $15,000.)

Use the sample *Basis for Lawsuit* document in Appendix 8 as a template to prepare your paperwork. Include all the pertinent facts and be sure to attach documentation as mentioned in the sample. Go to the small claims courthouse with your typed document and tell the court clerk that you are filing a Basis for Lawsuit. There may be additional forms to fill out at the courthouse, and there will probably be a nominal filing fee. The clerk should know exactly what needs to be done with your paperwork, and can answer all of your questions and even help you fill out the forms.

Taking legal action will help to bring about the change that is necessary in the way these companies operate. But more importantly for you, it will resolve the matter quickly. You also stand to be compensated for your frustration.

Suing in other courts

While small claims is quick and easy, you may want to consider suing in district, superior or federal court for the following reasons:

- ✧ You are limited to the amount allowed in your state. If the basis of your claim is the FDCPA, your actual damages may be more than small claims allows.
- ✧ Another disadvantage is that some small claims courts do not allow you legal representation should you need it.

✧ In addition, if you are suing with the FDCPA as the basis of your lawsuit, you can collect attorney fees as part of the settlement, which may entice a lawyer to take your case on contingency. Taking a case on contingency means that a lawyer only collects money from you IF you win in court. If you lose, you are not out any money.

✧ And still another is that *some* (I don't want to insult anyone here) small claims court judges are unknowledgeable about the FCRA and FDCPA laws and case rulings. Not that they are bad judges, it's just not their area of expertise. They are used to disputes with housing contractors, landlords and property disputes, not federal case law.

Can I only sue companies in my state?

Typically, the answer is yes. Some small claims courts won't even allow paperwork to be filed if the other party is out of town. Others may allow you to file in the state in which a contract was signed or where personal injury occurred. However, as long as a company has a registered agent in your state, you may sue them. A registered agent is an entity (physical office or person who represents the company in your state). To find the registered agent in your state, refer to Appendix 6 for state-specific Internet links or visit:

✧ The Better Business Bureau - http://www.bbb.org
✧ http://www.residentagentinfo.com

How much does it cost?

States have different filing fees, but generally the cost is between $10 and $50, with some businesses paying a slightly higher fee.

Serving the notice

In order for the judgment to be binding, the party being sued must be properly served. Depending on your state, either the court will serve the notice, or leave it up to you. ***It is vital to make sure the party is served properly.***

If your state makes it your responsibility to serve the party you are suing, ask for a list of the qualified people or services you can use to serve the paperwork.

What if I want to hire a lawyer, or at least consult with one, before going to trial?

The problem is that many lawyers aren't familiar with this kind of law and many only practice in a single state. But you can try it.

Where do you find a lawyer? The following links are an *excellent* resource for finding a lawyer in your area:

http://www.naca.net – National Association of Consumer Advocates
http://www.nclc.org/ - National Consumer Law Center

You must follow your state and county rules of court procedure

Following the court rules of procedure is vital. Rules of procedure include things like which forms to file, what kinds of disclosures you must make, how long you have to serve the person or company you are suing and what kinds of things must be covered in your basis of lawsuit.

If you don't follow these procedures, you could lose your case on a technicality. Fortunately, everything is posted on the internet these days and you can look it up fairly easily. Here's a good resource:

http://www.law.cornell.edu/topics/state_statutes.html#civil_procedure

THE IMPORTANCE OF DOCUMENTATION

This information is as vital as everything else in this book, so it gets its own dedicated section. Your documentation can be the difference between failure and success in any effort you make to clean up your credit. And in the event you decide to sue your creditors, it can be worth money!

Take these four little tips to heart and they will serve you well:

Keep a detailed phone log of all conversations.

Track the date, time, the name and title of the person you spoke with, and the details of phone conversations. It will help to jog your memory in the future, provide you with the details you need when you put the conversation in writing, and it could prove handy if you wind up taking your creditor to court.

Follow up all phone conversations in writing.

I can't tell you how many times people have told me that they can't understand why a deal negotiated over the phone with a creditor or a credit reporting agency didn't happen, or was lost or forgotten by the person or company making the deal.

Hello! There is no way you can prove any promise made over the phone. Whether you are writing to a collection agency, any of the credit bureaus, negotiating a settlement, validating a debt, or disputing a credit listing, you are not protected unless you have some record of the correspondence. You must have some written proof!

Send all mail certified "return receipt requested."

There are several ways to get proof of a promise or even to simply prove that your letter was received:

Send letters certified or registered mail. This requires a trip to the post office. Depending on the size of the letter and the distance it travels, you will spend no more than $3 per letter. You will be sent a receipt (a green postcard) that is your proof that your letter reached the intended destination.

Here's a nifty trick: If you are not sending any documentation along with your letter, the U.S. Postal Service just started a new service where you can upload a letter and they will print it out and send it for you certified mail (for an additional fee, of course). It's a great time saver since you don't need to stand in line at the post office. The website for this is: http://www.usps.gov.

It's relatively easy for a recipient to blow off receiving a certified letter. If problems arise delivering the letter (the intended recipient may have pretended to not be home when the postman rang the doorbell), it is sent back to a local post office. The recipient is notified that a letter is being held at this post office. If no one claims the letter after a certain number of days, it is returned to sender. However, even if the intended recipient avoids your letter, you will still have a receipt verifying you sent certified mail, along with the date you sent it.

If a collection agency or creditor refuses to accept your letter, you might need to get a bit sneakier. Try it again, but this time write "payment enclosed" on the envelope. Chances are, they will sign for that one!

You can send the letter UPS, Federal Express, or Priority or Express Mail, which will provide a tracking number.

Keep copies of everything!

Keep the credit reports you have requested, the notes you made while analyzing them, copies of the letters you send (including copies of any attachments you include), the "return receipts" you get back from the post office, and any correspondence you receive.

GLOSSARY

Annual Fee: A flat, yearly charge similar to a membership fee.

Amortization Schedule: A complete list of payments and the time the payments are due over the life of a loan.

Annual Percentage Rate (APR): A measure of the cost of credit that expresses the finance charge, which includes interest and may also include other charges, as a yearly rate.

Application Fee (Credit Cards): A one-time fee required when applying for a credit card or a loan. For credit cards, the fee usually is added to your credit card balance after the card has been issued.

Appraisals: Professional property appraisers will compare the value of one house to similar properties in the neighborhood or community to determine its value. Lenders use appraisals to be sure that the property is worth at least as much as the mortgage.

Automated Teller Machine (ATM) Card: A card used only to obtain cash, or retrieve information about a bank account, from an ATM machine; requires the use of a Personal Identification Number.

Bank Card: A credit card issued by a major banking institution.

Basis of Lawsuit: A document stating the reason for a lawsuit, outlining what results the plaintiff is seeking, and what laws have been violated.

Cash Advance Transaction Fee: A fee charged to a consumer for using a credit card credit line to get cash (not purchase goods or services). The fee may be either a percentage of the amount taken out or a flat fee per transaction.

Closing Costs: Money paid by the borrower or the seller in connection with the closing of a mortgage loan. This generally involves an origination fee, discount points, appraisal, credit report, title insurance, attorney's fees, survey, and pre-paid items such as tax and insurance escrow payments.

Consumer Credit Counseling Services (CCCS): Nonprofit organizations sponsored and funded at least in part by credit card companies to try and help consumers pay off their credit card debt.

Cost of Funds Index (COFI): The cost of funds is indexed to the average interest rate that banks in particular states pay their customers. One of the most common indexes is the 11th District Cost of Funds Index, which covers banks in California, Nevada, and Arizona.

Credit Bureau: The same as a Credit Reporting Agency (CRA).

Credit Inquiries: Every time you apply for credit, a copy of your credit report is pulled. The fact that your credit was pulled is recorded in your credit file along with the reason your credit was pulled.

Credit Report: An informational summary on how you have paid your debts, as well as your employment history, past addresses, and any civil or federal court records. This information is obtained and stored in a Credit Reporting Agency database.

Credit Reporting Agency (CRA): A privately owned, for-profit agency in the business of collecting and distributing consumer credit information, mostly concerning accounts and payment history. These agencies are subject to government regulations. Experian, Equifax, and TransUnion are the three biggest credit reporting agencies.

Debt: Money owed to another person or legal entity.

Debt Consolidation: A method of combining all debts into one umbrella debt and making one monthly payment to that umbrella debt.

Document Preparation Fees: The cost of preparing legal documents; usually refers to documents regarding a mortgage and sale of real property (real estate).

Down payment: The percentage of the purchase price that the buyer must pay in cash and may not borrow from the lender. The down payment amount, in addition to the mortgage, equals the purchase price of a property.

Equifax: One of the three major Credit Reporting Agencies.

Equity: The dollar amount difference between what a property (i.e., real estate, automobile) is worth and what is owed on that property.

Escrow: An account held by the lender into which a homeowner pays money for taxes and insurance.

Experian: One of the three major Credit Reporting Agencies.

Fair Credit Billing Act: A federal law regulating how a creditor can bill you for goods and services.

Fair Credit Reporting Act (FCRA): A federal law regulating how and what information credit reporting agencies can store and report about consumers. The FCRA is included in Appendix 1.

Fair Debt Collection Practices Act (FDCPA): A federal law regulating the means by which a bill collector can seek to collect an outstanding debt from a consumer. The FDCPA is included in Appendix 3.

Fair Isaac: The company that developed the basic credit scoring models (which are also called FICO).

Federal Trade Commission (FTC): The federal government agency responsible for monitoring and regulating all issues related to credit and consumer affairs in the United States.

FICO Score: A basic statistical credit-scoring model used by the credit bureaus. Variations are used by most creditors in the United States as internal decision-making tools when granting credit. FICO is short for functional intensity with correlation.

Finance Charge: The dollar amount you pay to use credit. Besides interest costs, it may include other charges associated with transactions such as cash advance fees.

Fixed Rate: An interest rate that remains constant over the life of a loan or credit line. Most often used in reference to a mortgage or car loan, but some credit cards have fixed rates as well.

Floating Rate: An interest rate that is tied to some published financial index, and varies in relation to this index. The rate is calculated by adding a fixed percentage to the financial index to which it is tied. The terms "floating" and "variable" rates are used interchangeably.

Grace Period: A time, about 25 days, during which you can pay your credit card bill without incurring a finance charge. Under almost all credit card plans, the grace period applies only if you pay your balance in full each month. It does not apply if you carry a balance forward. Also, the grace period does not apply to cash advances.

Homeowner's Insurance: Usually a part of any mortgage agreement. Most lenders require that you prepay the first year's premium for homeowner's insurance (sometimes called "hazard insurance") and bring proof of payment to the closing. This insures that the mortgage company's investment will be secured, even if the house is destroyed.

House Cards: Credit cards issued by department stores or other stores. The card can be used to purchase goods only at the store or chain that issued the card.

Identity Theft: A situation when a person's personal information is used by another to obtain credit fraudulently.

Interest Rate: The percentage of the loan that is charged to the debtor to borrow monies. Interest rates on credit card plans change over time. Some are explicitly tied to changes in other interest rates such as the prime rate or the Treasury Bill rate and are called "variable rate" plans. Others are not explicitly tied to changes in other interest rates and are called "fixed rate" plans.

Land Survey: Usually part of a mortgage agreement. Many mortgage lenders will require that the property be surveyed to make sure that no one has encroached on it and to verify the presence of the buildings and improvements on the property.

Late Payment Fee: Some credit cards charge a late payment fee in addition to the finance charges. A fee of $20 to $29 is common.

Loan: An agreement between a lender and borrower, the lender gives the borrower cash, and the borrower gives the lender a note which is a contract, legally binding him to repay the debt.

Loan Officer: An employee of a bank or a mortgage banker who sells loans to consumers.

London Inter-bank Offered Rate (LIBOR): This is the interest rate at which highly rated American and international banks lend funds to one another. LIBOR is an international index that follows the world economic condition.

Mortgage: A loan secured by real estate. If the borrower defaults on the loan, the lender can take the property by which the loan is secured.

Mortgage Insurance: If the down payment on purchasing a piece of real estate is less than 20%, many lenders will require that the debtor purchase private mortgage insurance (PMI) for the amount of the loan. This way, if the debtor defaults on the loan, the lender will be able to recover his money. These insurance premiums will continue until the principal payments plus down payment equal 20% of the selling price, but the law does allow lenders to continue requiring PMI all the way down to 50% equity for so-called high-risk borrowers. The premiums usually are added to any amount the debtor must escrow for taxes and homeowner's insurance.

Origination or Application Fees: These are fees for processing a mortgage application and may be a flat fee or a percentage of the mortgage.

Over-limit Fees: Many credit cards assess an over-limit fee if you charge something that takes you over your credit limit. The credit card company may or may not allow the charge if it assesses this fee. Common over-limit fees range from $20 to $29.

Par Rate: The interest rate of the loan when it is sold to a loan broker that neither costs extra in fees nor returns extras in commissions.

Personal Identification Number (PIN): A "password" that goes with your card and allows you to make certain types of electronic transactions involving your card. In some countries (notably France), most credit card purchases are validated with a PIN. Although you can still use your card without one, they may sometimes have to phone for authorization.

PITI: A mortgage loan payment that includes Principal, Interest, Taxes and Insurance.

Points: A point is equal to 1% of the mortgage loan. Points can be payable when the loan is approved, before or at closing. For FHA and VA mortgages, the seller—not the buyer—must pay the points. Even if you are not using an FHA or VA mortgage, you may want to negotiate points in the purchase offer. Some lenders will let you finance points, adding this cost to the mortgage, which will increase your interest costs. If you pay the points up front, they are deductible from your income taxes in the year they are paid. Different deductibility rules apply to second homes.

Prepaid Interest: The interest you pay at closing when purchasing a piece of real estate that covers the interest accrued on the mortgage until your first monthly mortgage payment is due. Your first regular mortgage payment is usually due about six to eight weeks after you close (for example, if you close in August, your first regular payment will be due in October; the October payment covers the cost of borrowing money for the month of September). Interest costs, however, start as soon as you close. The lender will calculate how much interest you owe for the fraction of the month in which you close (for example, if you close on August 25, you would owe interest for six days). In some cases this is due at closing.

Prorated Taxes: These monies due at the closing of a real estate sale are similar to Prepaid Interest in that you are paying at closing the taxes due on the property until your first monthly mortgage payment is due. Prorated taxes (such as school taxes and municipal taxes) may have to be split between you and the seller because they are due at different times of the year. For example, if taxes are due in October and you close in August, you would owe taxes for two months while the seller would owe taxes for the other 10 months. Prorated taxes usually are paid based on the number of days (not months) of ownership.

Recording Fees for Deed: Fees paid to the county clerk to record the deed and mortgage and change the property tax billing when a piece of real estate changes hands.

Residential Mortgage Credit Reporting (RMCR): A credit report that combines all of the information from the three credit bureaus about one person into one report. The information is presented in a standard format that the mortgage company likes.

RESPA: The Real Estate Settlement Procedures Act; a federal law that allows consumers to review information on known or estimated settlement costs once after application, and once prior to or at settlement.

Secured Credit Cards: Credit cards that are "backed up" by a savings account or other investment to secure the credit line. If the consumer fails to make payments on the secured card, the funds or assets used to secure the card are then used to pay off the debt.

Sexiness: Arousing desire or interest; attractiveness.

Termite and Water Inspections: If you apply for an FHA or VA mortgage, the lender will require a termite inspection. In many rural areas, lenders will require a water test to make sure the well and water system will maintain an adequate supply of water to the house (this usually is a test for quantity, not a test for water quality).

Title Insurance: Even though there is a title search for any obstacle (i.e., liens, lawsuits), many lenders require insurance so that should a problem arise, they can recover their mortgage investment. This is a one-time insurance premium, usually paid at closing; it is insurance for the lender only, not for the purchaser. The seller of a home also usually is required to purchase title insurance to protect the purchaser of the home in case unrecorded liens are discovered after the purchase of a home is completed (and title transfers).

Title Search: Usually your attorney or the title company will conduct or arrange for the title search to make sure there are no obstacles (i.e., liens, lawsuits) to your owning a piece of property.

TransUnion: One of the three major Credit Reporting Agencies.

Uniform Settlement Statement: A closing statement provided by the escrow company that outlines all costs associated with a mortgage loan transaction.

Variable Rate: An interest rate that is tied to some published financial index, and varies in relation to this index. The rate is calculated by adding a fixed percentage to the financial index to which it is tied. The terms "floating" and "variable" rates are used interchangeably.

APPENDIX 1: FAIR CREDIT REPORTING ACT

Source: http://www.ftc.gov/os/statutes/031224fcra.pdf

As a public service, the staff of the Federal Trade Commission (FTC) has prepared the following complete text of the Fair Credit Reporting Act (FCRA), 15 U.S.C. § 1681 et seq. Although staff generally followed the format of the U.S. Code as published by the Government Printing Office, the format of this text does differ in minor ways from the Code (and from West's U.S. Code Annotated). For example, this version uses FCRA section numbers (§§ 601-625) in the headings. (The relevant U.S. Code citation is included with each section heading and each reference to the FCRA in the text.) Although the staff has made every effort to transcribe the statutory material accurately, this compendium is intended only as a convenience for the public and not a substitute for the text in the U. S. Code.

This version of the FCRA includes the amendments to the FCRA set forth in the Consumer Credit Reporting Reform Act of 1996 (Public Law 104-208, the Omnibus Consolidated Appropriations Act for Fiscal Year 1997, Title II, Subtitle D, Chapter 1), Section 311 of the Intelligence Authorization for Fiscal Year 1998 (Public Law 105-107), the Consumer Reporting Employment Clarification Act of 1998 (Public Law 105-347), Section 506 of the Gramm-Leach-Bliley Act (Public Law 106-102), Sections 358(g) and 505(c) of the Uniting and Strengthening America by Providing Appropriate Tools Required to Intercept and Obstruct Terrorism Act of 2001 (USA PATRIOT Act) (Public Law 107-56), and the Fair and Accurate Credit Transactions Act of 2003 (FACT Act) (Public Law 108-159).

Many of the provisions added by the FACT Act will become effective at different times between December 31, 2003, and December 1, 2004, depending on the results of rulemaking proceedings announced by the Federal Trade Commission and Federal Reserve Board on December 16, 2003. See http://www.ftc.gov/opa/2003/12/fyi0372.htm. The effective dates will be made final by the Commission and Board no later than February 4, 2003.

TABLE OF CONTENTS

§ 601. Short title

This title may be cited as the "Fair Credit Reporting Act".

§ 602. Congressional findings and statement of purpose [15 U.S.C. § 1681]

(a) *Accuracy and fairness of credit reporting.* The Congress makes the following findings:

(1) The banking system is dependent upon fair and accurate credit reporting. Inaccurate credit reports directly impair the efficiency of the banking system, and unfair credit reporting methods undermine the public confidence which is essential to the continued functioning of the banking system.

(2) An elaborate mechanism has been developed for investigating and evaluating the credit worthiness, credit standing, credit capacity, character, and general reputation of consumers.

(3) Consumer reporting agencies have assumed a vital role in assembling and evaluating consumer credit and other information on consumers.

(4) There is a need to insure that consumer reporting agencies exercise their grave responsibilities with fairness, impartiality, and a respect for the consumer's right to privacy.

(b) *Reasonable procedures.* It is the purpose of this title to require that consumer reporting agencies adopt reasonable procedures for meeting the needs of commerce for consumer credit, personnel, insurance, and other information in a manner which is fair and equitable to the consumer, with regard to the confidentiality, accuracy, relevancy, and proper utilization of such information in accordance with the requirements of this title.

§ 603. Definitions; rules of construction [15 U.S.C. § 1681a]

(a) Definitions and rules of construction set forth in this section are applicable for the purposes of this title.

(b) The term "person" means any individual, partnership, corporation, trust, estate, cooperative, association, government or governmental subdivision or agency, or other entity.

(c) The term "consumer" means an individual.

(d) Consumer Report

(1) *In general.* The term "consumer report" means any written, oral, or other communication of any information by a consumer reporting agency bearing on a consumer's credit worthiness, credit standing, credit capacity, character, general reputation, personal characteristics, or mode of living which is used or expected to be used or collected in whole or in part for the purpose of serving as a factor in establishing the consumer's eligibility for

(A) subject to section 624, credit or insurance to be used primarily for personal, family, or household purposes;

(B) employment purposes; or

(C) any other purpose authorized under section 604 [§ 1681b].

(2) *Exclusions.* Except as provided in paragraph (3), the term "consumer report" does not include

(A) subject to section 624, any

(i) report containing information solely as to transactions or experiences between the consumer and the person making the report;

(ii) communication of that information among persons related by common ownership or affiliated by corporate control; or

(iii) communication of other information among persons related by common ownership or affiliated by corporate control, if it is clearly and conspicuously disclosed to the consumer that the information may be communicated among such persons and the consumer is given the opportunity, before the time that the information is initially communicated, to direct that such information not be communicated among such persons;

(B) any authorization or approval of a specific extension of credit directly or indirectly by the issuer of a credit card or similar device;

(C) any report in which a person who has been requested by a third party to make a specific extension of credit directly or indirectly to a consumer conveys his or her decision with respect to such request, if the third party advises the consumer of the name and address of the person to whom the request was made, and such person makes the disclosures to the consumer required under section 615 [§ 1681m]; or

(D) a communication described in subsection (o) or (x).

(3) *Restriction on sharing of medical information.* Except for information or any communication of information disclosed as provided in section 604(g)(3), the exclusions in paragraph (2) shall not apply with respect to information disclosed to any person related by common ownership or affiliated by corporate control, if the information is—

(A) medical information;

(B) an individualized list or description based on the payment transactions of the consumer for medical products or services; or

(C) an aggregate list of identified consumers based on payment transactions for medical products or services.

(e) The term "investigative consumer report" means a consumer report or portion thereof in which information on a consumer's character, general reputation, personal characteristics, or mode of living is obtained through personal interviews with neighbors, friends, or associates of the consumer reported on or with others with whom he is acquainted or who may have knowledge concerning any such items of information. However, such information shall not include specific factual information on a consumer's credit record obtained directly from a creditor of the consumer or from a consumer reporting agency when such information was obtained directly from a creditor of the consumer or from the consumer.

(f) The term "consumer reporting agency" means any person which, for monetary fees, dues, or on a cooperative nonprofit basis, regularly engages in whole or in part in the practice of assembling or evaluating consumer credit information or other information on consumers for the purpose of furnishing consumer reports to third parties, and which uses any means or facility of interstate commerce for the purpose of preparing or furnishing consumer reports.

(g) The term "file," when used in connection with information on any consumer, means all of the information on that consumer recorded and retained by a consumer reporting agency regardless of how the information is stored.

(h) The term "employment purposes" when used in connection with a consumer report means a report used for the purpose of evaluating a consumer for employment, promotion, reassignment or retention as an employee.

(i) The term "medical information" --

(1) means information or data, whether oral or recorded, in any form or medium, created by or derived from a health care provider or the consumer, that relates to--

(A) the past, present, or future physical, mental, or behavioral health or condition of an individual;

(B) the provision of health care to an individual; or

(C) the payment for the provision of health care to an individual.

(2) does not include the age or gender of a consumer, demographic information about the consumer, including a consumer's residence address or e-mail address, or any other information about a consumer that does not relate to the physical, mental, or behavioral health or condition of a consumer, including the existence or value of any insurance policy.

(j) Definitions Relating to Child Support Obligations

(1) The "overdue support" has the meaning given to such term in section 666(e) of title 42 [Social Security Act, 42 U.S.C. § 666(e)].

(2) The term "State or local child support enforcement agency" means a State or local agency which administers a State or local program for establishing and enforcing child support obligations.

(k) Adverse Action

(1) *Actions included.* The term "adverse action"

(A) has the same meaning as in section 701(d)(6) of the Equal Credit Opportunity Act; and

(B) means

(i) a denial or cancellation of, an increase in any charge for, or a reduction or other adverse or unfavorable change in the terms of coverage or amount of, any insurance, existing or applied for, in connection with the underwriting of insurance;

(ii) a denial of employment or any other decision for employment purposes that adversely affects any current or prospective employee;

(iii) a denial or cancellation of, an increase in any charge for, or any other adverse or unfavorable change in the terms of, any license or benefit described in section 604(a)(3)(D) [§ 1681b]; and

(iv) an action taken or determination that is

(I) made in connection with an application that was made by, or a transaction that was initiated by, any consumer, or in connection with a review of an account under section 604(a)(3)(F)(ii)[§ 1681b]; and

(II) adverse to the interests of the consumer.

(2) *Applicable findings*, decisions, commentary, and orders. For purposes of any determination of whether an action is an adverse action under paragraph (1)(A), all appropriate final findings, decisions, commentary, and orders issued under section 701(d)(6) of the Equal Credit Opportunity Act by the Board of Governors of the Federal Reserve System or any court shall apply.

(l) The term "firm offer of credit or insurance" means any offer of credit or insurance to a consumer that will be honored if the consumer is determined, based on information in a consumer report on the consumer, to meet the specific criteria used to select the consumer for the offer, except that the offer may be further conditioned on one or more of the following:

(1) The consumer being determined, based on information in the consumer's application for the credit or insurance, to meet specific criteria bearing on credit worthiness or insurability, as applicable, that are established

(A) before selection of the consumer for the offer; and

(B) for the purpose of determining whether to extend credit or insurance pursuant to the offer.

(2) Verification

(A) that the consumer continues to meet the specific criteria used to select the consumer for the offer, by using information in a consumer report on the consumer, information in the consumer's application for the credit or insurance, or other information bearing on the credit worthiness or insurability of the consumer; or

(B) of the information in the consumer's application for the credit or insurance, to determine that the consumer meets the specific criteria bearing on credit worthiness or insurability.

(3) The consumer furnishing any collateral that is a requirement for the extension of the credit or insurance that was

(A) established before selection of the consumer for the offer of credit or insurance; and

(B) disclosed to the consumer in the offer of credit or insurance.

(m) The term "credit or insurance transaction that is not initiated by the consumer" does not include the use of a consumer report by a person with which the consumer has an account or insurance policy, for purposes of

(1) reviewing the account or insurance policy; or

(2) collecting the account.

(n) The term "State" means any State, the Commonwealth of Puerto Rico, the District of Columbia, and any territory or possession of the United States.

(o) *Excluded communications.* A communication is described in this subsection if it is a communication

(1) that, but for subsection (d)(2)(D), would be an investigative consumer report;

(2) that is made to a prospective employer for the purpose of

(A) procuring an employee for the employer; or

(B) procuring an opportunity for a natural person to work for the employer;

(3) that is made by a person who regularly performs such procurement;

(4) that is not used by any person for any purpose other than a purpose described in subparagraph (A) or (B) of paragraph (2); and

(5) with respect to which

    (A) the consumer who is the subject of the communication

        (i) consents orally or in writing to the nature and scope of the communication, before the collection of any information for the purpose of making the communication;

        (ii) consents orally or in writing to the making of the communication to a prospective employer, before the making of the communication; and

        (iii) in the case of consent under clause (i) or (ii) given orally, is provided written confirmation of that consent by the person making the communication, not later than 3 business days after the receipt of the consent by that person;

    (B) the person who makes the communication does not, for the purpose of making the communication, make any inquiry that if made by a prospective employer of the consumer who is the subject of the communication would violate any applicable Federal or State equal employment opportunity law or regulation; and

    (C) the person who makes the communication

        (i) discloses in writing to the consumer who is the subject of the communication, not later than 5 business days after receiving any request from the consumer for such disclosure, the nature and substance of all information in the consumer's file at the time of the request, except that the sources of any information that is acquired solely for use in making the communication and is actually used for no other purpose, need not be disclosed other than under appropriate discovery procedures in any court of competent jurisdiction in which an action is brought; and

        (ii) notifies the consumer who is the subject of the communication, in writing, of the consumer's right to request the information described in clause (i).

(p) The term "consumer reporting agency that compiles and maintains files on consumers on a nationwide basis" means a consumer reporting agency that regularly engages in the practice of assembling or evaluating, and maintaining, for the purpose of furnishing consumer reports to third parties bearing on a consumer's credit worthiness, credit standing, or credit capacity, each of the following regarding consumers residing nationwide:

    (1) Public record information.

    (2) Credit account information from persons who furnish that information regularly and in the ordinary course of business.

(q) Definitions relating to fraud alerts.

    (1) The term "active duty military consumer" means a consumer in military service who--

        (A) is on active duty (as defined in section 101(d)(1) of title 10, United States Code) or is a reservist performing duty under a call or order to active duty under a provision of law referred to in section 101(a)(13) of title 10, United States Code; and

(B) is assigned to service away from the usual duty station of the consumer.

(2) The terms "fraud alert" and "active duty alert" mean a statement in the file of a consumer that--

(A) notifies all prospective users of a consumer report relating to the consumer that the consumer may be a victim of fraud, including identity theft, or is an active duty military consumer, as applicable; and

(B) is presented in a manner that facilitates a clear and conspicuous view of the statement described in subparagraph (A) by any person requesting such consumer report.

(3) The term "identity theft" means a fraud committed using the identifying information of another person, subject to such further definition as the Commission may prescribe, by regulation.

(4) The term "identity theft report" has the meaning given that term by rule of the Commission, and means, at a minimum, a report--

(A) that alleges an identity theft;

(B) that is a copy of an official, valid report filed by a consumer with an appropriate Federal, State, or local law enforcement agency, including the United States Postal Inspection Service, or such other government agency deemed appropriate by the Commission; and

(C) the filing of which subjects the person filing the report to criminal penalties relating to the filing of false information if, in fact, the information in the report is false.

(5) The term "new credit plan" means a new account under an open end credit plan (as defined in section 103(i) of the Truth in Lending Act) or a new credit transaction not under an open end credit plan.

(r) Credit and Debit Related Terms

(1) The term "card issuer" means--

(A) a credit card issuer, in the case of a credit card; and

(B) a debit card issuer, in the case of a debit card.

(2) The term "credit card" has the same meaning as in section 103 of the Truth in Lending Act.

(3) The term "debit card" means any card issued by a financial institution to a consumer for use in initiating an electronic fund transfer from the account of the consumer at such financial institution, for the purpose of transferring money between accounts or obtaining money, property, labor, or services.

(4) The terms "account" and "electronic fund transfer" have the same meanings as in section 903 of the Electronic Fund Transfer Act.

(5) The terms "credit" and "creditor" have the same meanings as in section 702 of the Equal Credit Opportunity Act.

(s) The term "Federal banking agency" has the same meaning as in section 3 of the Federal Deposit Insurance Act.

(t) The term "financial institution" means a State or National bank, a State or Federal savings and loan association, a mutual savings bank, a State or Federal credit union, or any other person that, directly or indirectly, holds a transaction account (as defined in section 19(b) of the Federal Reserve Act) belonging to a consumer.

(u) The term "reseller" means a consumer reporting agency that--

(1) assembles and merges information contained in the database of another consumer reporting agency or multiple consumer reporting agencies concerning any consumer for purposes of furnishing such information to any third party, to the extent of such activities; and

(2) does not maintain a database of the assembled or merged information from which new consumer reports are produced.

(v) The term "Commission" means the Federal Trade Commission.

(w) The term "nationwide specialty consumer reporting agency" means a consumer reporting agency that compiles and maintains files on consumers on a nationwide basis relating to--

(1) medical records or payments;

(2) residential or tenant history;

(3) check writing history;

(4) employment history; or

(5) insurance claims.

(x) Exclusion of Certain Communications for Employee Investigations

(1) A communication is described in this subsection if--

(A) but for subsection (d)(2)(D), the communication would be a consumer report;

(B) the communication is made to an employer in connection with an investigation of–

(i) suspected misconduct relating to employment; or

(ii) compliance with Federal, State, or local laws and regulations, the rules of a self-regulatory organization, or any preexisting written policies of the employer;

(C) the communication is not made for the purpose of investigating a consumer's credit worthiness, credit standing, or credit capacity; and

(D) the communication is not provided to any person except--

(i) to the employer or an agent of the employer;

(ii) to any Federal or State officer, agency, or department, or any officer, agency, or department of a unit of general local government;

(iii) to any self-regulatory organization with regulatory authority over the activities of the employer or employee;

(iv) as otherwise required by law; or

(v) pursuant to section 608.

(2) *Subsequent disclosure.* After taking any adverse action based in whole or in part on a communication described in paragraph (1), the employer shall disclose to the consumer a summary containing the nature and substance of the communication upon which the adverse action is based, except that the sources of information acquired solely for use in preparing what would be but for subsection (d)(2)(D) an investigative consumer report need not be disclosed.

(3) For purposes of this subsection, the term "self-regulatory organization" includes any self-regulatory organization (as defined in section 3(a)(26) of the

Securities Exchange Act of 1934), any entity established under title I of the Sarbanes-Oxley Act of 2002, any board of trade designated by the Commodity Futures Trading Commission, and any futures association registered with such Commission.

§ 604. Permissible purposes of consumer reports [15 U.S.C. § 1681b]

(a) *In general.* Subject to subsection (c), any consumer reporting agency may furnish a consumer report under the following circumstances and no other:

(1) In response to the order of a court having jurisdiction to issue such an order, or a subpoena issued in connection with proceedings before a Federal grand jury.

(2) In accordance with the written instructions of the consumer to whom it relates.

(3) To a person which it has reason to believe

(A) intends to use the information in connection with a credit transaction involving the consumer on whom the information is to be furnished and involving the extension of credit to, or review or collection of an account of, the consumer; or

(B) intends to use the information for employment purposes; or

(C) intends to use the information in connection with the underwriting of insurance involving the consumer; or

(D) intends to use the information in connection with a determination of the consumer's eligibility for a license or other benefit granted by a governmental instrumentality required by law to consider an applicant's financial responsibility or status; or

(E) intends to use the information, as a potential investor or servicer, or current insurer, in connection with a valuation of, or an assessment of the credit or prepayment risks associated with, an existing credit obligation; or

(F) otherwise has a legitimate business need for the information

(i) in connection with a business transaction that is initiated by the consumer; or

(ii) to review an account to determine whether the consumer continues to meet the terms of the account.

(4) In response to a request by the head of a State or local child support enforcement agency (or a State or local government official authorized by the head of such an agency), if the person making the request certifies to the consumer reporting agency that

(A) the consumer report is needed for the purpose of establishing an individual's capacity to make child support payments or determining the appropriate level of such payments;

(B) the paternity of the consumer for the child to which the obligation relates has been established or acknowledged by the consumer in accordance with State laws under which the obligation arises (if required by those laws);

(C) the person has provided at least 10 days' prior notice to the consumer whose report is requested, by certified or registered mail to the last known address of the consumer, that the report will be requested; and

(D) the consumer report will be kept confidential, will be used solely for a purpose described in subparagraph (A), and will not be used in connection with any other civil, administrative, or criminal proceeding, or for any other purpose.

(5) To an agency administering a State plan under Section 454 of the Social Security Act (42 U.S.C. § 654) for use to set an initial or modified child support award.

(b) Conditions for Furnishing and Using Consumer Reports for Employment Purposes.

(1) *Certification from user.* A consumer reporting agency may furnish a consumer report for employment purposes only if

(A) the person who obtains such report from the agency certifies to the agency that

(i) the person has complied with paragraph (2) with respect to the consumer report, and the person will comply with paragraph (3) with respect to the consumer report if paragraph (3) becomes applicable; and

(ii) information from the consumer report will not be used in violation of any applicable Federal or State equal employment opportunity law or regulation; and

(B) the consumer reporting agency provides with the report, or has previously provided, a summary of the consumer's rights under this title, as prescribed by the Federal Trade Commission under section 609(c)(3) [§ 1681g].

(2) Disclosure to Consumer.

(A) *In general.* Except as provided in subparagraph (B), a person may not procure a consumer report, or cause a consumer report to be procured, for employment purposes with respect to any consumer, unless--

(i) a clear and conspicuous disclosure has been made in writing to the consumer at any time before the report is procured or caused to be procured, in a document that consists solely of the disclosure, that a consumer report may be obtained for employment purposes; and

(ii) the consumer has authorized in writing (which authorization may be made on the document referred to in clause (i)) the procurement of the report by that person.

(B) *Application by mail, telephone, computer, or other similar means.* If a consumer described in subparagraph (C) applies for employment by mail, telephone, computer, or other similar means, at any time before a consumer report is procured or caused to be procured in connection with that application--

(i) the person who procures the consumer report on the consumer for employment purposes shall provide to the consumer, by oral, written, or electronic means, notice that a consumer report may be obtained for employment purposes, and a summary of the consumer's rights under section 615(a)(3); and

(ii) the consumer shall have consented, orally, in writing, or electronically to the procurement of the report by that person.

(C) *Scope.* Subparagraph (B) shall apply to a person procuring a consumer report on a consumer in connection with the consumer's application for employment only if--

(i) the consumer is applying for a position over which the Secretary of Transportation has the power to establish qualifications and maximum hours of service pursuant to the provisions of section 31502 of title 49, or a position subject to safety regulation by a State transportation agency; and

(ii) as of the time at which the person procures the report or causes the report to be procured the only interaction between the consumer and the person in connection with that employment application has been by mail, telephone, computer, or other similar means.

(3) Conditions on use for adverse actions.

(A) *In general.* Except as provided in subparagraph (B), in using a consumer report for employment purposes, before taking any adverse action based in whole or in part on the report, the person intending to take such adverse action shall provide to the consumer to whom the report relates--

(i) a copy of the report; and

(ii) a description in writing of the rights of the consumer under this title, as prescribed by the Federal Trade Commission under section 609(c)(3).

(B) Application by mail, telephone, computer, or other similar means.

(i) If a consumer described in subparagraph (C) applies for employment by mail, telephone, computer, or other similar means, and if a person who has procured a consumer report on the consumer for employment purposes takes adverse action on the employment application based in whole or in part on the report, then the person must provide to the consumer to whom the report relates, in lieu of the notices required under subparagraph (A) of this section and under section 615(a), within 3 business days of taking such action, an oral, written or electronic notification--

(I) that adverse action has been taken based in whole or in part on a consumer report received from a consumer reporting agency;

(II) of the name, address and telephone number of the consumer reporting agency that furnished the consumer report (including a toll-free telephone number established by the agency if the agency compiles and maintains files on consumers on a nationwide basis);

(III) that the consumer reporting agency did not make the decision to take the adverse action and is unable to provide to the consumer the specific reasons why the adverse action was taken; and

(IV) that the consumer may, upon providing proper identification, request a free copy of a report and may dispute with the consumer reporting agency the accuracy or completeness of any information in a report.

(ii) If, under clause (B)(i)(IV), the consumer requests a copy of a consumer report from the person who procured the report, then, within 3 business days of receiving the consumer's request, together with proper identification, the person must send or provide to the consumer a copy of a report and a copy of the consumer's rights as prescribed by the Federal Trade Commission under section 609(c)(3).

(C) *Scope.* Subparagraph (B) shall apply to a person procuring a consumer report on a consumer in connection with the consumer's application for employment only if--

(i) the consumer is applying for a position over which the Secretary of Transportation has the power to establish qualifications and maximum hours of service pursuant to the provisions of section 31502 of title 49, or a position subject to safety regulation by a State transportation agency; and

(ii) as of the time at which the person procures the report or causes the report to be procured the only interaction between the consumer and the person in connection with that employment application has been by mail, telephone, computer, or other similar means.

(4) Exception for national security investigations.

(A) *In general.* In the case of an agency or department of the United States Government which seeks to obtain and use a consumer report for employment purposes, paragraph (3) shall not apply to any adverse action by such agency or department which is based in part on such consumer report, if the head of such agency or department makes a written finding that--

(i) the consumer report is relevant to a national security investigation of such agency or department;

(ii) the investigation is within the jurisdiction of such agency or department;

(iii) there is reason to believe that compliance with paragraph (3) will--

(I) endanger the life or physical safety of any person;

(II) result in flight from prosecution;

(III) result in the destruction of, or tampering with, evidence relevant to the investigation;

(IV) result in the intimidation of a potential witness relevant to the investigation;

(V) result in the compromise of classified information; or

(VI) otherwise seriously jeopardize or unduly delay the investigation or another official proceeding.

(B) *Notification of consumer upon conclusion of investigation.* Upon the conclusion of a national security investigation described in subparagraph (A), or upon the determination that the exception under subparagraph (A) is no longer required for the reasons set forth in such subparagraph, the official exercising the authority in such subparagraph shall provide to the consumer who is the subject of the consumer report with regard to which such finding was made--

(i) a copy of such consumer report with any classified information redacted as necessary;

(ii) notice of any adverse action which is based, in part, on the consumer report; and

(iii) the identification with reasonable specificity of the nature of the investigation for which the consumer report was sought.

(C) *Delegation by head of agency or department.* For purposes of subparagraphs (A) and (B), the head of any agency or department of the United States Government may delegate his or her authorities under this paragraph to an official of such agency or department who has personnel security responsibilities and is a member of the Senior Executive Service or equivalent civilian or military rank.

(D) *Report to the Congress.* Not later than January 31 of each year, the head of each agency and department of the United States Government that exercised authority under this paragraph during the preceding year shall submit a report to the Congress on the number of times the department or agency exercised such authority during the year.

(E) *Definitions.* For purposes of this paragraph, the following definitions shall apply:

(i) The term "classified information" means information that is protected from unauthorized disclosure under Executive Order No. 12958 or successor orders.

(ii) The term "national security investigation" means any official inquiry by an agency or department of the United States Government to determine the eligibility of a consumer to receive access or continued access to classified information or to determine whether classified information has been lost or compromised.

(c) Furnishing reports in connection with credit or insurance transactions that are not initiated by the consumer.

(1) *In general.* A consumer reporting agency may furnish a consumer report relating to any consumer pursuant to subparagraph (A) or (C) of subsection (a)(3) in connection with any credit or insurance transaction that is not initiated by the consumer only if

(A) the consumer authorizes the agency to provide such report to such person; or

(B) (i) the transaction consists of a firm offer of credit or insurance;

(ii) the consumer reporting agency has complied with subsection (e); and

(iii) there is not in effect an election by the consumer, made in accordance with subsection (e), to have the consumer's name and address excluded from lists of names provided by the agency pursuant to this paragraph.

(2) *Limits on information received under paragraph (1)(B).* A person may receive pursuant to paragraph (1)(B) only

(A) the name and address of a consumer;

(B) an identifier that is not unique to the consumer and that is used by the person solely for the purpose of verifying the identity of the consumer; and

(C) other information pertaining to a consumer that does not identify the relationship or experience of the consumer with respect to a particular creditor or other entity.

(3) *Information regarding inquiries.* Except as provided in section 609(a)(5) [§1681g], a consumer reporting agency shall not furnish to any person a record of inquiries in connection with a credit or insurance transaction that is not initiated by a consumer.

(d) Reserved.

(e) Election of consumer to be excluded from lists.

(1) *In general.* A consumer may elect to have the consumer's name and address excluded from any list provided by a consumer reporting agency under subsection (c)(1)(B) in connection with a credit or insurance transaction that is not initiated by the consumer, by notifying the agency in accordance with paragraph (2) that the consumer does not consent to any use of a consumer report relating to the consumer in connection with any credit or insurance transaction that is not initiated by the consumer.

(2) *Manner of notification.* A consumer shall notify a consumer reporting agency under paragraph (1)

(A) through the notification system maintained by the agency under paragraph (5); or

(B) by submitting to the agency a signed notice of election form issued by the agency for purposes of this subparagraph.

(3) *Response of agency after notification through system.* Upon receipt of notification of the election of a consumer under paragraph (1) through the notification system maintained by the agency under paragraph (5), a consumer reporting agency shall

(A) inform the consumer that the election is effective only for the 5-year period following the election if the consumer does not submit to the agency a signed notice of election form issued by the agency for purposes of paragraph (2)(B); and

(B) provide to the consumer a notice of election form, if requested by the consumer, not later than 5 business days after receipt of the notification of the election through the system established under paragraph (5), in the case of a request made at the time the consumer provides notification through the system.

(4) *Effectiveness of election.* An election of a consumer under paragraph (1)

(A) shall be effective with respect to a consumer reporting agency beginning 5 business days after the date on which the consumer notifies the agency in accordance with paragraph (2);

(B) shall be effective with respect to a consumer reporting agency

(i) subject to subparagraph (C), during the 5-year period beginning 5 business days after the date on which the consumer notifies the agency of the election, in the case of an election for which a consumer notifies the agency only in accordance with paragraph (2)(A); or

(ii) until the consumer notifies the agency under subparagraph (C), in the case of an election for which a consumer notifies the agency in accordance with paragraph (2)(B);

(C) shall not be effective after the date on which the consumer notifies the agency, through the notification system established by the agency under paragraph (5), that the election is no longer effective; and

(D) shall be effective with respect to each affiliate of the agency.

(5) Notification System

(A) *In general.* Each consumer reporting agency that, under subsection (c)(1)(B), furnishes a consumer report in connection with a credit or insurance transaction that is not initiated by a consumer, shall

(i) establish and maintain a notification system, including a toll-free telephone number, which permits any consumer whose consumer report is maintained by the agency to notify the agency, with appropriate identification, of the consumer's election to have the consumer's name and address excluded from any such list of names and addresses provided by the agency for such a transaction; and

(ii) publish by not later than 365 days after the date of enactment of the Consumer Credit Reporting Reform Act of 1996, and not less than annually thereafter, in a publication of general circulation in the area served by the agency

(I) a notification that information in consumer files maintained by the agency may be used in connection with such transactions; and

(II) the address and toll-free telephone number for consumers to use to notify the agency of the consumer's election under clause (I).

(B) *Establishment and maintenance as compliance.* Establishment and maintenance of a notification system (including a toll-free telephone number) and publication by a consumer reporting agency on the agency's own behalf and on behalf of any of its affiliates in accordance with this paragraph is deemed to be compliance with this paragraph by each of those affiliates.

(6) *Notification system by agencies that operate nationwide.* Each consumer reporting agency that compiles and maintains files on consumers on a nationwide basis shall establish and maintain a notification system for purposes of paragraph (5) jointly with other such consumer reporting agencies.

(f) *Certain use or obtaining of information prohibited.* A person shall not use or obtain a consumer report for any purpose unless

(1) the consumer report is obtained for a purpose for which the consumer report is authorized to be furnished under this section; and

(2) the purpose is certified in accordance with section 607 [§ 1681e] by a prospective user of the report through a general or specific certification.

(g) Protection of Medical Information

(1) *Limitation on consumer reporting agencies.* A consumer reporting agency shall not furnish for employment purposes, or in connection with a credit or insurance transaction, a consumer report that contains medical information (other than medical contact information treated in the manner required under section 605(a)(6)) about a consumer, unless--

(A) if furnished in connection with an insurance transaction, the consumer affirmatively consents to the furnishing of the report;

(B) if furnished for employment purposes or in connection with a credit transaction--

(i) the information to be furnished is relevant to process or effect the employment or credit transaction; and

(ii) the consumer provides specific written consent for the furnishing of the report that describes in clear and conspicuous language the use for which the information will be furnished; or

(C) the information to be furnished pertains solely to transactions, accounts, or balances relating to debts arising from the receipt of medical services, products, or devises, where such information, other than account status or amounts, is restricted or reported using codes that do not identify, or do not provide information sufficient to infer, the specific provider or the nature of such services, products, or devices, as provided in section 605(a)(6).

(2) *Limitation on creditors.* Except as permitted pursuant to paragraph (3)(C) or regulations prescribed under paragraph (5)(A), a creditor shall not obtain or use medical information (other than medical contact information treated in the manner required under section 605(a)(6)) pertaining to a consumer in connection with any determination of the consumer's eligibility, or continued eligibility, for credit.

(3) *Actions authorized by federal law, insurance activities and regulatory determinations.* Section 603(d)(3) shall not be construed so as to treat information or any communication of information as a consumer report if the information or communication is disclosed--

(A) in connection with the business of insurance or annuities, including the activities described in section 18B of the model Privacy of Consumer Financial and Health Information Regulation issued by the National Association of Insurance Commissioners (as in effect on January 1, 2003);

(B) for any purpose permitted without authorization under the Standards for Individually Identifiable Health Information promulgated by the Department of Health and Human Services pursuant to the Health Insurance Portability and Accountability Act of 1996, or referred to under section 1179 of such Act, or described in section 502(e) of Public Law 106-102; or

(C) as otherwise determined to be necessary and appropriate, by regulation or order and subject to paragraph (6), by the Commission, any Federal banking agency or the National Credit Union Administration (with respect to any financial institution subject to the jurisdiction of such agency or Administration under paragraph (1), (2), or (3) of section 621(b), or the applicable State insurance authority (with respect to any person engaged in providing insurance or annuities).

(4) *Limitation on redisclosure of medical information.* Any person that receives medical information pursuant to paragraph (1) or (3) shall not disclose such information to any other person, except as necessary to carry out the purpose for which the information was initially disclosed, or as otherwise permitted by statute, regulation, or order.

(5) Regulations and Effective Date for Paragraph (2)

(A) *Regulations required.* Each Federal banking agency and the National Credit Union Administration shall, subject to paragraph (6) and after notice and opportunity for comment, prescribe regulations that permit transactions under paragraph (2) that are determined to be necessary and appropriate to protect legitimate operational, transactional, risk, consumer, and other needs (and which shall include permitting actions necessary for administrative verification purposes), consistent with the intent of paragraph (2) to restrict the use of medical information for inappropriate purposes.

(B) *Final regulations required.* The Federal banking agencies and the National Credit Union Administration shall issue the regulations required under subparagraph (A) in final form before the end of the 6-month period beginning on the date of enactment of the Fair and Accurate Credit Transactions Act of 2003.

(6) *Coordination with other laws.* No provision of this subsection shall be construed as altering, affecting, or superseding the applicability of any other provision of Federal law relating to medical confidentiality.

§ 605. Requirements relating to information contained in consumer reports [15 U.S.C. §1681c]

(a) Information excluded from consumer reports. Except as authorized under subsection (b) of this section, no consumer reporting agency may make any consumer report containing any of the following items of information:

(1) Cases under title 11 [United States Code] or under the Bankruptcy Act that, from the date of entry of the order for relief or the date of adjudication, as the case may be, antedate the report by more than 10 years.

(2) Civil suits, civil judgments, and records of arrest that from date of entry, antedate the report by more than seven years or until the governing statute of limitations has expired, whichever is the longer period.

(3) Paid tax liens which, from date of payment, antedate the report by more than seven years.

(4) Accounts placed for collection or charged to profit and loss which antedate the report by more than seven years.[1]

(5) Any other adverse item of information, other than records of convictions of crimes which antedates the report by more than seven years.[2]

(6) The name, address, and telephone number of any medical information furnisher that has notified the agency of its status, unless--

(A) such name, address, and telephone number are restricted or reported using codes that do not identify, or provide information sufficient to infer, the specific provider or the nature of such services, products, or devices to a person other than the consumer; or

(B) the report is being provided to an insurance company for a purpose relating to engaging in the business of insurance other than property and casualty insurance.

(b) *Exempted cases.* The provisions of paragraphs (1) through (5) of subsection (a) of this section are not applicable in the case of any consumer credit report to be used in connection with

(1) a credit transaction involving, or which may reasonably be expected to involve, a principal amount of $150,000 or more;

(2) the underwriting of life insurance involving, or which may reasonably be expected to involve, a face amount of $150,000 or more; or

(3) the employment of any individual at an annual salary which equals, or which may reasonably be expected to equal $75,000, or more.

(c) Running of Reporting Period

(1) *In general.* The 7-year period referred to in paragraphs (4) and (6)2 of subsection (a) shall begin, with respect to any delinquent account that is placed for collection (internally or by referral to a third party, whichever is earlier), charged to profit and loss, or subjected to any similar action, upon the expiration of the 180-day period beginning on the date of the commencement of the delinquency which immediately preceded the collection activity, charge to profit and loss, or similar action.

(2) *Effective date.* Paragraph (1) shall apply only to items of information added to the file of a consumer on or after the date that is 455 days after the date of enactment of the Consumer Credit Reporting Reform Act of 1996.

(d) Information Required to be Disclosed

(1) *Title 11 information.* Any consumer reporting agency that furnishes a consumer report that contains information regarding any case involving the consumer that arises under title 11, United States Code, shall include in the report an identification of the chapter of such title 11 under which such case arises if provided by the source of the information. If any case arising or filed

---

[1] The reporting periods have been lengthened for certain adverse information pertaining to U.S. Government insured or guaranteed student loans, or pertaining to national direct student loans. See sections 430A(f) and 463(c)(3) of the Higher Education Act of 1965, 20 U.S.C. 1080a(f) and 20 U.S.C. 1087cc(c)(3), respectively.

[2] This provision, added in September 1996, should read "paragraphs (4) and *(5)*...." Prior Section 605(a)(6) was amended and re-designated as Section 605(a)(5) in November 1998. The current Section 605(a)(6), added in December 2003 and now containing no reference to any 7-year period, is obviously inapplicable.

under title 11, United States Code, is withdrawn by the consumer before a final judgment, the consumer reporting agency shall include in the report that such case or filing was withdrawn upon receipt of documentation certifying such withdrawal.

(2) *Key factor in credit score information.* Any consumer reporting agency that furnishes a consumer report that contains any credit score or any other risk score or predictor on any consumer shall include in the report a clear and conspicuous statement that a key factor (as defined in section 609(f)(2)(B)) that adversely affected such score or predictor was the number of enquiries, if such a predictor was in fact a key factor that adversely affected such score. This paragraph shall not apply to a check services company, acting as such, which issues authorizations for the purpose of approving or processing negotiable instruments, electronic fund transfers, or similar methods of payments, but only to the extent that such company is engaged in such activities.

(e) *Indication of closure of account by consumer.* If a consumer reporting agency is notified pursuant to section 623(a)(4) [§ 1681s-2] that a credit account of a consumer was voluntarily closed by the consumer, the agency shall indicate that fact in any consumer report that includes information related to the account.

(f) *Indication of dispute by consumer.* If a consumer reporting agency is notified pursuant to section 623(a)(3) [§ 1681s-2] that information regarding a consumer who was furnished to the agency is disputed by the consumer, the agency shall indicate that fact in each consumer report that includes the disputed information.

(g) Truncation of Credit Card and Debit Card Numbers

(1) *In general.* Except as otherwise provided in this subsection, no person that accepts credit cards or debit cards for the transaction of business shall print more than the last 5 digits of the card number or the expiration date upon any receipt provided to the cardholder at the point of the sale or transaction.

(2) *Limitation.* This subsection shall apply only to receipts that are electronically printed, and shall not apply to transactions in which the sole means of recording a credit card or debit card account number is by handwriting or by an imprint or copy of the card.

(3) *Effective date.* This subsection shall become effective--

(A) 3 years after the date of enactment of this subsection, with respect to any cash register or other machine or device that electronically prints receipts for credit card or debit card transactions that is in use before January 1, 2005; and

(B) 1 year after the date of enactment of this subsection, with respect to any cash register or other machine or device that electronically prints receipts for credit card or debit card transactions that is first put into use on or after January 1, 2005.

(h) Notice of Discrepancy in Address

(1) *In general.* If a person has requested a consumer report relating to a consumer from a consumer reporting agency described in section 603(p), the request includes an address for the consumer that substantially differs from the addresses in the file of the consumer, and the agency provides a consumer

report in response to the request, the consumer reporting agency shall notify the requester of the existence of the discrepancy.

(2) Regulations

    (A) *Regulations required.* The Federal banking agencies, the National Credit Union Administration, and the Commission shall jointly, with respect to the entities that are subject to their respective enforcement authority under section 621, prescribe regulations providing guidance regarding reasonable policies and procedures that a user of a consumer report should employ when such user has received a notice of discrepancy under paragraph (1).

    (B) *Policies and procedures to be included.* The regulations prescribed under subparagraph (A) shall describe reasonable policies and procedures for use by a user of a consumer report--

        (i) to form a reasonable belief that the user knows the identity of the person to whom the consumer report pertains; and

        (ii) if the user establishes a continuing relationship with the consumer, and the user regularly and in the ordinary course of business furnishes information to the consumer reporting agency from which the notice of discrepancy pertaining to the consumer was obtained, to reconcile the address of the consumer with the consumer reporting agency by furnishing such address to such consumer reporting agency as part of information regularly furnished by the user for the period in which the relationship is established.

§ 605A. Identity theft prevention; fraud alerts and active duty alerts [15 U.S.C. §1681c-1]

(a) One-call Fraud Alerts

    (1) *Initial alerts.* Upon the direct request of a consumer, or an individual acting on behalf of or as a personal representative of a consumer, who asserts in good faith a suspicion that the consumer has been or is about to become a victim of fraud or related crime, including identity theft, a consumer reporting agency described in section 603(p) that maintains a file on the consumer and has received appropriate proof of the identity of the requester shall--

    (A) include a fraud alert in the file of that consumer, and also provide that alert along with any credit score generated in using that file, for a period of not less than 90 days, beginning on the date of such request, unless the consumer or such representative requests that such fraud alert be removed before the end of such period, and the agency has received appropriate proof of the identity of the requester for such purpose; and

    (B) refer the information regarding the fraud alert under this paragraph to each of the other consumer reporting agencies described in section 603(p), in accordance with procedures developed under section 621(f).

(2) *Access to free reports.* In any case in which a consumer reporting agency includes a fraud alert in the file of a consumer pursuant to this subsection, the consumer reporting agency shall--

    (A) disclose to the consumer that the consumer may request a free copy of the file of the consumer pursuant to section 612(d); and

(B) provide to the consumer all disclosures required to be made under section 609, without charge to the consumer, not later than 3 business days after any request described in subparagraph (A).

(b) Extended Alerts

(1) *In general.* Upon the direct request of a consumer, or an individual acting on behalf of or as a personal representative of a consumer, who submits an identity theft report to a consumer reporting agency described in section 603(p) that maintains a file on the consumer, if the agency has received appropriate proof of the identity of the requester, the agency shall--

(A) include a fraud alert in the file of that consumer, and also provide that alert along with any credit score generated in using that file, during the 7-year period beginning on the date of such request, unless the consumer or such representative requests that such fraud alert be removed before the end of such period and the agency has received appropriate proof of the identity of the requester for such purpose;

(B) during the 5-year period beginning on the date of such request, exclude the consumer from any list of consumers prepared by the consumer reporting agency and provided to any third party to offer credit or insurance to the consumer as part of a transaction that was not initiated by the consumer, unless the consumer or such representative requests that such exclusion be rescinded before the end of such period; and

(C) refer the information regarding the extended fraud alert under this paragraph to each of the other consumer reporting agencies described in section 603(p), in accordance with procedures developed under section 621(f).

(2) *Access to free reports.* In any case in which a consumer reporting agency includes a fraud alert in the file of a consumer pursuant to this subsection, the consumer reporting agency shall--

(A) disclose to the consumer that the consumer may request 2 free copies of the file of the consumer pursuant to section 612(d) during the 12-month period beginning on the date on which the fraud alert was included in the file; and

(B) provide to the consumer all disclosures required to be made under section 609, without charge to the consumer, not later than 3 business days after any request described in subparagraph (A).

(c) *Active duty alerts.* Upon the direct request of an active duty military consumer, or an individual acting on behalf of or as a personal representative of an active duty military consumer, a consumer reporting agency described in section 603(p) that maintains a file on the active duty military consumer and has received appropriate proof of the identity of the requester shall--

(1) include an active duty alert in the file of that active duty military consumer, and also provide that alert along with any credit score generated in using that file, during a period of not less than 12 months, or such longer period as the Commission shall determine, by regulation, beginning on the date of the request, unless the active duty military consumer or such representative requests that such fraud alert be removed before the end of

such period, and the agency has received appropriate proof of the identity of the requester for such purpose;

(2) during the 2-year period beginning on the date of such request, exclude the active duty military consumer from any list of consumers prepared by the consumer reporting agency and provided to any third party to offer credit or insurance to the consumer as part of a transaction that was not initiated by the consumer, unless the consumer requests that such exclusion be rescinded before the end of such period; and

(3) refer the information regarding the active duty alert to each of the other consumer reporting agencies described in section 603(p), in accordance with procedures developed under section 621(f).

(d) *Procedures.* Each consumer reporting agency described in section 603(p) shall establish policies and procedures to comply with this section, including procedures that inform consumers of the availability of initial, extended, and active duty alerts and procedures that allow consumers and active duty military consumers to request initial, extended, or active duty alerts (as applicable) in a simple and easy manner, including by telephone.

(e) *Referrals of alerts.* Each consumer reporting agency described in section 603(p) that receives a referral of a fraud alert or active duty alert from another consumer reporting agency pursuant to this section shall, as though the agency received the request from the consumer directly, follow the procedures required under--

(1) paragraphs (1)(A) and (2) of subsection (a), in the case of a referral under subsection (a)(1)(B);

(2) paragraphs (1)(A), (1)(B), and (2) of subsection (b), in the case of a referral under subsection (b)(1)(C); and

(3) paragraphs (1) and (2) of subsection (c), in the case of a referral under subsection (c)(3).

(f) *Duty of reseller to reconvey alert.* A reseller shall include in its report any fraud alert or active duty alert placed in the file of a consumer pursuant to this section by another consumer reporting agency.

(g) *Duty of other consumer reporting agencies to provide contact information.* If a consumer contacts any consumer reporting agency that is not described in section 603(p) to communicate a suspicion that the consumer has been or is about to become a victim of fraud or related crime, including identity theft, the agency shall provide information to the consumer on how to contact the Commission and the consumer reporting agencies described in section 603(p) to obtain more detailed information and request alerts under this section.

(h) Limitations on Use of Information for Credit Extensions

(1) Requirements for initial and active duty alerts-

(A) *Notification.* Each initial fraud alert and active duty alert under this section shall include information that notifies all prospective users of a consumer report on the consumer to which the alert relates that the consumer does not authorize the establishment of any new credit plan or extension of credit, other than under an open-end credit plan (as defined in section 103(i)), in the name of the consumer, or issuance of an additional card on an existing credit account requested by a consumer, or any increase in credit limit on an existing credit account requested by a consumer, except in accordance with subparagraph (B).

(B) Limitation on Users

(i) *In general.* No prospective user of a consumer report that includes an initial fraud alert or an active duty alert in accordance with this section may establish a new credit plan or extension of credit, other than under an open-end credit plan (as defined in section 103(i)), in the name of the consumer, or issue an additional card on an existing credit account requested by a consumer, or grant any increase in credit limit on an existing credit account requested by a consumer, unless the user utilizes reasonable policies and procedures to form a reasonable belief that the user knows the identity of the person making the request.

(ii) *Verification.* If a consumer requesting the alert has specified a telephone number to be used for identity verification purposes, before authorizing any new credit plan or extension described in clause (i) in the name of such consumer, a user of such consumer report shall contact the consumer using that telephone number or take reasonable steps to verify the consumer's identity and confirm that the application for a new credit plan is not the result of identity theft.

(2) Requirements for Extended Alerts

(A) *Notification.* Each extended alert under this section shall include information that provides all prospective users of a consumer report relating to a consumer with–

(i) notification that the consumer does not authorize the establishment of any new credit plan or extension of credit described in clause (i), other than under an open-end credit plan (as defined in section 103(i)), in the name of the consumer, or issuance of an additional card on an existing credit account requested by a consumer, or any increase in credit limit on an existing credit account requested by a consumer, except in accordance with subparagraph (B); and

(ii) a telephone number or other reasonable contact method designated by the consumer.

(B) *Limitation on users.* No prospective user of a consumer report or of a credit score generated using the information in the file of a consumer that includes an extended fraud alert in accordance with this section may establish a new credit plan or extension of credit, other than under an open-end credit plan (as defined in section 103(i)), in the name of the consumer, or issue an additional card on an existing credit account requested by a consumer, or any increase in credit limit on an existing credit account requested by a consumer, unless the user contacts the consumer in person or using the contact method described in subparagraph (A)(ii) to confirm that the application for a new credit plan or increase in credit limit, or request for an additional card is not the result of identity theft.

§ 605B. Block of information resulting from identity theft [15 U.S.C. §1681c-2]

(a) *Block*. Except as otherwise provided in this section, a consumer reporting agency shall block the reporting of any information in the file of a consumer that the consumer identifies as information that resulted from an alleged identity theft, not later than 4 business days after the date of receipt by such agency of--

(1) appropriate proof of the identity of the consumer;

(2) a copy of an identity theft report;

(3) the identification of such information by the consumer; and

(4) a statement by the consumer that the information is not information relating to any transaction by the consumer.

(b) *Notification*. A consumer reporting agency shall promptly notify the furnisher of information identified by the consumer under subsection (a)—

(1) that the information may be a result of identity theft;

(2) that an identity theft report has been filed;

(3) that a block has been requested under this section; and

(4) of the effective dates of the block.

(c) Authority to Decline or Rescind

(1) *In general*. A consumer reporting agency may decline to block, or may rescind any block, of information relating to a consumer under this section, if the consumer reporting agency reasonably determines that--

(A) the information was blocked in error or a block was requested by the consumer in error;

(B) the information was blocked, or a block was requested by the consumer, on the basis of a material misrepresentation of fact by the consumer relevant to the request to block; or

(C) the consumer obtained possession of goods, services, or money as a result of the blocked transaction or transactions.

(2) *Notification to consumer*. If a block of information is declined or rescinded under this subsection, the affected consumer shall be notified promptly, in the same manner as consumers are notified of the reinsertion of information under section 611(a)(5)(B).

(3) *Significance of block*. For purposes of this subsection, if a consumer reporting agency rescinds a block, the presence of information in the file of a consumer prior to the blocking of such information is not evidence of whether the consumer knew or should have known that the consumer obtained possession of any goods, services, or money as a result of the block.

(d) Exception for Resellers

(1) *No reseller file*. This section shall not apply to a consumer reporting agency, if the consumer reporting agency--

(A) is a reseller;

(B) is not, at the time of the request of the consumer under subsection (a), otherwise furnishing or reselling a consumer report concerning the information identified by the consumer; and

(C) informs the consumer, by any means, that the consumer may report the identity theft to the Commission to obtain consumer information regarding identity theft.

(2) *Reseller with file.* The sole obligation of the consumer reporting agency under this section, with regard to any request of a consumer under this section, shall be to block the consumer report maintained by the consumer reporting agency from any subsequent use, if--

(A) the consumer, in accordance with the provisions of subsection (a), identifies, to a consumer reporting agency, information in the file of the consumer that resulted from identity theft; and

(B) the consumer reporting agency is a reseller of the identified information.

(3) *Notice.* In carrying out its obligation under paragraph (2), the reseller shall promptly provide a notice to the consumer of the decision to block the file. Such notice shall contain the name, address, and telephone number of each consumer reporting agency from which the consumer information was obtained for resale.

(e) *Exception for verification companies.* The provisions of this section do not apply to a check services company, acting as such, which issues authorizations for the purpose of approving or processing negotiable instruments, electronic fund transfers, or similar methods of payments, except that, beginning 4 business days after receipt of information described in paragraphs (1) through (3) of subsection (a), a check services company shall not report to a national consumer reporting agency described in section 603(p), any information identified in the subject identity theft report as resulting from identity theft.

(f) *Access to blocked information by law enforcement agencies.* No provision of this section shall be construed as requiring a consumer reporting agency to prevent a Federal, State, or local law enforcement agency from accessing blocked information in a consumer file to which the agency could otherwise obtain access under this title.

§ 606. Disclosure of investigative consumer reports [15 U.S.C. § 1681d]

(a) *Disclosure of fact of preparation.* A person may not procure or cause to be prepared an investigative consumer report on any consumer unless

(1) it is clearly and accurately disclosed to the consumer that an investigative consumer report including information as to his character, general reputation, personal characteristics and mode of living, whichever are applicable, may be made, and such disclosure

(A) is made in a writing mailed, or otherwise delivered, to the consumer, not later than three days after the date on which the report was first requested, and

(B) includes a statement informing the consumer of his right to request the additional disclosures provided for under subsection (b) of this section and the written summary of the rights of the consumer prepared pursuant to section 609(c) [§ 1681g]; and

(2) the person certifies or has certified to the consumer reporting agency that

(A) the person has made the disclosures to the consumer required by paragraph(1); and

(B) the person will comply with subsection (b).

(b) *Disclosure on request of nature and scope of investigation.* Any person who procures or causes to be prepared an investigative consumer report on any consumer shall, upon written request made by the consumer within a reasonable period of time after the receipt by him of the disclosure required by subsection (a)(1) of this section, make a complete and accurate disclosure of the nature and scope of the investigation requested. This disclosure shall be made in a writing mailed, or otherwise delivered, to the consumer not later than five days after the date on which the request for such disclosure was received from the consumer or such report was first requested, whichever is the later.

(c) *Limitation on liability upon showing of reasonable procedures for compliance with provisions.* No person may be held liable for any violation of subsection (a) or (b) of this section if he shows by a preponderance of the evidence that at the time of the violation he maintained reasonable procedures to assure compliance with subsection (a) or (b) of this section.

(d) Prohibitions

(1) *Certification.* A consumer reporting agency shall not prepare or furnish investigative consumer report unless the agency has received a certification under subsection (a)(2) from the person who requested the report.

(2) *Inquiries.* A consumer reporting agency shall not make an inquiry for the purpose of preparing an investigative consumer report on a consumer for employment purposes if the making of the inquiry by an employer or prospective employer of the consumer would violate any applicable Federal or State equal employment opportunity law or regulation.

(3) *Certain public record information.* Except as otherwise provided in section 613 [§ 1681k], a consumer reporting agency shall not furnish an investigative consumer report that includes information that is a matter of public record and that relates to an arrest, indictment, conviction, civil judicial action, tax lien, or out standing judgment, unless the agency has verified the accuracy of the information during the 30-day period ending on the date on which the report is furnished.

(4) *Certain adverse information.* A consumer reporting agency shall not prepare or furnish an investigative consumer report on a consumer that contains information that is adverse to the interest of the consumer and that is obtained through a personal interview with a neighbor, friend, or associate of the consumer or with another person with whom the consumer is acquainted or who has knowledge of such item of information, unless

(A) the agency has followed reasonable procedures to obtain confirmation of the information, from an additional source that has independent and direct knowledge of the information; or

(B) the person interviewed is the best possible source of the information.

§ 607. Compliance procedures [15 U.S.C. § 1681e]

(a) *Identity and purposes of credit users.* Every consumer reporting agency shall maintain reasonable procedures designed to avoid violations of section 605 [§ 1681c] and to limit the furnishing of consumer reports to the purposes listed under section 604 [§ 1681b] of this title. These procedures shall require that prospective users of the information identify themselves, certify the purposes for which the information is sought, and certify that the information will be used for no other purpose. Every consumer reporting agency shall make a reasonable effort to verify the identity of a new prospective user and the uses certified by such prospective user prior to furnishing such user a consumer report. No consumer reporting agency may furnish a consumer report to any person if it has reasonable grounds for believing that the consumer report will not be used for a purpose listed in section 604 [§ 1681b] of this title.

(b) *Accuracy of report*. Whenever a consumer reporting agency prepares a consumer report it shall follow reasonable procedures to assure maximum possible accuracy of the information concerning the individual about whom the report relates.

(c) *Disclosure of consumer reports by users allowed*. A consumer reporting agency may not prohibit a user of a consumer report furnished by the agency on a consumer from disclosing the contents of the report to the consumer, if adverse action against the consumer has been taken by the user based in whole or in part on the report.

(d) Notice to Users and Furnishers of Information

(1) *Notice requirement*. A consumer reporting agency shall provide to any person

(A) who regularly and in the ordinary course of business furnishes information to the agency with respect to any consumer; or

(B) to whom a consumer report is provided by the agency;

a notice of such person's responsibilities under this title.

(2) *Content of notice*. The Federal Trade Commission shall prescribe the content of notices under paragraph (1), and a consumer reporting agency shall be in compliance with this subsection if it provides a notice under paragraph (1) that is substantially similar to the Federal Trade Commission prescription under this paragraph.

(e) Procurement of Consumer Report for Resale

(1) *Disclosure*. A person may not procure a consumer report for purposes of reselling the report (or any information in the report) unless the person discloses to the consumer reporting agency that originally furnishes the report

(A) the identity of the end-user of the report (or information); and

(B) each permissible purpose under section 604 [§ 1681b] for which the report is furnished to the end-user of the report (or information).

(2) *Responsibilities of procurers for resale*. A person who procures a consumer report for purposes of reselling the report (or any information in the report) shall

(A) establish and comply with reasonable procedures designed to ensure that the report (or information) is resold by the person only for a purpose for which the report may be furnished under section 604 [§ 1681b], including by requiring that each person to which the report (or information) is resold and that resells or provides the report (or information) to any other person

(i) identifies each end user of the resold report (or information);

(ii) certifies each purpose for which the report (or information) will be used; and

(iii) certifies that the report (or information) will be used for no other purpose; and

(B) before reselling the report, make reasonable efforts to verify the identifications and certifications made under subparagraph (A).

(3) *Resale of consumer report to a federal agency or department.* Notwithstanding paragraph (1) or (2), a person who procures a consumer report for purposes of reselling the report (or any information in the report) shall not disclose the identity of the end-user of the report under paragraph (1) or (2) if--

(A) the end user is an agency or department of the United States Government which procures the report from the person for purposes of determining the eligibility of the consumer concerned to receive access or continued access to classified information (as defined in section 604(b)(4)(E)(i)); and

(B) the agency or department certifies in writing to the person reselling the report that nondisclosure is necessary to protect classified information or the safety of persons employed by or contracting with, or undergoing investigation for work or contracting with the agency or department.

§ 608. Disclosures to governmental agencies [15 U.S.C. § 1681f]

Notwithstanding the provisions of section 604 [§ 1681b] of this title, a consumer reporting agency may furnish identifying information respecting any consumer, limited to his name, address, former addresses, places of employment, or former places of employment, to a governmental agency.

§ 609. Disclosures to consumers [15 U.S.C. § 1681g]

(a) *Information on file; sources; report recipients.* Every consumer reporting agency shall, upon request, and subject to 610(a)(1) [§ 1681h], clearly and accurately disclose to the consumer:

(1) All information in the consumer's file at the time of the request except that--

(A) if the consumer to whom the file relates requests that the first 5 digits of the social security number (or similar identification number) of the consumer not be included in the disclosure and the consumer reporting agency has received appropriate proof of the identity of the requester, the consumer reporting agency shall so truncate such number in such disclosure; and

(B) nothing in this paragraph shall be construed to require a consumer reporting agency to disclose to a consumer any information concerning credit scores or any other risk scores or predictors relating to the consumer.

(2) The sources of the information; except that the sources of information acquired solely for use in preparing an investigative consumer report and actually use for no other purpose need not be disclosed: Provided, That in the

event an action is brought under this title, such sources shall be available to the plaintiff under appropriate discovery procedures in the court in which the action is brought.

(3) (A) Identification of each person (including each end-user identified under section 607(e)(1) [§ 1681e]) that procured a consumer report

(i) for employment purposes, during the 2-year period preceding the date on which the request is made; or

(ii) for any other purpose, during the 1-year period preceding the date on which the request is made.

(B) An identification of a person under subparagraph (A) shall include

(i) the name of the person or, if applicable, the trade name (written in full) under which such person conducts business; and

(ii) upon request of the consumer, the address and telephone number of the person.

(C) Subparagraph (A) does not apply if--

(i) the end user is an agency or department of the United States Government that procures the report from the person for purposes of determining the eligibility of the consumer to whom the report relates to receive access or continued access to classified information (as defined in section 604(b)(4)(E)(i)); and

(ii) the head of the agency or department makes a written finding as prescribed under section 604(b)(4)(A).

(4) The dates, original payees, and amounts of any checks upon which is based any adverse characterization of the consumer, included in the file at the time of the disclosure.

(5) A record of all inquiries received by the agency during the 1-year period preceding the request that identified the consumer in connection with a credit or insurance transaction that was not initiated by the consumer.

(6) If the consumer requests the credit file and not the credit score, a statement that the consumer may request and obtain a credit score.

(b) *Exempt information.* The requirements of subsection (a) of this section respecting the disclosure of sources of information and the recipients of consumer reports do not apply to information received or consumer reports furnished prior to the effective date of this title except to the extent that the matter involved is contained in the files of the consumer reporting agency on that date.

(c) Summary of Rights to Obtain and Dispute Information in Consumer Reports and to Obtain Credit Scores

(1) Commission Summary of Rights Required

(A) *In general.* The Commission shall prepare a model summary of the rights of consumers under this title.

(B) *Content of summary.* The summary of rights prepared under subparagraph (A) shall include a description of–

(i) the right of a consumer to obtain a copy of a consumer report under subsection (a) from each consumer reporting agency;

(ii) the frequency and circumstances under which a consumer is entitled to receive a consumer report without charge under section 612;

(iii) the right of a consumer to dispute information in the file of the consumer under section 611;

(iv) the right of a consumer to obtain a credit score from a consumer reporting agency, and a description of how to obtain a credit score;

(v) the method by which a consumer can contact, and obtain a consumer report from, a consumer reporting agency without charge, as provided in the regulations of the Commission prescribed under section 211(c)

of the Fair and Accurate Credit Transactions Act of 2003; and

(vi) the method by which a consumer can contact, and obtain a consumer report from, a consumer reporting agency described in section 603(w), as provided in the regulations of the Commission prescribed under section 612(a)(1)(C).

(C) *Availability of summary of rights.* The Commission shall--

(i) actively publicize the availability of the summary of rights prepared under this paragraph;

(ii) conspicuously post on its Internet website the availability of such summary of rights; and

(iii) promptly make such summary of rights available to consumers, on request.

(2) *Summary of rights required to be included with agency disclosures.* A consumer reporting agency shall provide to a consumer, with each written disclosure by the agency to the consumer under this section--

(A) the summary of rights prepared by the Commission under paragraph (1);

(B) in the case of a consumer reporting agency described in section 603(p), a toll-free telephone number established by the agency, at which personnel are accessible to consumers during normal business hours;

(C) a list of all Federal agencies responsible for enforcing any provision of this title, and the address and any appropriate phone number of each such agency, in a form that will assist the consumer in selecting the appropriate agency;

(D) a statement that the consumer may have additional rights under State law, and that the consumer may wish to contact a State or local consumer protection agency or a State attorney general (or the equivalent thereof) to learn of those rights; and

(E) a statement that a consumer reporting agency is not required to remove accurate derogatory information from the file of a consumer, unless the information is outdated under section 605 or cannot be verified.

(d) Summary of Rights of Identity Theft Victims

(1) *In general.* The Commission, in consultation with the Federal banking agencies and the National Credit Union Administration, shall prepare a model summary of the rights of consumers under this title with respect to the procedures for remedying the effects of fraud or identity theft involving credit, an electronic fund transfer, or an account or transaction at or with a financial institution or other creditor.

(2) *Summary of rights and contact information.* Beginning 60 days after the date on which the model summary of rights is prescribed in final form by the Commission pursuant to paragraph (1), if any consumer contacts a consumer reporting agency and expresses a belief that the consumer is a victim of fraud or identity theft involving credit, an electronic fund transfer, or an account or transaction at or with a financial institution or other creditor, the consumer reporting agency shall, in addition to any other action that the agency may take, provide the consumer with a summary of rights that contains all of the information required by the Commission under paragraph (1), and information on how to contact the Commission to obtain more detailed information.

(e) Information Available to Victims

(1) *In general.* For the purpose of documenting fraudulent transactions resulting from identity theft, not later than 30 days after the date of receipt of a request from a victim in accordance with paragraph (3), and subject to verification of the identity of the victim and the claim of identity theft in accordance with paragraph (2), a business entity that has provided credit to, provided for consideration products, goods, or services to, accepted payment from, or otherwise entered into a commercial transaction for consideration with, a person who has allegedly made unauthorized use of the means of identification of the victim, shall provide a copy of application and business transaction records in the control of the business entity, whether maintained by the business entity or by another person on behalf of the business entity, evidencing any transaction alleged to be a result of identity theft to--

(A) the victim;

(B) any Federal, State, or local government law enforcement agency or officer specified by the victim in such a request; or

(C) any law enforcement agency investigating the identity theft and authorized by the victim to take receipt of records provided under this subsection.

(2) *Verification of identity and claim.* Before a business entity provides any information under paragraph (1), unless the business entity, at its discretion, otherwise has a high degree of confidence that it knows the identity of the victim making a request under paragraph (1), the victim shall provide to the business entity--

(A) as proof of positive identification of the victim, at the election of the business entity–

(i) the presentation of a government-issued identification card;

(ii) personally identifying information of the same type as was provided to the business entity by the unauthorized person; or

(iii) personally identifying information that the business entity typically requests from new applicants or for new transactions, at the time of the victim's request for information, including any documentation described in clauses (i) and (ii); and

(B) as proof of a claim of identity theft, at the election of the business entity--

(i) a copy of a police report evidencing the claim of the victim of identity theft; and

(ii) a properly completed--

(I) copy of a standardized affidavit of identity theft developed and made available by the Commission; or

(II) an affidavit of fact that is acceptable to the business entity for that purpose.

(3) *Procedures.* The request of a victim under paragraph (1) shall--

(A) be in writing;

(B) be mailed to an address specified by the business entity, if any; and

(C) if asked by the business entity, include relevant information about any transaction alleged to be a result of identity theft to facilitate compliance with this section including–

(i) if known by the victim (or if readily obtainable by the victim), the date of the application or transaction; and

(ii) if known by the victim (or if readily obtainable by the victim), any other identifying information such as an account or transaction number.

(4) *No charge to victim.* Information required to be provided under paragraph (1) shall be so provided without charge.

(5) *Authority to decline to provide information.* A business entity may decline to provide information under paragraph (1) if, in the exercise of good faith, the business entity determines that--

(A) this subsection does not require disclosure of the information;

(B) after reviewing the information provided pursuant to paragraph (2), the business entity does not have a high degree of confidence in knowing the true identity of the individual requesting the information;

(C) the request for the information is based on a misrepresentation of fact by the individual requesting the information relevant to the request for information; or

(D) the information requested is Internet navigational data or similar information about a person's visit to a website or online service.

(6) *Limitation on liability.* Except as provided in section 621, sections 616 and 617 do not apply to any violation of this subsection.

(7) *Limitation on civil liability.* No business entity may be held civilly liable under any provision of Federal, State, or other law for disclosure, made in good faith pursuant to this subsection.

(8) *No new recordkeeping obligation.* Nothing in this subsection creates an obligation on the part of a business entity to obtain, retain, or maintain information or records that are not otherwise required to be obtained, retained, or maintained in the ordinary course of its business or under other applicable law.

(9) Rule of Construction

(A) *In general.* No provision of subtitle A of title V of Public Law 106-102, prohibiting the disclosure of financial information by a business entity to third parties shall be used to deny disclosure of information to the victim under this subsection.

(B) *Limitation.* Except as provided in subparagraph (A), nothing in this subsection permits a business entity to disclose information, including information to law enforcement under subparagraphs (B) and (C) of paragraph (1), that the business entity is otherwise prohibited from disclosing under any other applicable provision of Federal or State law.

(10) *Affirmative defense.* In any civil action brought to enforce this subsection, it is an affirmative defense (which the defendant must establish by a preponderance of the evidence) for a business entity to file an affidavit or answer stating that--

(A) the business entity has made a reasonably diligent search of its available business records; and

(B) the records requested under this subsection do not exist or are not reasonably available.

(11) *Definition of victim.* For purposes of this subsection, the term "victim" means a consumer whose means of identification or financial information has been used or transferred (or has been alleged to have been used or transferred) without the authority of that consumer, with the intent to commit, or to aid or abet, an identity theft or a similar crime.

(12) *Effective date.* This subsection shall become effective 180 days after the date of enactment of this subsection.

(13) *Effectiveness study.* Not later than 18 months after the date of enactment of this subsection, the Comptroller General of the United States shall submit a report to Congress assessing the effectiveness of this provision.

(f) Disclosure of Credit Scores

(1) *In general.* Upon the request of a consumer for a credit score, a consumer reporting agency shall supply to the consumer a statement indicating that the information and credit scoring model may be different than the credit score that may be used by the lender, and a notice which shall include--

(A) the current credit score of the consumer or the most recent credit score of the consumer that was previously calculated by the credit reporting agency for a purpose related to the extension of credit;

(B) the range of possible credit scores under the model used;

(C) all of the key factors that adversely affected the credit score of the consumer in the model used, the total number of which shall not exceed 4, subject to paragraph (9);

(D) the date on which the credit score was created; and

(E) the name of the person or entity that provided the credit score or credit file upon which the credit score was created.

(2) *Definitions.* For purposes of this subsection, the following definitions shall apply:

(A) The term "credit score" --

(i) means a numerical value or a categorization derived from a statistical tool or modeling system used by a person who makes or arranges a loan to predict the likelihood of certain credit behaviors, including default (and the numerical value or the categorization derived from such analysis may also be referred to as a "risk predictor" or "risk score"); and

(ii) does not include--

(I) any mortgage score or rating of an automated underwriting system that considers one or more factors in addition to credit information, including the loan to value ratio, the amount of down payment, or the financial assets of a consumer; or

(II) any other elements of the underwriting process or underwriting decision.

(B) The term "key factors" means all relevant elements or reasons adversely affecting the credit score for the particular individual, listed in the order of their importance based on their effect on the credit score.

(3) *Timeframe and manner of disclosure.* The information required by this subsection shall be provided in the same timeframe and manner as the information described in subsection (a).

(4) *Applicability to certain uses.* This subsection shall not be construed so as to compel a consumer reporting agency to develop or disclose a score if the agency does not—

(A) distribute scores that are used in connection with residential real property loans; or

(B) develop scores that assist credit providers in understanding the general credit behavior of a consumer and predicting the future credit behavior of the consumer.

(5) Applicability to credit scores developed by another person.

(A) *In general.* This subsection shall not be construed to require a consumer reporting agency that distributes credit scores developed by another person or entity to provide a further explanation of them, or to process a dispute arising pursuant to section 611, except that the consumer reporting agency shall provide the consumer with the name and address and website for contacting the person or entity who developed the score or developed the methodology of the score.

(B) *Exception.* This paragraph shall not apply to a consumer reporting agency that develops or modifies scores that are developed by another person or entity.

(6) *Maintenance of credit scores not required.* This subsection shall not be construed to require a consumer reporting agency to maintain credit scores in its files.

(7) *Compliance in certain cases.* In complying with this subsection, a consumer reporting agency shall--

(A) supply the consumer with a credit score that is derived from a credit scoring model that is widely distributed to users by that consumer reporting agency in connection with residential real property loans or with a credit score that assists the consumer in understanding the credit scoring assessment of the credit behavior of the consumer and predictions about the future credit behavior of the consumer; and

(B) a statement indicating that the information and credit scoring model may be different than that used by the lender.

(8) *Fair and reasonable fee.* A consumer reporting agency may charge a fair and reasonable fee, as determined by the Commission, for providing the information required under this subsection.

(9) *Use of enquiries as a key factor.* If a key factor that adversely affects the credit score of a consumer consists of the number of enquiries made with respect to a consumer report, that factor shall be included in the disclosure pursuant to paragraph (1)(C) without regard to the numerical limitation in such paragraph.

(g) Disclosure of Credit Scores by Certain Mortgage Lenders

(1) *In general.* Any person who makes or arranges loans and who uses a consumer credit score, as defined in subsection (f), in connection with an application initiated or sought by a consumer for a closed end loan or the establishment of an open end loan for a consumer purpose that is secured by 1 to 4 units of residential real property (hereafter in this subsection referred to as the "lender") shall provide the following to the consumer as soon as reasonably practicable:

(A) Information Required under Subsection (f)

(i) *In general.* A copy of the information identified in subsection (f) that was obtained from a consumer reporting agency or was developed and used by the user of the information.

(ii) *Notice under subparagraph (D).* In addition to the information provided to it by a third party that provided the credit score or scores, a lender is only required to provide the notice contained in subparagraph (D).

(B) Disclosures in Case of Automated Underwriting System

(i) *In general.* If a person that is subject to this subsection uses an automated underwriting system to underwrite a loan, that person may satisfy the obligation to provide a credit score by disclosing a credit score and associated key factors supplied by a consumer reporting agency.

(ii) *Numerical credit score.* However, if a numerical credit score is generated by an automated underwriting system used by an enterprise, and that score is disclosed to the person, the score shall be disclosed to the consumer consistent with subparagraph (C).

(iii) *Enterprise defined.* For purposes of this subparagraph, the term "enterprise" has the same meaning as in paragraph (6) of section 1303 of the Federal Housing Enterprises Financial Safety and Soundness Act of 1992.

(C) *Disclosures of credit scores not obtained from a consumer reporting agency.* A person that is subject to the provisions of this subsection and that uses a credit score, other than a credit score provided by a consumer reporting agency, may satisfy the obligation to provide a credit score by disclosing a credit score and associated key factors supplied by a consumer reporting agency.

(D) *Notice to home loan applicants.* A copy of the following notice, which shall include the name, address, and telephone number of each consumer reporting agency providing a credit score that was used:

"Notice To The Home Loan Applicant

"In connection with your application for a home loan, the lender must disclose to you the score that a consumer reporting agency distributed to users and the lender used in connection with your home loan, and the key factors affecting your credit scores.

"The credit score is a computer generated summary calculated at the time of the request and based on information that a consumer reporting agency or lender has on file. The scores are based on data about your credit history and payment patterns. Credit scores are important because they are used to assist the lender in determining whether you will obtain a loan. They may also be used to determine what interest rate you may be offered on the mortgage. Credit scores can change over time, depending on your conduct, how your credit history and payment patterns change, and how credit scoring technologies change.

"Because the score is based on information in your credit history, it is very important that you review the credit-related information that is being furnished to make sure it is accurate. Credit records may vary from one company to another.

"If you have questions about your credit score or the credit information that is furnished to you, contact the consumer reporting agency at the address and telephone number provided with this notice, or contact the lender, if the lender developed or generated the credit score. The consumer reporting agency plays no part in the decision to take any action on the loan application and is unable to provide you with specific reasons for the decision on a loan application.

"If you have questions concerning the terms of the loan, contact the lender."

(E) *Actions not required under this subsection.* This subsection shall not require any person to–

(i) explain the information provided pursuant to subsection (f);

(ii) disclose any information other than a credit score or key factors, as defined in subsection (f);

(iii) disclose any credit score or related information obtained by the user after a loan has closed;

(iv) provide more than 1 disclosure per loan transaction; or

(v) provide the disclosure required by this subsection when another person has made the disclosure to the consumer for that loan transaction.

(F) No Obligation for Content

(i) *In general.* The obligation of any person pursuant to this subsection shall be limited solely to providing a copy of the information that was received from the consumer reporting agency.

(ii) *Limit on liability.* No person has liability under this subsection for the content of that information or for the omission of any information within the report provided by the consumer reporting agency.

(G) *Person defined as excluding enterprise.* As used in this subsection, the term "person" does not include an enterprise (as defined in paragraph (6) of section 1303 of the Federal Housing Enterprises Financial Safety and Soundness Act of 1992).

(2) Prohibition on Disclosure Clauses Null and Void

(A) *In general.* Any provision in a contract that prohibits the disclosure of a credit score by a person who makes or arranges loans or a consumer reporting agency is void.

(B) *No liability for disclosure under this subsection-* A lender shall not have liability under any contractual provision for disclosure of a credit score pursuant to this subsection.

§ 610. Conditions and form of disclosure to consumers [15 U.S.C. § 1681h]

(a) In General

(1) *Proper identification.* A consumer reporting agency shall require, as a condition of making the disclosures required under section 609 [§ 1681g], that the consumer furnish proper identification.

(2) *Disclosure in writing.* Except as provided in subsection (b), the disclosures required to be made under section 609 [§ 1681g] shall be provided under that section in writing.

(b) Other Forms of Disclosure

(1) *In general.* If authorized by a consumer, a consumer reporting agency may make the disclosures required under 609 [§ 1681g]

(A) other than in writing; and

(B) in such form as may be

(i) specified by the consumer in accordance with paragraph (2); and

(ii) available from the agency.

(2) *Form.* A consumer may specify pursuant to paragraph (1) that disclosures under section 609 [§ 1681g] shall be made

(A) in person, upon the appearance of the consumer at the place of business of the consumer reporting agency where disclosures are regularly provided, during normal business hours, and on reasonable notice;

(B) by telephone, if the consumer has made a written request for disclosure by telephone;

(C) by electronic means, if available from the agency; or

(D) by any other reasonable means that is available from the agency.

(c) *Trained personnel.* Any consumer reporting agency shall provide trained personnel to explain to the consumer any information furnished to him pursuant to section 609 [§ 1681g] of this title.

(d) *Persons accompanying consumer.* The consumer shall be permitted to be accompanied by one other person of his choosing, who shall furnish reasonable identification. A consumer reporting agency may require the consumer to furnish a written statement granting permission to the consumer reporting agency to discuss the consumer's file in such person's presence.

(e) *Limitation of liability.* Except as provided in sections 616 and 617 [§§ 1681n and 1681o] of this title, no consumer may bring any action or proceeding in the nature of defamation, invasion of privacy, or negligence with respect to the reporting of information against any consumer reporting agency, any user of information, or any person who furnishes information to a consumer reporting agency, based on information disclosed pursuant to section 609, 610, or 615 [§§ 1681g, 1681h, or 1681m] of this title or based on information disclosed by a user of a consumer report to or for a consumer against whom the user has taken adverse action, based in whole or in part on the report, except as to false information furnished with malice or willful intent to injure such consumer.

§ 611. Procedure in case of disputed accuracy [15 U.S.C. § 1681i]

(a) Reinvestigations of Disputed Information

   (1) Reinvestigation Required

      (A) *In general.* Subject to subsection (f), if the completeness or accuracy of any item of information contained in a consumer's file at a consumer reporting agency is disputed by the consumer and the consumer notifies the agency directly, or indirectly through a reseller, of such dispute, the agency shall, free of charge, conduct a reasonable reinvestigation to determine whether the disputed information is inaccurate and record the current status of the disputed information, or delete the item from the file in accordance with paragraph (5), before the end of the 30-day period beginning on the date on which the agency receives the notice of the dispute from the consumer or reseller.

      (B) *Extension of period to reinvestigate.* Except as provided in subparagraph (C), the 30-day period described in subparagraph (A) may be extended for not more than 15 additional days if the consumer reporting agency receives information from the consumer during that 30-day period that is relevant to the reinvestigation.

      (C) *Limitations on extension of period to reinvestigate.* Subparagraph (B) shall not apply to any reinvestigation in which, during the 30-day period described in subparagraph (A), the information that is the subject of the reinvestigation is found to be inaccurate or incomplete or the consumer reporting agency determines that the information cannot be verified.

   (2) Prompt Notice of Dispute to Furnisher of Information

      (A) *In general.* Before the expiration of the 5-business-day period beginning on the date on which a consumer reporting agency receives notice of a dispute from any consumer or a reseller in accordance with paragraph (1), the agency shall provide notification of the dispute to any person who provided any item of information in dispute, at the address and in the manner established with the person. The notice shall include all relevant information regarding the dispute that the agency has received from the consumer or reseller.

      (B) *Provision of other information.* The consumer reporting agency shall promptly provide to the person who provided the information in dispute all relevant information regarding the dispute that is received by the agency from the consumer or the reseller after the period referred to in subparagraph (A) and before the end of the period referred to in paragraph (1)(A).

(3) Determination That Dispute Is Frivolous or Irrelevant

(A) *In general.* Notwithstanding paragraph (1), a consumer reporting agency may terminate a reinvestigation of information disputed by a consumer under that paragraph if the agency reasonably determines that the dispute by the consumer is frivolous or irrelevant, including by reason of a failure by a consumer to provide sufficient information to investigate the disputed information.

(B) *Notice of determination.* Upon making any determination in accordance with subparagraph (A) that a dispute is frivolous or irrelevant, a consumer reporting agency shall notify the consumer of such determination not later than 5 business days after making such determination, by mail or, if authorized by the consumer for that purpose, by any other means available to the agency.

(C) *Contents of notice.* A notice under subparagraph (B) shall include

(i) the reasons for the determination under subparagraph (A); and

(ii) identification of any information required to investigate the disputed information, which may consist of a standardized form describing the general nature of such information.

(4) *Consideration of consumer information.* In conducting any reinvestigation under paragraph (1) with respect to disputed information in the file of any consumer, the consumer reporting agency shall review and consider all relevant information submitted by the consumer in the period described in paragraph (1)(A) with respect to such disputed information.

(5) Treatment of Inaccurate or Unverifiable Information

(A) *In general.* If, after any reinvestigation under paragraph (1) of any information disputed by a consumer, an item of the information is found to be inaccurate or incomplete or cannot be verified, the consumer reporting agency shall–

(i) promptly delete that item of information from the file of the consumer, or modify that item of information, as appropriate, based on the results of the reinvestigation; and

(ii) promptly notify the furnisher of that information that the information has been modified or deleted from the file of the consumer.

(B) *Requirements Relating to Reinsertion of Previously Deleted Material*

(i) Certification of accuracy of information. If any information is deleted from a consumer's file pursuant to subparagraph (A), the information may not be reinserted in the file by the consumer reporting agency unless the person who furnishes the information certifies that the information is complete and accurate.

(ii) Notice to consumer. If any information that has been deleted from a consumer's file pursuant to subparagraph (A) is reinserted in the file, the consumer reporting agency shall notify the consumer of the reinsertion in writing not later than 5 business days after the reinsertion or, if authorized by the consumer for that purpose, by any other means available to the agency.

(iii) Additional information. As part of, or in addition to, the notice under clause (ii), a consumer reporting agency shall provide to a consumer in writing not later than 5 business days after the date of the reinsertion

(I) a statement that the disputed information has been reinserted;

(II) the business name and address of any furnisher of information contacted and the telephone number of such furnisher, if reasonably available, or of any furnisher of information that contacted the consumer reporting agency, in connection with the reinsertion of such information; and

(III) a notice that the consumer has the right to add a statement to the consumer's file disputing the accuracy or completeness of the disputed information.

(C) *Procedures to prevent reappearance.* A consumer reporting agency shall maintain reasonable procedures designed to prevent the reappearance in a consumer's file, and in consumer reports on the consumer, of information that is deleted pursuant to this paragraph (other than information that is reinserted in accordance with subparagraph (B)(i)).

(D) *Automated reinvestigation system.* Any consumer reporting agency that compiles and maintains files on consumers on a nationwide basis shall implement an automated system through which furnishers of information to that consumer reporting agency may report the results of a reinvestigation that finds incomplete or inaccurate information in a consumer's file to other such consumer reporting agencies.

(6) Notice of Results of Reinvestigation

(A) *In general.* A consumer reporting agency shall provide written notice to a consumer of the results of a reinvestigation under this subsection not later than 5 business days after the completion of the reinvestigation, by mail or, if authorized by the consumer for that purpose, by other means available to the agency.

(B) *Contents.* As part of, or in addition to, the notice under subparagraph (A), a consumer reporting agency shall provide to a consumer in writing before the expiration of the 5-day period referred to in subparagraph (A)

(i) a statement that the reinvestigation is completed;

(ii) a consumer report that is based upon the consumer's file as that file is revised as a result of the reinvestigation;

(iii) a notice that, if requested by the consumer, a description of the procedure used to determine the accuracy and completeness of the information shall be provided to the consumer by the agency, including the business name and address of any furnisher of information contacted in connection with such information and the telephone number of such furnisher, if reasonably available;

(iv) a notice that the consumer has the right to add a statement to the consumer's file disputing the accuracy or completeness of the information; and

(v) a notice that the consumer has the right to request under subsection (d) that the consumer reporting agency furnish notifications under that subsection.

(7) *Description of reinvestigation procedure.* A consumer reporting agency shall provide to a consumer a description referred to in paragraph (6)(B)(iii) by not later than 15 days after receiving a request from the consumer for that description.

(8) *Expedited dispute resolution.* If a dispute regarding an item of information in a consumer's file at a consumer reporting agency is resolved in accordance with paragraph (5)(A) by the deletion of the disputed information by not later than 3 business days after the date on which the agency receives notice of the dispute from the consumer in accordance with paragraph (1)(A), then the agency shall not be required to comply with paragraphs (2), (6), and (7) with respect to that dispute if the agency

(A) provides prompt notice of the deletion to the consumer by telephone;

(B) includes in that notice, or in a written notice that accompanies a confirmation and consumer report provided in accordance with subparagraph (C), a statement of the consumer's right to request under subsection (d) that the agency furnish notifications under that subsection; and

(C) provides written confirmation of the deletion and a copy of a consumer report on the consumer that is based on the consumer's file after the deletion, not later than 5 business days after making the deletion.

(b) *Statement of dispute.* If the reinvestigation does not resolve the dispute, the consumer may file a brief statement setting forth the nature of the dispute. The consumer reporting agency may limit such statements to not more than one hundred words if it provides the consumer with assistance in writing a clear summary of the dispute.

(c) *Notification of consumer dispute in subsequent consumer reports.* Whenever a statement of a dispute is filed, unless there is reasonable grounds to believe that it is frivolous or irrelevant, the consumer reporting agency shall, in any subsequent report containing the information in question, clearly note that it is disputed by the consumer and provide either the consumer's statement or a clear and accurate codification or summary thereof.

(d) *Notification of deletion of disputed information.* Following any deletion of information which is found to be inaccurate or whose accuracy can no longer be verified or any notation as to disputed information, the consumer reporting agency shall, at the request of the consumer, furnish notification that the item has been deleted or the statement, codification or summary pursuant to subsection (b) or (c) of this section to any person specifically designated by the consumer who has within two years prior thereto received a consumer report for employment purposes, or within six months prior thereto received a consumer report for any other purpose, which contained the deleted or disputed information.

(e) Treatment of Complaints and Report to Congress

   (1) *In general*. The Commission shall--

      (A) compile all complaints that it receives that a file of a consumer that is maintained by a consumer reporting agency described in section 603(p) contains incomplete or inaccurate information, with respect to which, the consumer appears to have disputed the completeness or accuracy with the consumer reporting agency or otherwise utilized the procedures provided by subsection (a); and (B) transmit each such complaint to each consumer reporting agency involved.

   (2) *Exclusion*. Complaints received or obtained by the Commission pursuant to its investigative authority under the Federal Trade Commission Act shall not be subject to paragraph (1).

   (3) *Agency responsibilities*. Each consumer reporting agency described in section 603(p) that receives a complaint transmitted by the Commission pursuant to paragraph (1) shall--

      (A) review each such complaint to determine whether all legal obligations imposed on the consumer reporting agency under this title (including any obligation imposed by an applicable court or administrative order) have been met with respect to the subject matter of the complaint;

      (B) provide reports on a regular basis to the Commission regarding the determinations of and actions taken by the consumer reporting agency, if any, in connection with its review of such complaints; and

      (C) maintain, for a reasonable time period, records regarding the disposition of each such complaint that is sufficient to demonstrate compliance with this subsection.

   (4) *Rulemaking authority*. The Commission may prescribe regulations, as appropriate to implement this subsection.

   (5) *Annual report*. The Commission shall submit to the Committee on Banking, Housing, and Urban Affairs of the Senate and the Committee on Financial Services of the House of Representatives an annual report regarding information gathered by the Commission under this subsection.

(f) Reinvestigation Requirement Applicable to Resellers

   (1) *Exemption from general reinvestigation requirement*. Except as provided in paragraph (2), a reseller shall be exempt from the requirements of this section.

   (2) *Action required upon receiving notice of a dispute*. If a reseller receives a notice from a consumer of a dispute concerning the completeness or accuracy of any item of information contained in a consumer report on such consumer produced by the reseller, the reseller shall, within 5 business days of receiving the notice, and free of charge–

      (A) determine whether the item of information is incomplete or inaccurate as a result of an act or omission of the reseller; and

      (B) if

         (i) the reseller determines that the item of information is incomplete or inaccurate as a result of an act or omission of the reseller, not later than 20 days after receiving the notice, correct the information in the consumer report or delete it; or

(ii) if the reseller determines that the item of information is not incomplete or inaccurate as a result of an act or omission of the reseller, convey the notice of the dispute, together with all relevant information provided by the consumer, to each consumer reporting agency that provided the reseller with the information that is the subject of the dispute, using an address or a notification mechanism specified by the consumer reporting agency for such notices.

(3) *Responsibility of consumer reporting agency to notify consumer through reseller.* Upon the completion of a reinvestigation under this section of a dispute concerning the completeness or accuracy of any information in the file of a consumer by a consumer reporting agency that received notice of the dispute from a reseller under paragraph (2)--

(A) the notice by the consumer reporting agency under paragraph (6), (7), or (8) of subsection (a) shall be provided to the reseller in lieu of the consumer; and

(B) the reseller shall immediately reconvey such notice to the consumer, including any notice of a deletion by telephone in the manner required under paragraph (8)(A).

(4) *Reseller reinvestigations.* No provision of this subsection shall be construed as prohibiting a reseller from conducting a reinvestigation of a consumer dispute directly.

§ 612. Charges for certain disclosures [15 U.S.C. § 1681j]

(a) Free Annual Disclosure

(1) Nationwide Consumer Reporting Agencies

(A) *In general.* All consumer reporting agencies described in subsections (p) and (w) of section 603 shall make all disclosures pursuant to section 609 once during any 12-month period upon request of the consumer and without charge to the consumer.

(B) *Centralized source.* Subparagraph (A) shall apply with respect to a consumer reporting agency described in section 603(p) only if the request from the consumer is made using the centralized source established for such purpose in accordance with section 211(c) of the Fair and Accurate Credit Transactions Act of 2003.

(C) Nationwide Specialty Consumer Reporting Agency

(i) *In general.* The Commission shall prescribe regulations applicable to each consumer reporting agency described in section 603(w) to require the establishment of a streamlined process for consumers to request consumer reports under subparagraph (A), which shall include, at a minimum, the establishment by each such agency of a toll-free telephone number for such requests.

(ii) *Considerations.* In prescribing regulations under clause (i), the Commission shall consider–

(I) the significant demands that may be placed on consumer reporting agencies in providing such consumer reports;

(II) appropriate means to ensure that consumer reporting agencies can satisfactorily meet those demands, including the efficacy of a system of staggering the availability to consumers of such consumer reports; and

(III) the ease by which consumers should be able to contact consumer reporting agencies with respect to access to such consumer reports.

(iii) *Date of issuance.* The Commission shall issue the regulations required by this subparagraph in final form not later than 6 months after the date of enactment of the Fair and Accurate Credit Transactions Act of 2003.

(iv) *Consideration of ability to comply.* The regulations of the Commission under this subparagraph shall establish an effective date by which each nationwide specialty consumer reporting agency (as defined in section 603(w)) shall be required to comply with subsection (a), which effective date--

(I) shall be established after consideration of the ability of each nationwide specialty consumer reporting agency to comply with subsection (a); and

(II) shall be not later than 6 months after the date on which such regulations are issued in final form (or such additional period not to exceed 3 months, as the Commission determines appropriate).

(2) *Timing.* A consumer reporting agency shall provide a consumer report under paragraph (1) not later than 15 days after the date on which the request is received under paragraph (1).

(3) *Reinvestigations.* Notwithstanding the time periods specified in section 611(a)(1), a reinvestigation under that section by a consumer reporting agency upon a request of a consumer that is made after receiving a consumer report under this subsection shall be completed not later than 45 days after the date on which the request is received.

(4) *Exception for first 12 months of operation.* This subsection shall not apply to a consumer reporting agency that has not been furnishing consumer reports to third parties on a continuing basis during the 12-month period preceding a request under paragraph (1), with respect to consumers residing nationwide.

(b) *Free disclosure after adverse notice to consumer.* Each consumer reporting agency that maintains a file on a consumer shall make all disclosures pursuant to section 609 [§ 1681g] without charge to the consumer if, not later than 60 days after receipt by such consumer of a notification pursuant to section 615 [§ 1681m], or of a notification from a debt collection agency affiliated with that consumer reporting agency stating that the consumer's credit rating may be or has been adversely affected, the consumer makes a request under section 609 [§ 1681g].

(c) *Free disclosure under certain other circumstances.* Upon the request of the consumer, a consumer reporting agency shall make all disclosures pursuant to section 609 [§ 1681g] once during any 12-month period without charge to that consumer if the consumer certifies in writing that the consumer

(1) is unemployed and intends to apply for employment in the 60-day period beginning on the date on which the certification is made;

(2) is a recipient of public welfare assistance; or

(3) has reason to believe that the file on the consumer at the agency contains inaccurate information due to fraud.

(d) *Free disclosures in connection with fraud alerts.* Upon the request of a consumer, a consumer reporting agency described in section 603(p) shall make all disclosures pursuant to section 609 without charge to the consumer, as provided in subsections (a)(2) and (b)(2) of section 605A, as applicable.

(e) *Other charges prohibited.* A consumer reporting agency shall not impose any charge on a consumer for providing any notification required by this title or making any disclosure required by this title, except as authorized by subsection (f).

(f) Reasonable Charges Allowed for Certain Disclosures

(1) *In general.* In the case of a request from a consumer other than a request that is covered by any of subsections (a) through (d), a consumer reporting agency may

impose a reasonable charge on a consumer

(A) for making a disclosure to the consumer pursuant to section 609 [§ 1681g], which charge

(i) shall not exceed $8;[3] and

(ii) shall be indicated to the consumer before making the disclosure; and

(B) for furnishing, pursuant to 611(d) [§ 1681i], following a reinvestigation under section 611(a) [§ 1681i], a statement, codification, or summary to a person designated by the consumer under that section after the 30-day period beginning on the date of notification of the consumer under paragraph (6) or (8) of section 611(a) [§ 1681i] with respect to the reinvestigation, which charge

(i) shall not exceed the charge that the agency would impose on each designated recipient for a consumer report; and

(ii) shall be indicated to the consumer before furnishing such information.

(2) *Modification of amount.* The Federal Trade Commission shall increase the amount referred to in paragraph (1)(A)(I) on January 1 of each year, based proportionally on changes in the Consumer Price Index, with fractional changes rounded to the nearest fifty cents.

---

[3] The Federal Trade Commission increased the maximum allowable charge to $9.00, effective January 1, 2002. 66 Fed. Reg. 63545 (Dec. 7, 2001).

§ 613. Public record information for employment purposes [15 U.S.C. § 1681k]

(a) *In general.* A consumer reporting agency which furnishes a consumer report for employment purposes and which for that purpose compiles and reports items of information on consumers which are matters of public record and are likely to have an adverse effect upon a consumer's ability to obtain employment shall

(1) at the time such public record information is reported to the user of such consumer report, notify the consumer of the fact that public record information is being reported by the consumer reporting agency, together with the name and address of the person to whom such information is being reported; or

(2) maintain strict procedures designed to insure that whenever public record information which is likely to have an adverse effect on a consumer's ability to obtain employment is reported it is complete and up to date. For purposes of this paragraph, items of public record relating to arrests, indictments, convictions, suits, tax liens, and outstanding judgments shall be considered up to date if the current public record status of the item at the time of the report is reported.

(b) *Exemption for national security investigations.* Subsection (a) does not apply in the case of an agency or department of the United States Government that seeks to obtain and use a consumer report for employment purposes, if the head of the agency or department makes a written finding as prescribed under section 604(b)(4)(A).

§ 614. Restrictions on investigative consumer reports [15 U.S.C. § 168*l*l]

Whenever a consumer reporting agency prepares an investigative consumer report, no adverse information in the consumer report (other than information which is a matter of public record) may be included in a subsequent consumer report unless such adverse information has been verified in the process of making such subsequent consumer report, or the adverse information was received within the three-month period preceding the date the subsequent report is furnished.

§ 615. Requirements on users of consumer reports [15 U.S.C. § 1681m]

(a) *Duties of users taking adverse actions on the basis of information contained in consumer reports.* If any person takes any adverse action with respect to any consumer that is based in whole or in part on any information contained in a consumer report, the person shall

(1) provide oral, written, or electronic notice of the adverse action to the consumer;

(2) provide to the consumer orally, in writing, or electronically

(A) the name, address, and telephone number of the consumer reporting agency (including a toll-free telephone number established by the agency if the agency compiles and maintains files on consumers on a nationwide basis) that furnished the report to the person; and

(B) a statement that the consumer reporting agency did not make the decision to take the adverse action and is unable to provide the consumer the specific reasons why the adverse action was taken; and

(3) provide to the consumer an oral, written, or electronic notice of the consumer's right

(A) to obtain, under section 612 [§ 1681j], a free copy of a consumer report on the consumer from the consumer reporting agency referred to in paragraph (2), which notice shall include an indication of the 60-day period under that section for obtaining such a copy; and

(B) to dispute, under section 611 [§ 1681i], with a consumer reporting agency the accuracy or completeness of any information in a consumer report furnished by the agency.

(b) Adverse Action Based on Information Obtained from Third Parties Other than Consumer Reporting Agencies

(1) *In general.* Whenever credit for personal, family, or household purposes involving a consumer is denied or the charge for such credit is increased either wholly or partly because of information obtained from a person other than a consumer reporting agency bearing upon the consumer's credit worthiness, credit standing, credit capacity, character, general reputation, personal characteristics, or mode of living, the user of such information shall, within a reasonable period of time, upon the consumer's written request for the reasons for such adverse action received within sixty days after learning of such adverse action, disclose the nature of the information to the consumer. The user of such information shall clearly and accurately disclose to the consumer his right to make such written request at the time such adverse action is communicated to the consumer.

(2) Duties of Person Taking Certain Actions Based on Information Provided by Affiliate

(A) *Duties, generally.* If a person takes an action described in subparagraph (B) with respect to a consumer, based in whole or in part on information described in subparagraph (C), the person shall

(i) notify the consumer of the action, including a statement that the consumer may obtain the information in accordance with clause (ii); and

(ii) upon a written request from the consumer received within 60 days after transmittal of the notice required by clause (I), disclose to the consumer the nature of the information upon which the action is based by not later than 30 days after receipt of the request.

(B) *Action described.* An action referred to in subparagraph (A) is an adverse action described in section 603(k)(1)(A) [§ 1681a], taken in connection with a transaction initiated by the consumer, or any adverse action described in clause (i) or (ii) of section 603(k)(1)(B) [§ 1681a].

(C) Information described. Information referred to in subparagraph (A)

(i) except as provided in clause (ii), is information that

(I) is furnished to the person taking the action by a person related by common ownership or affiliated by common corporate control to the person taking the action; and

(II) bears on the credit worthiness, credit standing, credit capacity, character, general reputation, personal characteristics, or mode of living of the consumer; and

(ii) does not include

(I) information solely as to transactions or experiences between the consumer and the person furnishing the information; or

(II) information in a consumer report.

(c) *Reasonable procedures to assure compliance.* No person shall be held liable for any violation of this section if he shows by a preponderance of the evidence that at the time of the alleged violation he maintained reasonable procedures to assure compliance with the provisions of this section.

(d) Duties of Users Making Written Credit or Insurance Solicitations on the Basis of Information Contained in Consumer Files

(1) *In general.* Any person who uses a consumer report on any consumer in connection with any credit or insurance transaction that is not initiated by the consumer, that is provided to that person under section 604(c)(1)(B) [§ 1681b], shall provide with each written solicitation made to the consumer regarding the transaction a clear and conspicuous statement that

(A) information contained in the consumer's consumer report was used in connection with the transaction;

(B) the consumer received the offer of credit or insurance because the consumer satisfied the criteria for credit worthiness or insurability under which the consumer was selected for the offer;

(C) if applicable, the credit or insurance may not be extended if, after the consumer responds to the offer, the consumer does not meet the criteria used to select the consumer for the offer or any applicable criteria bearing on credit worthiness or insurability or does not furnish any required collateral;

(D) the consumer has a right to prohibit information contained in the consumer's file with any consumer reporting agency from being used in connection with any credit or insurance transaction that is not initiated by the consumer; and

(E) the consumer may exercise the right referred to in subparagraph (D) by notifying a notification system established under section 604(e) [§ 1681b].

(2) *Disclosure of address and telephone number; format.* A statement under paragraph (1) shall--

(A) include the address and toll-free telephone number of the appropriate notification system established under section 604(e); and

(B) be presented in such format and in such type size and manner as to be simple and easy to understand, as established by the Commission, by rule, in consultation with the Federal banking agencies and the National Credit Union Administration.

(3) *Maintaining criteria on file.* A person who makes an offer of credit or insurance to a consumer under a credit or insurance transaction described in paragraph (1) shall maintain on file the criteria used to select the consumer to receive the offer, all criteria bearing on credit worthiness or insurability, as

applicable, that are the basis for determining whether or not to extend credit or insurance pursuant to the offer, and any requirement for the furnishing of collateral as a condition of the extension of credit or insurance, until the expiration of the 3-year period beginning on the date on which the offer is made to the consumer.

(4) *Authority of federal agencies regarding unfair or deceptive acts or practices not affected.* This section is not intended to affect the authority of any Federal or State agency to enforce a prohibition against unfair or deceptive acts or practices, including the making of false or misleading statements in connection with a credit or insurance transaction that is not initiated by the consumer.

(e) Red Flag Guidelines and Regulations Required

(1) *Guidelines.* The Federal banking agencies, the National Credit Union Administration, and the Commission shall jointly, with respect to the entities that are subject to their respective enforcement authority under section 621–

(A) establish and maintain guidelines for use by each financial institution and each creditor regarding identity theft with respect to account holders at, or customers of, such entities, and update such guidelines as often as necessary;

(B) prescribe regulations requiring each financial institution and each creditor to establish reasonable policies and procedures for implementing the guidelines established pursuant to subparagraph (A), to identify possible risks to account holders or customers or to the safety and soundness of the institution or customers; and

(C) prescribe regulations applicable to card issuers to ensure that, if a card issuer receives notification of a change of address for an existing account, and within a short period of time (during at least the first 30 days after such notification is received) receives a request for an additional or replacement card for the same account, the card issuer may not issue the additional or replacement card, unless the card issuer, in accordance with reasonable policies and procedures--

(i) notifies the cardholder of the request at the former address of the cardholder and provides to the cardholder a means of promptly reporting incorrect address changes;

(ii) notifies the cardholder of the request by such other means of communication as the cardholder and the card issuer previously agreed to; or

(iii) uses other means of assessing the validity of the change of address, in accordance with reasonable policies and procedures established by the card issuer in accordance with the regulations prescribed under subparagraph (B).

(2) Criteria

(A) *In general.* In developing the guidelines required by paragraph (1)(A), the agencies described in paragraph (1) shall identify patterns, practices, and specific forms of activity that indicate the possible existence of identity theft.

(B) *Inactive accounts.* In developing the guidelines required by paragraph (1)(A), the agencies described in paragraph (1) shall consider including reasonable guidelines providing that when a transaction occurs with respect to a credit or deposit account that has been inactive for more than 2 years, the creditor or financial institution shall follow reasonable policies and procedures that provide for notice to be given to a consumer in a manner reasonably designed to reduce the likelihood of identity theft with respect to such account.

(3) *Consistency with verification requirements.* Guidelines established pursuant to paragraph (1) shall not be inconsistent with the policies and procedures required under section 5318(l) of title 31, United States Code.

(f) Prohibition on Sale or Transfer of Debt Caused by Identity Theft

(1) *In general.* No person shall sell, transfer for consideration, or place for collection a debt that such person has been notified under section 605B has resulted from identity theft.

(2) *Applicability.* The prohibitions of this subsection shall apply to all persons collecting a debt described in paragraph (1) after the date of a notification under paragraph (1).

(3) *Rule of construction.* Nothing in this subsection shall be construed to prohibit--

(A) the repurchase of a debt in any case in which the assignee of the debt requires such repurchase because the debt has resulted from identity theft;

(B) the securitization of a debt or the pledging of a portfolio of debt as collateral in connection with a borrowing; or

(C) the transfer of debt as a result of a merger, acquisition, purchase and assumption transaction, or transfer of substantially all of the assets of an entity.

(g) *Debt collector communications concerning identity theft.* If a person acting as a debt collector (as that term is defined in title VIII) on behalf of a third party that is a creditor or other user of a consumer report is notified that any information relating to a debt that the person is attempting to collect may be fraudulent or may be the result of identity theft, that person shall--

(1) notify the third party that the information may be fraudulent or may be the result of identity theft; and

(2) upon request of the consumer to whom the debt purportedly relates, provide to the consumer all information to which the consumer would otherwise be entitled if the consumer were not a victim of identity theft, but wished to dispute the debt under provisions of law applicable to that person.

(h) Duties of Users in Certain Credit Transactions

(1) *In general.* Subject to rules prescribed as provided in paragraph (6), if any person uses a consumer report in connection with an application for, or a grant, extension, or other provision of, credit on material terms that are materially less favorable than the most favorable terms available to a substantial proportion of consumers from or through that person, based in whole or in part on a consumer report, the person shall provide an oral,

written, or electronic notice to the consumer in the form and manner required by regulations prescribed in accordance with this subsection.

(2) *Timing.* The notice required under paragraph (1) may be provided at the time of an application for, or a grant, extension, or other provision of, credit or the time of communication of an approval of an application for, or grant, extension, or other provision of, credit, except as provided in the regulations prescribed under paragraph (6).

(3) *Exceptions.* No notice shall be required from a person under this subsection if–

(A) the consumer applied for specific material terms and was granted those terms, unless those terms were initially specified by the person after the transaction was initiated by the consumer and after the person obtained a consumer report; or

(B) the person has provided or will provide a notice to the consumer under subsection (a) in connection with the transaction.

(4) *Other notice not sufficient.* A person that is required to provide a notice under subsection (a) cannot meet that requirement by providing a notice under this subsection.

(5) *Content and delivery of notice.* A notice under this subsection shall, at a minimum–

(A) include a statement informing the consumer that the terms offered to the consumer are set based on information from a consumer report;

(B) identify the consumer reporting agency furnishing the report;

(C) include a statement informing the consumer that the consumer may obtain a copy of a consumer report from that consumer reporting agency without charge; and

(D) include the contact information specified by that consumer reporting agency for obtaining such consumer reports (including a toll-free telephone number established by the agency in the case of a consumer reporting agency described in section 603(p)).

(6) Rulemaking

(A) *Rules required.* The Commission and the Board shall jointly prescribe rules.

(B) *Content.* Rules required by subparagraph (A) shall address, but are not limited to–

(i) the form, content, time, and manner of delivery of any notice under this subsection;

(ii) clarification of the meaning of terms used in this subsection, including what credit terms are material, and when credit terms are materially less favorable;

(iii) exceptions to the notice requirement under this subsection for classes of persons or transactions regarding which the agencies determine that notice would not significantly benefit consumers;

(iv) a model notice that may be used to comply with this subsection; and

(v) the timing of the notice required under paragraph (1), including the circumstances under which the notice must be provided after the terms offered to the consumer were set based on information from a consumer report.

(7) *Compliance.* A person shall not be liable for failure to perform the duties required by this section if, at the time of the failure, the person maintained reasonable policies and procedures to comply with this section.

(8) Enforcement

(A) *No civil actions.* Sections 616 and 617 shall not apply to any failure by any person to comply with this section.

(B) *Administrative enforcement.* This section shall be enforced exclusively under section 621 by the Federal agencies and officials identified in that section.

§ 616. Civil liability for willful noncompliance [15 U.S.C. § 1681n]

(a) *In general.* Any person who willfully fails to comply with any requirement imposed under this title with respect to any consumer is liable to that consumer in an amount equal to the sum of

(1) (A) any actual damages sustained by the consumer as a result of the failure or damages of not less than $100 and not more than $1,000; or

(B) in the case of liability of a natural person for obtaining a consumer report under false pretenses or knowingly without a permissible purpose, actual damages sustained by the consumer as a result of the failure or $1,000, whichever is greater;

(2) such amount of punitive damages as the court may allow; and

(3) in the case of any successful action to enforce any liability under this section, the costs of the action together with reasonable attorney's fees as determined by the court.

(b) *Civil liability for knowing noncompliance.* Any person who obtains a consumer report from a consumer reporting agency under false pretenses or knowingly without a permissible purpose shall be liable to the consumer reporting agency for actual damages sustained by the consumer reporting agency or $1,000, whichever is greater.

(c) *Attorney's fees.* Upon a finding by the court that an unsuccessful pleading, motion, or other paper filed in connection with an action under this section was filed in bad faith or for purposes of harassment, the court shall award to the prevailing party attorney's fees reasonable in relation to the work expended in responding to the pleading, motion, or other paper.

§ 617. Civil liability for negligent noncompliance [15 U.S.C. § 1681o]

(a) *In general.* Any person who is negligent in failing to comply with any requirement imposed under this title with respect to any consumer is liable to that consumer in an amount equal to the sum of

(1) any actual damages sustained by the consumer as a result of the failure; and

(2) in the case of any successful action to enforce any liability under this section, the costs of the action together with reasonable attorney's fees as determined by the court.

(b) *Attorney's fees.* On a finding by the court that an unsuccessful pleading, motion, or other paper filed in connection with an action under this section was filed in bad faith or for purposes of harassment, the court shall award to the prevailing party attorney's fees reasonable in relation to the work expended in responding to the pleading, motion, or other paper.

§ 618. Jurisdiction of courts; limitation of actions [15 U.S.C. § 1681p]

An action to enforce any liability created under this title may be brought in any appropriate United States district court, without regard to the amount in controversy, or in any other court of competent jurisdiction, not later than the earlier of (1) 2 years after the date of discovery by the plaintiff of the violation that is the basis for such liability; or (2) 5 years after the date on which the violation that is the basis for such liability occurs.

§ 619. Obtaining information under false pretenses [15 U.S.C. § 1681q]

Any person who knowingly and willfully obtains information on a consumer from a consumer reporting agency under false pretenses shall be fined under title 18, United States Code, imprisoned for not more than 2 years, or both.

§ 620. Unauthorized disclosures by officers or employees [15 U.S.C. § 1681r]

Any officer or employee of a consumer reporting agency who knowingly and willfully provides information concerning an individual from the agency's files to a person not authorized to receive that information shall be fined under title 18, United States Code, imprisoned for not more than 2 years, or both.

§ 621. Administrative enforcement [15 U.S.C. § 1681s]

(a) (1) *Enforcement by Federal Trade Commission.* Compliance with the requirements imposed under this title shall be enforced under the Federal Trade Commission Act [15 U.S.C. §§ 41 et seq.] by the Federal Trade Commission with respect to consumer reporting agencies and all other persons subject thereto, except to the extent that enforcement of the requirements imposed under this title is specifically committed to some other government agency under subsection (b) hereof. For the purpose of the exercise by the Federal Trade Commission of its functions and powers under the Federal Trade Commission Act, a violation of any requirement or prohibition imposed under this title shall constitute an unfair or deceptive act or practice in commerce in violation of section 5(a) of the Federal Trade Commission Act [15 U.S.C. § 45(a)] and shall be subject to enforcement by the Federal Trade Commission under section 5(b) thereof [15 U.S.C. § 45(b)] with respect to any consumer reporting agency or person subject to enforcement by the Federal Trade Commission pursuant to this subsection, irrespective of whether that person is engaged in commerce or meets any other jurisdictional tests in the Federal Trade Commission Act. The Federal Trade Commission shall have such procedural, investigative, and enforcement powers, including the power to issue procedural rules in enforcing compliance with the requirements imposed under this title and to require the filing of reports, the production of documents, and the appearance of witnesses as though the applicable terms and conditions of the Federal Trade Commission Act were part of this title. Any person violating any of the provisions of this title shall be subject to the penalties and entitled to the privileges and immunities provided in the Federal Trade Commission Act as though the applicable terms and provisions thereof were part of this title.

(2) (A) In the event of a knowing violation, which constitutes a pattern or practice of violations of this title, the Commission may commence a civil action to recover a civil penalty in a district court of the United States against any person that violates this title. In such action, such person shall be liable for a civil penalty of not more than $2,500 per violation.

> (B) In determining the amount of a civil penalty under subparagraph (A), the court shall take into account the degree of culpability, any history of prior such conduct, ability to pay, effect on ability to continue to do business, and such other matters as justice may require.

(3) Notwithstanding paragraph (2), a court may not impose any civil penalty on a person for a violation of section 623(a)(1) [§ 1681s-2] unless the person has been enjoined from committing the violation, or ordered not to commit the violation, in an action or proceeding brought by or on behalf of the Federal Trade Commission, and has violated the injunction or order, and the court may not impose any civil penalty for any violation occurring before the date of the violation of the injunction or order.

(b) *Enforcement by other agencies.* Compliance with the requirements imposed under this title with respect to consumer reporting agencies, persons who use consumer reports from such agencies, persons who furnish information to such agencies, and users of information that are subject to subsection (d) of section 615 [§ 1681m] shall be enforced under

> (1) section 8 of the Federal Deposit Insurance Act [12 U.S.C. § 1818], in the case of
>
> > (A) national banks, and Federal branches and Federal agencies of foreign banks, by the Office of the Comptroller of the Currency;
> >
> > (B) member banks of the Federal Reserve System (other than national banks), branches and agencies of foreign banks (other than Federal branches, Federal agencies, and insured State branches of foreign banks), commercial lending companies owned or controlled by foreign banks, and organizations operating under section 25 or 25A of the Federal Reserve Act [12 U.S.C. §§ 601 et seq., §§ 611 et seq], by the Board of Governors of the Federal Reserve System; and
> >
> > (C) banks insured by the Federal Deposit Insurance Corporation (other than members of the Federal Reserve System) and insured State branches of foreign banks, by the Board of Directors of the Federal Deposit Insurance Corporation;
>
> (2) section 8 of the Federal Deposit Insurance Act [12 U.S.C. § 1818], by the Director of the Office of Thrift Supervision, in the case of a savings association the deposits of which are insured by the Federal Deposit Insurance Corporation;

(3) the Federal Credit Union Act [12 U.S.C. §§ 1751 et seq.], by the Administrator of the National Credit Union Administration [National Credit Union Administration Board] with respect to any Federal credit union;

(4) subtitle IV of title 49 [49 U.S.C. §§ 10101 et seq.], by the Secretary of Transportation, with respect to all carriers subject to the jurisdiction of the Surface Transportation Board;

(5) the Federal Aviation Act of 1958 [49 U.S.C. Appx §§ 1301 et seq.], by the Secretary of Transportation with respect to any air carrier or foreign air carrier subject to that Act [49 U.S.C. Appx §§ 1301 et seq.]; and

(6) the Packers and Stockyards Act, 1921 [7 U.S.C. §§ 181 et seq.] (except as provided in section 406 of that Act [7 U.S.C. §§ 226 and 227]), by the Secretary of Agriculture with respect to any activities subject to that Act.

The terms used in paragraph (1) that are not defined in this title or otherwise defined in section 3(s) of the Federal Deposit Insurance Act (12 U.S.C. §1813(s)) shall have the meaning given to them in section 1(b) of the International Banking Act of 1978 (12 U.S.C. § 3101).

(c) State Action for Violations

(1) *Authority of states.* In addition to such other remedies as are provided under State law, if the chief law enforcement officer of a State, or an official or agency designated by a State, has reason to believe that any person has violated or is violating this title, the State

(A) may bring an action to enjoin such violation in any appropriate United States district court or in any other court of competent jurisdiction;

(B) subject to paragraph (5), may bring an action on behalf of the residents of the State to recover

(i) damages for which the person is liable to such residents under sections 616 and 617 [§§ 1681n and 1681o] as a result of the violation;

(ii) in the case of a violation described in any of paragraphs (1) through (3) of section 623(c), damages for which the person would, but for section 623(c) [§ 1681s-2], be liable to such residents as a result of the violation; or

(iii) damages of not more than $1,000 for each willful or negligent violation; and

(C) in the case of any successful action under subparagraph (A) or (B), shall be awarded the costs of the action and reasonable attorney fees as determined by the court.

(2) *Rights of federal regulators.* The State shall serve prior written notice of any action under paragraph (1) upon the Federal Trade Commission or the appropriate Federal regulator determined under subsection (b) and provide the Commission or appropriate Federal regulator with a copy of its complaint, except in any case in which such prior notice is not feasible, in which case the State shall serve such notice immediately upon instituting such action. The Federal Trade Commission or appropriate Federal regulator shall have the right

(A) to intervene in the action;

(B) upon so intervening, to be heard on all matters arising therein;

(C) to remove the action to the appropriate United States district court; and

(D) to file petitions for appeal.

(3) *Investigatory powers.* For purposes of bringing any action under this subsection, nothing in this subsection shall prevent the chief law enforcement officer, or an official or agency designated by a State, from exercising the powers conferred on the chief law enforcement officer or such official by the laws of such State to conduct investigations or to administer oaths or affirmations or to compel the attendance of witnesses or the production of documentary and other evidence.

(4) *Limitation on state action while federal action pending.* If the Federal Trade Commission or the appropriate Federal regulator has instituted a civil action or an administrative action under section 8 of the Federal Deposit Insurance Act for a violation of this title, no State may, during the pendency of such action, bring an action under this section against any defendant named in the complaint of the Commission or the appropriate Federal regulator for any violation of this title that is alleged in that complaint.

(5) Limitations on State Actions for Certain Violations

(A) *Violation of injunction required.* A State may not bring an action against a person under paragraph (1)(B) for a violation described in any of paragraphs (1) through (3) of section 623(c), unless

(i) the person has been enjoined from committing the violation, in an action brought by the State under paragraph (1)(A); and

(ii) the person has violated the injunction.

(B) *Limitation on damages recoverable.* In an action against a person under paragraph (1)(B) for a violation described in any of paragraphs (1) through (3) of section 623(c), a State may not recover any damages incurred before the date of the violation of an injunction on which the action is based.

(d) *Enforcement under other authority.* For the purpose of the exercise by any agency referred to in subsection (b) of this section of its powers under any Act referred to in that subsection, a violation of any requirement imposed under this title shall be deemed to be a violation of a requirement imposed under that Act. In addition to its powers under any provision of law specifically referred to in subsection (b) of this section, each of the agencies referred to in that subsection may exercise, for the purpose of enforcing compliance with any requirement imposed under this title any other authority conferred on it by law.

(e) Regulatory authority

(1) The Federal banking agencies referred to in paragraphs (1) and (2) of subsection (b) shall jointly prescribe such regulations as necessary to carry out the purposes of this Act with respect to any persons identified under paragraphs (1) and (2) of subsection (b), and the Board of Governors of the Federal Reserve System shall have authority to prescribe regulations consistent with such joint regulations with respect to bank holding companies

and affiliates (other than depository institutions and consumer reporting agencies) of such holding companies.

(2) The Board of the National Credit Union Administration shall prescribe such regulations as necessary to carry out the purposes of this Act with respect to any persons identified under paragraph (3) of subsection (b).

(f) Coordination of Consumer Complaint Investigations

(1) *In general.* Each consumer reporting agency described in section 603(p) shall develop and maintain procedures for the referral to each other such agency of any consumer complaint received by the agency alleging identity theft, or requesting a fraud alert under section 605A or a block under section 605B.

(2) *Model form and procedure for reporting identity theft.* The Commission, in consultation with the Federal banking agencies and the National Credit Union Administration, shall develop a model form and model procedures to be used by consumers who are victims of identity theft for contacting and informing creditors and consumer reporting agencies of the fraud.

(3) *Annual summary reports.* Each consumer reporting agency described in section 603(p) shall submit an annual summary report to the Commission on consumer complaints received by the agency on identity theft or fraud alerts.

(g) *FTC regulation of coding of trade names.* If the Commission determines that a person described in paragraph (9) of section 623(a) has not met the requirements of such paragraph, the Commission shall take action to ensure the person's compliance with such paragraph, which may include issuing model guidance or prescribing reasonable policies and procedures, as necessary to ensure that such person complies with such paragraph.

§ 622. Information on overdue child support obligations [15 U.S.C. § 1681s-1]

Notwithstanding any other provision of this title, a consumer reporting agency shall include in any consumer report furnished by the agency in accordance with section 604 [§ 1681b] of this title, any information on the failure of the consumer to pay overdue support which

(1) is provided

(A) to the consumer reporting agency by a State or local child support enforcement agency; or

(B) to the consumer reporting agency and verified by any local, State, or Federal government agency; and

(2) antedates the report by 7 years or less.

§ 623. Responsibilities of furnishers of information to consumer reporting agencies [15 U.S.C. § 1681s-2]

(a) Duty of Furnishers of Information to Provide Accurate Information

(1) Prohibition

(A) *Reporting information with actual knowledge of errors.* A person shall not furnish any information relating to a consumer to any consumer reporting agency if the person knows or has reasonable cause to believe that the information is inaccurate.

(B) *Reporting information after notice and confirmation of errors.* A person shall not furnish information relating to a consumer to any consumer reporting agency if

(i) the person has been notified by the consumer, at the address specified by the person for such notices, that specific information is inaccurate; and

(ii) the information is, in fact, inaccurate.

(C) *No address requirement.* A person who clearly and conspicuously specifies to the consumer an address for notices referred to in subparagraph (B) shall not be subject to subparagraph (A); however, nothing in subparagraph (B) shall require a person to specify such an address.

(D) *Definition.* For purposes of subparagraph (A), the term "reasonable cause to believe that the information is inaccurate" means having specific knowledge, other than solely allegations by the consumer, that would cause a reasonable person to have substantial doubts about the accuracy of the information.

(2) *Duty to correct and update information.* A person who

(A) regularly and in the ordinary course of business furnishes information to one or more consumer reporting agencies about the person's transactions or experiences with any consumer; and

(B) has furnished to a consumer reporting agency information that the person determines is not complete or accurate, shall promptly notify the consumer reporting agency of that determination and provide to the agency any corrections to that information, or any additional information, that is necessary to make the information provided by the person to the agency complete and accurate, and shall not thereafter furnish to the agency any of the information that remains not complete or accurate.

(3) *Duty to provide notice of dispute.* If the completeness or accuracy of any information furnished by any person to any consumer reporting agency is disputed to such person by a consumer, the person may not furnish the information to any consumer reporting agency without notice that such information is disputed by the consumer.

(4) *Duty to provide notice of closed accounts.* A person who regularly and in the ordinary course of business furnishes information to a consumer reporting agency regarding a consumer who has a credit account with that person shall notify the agency of the voluntary closure of the account by the consumer, in information regularly furnished for the period in which the account is closed.

(5) Duty to Provide Notice of Delinquency of Accounts

(A) *In general.* A person who furnishes information to a consumer reporting agency regarding a delinquent account being placed for collection, charged to profit or loss, or subjected to any similar action shall, not later than 90 days after furnishing the information, notify the agency of the date of delinquency on the account, which shall be the month and year of the commencement of the delinquency on the account that immediately preceded the action.

(B) *Rule of construction.* For purposes of this paragraph only, and provided that the consumer does not dispute the information, a person that furnishes information on a delinquent account that is placed for collection, charged for profit or loss, or subjected to any similar action, complies with this paragraph, if--

(i) the person reports the same date of delinquency as that provided by the creditor to which the account was owed at the time at which the commencement of the delinquency occurred, if the creditor previously reported that date of delinquency to a consumer reporting agency;

(ii) the creditor did not previously report the date of delinquency to a consumer reporting agency, and the person establishes and follows reasonable procedures to obtain the date of delinquency from the creditor or another reliable source and reports that date to a consumer reporting agency as the date of delinquency; or

(iii) the creditor did not previously report the date of delinquency to a consumer reporting agency and the date of delinquency cannot be reasonably obtained as provided in clause (ii), the person establishes and follows reasonable procedures to ensure the date reported as the date of delinquency precedes the date on which the account is placed for collection, charged to profit or loss, or subjected to any similar action, and reports such date to the credit reporting agency.

(6) Duties of Furnishers Upon Notice of Identity Theft-Related Information

(A) *Reasonable procedures.* A person that furnishes information to any consumer reporting agency shall have in place reasonable procedures to respond to any notification that it receives from a consumer reporting agency under section 605B relating to information resulting from identity theft, to prevent that person from refurnishing such blocked information.

(B) *Information alleged to result from identity theft.* If a consumer submits an identity theft report to a person who furnishes information to a consumer reporting agency at the address specified by that person for receiving such reports stating that information maintained by such person that purports to relate to the consumer resulted from identity theft, the person may not furnish such information that purports to relate to the consumer to any consumer reporting agency, unless the person subsequently knows or is informed by the consumer that the information is correct.

(7) Negative Information

(A) Notice to Consumer Required

(i) *In general.* If any financial institution that extends credit and regularly and in the ordinary course of business furnishes information to a consumer reporting agency described in section 603(p) furnishes negative information to such an agency regarding credit extended to a customer, the financial institution shall provide a notice of such furnishing of negative information, in writing, to the customer.

(ii) *Notice effective for subsequent submissions.* After providing such notice, the financial institution may submit additional negative information to a consumer reporting agency described in section 603(p) with respect to the same transaction, extension of credit, account, or customer without providing additional notice to the customer.

(B) Time of Notice

(i) *In general.* The notice required under subparagraph (A) shall be provided to the customer prior to, or no later than 30 days after, furnishing the negative information to a consumer reporting agency described in section 603(p).

(ii) *Coordination with new account disclosures.* If the notice is provided to the customer prior to furnishing the negative information to a consumer reporting agency, the notice may not be included in the initial disclosures provided under section 127(a) of the Truth in Lending Act.

(C) Coordination with other disclosures- The notice required under subparagraph (A)--

(i) may be included on or with any notice of default, any billing statement, or any other materials provided to the customer; and

(ii) must be clear and conspicuous.

(D) Model Disclosure

(i) *Duty of board to prepare.* The Board shall prescribe a brief model disclosure a financial institution may use to comply with subparagraph (A), which shall not exceed 30 words.

(ii) *Use of model not required.* No provision of this paragraph shall be construed as requiring a financial institution to use any such model form prescribed by the Board.

(iii) *Compliance using model.* A financial institution shall be deemed to be in compliance with subparagraph (A) if the financial institution uses any such model form prescribed by the Board, or the financial institution uses any such model form and rearranges its format.

(E) *Use of notice without submitting negative information.* No provision of this paragraph shall be construed as requiring a financial institution that has provided a customer with a notice described in subparagraph (A) to furnish negative information about the customer to a consumer reporting agency.

(F) *Safe harbor.* A financial institution shall not be liable for failure to perform the duties required by this paragraph if, at the time of the failure, the financial institution maintained reasonable policies and procedures to comply with this paragraph or the financial institution reasonably believed that the institution is prohibited, by law, from contacting the consumer.

(G) *Definitions.* For purposes of this paragraph, the following definitions shall apply:

(i) The term "negative information" means information concerning a customer's delinquencies, late payments, insolvency, or any form of default.

(ii) The terms "customer" and "financial institution" have the same meanings as in section 509 Public Law 106-102.

(8) Ability of Consumer to Dispute Information Directly with Furnisher

(A) *In general.* The Federal banking agencies, the National Credit Union Administration, and the Commission shall jointly prescribe regulations that shall identify the circumstances under which a furnisher shall be required to reinvestigate a dispute concerning the accuracy of information contained in a consumer report on the consumer, based on a direct request of a consumer.

(B) *Considerations.* In prescribing regulations under subparagraph (A), the agencies shall weigh--

(i) the benefits to consumers with the costs on furnishers and the credit reporting system;

(ii) the impact on the overall accuracy and integrity of consumer reports of any such requirements;

(iii) whether direct contact by the consumer with the furnisher would likely result in the most expeditious resolution of any such dispute; and

(iv) the potential impact on the credit reporting process if credit repair organizations, as defined in section 403(3), including entities that would be a credit repair organization, but for section 403(3)(B)(i), are able to circumvent the prohibition in subparagraph (G).

(C) *Applicability.* Subparagraphs (D) through (G) shall apply in any circumstance identified under the regulations promulgated under subparagraph (A).

(D) *Submitting a notice of dispute-* A consumer who seeks to dispute the accuracy of information shall provide a dispute notice directly to such person at the address specified by the person for such notices that--

(i) identifies the specific information that is being disputed;

(ii) explains the basis for the dispute; and

(iii) includes all supporting documentation required by the furnisher to substantiate the basis of the dispute.

(E) *Duty of person after receiving notice of dispute.* After receiving a notice of dispute from a consumer pursuant to subparagraph (D), the person that provided the information in dispute to a consumer reporting agency shall--

(i) conduct an investigation with respect to the disputed information;

(ii) review all relevant information provided by the consumer with the notice;

(iii) complete such person's investigation of the dispute and report the results of the investigation to the consumer before the expiration of the period under section 611(a)(1) within which a consumer reporting agency would be required to complete its action if the consumer had elected to dispute the information under that section; and

(iv) if the investigation finds that the information reported was inaccurate, promptly notify each consumer reporting agency to which the person furnished the inaccurate information of that determination and provide to the agency any correction to that information that is necessary to make the information provided by the person accurate.

(F) Frivolous or Irrelevant Dispute

(i) *In general.* This paragraph shall not apply if the person receiving a notice of a dispute from a consumer reasonably determines that the dispute is frivolous or irrelevant, including--

(I) by reason of the failure of a consumer to provide sufficient information to investigate the disputed information; or

(II) the submission by a consumer of a dispute that is substantially the same as a dispute previously submitted by or for the consumer, either directly to the person or through a consumer reporting agency under subsection (b), with respect to which the person has already performed the person's duties under this paragraph or subsection (b), as applicable.

(ii) *Notice of determination.* Upon making any determination under clause (i) that a dispute is frivolous or irrelevant, the person shall notify the consumer of such determination not later than 5 business days after making such determination, by mail or, if authorized by the consumer for that purpose, by any other means available to the person.

(iii) *Contents of notice.* A notice under clause (ii) shall include--

(I) the reasons for the determination under clause (i); and

(II) identification of any information required to investigate the disputed information, which may consist of a standardized form describing the general nature of such information.

(G) *Exclusion of credit repair organizations.* This paragraph shall not apply if the notice of the dispute is submitted by, is prepared on behalf of the consumer by, or is submitted on a form supplied to the consumer by, a credit repair organization, as defined in section 403(3), or an entity that would be a credit repair organization, but for section 403(3)(B)(i).

(9) *Duty to provide notice of status as medical information furnisher.* A person whose primary business is providing medical services, products, or devices, or the person's agent or assignee, who furnishes information to a consumer reporting agency on a consumer shall be considered a medical information furnisher for purposes of this title, and shall notify the agency of such status.

(b) Duties of Furnishers of Information upon Notice of Dispute

(1) *In general.* After receiving notice pursuant to section 611(a)(2) [§ 1681i] of a dispute with regard to the completeness or accuracy of any information provided by a person to a consumer reporting agency, the person shall

(A) conduct an investigation with respect to the disputed information;

(B) review all relevant information provided by the consumer reporting agency pursuant to section 611(a)(2) [§ 1681i];

(C) report the results of the investigation to the consumer reporting agency;

(D) if the investigation finds that the information is incomplete or inaccurate, report those results to all other consumer reporting agencies to which the person furnished the information and that compile and maintain files on consumers on a nationwide basis; and

(E) if an item of information disputed by a consumer is found to be inaccurate or incomplete or cannot be verified after any reinvestigation under paragraph (1), for purposes of reporting to a consumer reporting agency only, as appropriate, based on the results of the reinvestigation promptly–

(i) modify that item of information;

(ii) delete that item of information; or

(iii) permanently block the reporting of that item of information.

(2) *Deadline.* A person shall complete all investigations, reviews, and reports required under paragraph (1) regarding information provided by the person to a consumer reporting agency, before the expiration of the period under section 611(a)(1) [§ 1681i] within which the consumer reporting agency is required to complete actions required by that section regarding that information.

(c) *Limitation on liability.* Except as provided in section 621(c)(1)(B), sections 616 and 617 do not apply to any violation of--

(1) subsection (a) of this section, including any regulations issued thereunder;

(2) subsection (e) of this section, except that nothing in this paragraph shall limit, expand, or otherwise affect liability under section 616 or 617, as applicable, for violations of subsection (b) of this section; or

(3) subsection (e) of section 615.

(d) *Limitation on enforcement.* The provisions of law described in paragraphs (1) through (3) of subsection (c) (other than with respect to the exception described in paragraph (2) of subsection (c)) shall be enforced exclusively as provided under section 621 by the Federal agencies and officials and the State officials identified in section 621.

(e) Accuracy Guidelines and Regulations Required

(1) *Guidelines.* The Federal banking agencies, the National Credit Union Administration, and the Commission shall, with respect to the entities that are subject to their respective enforcement authority under section 621, and in coordination as described in paragraph (2)--

(A) establish and maintain guidelines for use by each person that furnishes information to a consumer reporting agency regarding the accuracy and integrity of the information relating to consumers that such entities furnish to consumer reporting agencies, and update such guidelines as often as necessary; and

(B) prescribe regulations requiring each person that furnishes information to a consumer reporting agency to establish reasonable policies and procedures for implementing the guidelines established pursuant to subparagraph (A).

(2) *Coordination.* Each agency required to prescribe regulations under paragraph (1) shall consult and coordinate with each other such agency so that, to the extent possible, the regulations prescribed by each such entity are consistent and comparable with the regulations prescribed by each other such agency.

(3) *Criteria.* In developing the guidelines required by paragraph (1)(A), the agencies described in paragraph (1) shall--

(A) identify patterns, practices, and specific forms of activity that can compromise the accuracy and integrity of information furnished to consumer reporting agencies;

(B) review the methods (including technological means) used to furnish information relating to consumers to consumer reporting agencies;

(C) determine whether persons that furnish information to consumer reporting agencies maintain and enforce policies to assure the accuracy and integrity of information furnished to consumer reporting agencies; and

(D) examine the policies and processes that persons that furnish information to consumer reporting agencies employ to conduct reinvestigations and correct inaccurate information relating to consumers that has been furnished to consumer reporting agencies.

§ 624. Affiliate sharing [15 U.S.C. § 1681s-3]

(a) Special Rule for Solicitation for Purposes of Marketing

(1) *Notice.* Any person that receives from another person related to it by common ownership or affiliated by corporate control a communication of information that would be a consumer report, but for clauses (i), (ii), and (iii) of section 603(d)(2)(A), may not use the information to make a solicitation for marketing purposes to a consumer about its products or services, unless--

(A) it is clearly and conspicuously disclosed to the consumer that the information may be communicated among such persons for purposes of making such solicitations to the consumer; and

(B) the consumer is provided an opportunity and a simple method to prohibit the making of such solicitations to the consumer by such person.

(2) Consumer Choice

(A) *In general.* The notice required under paragraph (1) shall allow the consumer the opportunity to prohibit all solicitations referred to in such paragraph, and may allow the consumer to choose from different options when electing to prohibit the sending of such solicitations, including options regarding the types of entities and information covered, and which methods of delivering solicitations the consumer elects to prohibit.

(B) *Format.* Notwithstanding subparagraph (A), the notice required under paragraph (1) shall be clear, conspicuous, and concise, and any method provided under paragraph (1)(B) shall be simple. The regulations prescribed to implement this section shall provide specific guidance regarding how to comply with such standards.

(3) Duration

(A) *In general.* The election of a consumer pursuant to paragraph (1)(B) to prohibit the making of solicitations shall be effective for at least 5 years, beginning on the date on which the person receives the election of the consumer, unless the consumer requests that such election be revoked.

(B) *Notice upon expiration of effective period.* At such time as the election of a consumer pursuant to paragraph (1)(B) is no longer effective, a person may not use information that the person receives in the manner described in paragraph (1) to make any solicitation for marketing purposes to the consumer, unless the consumer receives a notice and an opportunity, using a simple method, to extend the opt-out for another period of at least 5 years, pursuant to the procedures described in paragraph (1).

(4) *Scope.* This section shall not apply to a person–

(A) using information to make a solicitation for marketing purposes to a consumer with whom the person has a pre-existing business relationship;

(B) using information to facilitate communications to an individual for whose benefit the person provides employee benefit or other services pursuant to a contract with an employer related to and arising out of the current employment relationship or status of the individual as a participant or beneficiary of an employee benefit plan;

(C) using information to perform services on behalf of another person related by common ownership or affiliated by corporate control, except that this subparagraph shall not be construed as permitting a person to send solicitations on behalf of another person, if such other person would not be permitted to send the solicitation on its own behalf as a result of the election of the consumer to prohibit solicitations under paragraph (1)(B);

(D) using information in response to a communication initiated by the consumer;

(E) using information in response to solicitations authorized or requested by the consumer; or

(F) if compliance with this section by that person would prevent compliance by that person with any provision of State insurance laws pertaining to unfair discrimination in any State in which the person is lawfully doing business.

(5) *No retroactivity.* This subsection shall not prohibit the use of information to send a solicitation to a consumer if such information was received prior to the date on which persons are required to comply with regulations implementing this subsection.

(b) *Notice for other purposes permissible.* A notice or other disclosure under this section may be coordinated and consolidated with any other notice required to be issued under any other provision of law by a person that is subject to this section, and a notice or other disclosure that is equivalent to the notice required by subsection (a), and that is provided by a person described in subsection (a) to a consumer together with disclosures required by any other provision of law, shall satisfy the requirements of subsection (a).

(c) *User requirements.* Requirements with respect to the use by a person of information received from another person related to it by common ownership or affiliated by corporate control, such as the requirements of this section, constitute requirements with respect to the exchange of information among persons affiliated by common ownership or common corporate control, within the meaning of section 625(b)(2).

(d) *Definitions.* For purposes of this section, the following definitions shall apply:

(1) The term "pre-existing business relationship" means a relationship between a person, or a person's licensed agent, and a consumer, based on--

(A) a financial contract between a person and a consumer which is in force;

(B) the purchase, rental, or lease by the consumer of that person's goods or services, or a financial transaction (including holding an active account or a policy in force or having another continuing relationship) between the consumer and that person during the 18-month period immediately preceding the date on which the consumer is sent a solicitation covered by this section;

(C) an inquiry or application by the consumer regarding a product or service offered by that person, during the 3-month period immediately preceding the date on which the consumer is sent a solicitation covered by this section; or

(D) any other pre-existing customer relationship defined in the regulations implementing this section.

(2) The term "solicitation" means the marketing of a product or service initiated by a person to a particular consumer that is based on an exchange of information described in subsection (a), and is intended to encourage the consumer to purchase such product or service, but does not include communications that are directed at the general public or determined not to be a solicitation by the regulations prescribed under this section.

§ 625. Relation to State laws [15 U.S.C. § 1681t]

(a) *In general.* Except as provided in subsections (b) and (c), this title does not annul, alter, affect, or exempt any person subject to the provisions of this title from complying with the laws of any State with respect to the collection, distribution, or use of any information on consumers, or for the prevention or mitigation of identity theft, except to the extent that those laws are inconsistent with any provision of this title, and then only to the extent of the inconsistency.

(b) *General exceptions.* No requirement or prohibition may be imposed under the laws of any State

(1) with respect to any subject matter regulated under

(A) subsection (c) or (e) of section 604 [§ 1681b], relating to the prescreening of consumer reports;

(B) section 611 [§ 1681i], relating to the time by which a consumer reporting agency must take any action, including the provision of notification to a consumer or other person, in any procedure related to the disputed accuracy of information in a consumer's file, except that this subparagraph shall not apply to any State law in effect on the date of enactment of the Consumer Credit Reporting Reform Act of 1996;

(C) subsections (a) and (b) of section 615 [§ 1681m], relating to the duties of a person who takes any adverse action with respect to a consumer;

(D) section 615(d) [§ 1681m], relating to the duties of persons who use a consumer report of a consumer in connection with any credit or insurance transaction that is not initiated by the consumer and that consists of a firm offer of credit or insurance;

(E) section 605 [§ 1681c], relating to information contained in consumer reports, except that this subparagraph shall not apply to any State law in effect on the date of enactment of the Consumer Credit Reporting Reform Act of 1996;

(F) section 623 [§ 1681s-2], relating to the responsibilities of persons who furnish information to consumer reporting agencies, except that this paragraph shall not apply

 (i) with respect to section 54A(a) of chapter 93 of the Massachusetts Annotated Laws (as in effect on the date of enactment of the Consumer Credit Reporting Reform Act of 1996); or

 (ii) with respect to section 1785.25(a) of the California Civil Code (as in effect on the date of enactment of the Consumer Credit Reporting Reform Act of 1996);

(G) section 609(e), relating to information available to victims under section 609(e);

(H) section 624, relating to the exchange and use of information to make a solicitation for marketing purposes; or

(I) section 615(h), relating to the duties of users of consumer reports to provide notice with respect to terms in certain credit transactions;

(2) with respect to the exchange of information among persons affiliated by common ownership or common corporate control, except that this paragraph shall not apply with respect to subsection (a) or (c)(1) of section 2480e of title 9, Vermont Statutes Annotated (as in effect on the date of enactment of the Consumer Credit Reporting Reform Act of 1996);

(3) with respect to the disclosures required to be made under subsection (c), (d), (e), or (g) of section 609, or subsection (f) of section 609 relating to the disclosure of credit scores for credit granting purposes, except that this paragraph--

 (A) shall not apply with respect to sections 1785.10, 1785.16, and 1785.20.2 of the California Civil Code (as in effect on the date of enactment of the Fair and Accurate Credit Transactions Act of 2003) and section 1785.15 through section 1785.15.2 of such Code (as in effect on such date);

(B) shall not apply with respect to sections 5-3-106(2) and 212-14.3-104.3 of the Colorado Revised Statutes (as in effect on the date of enactment of the Fair and Accurate Credit Transactions Act of 2003); and

(C) shall not be construed as limiting, annulling, affecting, or superseding any provision of the laws of any State regulating the use in an insurance activity, or regulating disclosures concerning such use, of a credit-based insurance score of a consumer by any person engaged in the business of insurance;

(4) with respect to the frequency of any disclosure under section 612(a), except that this paragraph shall not apply–

(A) with respect to section 12-14.3-105(1)(d) of the Colorado Revised Statutes (as in effect on the date of enactment of the Fair and Accurate Credit Transactions Act of 2003);

(B) with respect to section 10-1-393(29)(C) of the Georgia Code (as in effect on the date of enactment of the Fair and Accurate Credit Transactions Act of 2003);

(C) with respect to section 1316.2 of title 10 of the Maine Revised Statutes (as in effect on the date of enactment of the Fair and Accurate Credit Transactions Act of 2003);

(D) with respect to sections 14-1209(a)(1) and 14-1209(b)(1)(i) of the Commercial Law Article of the Code of Maryland (as in effect on the date of enactment of the Fair and Accurate Credit Transactions Act of 2003);

(E) with respect to section 59(d) and section 59(e) of chapter 93 of the General Laws of Massachusetts (as in effect on the date of enactment of the Fair and Accurate Credit Transactions Act of 2003);

(F) with respect to section 56:11-37.10(a)(1) of the New Jersey Revised Statutes (as in effect on the date of enactment of the Fair and Accurate Credit Transactions Act of 2003); or

(G) with respect to section 2480c(a)(1) of title 9 of the Vermont Statutes Annotated (as in effect on the date of enactment of the Fair and Accurate Credit Transactions Act of 2003); or

(5) with respect to the conduct required by the specific provisions of--

(A) section 605(g);

(B) section 605A;

(C) section 605B;

(D) section 609(a)(1)(A);

(E) section 612(a);

(F) subsections (e), (f), and (g) of section 615;

(G) section 621(f);

(H) section 623(a)(6); or

(I) section 628.

(c) *Definition of firm offer of credit or insurance.* Notwithstanding any definition of the term "firm offer of credit or insurance" (or any equivalent term) under the laws of any State, the definition of that term contained in section 603(l) [§ 1681a] shall be construed to apply in the enforcement and interpretation of the laws of any State governing consumer reports.

(d) *Limitations.* Subsections (b) and (c) do not affect any settlement, agreement, or consent judgment between any State Attorney General and any consumer reporting agency in effect on the date of enactment of the Consumer Credit Reporting Reform Act of 1996.

§ 626. Disclosures to FBI for counterintelligence purposes [15 U.S.C. § 1681u]

(a) *Identity of financial institutions.* Notwithstanding section 604 [§ 1681b] or any other provision of this title, a consumer reporting agency shall furnish to the Federal Bureau of Investigation the names and addresses of all financial institutions (as that term is defined in section 1101 of the Right to Financial Privacy Act of 1978 [12 U.S.C. § 3401]) at which a consumer maintains or has maintained an account, to the extent that information is in the files of the agency, when presented with a written request for that information, signed by the Director of the Federal Bureau of Investigation, or the Director's designee in a position not lower than Deputy Assistant Director at Bureau headquarters or a Special Agent in Charge of a Bureau field office designated by the Director, which certifies compliance with this section. The Director or the Director's designee may make such a certification only if the Director or the Director's designee has determined in writing, that such information is sought for the conduct of an authorized investigation to protect against international terrorism or clandestine intelligence activities, provided that such an investigation of a United States person is not conducted solely upon the basis of activities protected by the first amendment to the Constitution of the United States.

(b) *Identifying information.* Notwithstanding the provisions of section 604 [§ 1681b] or any other provision of this title, a consumer reporting agency shall furnish identifying information respecting a consumer, limited to name, address, former addresses, places of employment, or former places of employment, to the Federal Bureau of Investigation when presented with a written request, signed by the Director or the Director's designee, which certifies compliance with this subsection. The Director or the Director's designee in a position not lower than Deputy Assistant Director at Bureau headquarters or a Special Agent in Charge of a Bureau field office designated by the Director may make such a certification only if the Director or the Director's designee has determined in writing that such information is sought for the conduct of an authorized investigation to protect against international terrorism or clandestine intelligence activities, provided that such an investigation of a United States person is not conducted solely upon the basis of activities protected by the first amendment to the Constitution of the United States.

(c) *Court order for disclosure of consumer reports.* Notwithstanding section 604 [§ 1681b] or any other provision of this title, if requested in writing by the Director of the Federal Bureau of Investigation, or a designee of the Director in a position not lower than Deputy Assistant Director at Bureau headquarters or a Special Agent in Charge of a Bureau field office designated by the Director, a court may issue an order ex parte directing a consumer reporting agency to furnish a consumer report to the Federal Bureau of Investigation, upon a showing in camera that the consumer report is sought for the conduct of an authorized investigation to protect against international terrorism or clandestine intelligence activities, provided that such an investigation of a United States person is not conducted solely upon the basis of activities protected by the first amendment to the Constitution of the United States. The terms of an order issued under this subsection shall not disclose that the order is issued for purposes of a counterintelligence investigation.

(d) *Confidentiality*. No consumer reporting agency or officer, employee, or agent of a consumer reporting agency shall disclose to any person, other than those officers, employees, or agents of a consumer reporting agency necessary to fulfill the requirement to disclose information to the Federal Bureau of Investigation under this section, that the Federal Bureau of Investigation has sought or obtained the identity of financial institutions or a consumer report respecting any consumer under subsection (a), (b), or (c), and no consumer reporting agency or officer, employee, or agent of a consumer reporting agency shall include in any consumer report any information that would indicate that the Federal Bureau of Investigation has sought or obtained such information or a consumer report.

(e) *Payment of fees*. The Federal Bureau of Investigation shall, subject to the availability of appropriations, pay to the consumer reporting agency assembling or providing report or information in accordance with procedures established under this section a fee for reimbursement for such costs as are reasonably necessary and which have been directly incurred in searching, reproducing, or transporting books, papers, records, or other data required or requested to be produced under this section.

(f) *Limit on dissemination*. The Federal Bureau of Investigation may not disseminate information obtained pursuant to this section outside of the Federal Bureau of Investigation, except to other Federal agencies as may be necessary for the approval or conduct of a foreign counterintelligence investigation, or, where the information concerns a person subject to the Uniform Code of Military Justice, to appropriate investigative authorities within the military department concerned as may be necessary for the conduct of a joint foreign counterintelligence investigation.

(g) *Rules of construction*. Nothing in this section shall be construed to prohibit information from being furnished by the Federal Bureau of Investigation pursuant to a subpoena or court order, in connection with a judicial or administrative proceeding to enforce the provisions of this Act. Nothing in this section shall be construed to authorize or permit the withholding of information from the Congress.

(h) *Reports to Congress*. On a semiannual basis, the Attorney General shall fully inform the Permanent Select Committee on Intelligence and the Committee on Banking, Finance and Urban Affairs of the House of Representatives, and the Select Committee on Intelligence and the Committee on Banking, Housing, and Urban Affairs of the Senate concerning all requests made pursuant to subsections (a), (b), and (c).

(i) *Damages*. Any agency or department of the United States obtaining or disclosing any consumer reports, records, or information contained therein in violation of this section is liable to the consumer to whom such consumer reports, records, or information relate in an amount equal to the sum of

(1) $100, without regard to the volume of consumer reports, records, or information involved;

(2) any actual damages sustained by the consumer as a result of the disclosure;

(3) if the violation is found to have been willful or intentional, such punitive damages as a court may allow; and

(4) in the case of any successful action to enforce liability under this subsection, the costs of the action, together with reasonable attorney fees, as determined by the court.

(j) *Disciplinary actions for violations.* If a court determines that any agency or department of the United States has violated any provision of this section and the court finds that the circumstances surrounding the violation raise questions of whether or not an officer or employee of the agency or department acted willfully or intentionally with respect to the violation, the agency or department shall promptly initiate a proceeding to determine whether or not disciplinary action is warranted against the officer or employee who was responsible for the violation.

(k) *Good-faith exception.* Notwithstanding any other provision of this title, any consumer reporting agency or agent or employee thereof making disclosure of consumer reports or identifying information pursuant to this subsection in good-faith reliance upon a certification of the Federal Bureau of Investigation pursuant to provisions of this section shall not be liable to any person for such disclosure under this title, the constitution of any State, or any law or regulation of any State or any political subdivision of any State.

(l) *Limitation of remedies.* Notwithstanding any other provision of this title, the remedies and sanctions set forth in this section shall be the only judicial remedies and sanctions for violation of this section.

(m) *Injunctive relief.* In addition to any other remedy contained in this section, injunctive relief shall be available to require compliance with the procedures of this section. In the event of any successful action under this subsection, costs together with reasonable attorney fees, as determined by the court, may be recovered.

§ 627. Disclosures to governmental agencies for counterterrorism purposes [15 U.S.C. §1681v]

(a) *Disclosure.* Notwithstanding section 604 or any other provision of this title, a consumer reporting agency shall furnish a consumer report of a consumer and all other information in a consumer's file to a government agency authorized to conduct investigations of, or intelligence or counterintelligence activities or analysis related to, international terrorism when presented with a written certification by such government agency that such information is necessary for the agency's conduct or such investigation, activity or analysis.

(b) *Form of certification.* The certification described in subsection (a) shall be signed by a supervisory official designated by the head of a Federal agency or an officer of a Federal agency whose appointment to office is required to be made by the President, by and with the advice and consent of the Senate.

(c) *Confidentiality.* No consumer reporting agency, or officer, employee, or agent of such consumer reporting agency, shall disclose to any person, or specify in any consumer report, that a government agency has sought or obtained access to information under subsection (a).

(d) *Rule of construction.* Nothing in section 626 shall be construed to limit the authority of the Director of the Federal Bureau of Investigation under this section.

(e) *Safe harbor.* Notwithstanding any other provision of this title, any consumer reporting agency or agent or employee thereof making disclosure of consumer reports or other information pursuant to this section in good-faith reliance upon a certification of a governmental agency pursuant to the provisions of this section shall not be liable to any person for such disclosure under this subchapter, the constitution of any State, or any law or regulation of any State or any political subdivision of any State.

§ 628. Disposal of records [15 U.S.C. §1681w]

(a) Regulations

(1) *In general.* Not later than 1 year after the date of enactment of this section, the Federal banking agencies, the National Credit Union Administration, and the Commission with respect to the entities that are subject to their respective enforcement authority under section 621, and the Securities and Exchange Commission, and in coordination as described in paragraph (2), shall issue final regulations requiring any person that maintains or otherwise possesses consumer information, or any compilation of consumer information, derived from consumer reports for a business purpose to properly dispose of any such information or compilation.

(2) *Coordination.* Each agency required to prescribe regulations under paragraph (1) shall–

(A) consult and coordinate with each other such agency so that, to the extent possible, the regulations prescribed by each such agency are consistent and comparable with the regulations by each such other agency; and

(B) ensure that such regulations are consistent with the requirements and regulations issued pursuant to Public Law 106-102 and other provisions of Federal law.

(3) *Exemption authority.* In issuing regulations under this section, the Federal banking agencies, the National Credit Union Administration, the Commission, and the Securities and Exchange Commission may exempt any person or class of persons from application of those regulations, as such agency deems appropriate to carry out the purpose of this section.

(b) *Rule of construction.* Nothing in this section shall be construed--

(1) to require a person to maintain or destroy any record pertaining to a consumer that is not imposed under other law; or

(2) to alter or affect any requirement imposed under any other provision of law to maintain or destroy such a record.

§ 629. Corporate and technological circumvention prohibited [15 U.S.C. §1681x]

The Commission shall prescribe regulations, to become effective not later than 90 days after the date of enactment of this section, to prevent a consumer reporting agency from circumventing or evading treatment as a consumer reporting agency described in section 603(p) for purposes of this title, including--

(1) by means of a corporate reorganization or restructuring, including a merger, acquisition, dissolution, divestiture, or asset sale of a consumer reporting agency; or

(2) by maintaining or merging public record and credit account information in a manner that is substantially equivalent to that described in paragraphs (1) and (2) of section 603(p), in the manner described in section 603(p).

Legislative History

House Reports: No. 91-975 (Comm. on Banking and Currency) and
                No. 91-1587 (Comm. of Conference)
Senate Reports: No. 91-1139 accompanying S. 3678 (Comm. on Banking and Currency)

Congressional Record, Vol. 116 (1970)
                May 25, considered and passed House.
                Sept. 18, considered and passed Senate, amended.
                Oct. 9, Senate agreed to conference report.
                Oct. 13, House agreed to conference report.

Enactment: Public Law No. 91-508 (October 26, 1970):

Amendments: Public Law Nos.   95-473 (October 17, 1978)
                              95-598 (November 6, 1978)
                              98-443 (October 4, 1984)
                              101-73 (August 9, 1989)
                              102-242 (December 19, 1991)
                              102-537 (October 27, 1992)
                              02-550 (October 28, 1992)
                              03-325 (September 23, 1994)
                              04-88 (December 29, 1995)
                              04-93 (January 6, 1996)
                              04-193 (August 22, 1996)
                              04-208 (September 30, 1996)
                              05-107 (November 20, 1997)
                              05-347 (November 2, 1998)
                              06-102 (November 12, 1999)
                              07-56 (October 26, 2001)
                              08-159 (December 4, 2003)

APPENDIX 2: FAIR CREDIT BILLING ACT

15 USC 1601 note

§ 301. Short Title
This title may be cited as the Fair Credit Billing Act.

§ 302. Declaration of purpose
The last sentence of section 102 of the Truth in Lending Act (15 U.S.C. 1601) is amended by striking out the period and inserting in lieu thereof a comma and the following: "and to protect the consumer against inaccurate and unfair credit billing and credit card practices."

§ 303. Definitions of creditor and open-end credit plan
The first sentence of section 103(f) of the Truth in Lending Act (15 U.S.C. 1602(f)) is amended to read as follows:

    i.   The term "creditor" refers only to creditors who regularly extend, or arrange for the extension of, credit which is payable by agreement in more than four installments or for which the payment of a finance charge is or may be required, whether in connection with loans, sales of property or services, or otherwise. For the purposes of the requirements imposed under Chapter 4 and sections 127(a) (6), 127(a) (7), 127(a) (8), 127(b) (1), 127(b) (2), 127(b) (3), 127(b) (9), and 127(b) (11) of Chapter 2 of this Title, the term "creditor" shall also include card issuers whether or not the amount due is payable by agreement in more than four installments or the payment of a finance charge is or may be required, and the Board shall, by regulation, apply these requirements to such card issuers, to the extent appropriate, even though the requirements are by their terms applicable only to creditors offering open end credit plans.

§ 304. Disclosure of fair credit billing rights

(a) Section 127(a) of the Truth in Lending Act (15 U.S.C. 1637(a)) is amended by adding at the end thereof a new paragraph as follows:

> "(8) A statement, in a form prescribed by regulations of the Board of the protection provided by sections 161 and 170 to an obligor and the creditor's responsibilities under sections 162 and 170. With respect to each of two billing cycles per year, at semiannual intervals, the creditor shall transmit such statement to each obligor to whom the creditor is required to transmit a statement pursuant to sections 127(b) for such billing cycle."

(b) Section 127(c) of such Act (15 U.S.C. 1637(c)) is amended to read:

> "(c) In the case of any existing account under an open end consumer credit plan having an outstanding balance of more than $1 at or after the close of the creditor's first full billing cycle under the plan after the effective date of subsection (a) or any amendments thereto, the items described in subsection (a), to the extent applicable and not previously disclosed, shall be disclosed in a notice mailed or delivered to the obligor not later than the time of mailing the next statement required by subsection (b)."

§ 305. Disclosure of billing contact

Section 127(b) of the Truth in Lending Act (15 U.S.C. 1637(b)) is amended by adding at the end thereof a new paragraph as follows:

> "(11) The address to be used by the creditor for the purpose of receiving billing inquiries from the obligor."

§ 306. Billing practices

The Truth in Lending Act (15 U.S.C. 1601-1665) is amended by adding at the end thereof a new chapter as follows:

Chapter 4 - CREDIT BILLING
Sec.
161. Correction of billing errors
162. Regulation of credit reports
163. Length of billing period
164. Prompt crediting of payments
165. Crediting excess payments
166. Prompt notification of returns
167. Use of cash discounts
168. Prohibition of tie-in services
169. Prohibition of offsets
170. Rights of credit card customers
171. Relation to State laws

§ 161. Correction of billing errors
ii (a) If a creditor, within sixty days after having transmitted to an obligor a statement of the obligor's account in connection with an extension of

consumer credit, receives at the address disclosed under section 127(b) (11) a written notice (other than notice on a payment stub or other payment medium supplied by the creditor if the creditor so stipulates with the disclosure required under section 127(a) (8)) from the obligor in which the obligor (1) sets forth or otherwise enables the creditor to identify the name and account number (if any) of the obligor,

(2) indicates the obligor's belief that the statement contains a billing error and the amount of such billing error, and

(3) sets forth the reasons for the obligor's belief (to the extent applicable) that the statement contains a billing error, the creditor shall, unless the obligor has, after giving such written notice and before the expiration of the time limits herein specified, agreed that the statement was correct

    (A) not later than thirty days after the receipt of the notice, send a written acknowledgment thereof to the obligor, unless the action required in subparagraph

    (B) is taken within such thirty-day period, and (B) not later than two complete billing cycles of the creditor (in no event later than ninety days) after the receipt of the notice and prior to taking any action to collect the amount, or any part thereof, indicated by the obligor under paragraph (2) either

    (i) make appropriate corrections in the account of the obligor, including the crediting of any finance charges on amounts erroneously billed, and transmit to the obligor a notification of such corrections and the creditor's explanation of any cage in the amount indicated by the obligor under paragraph (2) and, if any such change is made and the obligor so requests, copies of documentary evidence of the obligor's indebtedness; or

    (ii) send a written explanation or clarification to the obligor, after having conducted an investigation, setting forth to the extent applicable the reasons why the creditor believes the account of the obligor was correctly shown in the statement and, upon request of the obligor, provide copies of documentary evidence of the obligor's indebtedness. In the case of a billing error where the obligor alleges that the creditor's billing statement reflects goods not delivered to the obligor or his designee in accordance with the agreement made at the time of the transaction, a creditor may not construe such amount to be correctly shown unless he determines that such goods were actually delivered, mailed, or otherwise sent to the obligor and provides the obligor with a statement of such determination. After complying with the provisions of this subsection with respect to an alleged billing error, a creditor has no further responsibility under this section if the obligor continues to make substantially the same allegation with respect to such error.

(b) For the purpose of this section, a "billing error" consists of any of the following:

(1) A reflection on a statement of an extension of credit that was not made to the obligor or, if made, was not in the amount reflected on such statement.

(2) A reflection on a statement of an extension of credit for which the obligor requests additional clarification including documentary evidence thereof.

(3) A reflection on a statement of goods or services not accepted by the obligor or his designee or not delivered to the obligor or his designee in accordance with the agreement made at the time of a transaction.

(4) The creditor's failure to reflect properly on a statement a payment made by the obligor or a credit issued to the obligor.

(5) A computation error or similar error of an accounting nature of the creditor on a statement.

(6) Any other error described in regulations of the Board.

(c) For the purposes of this section, "action to collect the amount, or any part thereof, indicated by an obligor under paragraph (2)" does not include the sending of statements of account to the obligor following written notice from the obligor as specified under subsection (a) if

(1) the obligor's account is not restricted or closed because of the failure of the obligor to pay the amount indicated under paragraph (2) of subsection (a) and (2) the creditor indicates the payment of such amount is not required pending the creditor's compliance with this section. Nothing in this section shall be construed to prohibit any action by a creditor to collect any amount which has not been indicated by the obligor to contain a billing error.

(d) Pursuant to regulations of the Board, a creditor operating an open end consumer credit plan may not, prior to the sending of the written explanation or clarification required under paragraph (B) (ii), restrict or close an account with respect to which the obligor has indicated pursuant to subsection (a) that he believes such account to contain a billing error solely because of the obligor's failure to pay the amount indicated to be in error. Nothing in this subsection shall be deemed to prohibit a creditor from applying against the credit limit on the obligor's account the amount indicated to be in error.

(e) Any creditor who fails to comply with the requirements of this section or section 162 forfeits any right to collect from the obligor the amount indicated by the obligor under paragraph (2) of subsection (a) of this section, and any finance charges thereon, except that the amount required to be forfeited under this subsection may not exceed $50.

§ 162. Regulation of credit reports

(a) After receiving a notice from an obligor as provided in section 161(a), a creditor or his agent may not directly or indirectly threaten to report to any person adversely on the obligor's credit rating or credit standing because of the obligor's failure to pay the amount indicated by the obligor under section 161(a) (2) and such amount may not be reported as delinquent to any third party until the creditor has met the requirements of section 161 and has allowed the obligor the same number of days (not less than ten) thereafter to make payment as is provided under the credit agreement with the obligor for the payment of undisputed amounts.

(b) If a creditor receives a further written notice from an obligor that an amount is still in dispute within the time allowed for payment under subsection (a) of this section, a creditor may not report to any third party that the amount of the obligor is delinquent because the obligor has failed to pay an amount which he has indicated under section 161(a) (2), unless the creditor also reports that the amount is in dispute and, at the same time, notifies the obligor of the name and address of each party to whom the creditor is reporting information concerning the delinquency.

(c) A creditor shall report any subsequent resolution of any delinquencies reported pursuant to subsection (b) to the parties to whom such delinquencies were initially reported.

§ 163. Length of billing period

(a) If an open end consumer credit plan provides a time period within which an obligor may repay any portion of the credit extended without incurring an additional finance charge, such additional finance charge may not be imposed with respect to such portion of the credit extended for the billing cycle of which such period is a part unless a statement which includes the amount upon which the finance charge for that period is based was mailed at least fourteen days prior to the date specified in the statement by which payment must be made in order to avoid imposition of that finance charge.

(b) Subsection (a) does not apply in any case where a creditor has been prevented, delayed, or hindered in making timely mailing or delivery of such periodic statement within the time period specified in such subsection because of an act of God, war, natural disaster, strike, or other excusable or justifiable cause, as determined under regulations of the Board.

§ 164. Prompt crediting of payments

Payments received from an obligor under an open end consumer credit plan by the creditor shall be posted promptly to the obligor's account as specified in regulations of the Board. Such regulations shall prevent a finance charge from being imposed on any obligor if the creditor has received the obligor's payment in readily identifiable form in the amount, manner, location, and time indicated by the creditor to avoid the imposition thereof.

§ 165. Crediting excess payments

Whenever an obligor transmits funds to a creditor in excess of the total balance due on an open end consumer credit account, the creditor shall promptly (1) upon request of the obligor refund the amount of the overpayment, or (2) credit such amount to the obligor's account.

§ 166. Prompt notification of returns

With respect to any sales transaction where a credit card has been used to obtain credit, where the seller is a person other than the card issuer, and where the seller accepts or allows a return of the goods or forgiveness of a debit for services which were the subject of such sale, the seller shall promptly transmit to the credit card issuer, a credit statement with respect thereto and the credit card issuer shall credit the account of the obligor for the amount of the transaction.

§ 167. Use of cash discounts

(a) With respect to credit card which may be used for extensions of credit in sales transactions in which the seller is a person other than the card issuer, the card issuer may not, by contract or otherwise, prohibit any such seller from offering a discount to a cardholder to induce the cardholder to pay by cash, check, or similar means rather than use a credit card.

(b) With respect to any sales transaction, any discount not in excess of 5 per centum offered by the seller for the purpose of inducing payment by cash, check, or other means not involving the use of a credit card shall not constitute a finance charge as determined under section 106, if such discount is offered to all prospective buyers and its availability is disclosed to all prospective buyers clearly and conspicuously in accordance with regulations of the Board.

§ 168. Prohibition of tie-in services

Notwithstanding any agreement to the contrary, a card issuer may not require a seller, as a condition to participating in a credit card plan, to open an account with or procure any other service from the card issuer or its subsidiary or agent.

§ 169. Prohibition of offsets

(a) A card issuer may not take any action to offset a cardholder's indebtedness arising in connection with a consumer credit transaction under the relevant credit card plan against funds of the cardholder held on deposit with the card issuer unless

> (1) such action was previously authorized in writing by the cardholder in accordance with a credit plan whereby the cardholder agrees periodically to pay debts incurred in his open end credit account by permitting the card issuer periodically to

deduct all or a portion of such debt from the cardholder's deposit account, and

(2) such action with respect to any outstanding disputed amount not be taken by the card issuer upon request of the cardholder. In the case of any credit card account in existence on the effective date of this section, the previous written authorization referred to in clause (1) shall not be required until the date (after such effective date) when such account is renewed, but in no case later than one year after such effective date. Such written authorization shall be deemed to exist if the card issuer has previously notified the cardholder that the use of his credit card account will subject any funds which the card issuer holds in deposit accounts of such cardholder to offset against any amounts due and payable on his credit card account which have not been paid in accordance with the terms of the agreement between the card issuer and the cardholder.

(b) This section does not alter or affect the right under State law of a card issuer to attach or otherwise levy upon funds of a cardholder held on deposit with the card issuer if that remedy is constitutionally available to creditors generally.

§ 170. Rights of credit card customers

(a) Subject to the limitation contained in subsection (b), a card issuer who has issued a credit card to a cardholder pursuant to an open end consumer credit plan shall be subject to all claims (other than tort claims) and defenses arising out of any transaction in which the credit card is used as a method of payment or extension of credit if (1) the obligor has made a good faith attempt to obtain satisfactory resolution of a disagreement or problem relative to the transaction from the transaction exceeds $50; and (2) the place where the initial transaction occurred was in the same State as the mailing address previously provided by the cardholder or was within 100 miles from such address, except that the limitations set forth in clauses (2) and (3) with respect to an obligor's right to assert claims and defenses against a card issuer shall not be applicable to any transaction in which the person honoring the credit card (A) is the same person as the card issuer, (B) is controlled by the card issuer, (C) is under direct or indirect common control with the card issuer, (D) is a franchised dealer in the card issuer's products or services, or (E) has obtained the order for such transaction through a mail solicitation made by or participated in by the card issuer in which the cardholder is solicited to enter into such transaction by using the credit card issued by the card issuer.

(b) The amount of claims or defenses asserted by the cardholder may not exceed the amount of credit outstanding with respect to such transaction at the time the cardholder first notifies the card issuer or the person honoring the credit card of such claim or defense. For the purpose of determining the amount of credit outstanding in the preceding sentence, payments and credits to the cardholder's account are deemed to have been applied, in the order indicated, to the payment of:

    (1) late charges in the order of their entry to the account;

    (2) finance charges in order of their entry to the account; and

    (3) debits to the account other than those set forth above, in the order in which each debit entry to the account was made.

§ 171. Relation to State laws

(a) This chapter does not annul, alter, or affect, or exempt any person subject to the provisions of this chapter from complying with, the laws of any State with respect to credit billing practices, except to the extent that those laws are inconsistent with any provision of this chapter, and then only to the extent of the inconsistency. The Board is authorized to determine whether such inconsistencies exist. The Board may not determine that any State law is inconsistent with person honoring the credit card; the amount of the initial any provision of this chapter if the Board determines that such law gives greater protection to the consumer.

(b) The Board shall by regulation exempt from the requirements of this chapter any class of credit transactions within any State if it determines that under the law of that State that class of transactions is subject to requirements substantially similar to those imposed under this chapter or hat such law gives greater protection to the consumer, and that there is adequate provision for enforcement.

§ 307. Conforming amendments

(a) The table of chapter of the Truth in Lending Act is amended by adding immediately under item 3 the following:

"4. CREDIT BILLING . . . . 161"

(b) Section 111(d) of such Act (15 U.S.C. 1610(d)) is amended by striking out and 130 and inserting in lieu thereof a comma and the following: 130, and 166.

(c) Section 121(a) of such Act (15 U.S.C. 1631(a)) is amended--

    (1) by striking out and upon whom a finance charge is or may be imposed; and

    (2) by inserting "or Chapter 4" immediately after this chapter.

(d) Section 121(b) of such Act (15 U.S.C. 1631(b)) is amended by inserting "or Chapter 4" immediately after this chapter.

(e) Section 122(a) of such Act (15 U.S.C. 1632(a)) is amended by inserting "or Chapter 4" immediately after this chapter.

(f) Section 122(b) of such Act (15 U.S.C. 1632(b)) is amended by inserting "or Chapter 4" immediately after this chapter.

§ 308. Effective date

This title takes effect upon the expiration of one year after the date of its enactment.

APPENDIX 3: FAIR DEBT COLLECTION PRACTICES ACT

§ 801. Short Title [15 USC 1601 note]
This title may be cited as the "Fair Debt Collection Practices Act."

§ 802. Congressional findings and declarations of purpose [15 USC 1692]
(a) There is abundant evidence of the use of abusive, deceptive, and unfair debt collection practices by many debt collectors. Abusive debt collection practices contribute to the number of personal bankruptcies, to marital instability, to the loss of jobs, and to invasions of individual privacy.
(b) Existing laws and procedures for redressing these injuries are inadequate to protect consumers.
(c) Means other than misrepresentation or other abusive debt collection practices are available for the effective collection of debts.
(d) Abusive debt collection practices are carried on to a substantial extent in interstate commerce and through means and instrumentalities of such commerce. Even where abusive debt collection practices are purely intrastate in character, they nevertheless directly affect interstate commerce.
(e) It is the purpose of this title to eliminate abusive debt collection practices by debt collectors, to insure that those debt collectors who refrain from using abusive debt collection practices are not competitively disadvantaged, and to promote consistent State action to protect consumers against debt collection abuses.

§ 803. Definitions [15 USC 1692a]
As used in this title --
(1) The term "Commission" means the Federal Trade Commission.
(2) The term "communication" means the conveying of information regarding a debt directly or indirectly to any person through any medium.
(3) The term "consumer" means any natural person obligated or allegedly obligated to pay any debt.

(4) The term "creditor" means any person who offers or extends credit creating a debt or to whom a debt is owed, but such term does not include any person to the extent that he receives an assignment or transfer of a debt in default solely for the purpose of facilitating collection of such debt for another.

(5) The term "debt" means any obligation or alleged obligation of a consumer to pay money arising out of a transaction in which the money, property, insurance or services which are the subject of the transaction are primarily for personal, family, or household purposes, whether or not such obligation has been reduced to judgment.

(6) The term "debt collector" means any person who uses any instrumentality of interstate commerce or the mails in any business the principal purpose of which is the collection of any debts, or who regularly collects or attempts to collect, directly or indirectly, debts owed or due or asserted to be owed or due another. Notwithstanding the exclusion provided by clause (F) of the last sentence of this paragraph, the term includes any creditor who, in the process of collecting his own debts, uses any name other than his own which would indicate that a third person is collecting or attempting to collect such debts. For the purpose of section 808(6), such term also includes any person who uses any instrumentality of interstate commerce or the mails in any business the principal purpose of which is the enforcement of security interests. The term does not include --

(A) any officer or employee of a creditor while, in the name of the creditor, collecting debts for such creditor;

(B) any person while acting as a debt collector for another person, both of whom are related by common ownership or affiliated by corporate control, if the person acting as a debt collector does so only for persons to whom it is so related or affiliated and if the principal business of such person is not the collection of debts;

(C) any officer or employee of the United States or any State to the extent that collecting or attempting to collect any debt is in the performance of his official duties;

(D) any person while serving or attempting to serve legal process on any other person in connection with the judicial enforcement of any debt;

(E) any nonprofit organization which, at the request of consumers, performs bona fide consumer credit counseling and assists consumers in the liquidation of their debts by receiving payments from such consumers and distributing such amounts to creditors; and

(F) any person collecting or attempting to collect any debt owed or due or asserted to be owed or due another to the extent such activity (i) is incidental to a bona fide fiduciary obligation or a bona fide escrow arrangement; (ii) concerns a debt which was originated by such person; (iii) concerns a debt which was not in default at the time it was obtained by such person; or (iv) concerns a debt obtained by such person as a secured party in a commercial credit transaction involving the creditor.

(7) The term "location information" means a consumer's place of abode and his telephone number at such place, or his place of employment.

(8) The term "State" means any State, territory, or possession of the United States, the District of Columbia, the Commonwealth of Puerto Rico, or any political subdivision of any of the foregoing.

§ 804. Acquisition of location information [15 USC 1692b]

Any debt collector communicating with any person other than the consumer for the purpose of acquiring location information about the consumer shall --

(1) identify himself, state that he is confirming or correcting location information concerning the consumer, and, only if expressly requested, identify his employer;

(2) not state that such consumer owes any debt;

(3) not communicate with any such person more than once unless requested to do so by such person or unless the debt collector reasonably believes that the earlier response of such person is erroneous or incomplete and that such person now has correct or complete location information;

(4) not communicate by post card;

(5) not use any language or symbol on any envelope or in the contents of any communication effected by the mails or telegram that indicates that the debt collector is in the debt collection business or that the communication relates to the collection of a debt; and

(6) after the debt collector knows the consumer is represented by an attorney with regard to the subject debt and has knowledge of, or can readily ascertain, such attorney's name and address, not communicate with any person other than that attorney, unless the attorney fails to respond within a reasonable period of time to the communication from the debt collector.

§ 805. Communication in connection with debt collection [15 USC 1692c]

(a) COMMUNICATION WITH THE CONSUMER GENERALLY. Without the prior consent of the consumer given directly to the debt collector or the express permission of a court of competent jurisdiction, a debt collector may not communicate with a consumer in connection with the collection of any debt --

(1) at any unusual time or place or a time or place known or which should be known to be inconvenient to the consumer. In the absence of knowledge of circumstances to the contrary, a debt collector shall assume that the convenient time for communicating with a consumer is after 8 o'clock antemeridian and before 9 o'clock postmeridian, local time at the consumer's location;

(2) if the debt collector knows the consumer is represented by an attorney with respect to such debt and has knowledge of, or can readily ascertain, such attorney's name and address, unless the attorney fails to respond within a reasonable period of time to a communication from the debt collector or unless the attorney consents to direct communication with the consumer; or

(3) at the consumer's place of employment if the debt collector knows or has reason to know that the consumer's employer prohibits the consumer from receiving such communication.

(b) COMMUNICATION WITH THIRD PARTIES. Except as provided in section 804, without the prior consent of the consumer given directly to the debt collector, or the express permission of a court of competent jurisdiction, or as reasonably necessary to effectuate a post-judgment judicial remedy, a debt collector may not communicate, in connection with the collection of any debt, with any person other than a consumer, his attorney, a consumer reporting agency if otherwise permitted by law, the creditor, the attorney of the creditor, or the attorney of the debt collector.

(c) CEASING COMMUNICATION. If a consumer notifies a debt collector in writing that the consumer refuses to pay a debt or that the consumer wishes the debt collector to cease further communication with the consumer, the debt collector shall not communicate further with the consumer with respect to such debt, except --

(1) to advise the consumer that the debt collector's further efforts are being terminated;

(2) to notify the consumer that the debt collector or creditor may invoke specified remedies which are ordinarily invoked by such debt collector or creditor; or

(3) where applicable, to notify the consumer that the debt collector or creditor intends to invoke a specified remedy.

If such notice from the consumer is made by mail, notification shall be complete upon receipt.

(d) For the purpose of this section, the term "consumer" includes the consumer's spouse, parent (if the consumer is a minor), guardian, executor, or administrator.

§ 806. Harassment or abuse [15 USC 1692d]

A debt collector may not engage in any conduct the natural consequence of which is to harass, oppress, or abuse any person in connection with the collection of a debt. Without limiting the general application of the foregoing, the following conduct is a violation of this section:

(1) The use or threat of use of violence or other criminal means to harm the physical person, reputation, or property of any person.

(2) The use of obscene or profane language or language the natural consequence of which is to abuse the hearer or reader.

(3) The publication of a list of consumers who allegedly refuse to pay debts, except to a consumer reporting agency or to persons meeting the requirements of section 603(f) or 604(3)[1] of this Act.

(4) The advertisement for sale of any debt to coerce payment of the debt.

(5) Causing a telephone to ring or engaging any person in telephone conversation repeatedly or continuously with intent to annoy, abuse, or harass any person at the called number.

(6) Except as provided in section 804, the placement of telephone calls without meaningful disclosure of the caller's identity.

§ 807. False or misleading representations [15 USC 1962e]

A debt collector may not use any false, deceptive, or misleading representation or means in connection with the collection of any debt. Without limiting the general application of the foregoing, the following conduct is a violation of this section:

(1) The false representation or implication that the debt collector is vouched for, bonded by, or affiliated with the United States or any State, including the use of any badge, uniform, or facsimile thereof.

(2) The false representation of --

(A) the character, amount, or legal status of any debt; or

(B) any services rendered or compensation which may be lawfully received by any debt collector for the collection of a debt.

(3) The false representation or implication that any individual is an attorney or that any communication is from an attorney.

(4) The representation or implication that nonpayment of any debt will result in the arrest or imprisonment of any person or the seizure, garnishment, attachment, or sale of any property or wages of any person unless such action is lawful and the debt collector or creditor intends to take such action.

(5) The threat to take any action that cannot legally be taken or that is not intended to be taken.

(6) The false representation or implication that a sale, referral, or other transfer of any interest in a debt shall cause the consumer to --

(A) lose any claim or defense to payment of the debt; or

(B) become subject to any practice prohibited by this title.

(7) The false representation or implication that the consumer committed any crime or other conduct in order to disgrace the consumer.

(8) Communicating or threatening to communicate to any person credit information which is known or which should be known to be false, including the failure to communicate that a disputed debt is disputed.

(9) The use or distribution of any written communication which simulates or is falsely represented to be a document authorized, issued, or approved by any court, official, or agency of the United States or any State, or which creates a false impression as to its source, authorization, or approval.

(10) The use of any false representation or deceptive means to collect or attempt to collect any debt or to obtain information concerning a consumer.

(11) The failure to disclose in the initial written communication with the consumer and, in addition, if the initial communication with the consumer is oral, in that initial oral communication, that the debt collector is attempting to collect a debt and that any information obtained will be used for that purpose, and the failure to disclose in subsequent communications that the communication is from a debt collector, except that this paragraph shall not apply to a formal pleading made in connection with a legal action.

(12) The false representation or implication that accounts have been turned over to innocent purchasers for value.

(13) The false representation or implication that documents are legal process.

(14) The use of any business, company, or organization name other than the true name of the debt collector's business, company, or organization.

(15) The false representation or implication that documents are not legal process forms or do not require action by the consumer.

(16) The false representation or implication that a debt collector operates or is employed by a consumer reporting agency as defined by section 603(f) of this Act.

§ 808. Unfair practices [15 USC 1692f]

A debt collector may not use unfair or unconscionable means to collect or attempt to collect any debt. Without limiting the general application of the foregoing, the following conduct is a violation of this section:

(1) The collection of any amount (including any interest, fee, charge, or expense incidental to the principal obligation) unless such amount is expressly authorized by the agreement creating the debt or permitted by law.

(2) The acceptance by a debt collector from any person of a check or other payment instrument postdated by more than five days unless such person is notified in writing of the debt collector's intent to deposit such check or instrument not more than ten nor less than three business days prior to such deposit.

(3) The solicitation by a debt collector of any postdated check or other postdated payment instrument for the purpose of threatening or instituting criminal prosecution.

(4) Depositing or threatening to deposit any postdated check or other postdated payment instrument prior to the date on such check or instrument.

(5) Causing charges to be made to any person for communications by concealment of the true propose of the communication. Such charges include, but are not limited to, collect telephone calls and telegram fees.

(6) Taking or threatening to take any nonjudicial action to effect dispossession or disablement of property if --

(A) there is no present right to possession of the property claimed as collateral through an enforceable security interest;

(B) there is no present intention to take possession of the property; or

(C) the property is exempt by law from such dispossession or disablement.

(7) Communicating with a consumer regarding a debt by post card.

(8) Using any language or symbol, other than the debt collector's address, on any envelope when communicating with a consumer by use of the mails or by telegram, except that a debt collector may use his business name if such name does not indicate that he is in the debt collection business.

§ 809. Validation of debts [15 USC 1692g]

(a) Within five days after the initial communication with a consumer in connection with the collection of any debt, a debt collector shall, unless the following information is contained in the initial communication or the consumer has paid the debt, send the consumer a written notice containing --

(1) the amount of the debt;

(2) the name of the creditor to whom the debt is owed;

(3) a statement that unless the consumer, within thirty days after receipt of the notice, disputes the validity of the debt, or any portion thereof, the debt will be assumed to be valid by the debt collector;

(4) a statement that if the consumer notifies the debt collector in writing within the thirty-day period that the debt, or any portion thereof, is disputed, the debt collector will obtain verification of the debt or a copy of a judgment

against the consumer and a copy of such verification or judgment will be mailed to the consumer by the debt collector; and

(5) a statement that, upon the consumer's written request within the thirty-day period, the debt collector will provide the consumer with the name and address of the original creditor, if different from the current creditor.

(b) If the consumer notifies the debt collector in writing within the thirty-day period described in subsection (a) that the debt, or any portion thereof, is disputed, or that the consumer requests the name and address of the original creditor, the debt collector shall cease collection of the debt, or any disputed portion thereof, until the debt collector obtains verification of the debt or any copy of a judgment, or the name and address of the original creditor, and a copy of such verification or judgment, or name and address of the original creditor, is mailed to the consumer by the debt collector.

(c) The failure of a consumer to dispute the validity of a debt under this section may not be construed by any court as an admission of liability by the consumer.

§ 810. Multiple debts [15 USC 1692h]

If any consumer owes multiple debts and makes any single payment to any debt collector with respect to such debts, such debt collector may not apply such payment to any debt which is disputed by the consumer and, where applicable, shall apply such payment in accordance with the consumer's directions.

§ 811. Legal actions by debt collectors [15 USC 1692i]

(a) Any debt collector who brings any legal action on a debt against any consumer shall --

(1) in the case of an action to enforce an interest in real property securing the consumer's obligation, bring such action only in a judicial district or similar legal entity in which such real property is located; or

(2) in the case of an action not described in paragraph (1), bring such action only in the judicial district or similar legal entity --

(A) in which such consumer signed the contract sued upon; or

(B) in which such consumer resides at the commencement of the action.

(b) Nothing in this title shall be construed to authorize the bringing of legal actions by debt collectors.

§ 812. Furnishing certain deceptive forms [15 USC 1692j]

(a) It is unlawful to design, compile, and furnish any form knowing that such form would be used to create the false belief in a consumer that a person other than the creditor of such consumer is participating in the collection of or in an attempt to collect a debt such consumer allegedly owes such creditor, when in fact such person is not so participating.

(b) Any person who violates this section shall be liable to the same extent and in the same manner as a debt collector is liable under section 813 for failure to comply with a provision of this title.

§ 813. Civil liability [15 USC 1692k]

(a) Except as otherwise provided by this section, any debt collector who fails to comply with any provision of this title with respect to any person is liable to such person in an amount equal to the sum of --

(1) any actual damage sustained by such person as a result of such failure;

(2) (A) in the case of any action by an individual, such additional damages as the court may allow, but not exceeding $1,000; or

(B) in the case of a class action, (i) such amount for each named plaintiff as could be recovered under subparagraph (A), and (ii) such amount as the court may allow for all other class members, without regard to a minimum individual recovery, not to exceed the lesser of $500,000 or 1 per centum of the net worth of the debt collector; and

(3) in the case of any successful action to enforce the foregoing liability, the costs of the action, together with a reasonable attorney's fee as determined by the court. On a finding by the court that an action under this section was brought in bad faith and for the purpose of harassment, the court may award to the defendant attorney's fees reasonable in relation to the work expended and costs.

(b) In determining the amount of liability in any action under subsection (a), the court shall consider, among other relevant factors --

(1) in any individual action under subsection (a)(2)(A), the frequency and persistence of noncompliance by the debt collector, the nature of such noncompliance, and the extent to which such noncompliance was intentional; or

(2) in any class action under subsection (a)(2)(B), the frequency and persistence of noncompliance by the debt collector, the nature of such noncompliance, the resources of the debt collector, the number of persons adversely affected, and the extent to which the debt collector's noncompliance was intentional.

(c) A debt collector may not be held liable in any action brought under this title if the debt collector shows by a preponderance of evidence that the violation was not intentional and resulted from a bona fide error notwithstanding the maintenance of procedures reasonably adapted to avoid any such error.

(d) An action to enforce any liability created by this title may be brought in any appropriate United States district court without regard to the amount in controversy, or in any other court of competent jurisdiction, within one year from the date on which the violation occurs.

(e) No provision of this section imposing any liability shall apply to any act done or omitted in good faith in conformity with any advisory opinion of the Commission, notwithstanding that after such act or omission has occurred, such opinion is amended, rescinded, or determined by judicial or other authority to be invalid for any reason.

§ 814. Administrative enforcement [15 USC 1692l]

(a) Compliance with this title shall be enforced by the Commission, except to the extend that enforcement of the requirements imposed under this title is specifically committed to another agency under subsection (b). For purpose of the exercise by the Commission of its functions and powers under the Federal Trade Commission Act, a violation of this title shall be deemed an unfair or deceptive act or practice in violation of that Act. All of the functions and powers of the Commission under the Federal Trade Commission Act are available to the Commission to enforce compliance by any person with this title, irrespective of whether that person is engaged in commerce or meets any other jurisdictional tests in the Federal Trade Commission Act, including the power to enforce the provisions of this title in the same manner as if the violation had been a violation of a Federal Trade Commission trade regulation rule.

(b) Compliance with any requirements imposed under this title shall be enforced under --

(1) section 8 of the Federal Deposit Insurance Act, in the case of --

(A) national banks, by the Comptroller of the Currency;

(B) member banks of the Federal Reserve System (other than national banks), by the Federal Reserve Board; and

(C) banks the deposits or accounts of which are insured by the Federal Deposit Insurance Corporation (other than members of the Federal Reserve System), by the Board of Directors of the Federal Deposit Insurance Corporation;

(2) section 5(d) of the Home Owners Loan Act of 1933, section 407 of the National Housing Act, and sections 6(i) and 17 of the Federal Home Loan Bank Act, by the Federal Home Loan Bank Board (acting directing or through the Federal Savings and Loan Insurance Corporation), in the case of any institution subject to any of those provisions;

(3) the Federal Credit Union Act, by the Administrator of the National Credit Union Administration with respect to any Federal credit union;

(4) subtitle IV of Title 49, by the Interstate Commerce Commission with respect to any common carrier subject to such subtitle;

(5) the Federal Aviation Act of 1958, by the Secretary of Transportation with respect to any air carrier or any foreign air carrier subject to that Act; and

(6) the Packers and Stockyards Act, 1921 (except as provided in section 406 of that Act), by the Secretary of Agriculture with respect to any activities subject to that Act.

(c) For the purpose of the exercise by any agency referred to in subsection (b) of its powers under any Act referred to in that subsection, a violation of any requirement imposed under this title shall be deemed to be a violation of a requirement imposed under that Act. In addition to its powers under any provision of law specifically referred to in subsection (b), each of the agencies referred to in that subsection may exercise, for the purpose of enforcing compliance with any requirement imposed under this title any other authority conferred on it by law, except as provided in subsection (d).

(d) Neither the Commission nor any other agency referred to in subsection (b) may promulgate trade regulation rules or other regulations with respect to the collection of debts by debt collectors as defined in this title.

§ 815. Reports to Congress by the Commission [15 USC 1692m]

(a) Not later than one year after the effective date of this title and at one-year intervals thereafter, the Commission shall make reports to the Congress concerning the administration of its functions under this title, including such recommendations as the Commission deems necessary or appropriate. In addition, each report of the Commission shall include its assessment of the extent to which compliance with this title is being achieved and a summary of the enforcement actions taken by the Commission under section 814 of this title.

(b) In the exercise of its functions under this title, the Commission may obtain upon request the views of any other Federal agency which exercises enforcement functions under section 814 of this title.

§ 816. Relation to State laws [15 USC 1692n]

This title does not annul, alter, or affect, or exempt any person subject to the provisions of this title from complying with the laws of any State with respect to debt collection practices, except to the extent that those laws are inconsistent with any provision of this title, and then only to the extent of the inconsistency. For purposes of this section, a State law is not inconsistent with this title if the protection such law affords any consumer is greater than the protection provided by this title.

§ 817. Exemption for State regulation [15 USC 1692o]

The Commission shall by regulation exempt from the requirements of this title any class of debt collection practices within any State if the Commission determines that under the law of that State that class of debt collection practices is subject to requirements substantially similar to those imposed by this title, and that there is adequate provision for enforcement.

§ 818. Effective date [15 USC 1692 note]

This title takes effect upon the expiration of six months after the date of its enactment, but section 809 shall apply only with respect to debts for which the initial attempt to collect occurs after such effective date.

Approved September 20, 1977

ENDNOTES
1. So in original; however, should read "604(a)(3)."

LEGISLATIVE HISTORY:
Public Law 95-109 [H.R. 5294]
HOUSE REPORT No. 95-131 (Comm. on Banking, Finance, and Urban Affairs).
SENATE REPORT No. 95-382 (Comm. on Banking, Housing, and Urban Affairs).
CONGRESSIONAL RECORD, Vol. 123 (1977):
> Apr. 4, considered and passed House.
> Aug. 5, considered and passed Senate, amended.
> Sept. 8, House agreed to Senate amendment.
WEEKLY COMPILATION OF PRESIDENTIAL DOCUMENTS, Vol. 13, No. 39: Sept. 20, Presidential statement.
AMENDMENTS:
SECTION 621, SUBSECTIONS (b)(3), (b)(4) and (b)(5) were amended to transfer certain administrative enforcement responsibilities, pursuant to Pub. L. 95-473, § 3(b), Oct. 17, 1978. 92 Stat. 166; Pub. L. 95-630, Title V. § 501, November 10, 1978, 92 Stat. 3680; Pub. L. 98-443, § 9(h), Oct. 4, 1984, 98 Stat. 708.
SECTION 803, SUBSECTION (6), defining "debt collector," was amended to repeal the attorney at law exemption at former Section (6)(F) and to redesignate Section 803(6)(G) pursuant to Pub. L. 99-361, July 9, 1986, 100 Stat. 768. For legislative history, see H.R. 237, HOUSE REPORT No. 99-405 (Comm. on Banking, Finance and Urban Affairs). CONGRESSIONAL RECORD: Vol. 131 (1985): Dec. 2, considered and passed House. Vol. 132 (1986): June 26, considered and passed Senate.
SECTION 807, SUBSECTION (11), was amended to affect when debt collectors must state (a) that they are attempting to collect a debt and (b) that information obtained will be used for that purpose, pursuant to Pub. L. 104-208 § 2305, 110 Stat. 3009 (Sept. 30, 1996).

APPENDIX 4: STATE STATUTES OF LIMITATIONS

Below are the State Statutes of Limitations for various kinds of agreements. All figures are in years.

Oral Contract: You agree to pay money loaned to you by someone, but this contract or agreement is verbal (i.e., no written contract, "handshake agreement"). Remember a verbal contract is legal, if tougher to prove in court.

Written Contract: You agree to pay on a loan under the terms written in a document, which you and your debtor have signed.

Promissory Note: You agree to pay on a loan via a written contract, just like the written contract. The big difference between a promissory note and a regular written contract is that the scheduled payments and interest on the loan also is spelled out in the promissory note. A mortgage is an example of a promissory note.

Open-ended Accounts: These are revolving lines of credit with varying balances. The best example is a credit card account.

State	Oral	Written	Promissory	Open-ended Accounts
AL	6	6	6	3
AR	5	5	5	3
AK	6	6	3	3
AZ	3	6	6	3
CA	2	4	4	4
CO	6	6	6	3
CT	3	6	6	6
DE	3	3	3	4
DC	3	3	3	3
FL	4	5	5	4
GA	4	6	6	4
HI	6	6	6	6
IA	5	10	5	5

State	Oral	Written	Promissory	Open-ended Accounts
ID	4	5	5	4
IL	5	10	10	5
IN	6	10	10	6
KS	3	5	5	3
KY	5	15	15	5
LA	10	10	10	3
ME	6	6	6	6
MD	3	3	6	3
MA	6	6	6	6
MI	6	6	6	6
MN	6	6	6	6
MS	3	3	3	3
MO	5	10	10	5
MT	3	8	8	5
NC	3	3	5	4
ND	6	6	6	6
NE	4	5	5	4
NH	3	3	6	3
NJ	6	6	6	6
NM	4	6	6	4
NV	4	6	3	4
NY	6	6	6	6
OH	6	15	15	6
OK	3	5	5	3
OR	6	6	6	6
PA	4	6	4	6
RI	10	10	6	4
SC	3	3	3	3
SD	6	6	6	6
TN	6	4	6	6
TX	4	4	4	4
UT	4	6	6	4
VA	3	6	6	3
VT	6	6	5	4
WA	3	6	6	3
WI	6	6	10	6
WV	5	15	6	4
WY	8	10	10	8

APPENDIX 5: STATE STATUTES OF LIMITATIONS: JUDGMENTS

A judgment occurs when a creditor takes you to court, sues you, and wins his case against you. The creditor must do this before the statute of limitations has expired for the original debt.

Typically, the court will try and contact you via mail, but they do not need proof that you were contacted, and you do not have to be present for your creditor to win. The creditor only has to provide proof that the debt is owed. You want to avoid this at all costs; for it is after a judgment is issued that a creditor can seize bank accounts, assets, or garnish wages. In addition, it is easy to renew a judgment once its statute of limitations has passed. In effect, if the creditor is diligent about his renewals, you could find yourself in the position where a judgment against you never expires. A judgment will drop off your credit report after seven years, but your creditor can hound you until the debt is paid.

The state you use to determine the statute of limitations is the state in which the judgment was granted.

State	SOL (years)	Allowable % Interest Rate on the Judgment Amount
AL	20	12
AR	10	10.5
AK	5	10
AZ	10	5 above the Fed Rate
CA	10	10
CO	20	8
CT	20	10
DE	None	Legal + Fed Discount + 5%
DC	3	70% of interest rate or 6% if not specified
FL	20	10
GA	7	12

State	SOL (years)	Allowable % Interest Rate on the Judgment Amount
HI	10	10
IA	6	10.875
ID	20	9
IL	20	8
IN	20	10
KS	5	4% above the Fed Discount
KY	15	12
LA	10	9.75
ME	20	15% if under 30 months, T-bill rate if over 30 months
MD	12	10
MA	20	12
MI	10	6.953
MN	10	5%, changes yearly
MS	7	Amount in contract
MO	10	9
MT	10	10
NC	5	1% above bond equivalent yield
ND	6	2% above the Prime Rate
NE	20	10
NH	20	No Provisions
NJ	14	8.75% without a written contract
NM	20	9
NV	10	8
NY	10	12
OH	21	10
OK	5	4% over the T-bill Rate
OR	10	9%, renewable at 10 yrs
PA	4	6
RI	20	12
SC	10	14
SD	20	10
TN	10	10
TX	10	Can be 18% w/Agreement, 6% without
UT	8	Judgment Contract Rate
VA	8	12
VT	20	9
WA	10	12
WI	10	10

APPENDIX 6: STATE LAWS RELATING TO CREDIT

State	General Garnishment Exemptions	Bad Checks	Max Bad Debt Rates	Collection Agency Bond & License
AL	75% of wages are exempt from garnishment	Greater of $10 or Actual Bank Charges (Section 7-3-118)	Legal: 6% Judgment: 12%	Bond: No License: Yes Fee: $25 - Population under 20,000 $100 - Population over 20,000 Exemption for out-of-state collectors: Business License not required for out-of-state agency.
AR	$500 head of family; $200 single. Includes personal property except clothing.	Twice amount of check - prior to double charge - can start out with $15 charge per NSF check after 30 days.	Legal: 6% or 5 points above the Fed. Discount rate Judgment: Contract rate or 10% per annum whichever is greater	Bond: $5,000 to $25,000 License: Yes Fee: $125 - $5 each employee
AK	Federal Garnishment Returns*	Damages in amount equal to $100 or triple the amount of the check, whichever is greater, but no more than $1,000 over the	Legal: 10.5% Judgment: 10.5% or contractual	Bond: $5,000 License: Yes Fee: $100 - Application $200 - Agency Biennially

		amount of the check.		
AZ	Federal Garnishment Returns*	Twice the amount of check, costs of suit, reasonable attorney fees.	Legal: 10% Judgment: 10% or contractual	Bond: $10,000 minimum (based on gross income) License: Yes Fee: $1,500 Application Fee $600 Annual Fee $23 per Officers/Managers
CA	Federal Garnishment Restrictions*	Amount due, Treble damages - minimum $100 maximum $1,500 per check	Legal: 10% Judgment: 10% (Unless otherwise contracted)	No license or bond required.
CO	Federal Garnishment Restrictions*	Fees Bounced Check 3 years SOL UCC 4-3-11. Treble Damages & Reasonable	Legal: 8% Judgment:8% (or higher if specified in contract or note)	Bond: $12,000 - 20,000 License: Yes Fee: Determined by collection agency board Exemption for out-of-state collectors: Out of state collectors are exempt if [1] collecting only by interstate means (phone, fax, mail); [2] have no Colorado client; and [3] are regulated and licensed in the state in which they reside.
CT	25% you may garnish disposable earnings each week, or 40 x fed. min. hourly wage, whichever is less.	Personal liability of signatory on corporate claims unless signed in corporate capacity.	Legal:8% Judgment:10%	Bond:$5,000 License: Yes Fee: $200 Yearly $50 Investigation
DE	85% of disposable earnings or disposable earnings minus $150 weekly	Amount due, cost of suit, protest fees Bounced Check SOL § 3-118. 3 Years	Legal: Fed Reserve Discount Rate Plus 5% Points Judgment: Fed Reserve Discount Rate	Bond: No License: Merc. License Fee: $50 Yearly

	according to schedule.		Plus 5% Points	
DC	Federal Garnishment Restrictions* D.C. Government employees are not attachable.	Amount Due - Protest Fees	Legal: 6% Judgment: 70% of interest rates on taxes to IRS	Bond: No License: No Fee: No
FL	Federal Garnishment Restrictions* except 100% head of household. Liberal Homestead Exemption - 1st $1,000 of automobile	After 30 day demand-treble amount in addition to amount owed, bank & court costs & reasonable attorney fees.	Legal: 10% Judgment: 10% or up to 18% if contractual	Bond: Yes - $50,000 (Commercial) License: Yes Fee: Yes $200 - Registration $50 - Investigation $200 - Renewal Exemption for out-of-state collectors: Registration is required for out-of-state collectors if [1] soliciting accounts; [2] if client (creditor, its affiliate or subsidiary) has an office in Florida.
GA	Federal Garnishment Restrictions* City, County & State employees may be garnished.	After 10 day written demand double damages up to $500 and service charge of $20 or 5%, whichever is greater.	Legal: 7% Judgment: 12% Commercial Accounts: 18%	Bond: No License: No Fee: No
HI	General garnishment exemptions 95% of 1st $100, 90% of 2nd $100, 80% net wages in excess of $200 per mo. Or federal limits whichever is greater.	Damages equal to $100 or triple amount of check, not to exceed $500.	Legal: 10% Judgment: 10% (No Written Contract)	Collection agency bond & licenses Bond: $25,000 / $15,000 each branch License or registration: Required to solicit/collect
ID	Federal Garnishment	Triple amount of check up to $500	Legal: 12% Judgment:	Bond: $5,000 initial License: Yes

	Restrictions*	over the check amount	10.875% plus the base rate	Fee: $100 -permit fee $50 - renewal Exemption for out-of-state collectors: Out-of-state collectors may qualify for a special license if [1] only collecting for client; and [2] are licensed and bonded by any state
IA	Federal Garnishment Restrictions*	Triple check up to $500 over check amount	Legal: 5% Judgment: 10%	Bond: No License: No Fee: No
IL	15% of gross wages or disposable earnings for workweek up to 45 x fed. min. hourly wage, whichever is greater.	Triple check amount up to $500, attorney fees & court costs.	Legal: 5% Judgment: 9%	Bond: $25,000 License: Yes Fee: $750 - Original $750 - Renewal Exemption for out-of-state collectors: Out-of-state collectors may be exempt if [1] not soliciting accounts in Illinois; [2] their state of residence has laws which provide similar reciprocity (allow out-of-state agencies to collect only); and [3] the state in which the non-Illinois agency resides extends the same privileges to out-of-state agencies.
IN	75% of disposable earnings for workweek or the amount of 30 x fed. min. hourly wage, whichever is greater.	Triple check amount up to $500 over check amount, + attorney fees & interest up to 18% per annum or triple check amount + attorney fees and interest at 8% per annum	Legal: 8% Judgment: 8%	Bond: $5,000 each office License: Yes Fee: $100 plus $5 per annum, each unlicensed employee $30 branch office $80 - Renewal Exemption for out-of-state collectors:

				Out-of-state collectors are exempt from licensing if [1] collecting for a non-resident creditor; and [2] collection activities limited to interstate communications (phone, fax, mail).
KS	Federal Garnishment Restrictions* Plus other personal property, benefit exemptions, and homestead	Three times check amount not exceeding the check amount by $500 or $100 whichever is greater plus attorney fees	Legal: 10% Judgment: 12%	Bond: No License: No Fee: No
KY	75% of disposable income or 30 times the federal minimum hourly wage (whichever is greater)	N/A	Legal: 8% Judgment: 12%	Bond: No License: No Fee: No
LA	75% disposable earnings per work week, but not less than 30 x fed. min. hourly wage.	After 30 day written demand (certified or registered), twice check amount. Attorney fees & court costs	Legal: 9.75% Judgment: 9.75%	Bond: Yes - $10,000 License: Yes Fee: $200 Initial $200 Investigation $200 Renewal $100 Branch $100 Branch Renewal
ME	You may garnish 25% of disposable income or 40 times the federal minimum wages per week	Amount due, court costs, service costs & collection costs	Legal: 8% Post Judgment: 15% annual (less than $30,000) T-Bill rate over $30,000	Bond: $25,000 to $50,000 License: Yes Fee: $400 Yearly Exemption for out-of-state collectors: Contact state authority. Licensing

	(whichever is less) After judgment only.			authority is allowing some exemptions to out-of-state agencies that collect for non-resident creditors and are not soliciting.
MD	Greater of 75% or amount = to $145 x no. of wks. in which wages due were earned; except in Caroline, Worchester, Kent & Queen Anne's Counties, see federal law. Exemption is up to $3,000 in cash and/or property for non-wage property exemption.	After 30 day written notice, amount due, $25 fee, twice check amount up to $1,000. (At the discretion of the court.) Applies to COD sales only.	Legal: 6% Judgment: 10% or contractual	Bond: $5,000 License: Yes Fee: $200 each office
MA	$125 week	Amount due, costs of suit, protest fees Additional damages $100 - $500 can be assessed.	Legal: 6% Judgment: 12% Contract: 12%	Bond: $10,000 - $25,000 License: Yes Fee: Determined by commissioner
MI	Federal Garnishment Restrictions*	Twice the amount of check-not to exceed $500. Retail Claims - Notice Requirements.	Legal: 5% Judgment: 7.162 changes semi-annually Usury limit 25%	(RETAIL ONLY) Bond: $5,000 - $50,000 License: Yes Fee: $150 - Investigation $225 - Initial $125 - Annually Exemption for out-of-state collectors: Out-of-state collectors are exempt if [1] collecting by interstate means; and [2] have no clients in the state of

				Michigan.
MN	Greater of 75% or amount = to 40 x fed. min. hourly wage	$100 or up to 100% of the value of the check, whichever is greater, plus interest at the rate payable on judgments on the face amount of check, plus reasonable attorney fees if aggregate amount of checks within 6 month period is over $1,250.	Legal: 6% Judgment: 5% (Changes Yearly) Business or Agricultural Loan: 4.5% over federal discount rate	Bond: $5,000 to $20,000 License: Yes Fee: $1,000 - Initial $400 - Annual $10 - Per Collector
MS	Federal Garnishment Restrictions*	On checks up to and including $25, additional damages would be 100% of check amount. On checks from $25.01 to $200, additional damages would be 50% of check amount but not less than $25. On checks over $200 additional damages would be 25% of check amount.	Legal: 8% Judgment: Amount in contract if no contract amount court decides	Bond: No License: City-Business Fee: $15-$50
MO	Federal Garnishment Restrictions*; exempt 90% of week's net pay, head of household, single person w/o depend. = 75%	Three times face amount owed or $100 whichever is greater not to exceed $500 (exclusive of attorney fees)	Legal: 9% Judgment: 9%	Bond: No License: No Fee: No
MT	Federal Garnishment	$100 minimum or 3 times face	Legal: 10% Judgment: 10%	Bond: No License: No

	Restrictions*	value up to $500	A binding written agreement may provide for interest of 15% or 6% above prime	Fee: No Caveats: Foreign corporations should register with MT Sec. of State prior to any suit in MT Courts or risk dismissal. Attorney fees only if provided by a signed written agreement.
NC	100% of last 60 days' earnings for family support. Garnishment only by political subdivisions for taxes, ambulance fees, etc.	30 day written demand lesser of $500 or 3x check amount, but not less than $100.	Legal: 8% Judgment: 8%	Bond: $5,000 to $50,000 License: Yes Fee: $500 Exemption for out-of-state collectors: Contact state authorities. Unofficially, licensing authorities may allow out-of-state agencies to bypass requirements if they do not solicit in state and/or work for in-state clients.
ND	Greater of 75% or amount each wk. = to 40 x fed. min. hourly wage. Plus $20 each household dependent.	Amount due, collection fees of $20, and $100 or 3x check whichever is less.	Legal: 6% Judgment: 12%	Bond: $20,000 License: Yes Fee: $200 Exemption for out-of-state collectors: Out-of-state collectors may be exempt if [1] collecting only; [2] their office is located in a state that has a reciprocal law; and [3] the state has "enacted similar legislation."
NE	Greater of 75% disposable earnings (85% if head of household), or 30 x fed. minimum hourly wage.	Amount due, costs, protest fees	Legal: 12% per written instrument or contract rate Judgment: 1% above bond equivalent yield as published by U.S. Treasury	Bond: Based on Lic. Solic. Less Than 5 = $5,000, 5-15=$10,000, 16-Up=$15,000 License: Yes Fee: (not to exceed) $250 - Investigation $200 - Original $100 - Renewal

				$50 - Investigation Branch Office $35 - Original Branch Office Exemption for out-of-state collectors: Out-of-state collectors are exempt if [1] communicating by interstate means (phone, fax, mail); and [2] are "regulated" by the laws of another state.
NH	50 x fed. min. hourly wage - All future wages are exempt so that the court cannot issue an ongoing order.	Amount due, interest, court costs, reasonable costs of collection & $10 per day (max. $50)	Judgment: 7.6%	Bond: No License: No Fee: No
NJ	$142.50 wk. min. 10% of gross earnings $142.50 & over	N/A	Legal: 6% Judgment: No Statutory Provision	Bond: $5,000 Surety License: No Fee: No
NM	Greater of 75% or amount each wk. = to 40 x fed. min. hourly wage	Amount due, triple damages up to $500 per check. Complex requirements need to be met.	Judgment: 8.75% (in the absence of a written contract)	Bond: $5,000 minimum - based on volume License: Yes Fee: $500 - original collection agency or branch $300 - renewal collection agency or branch $100 - examination fee for manager's license $50 - manager renewal Exemption for out-of-state collectors: Out-of-state agency is exempt if [1]

				collecting by interstate means (phone, fax, mail); and [2] debt was incurred outside the state of NM.
NV	Garnish only. 25% of disposable earnings for each week or 30 times federal minimum hourly wage (whichever is less)	Amount due, protest fees three times check amount not more than $500, or less than $100	Legal: 2% Over Prime Judgment: 2% Over Prime	Bond: $25,000 to $50,000 License: Yes Fee: $250 - App. Survey $300 - Original $200 - Renewal Exemption for out-of-state collectors: Out-of-state collectors are exempt if [1] collecting by interstate means (phone, fax, mail); and [2] collecting for an out-of-state client.
NY	90% of earnings, except 1st $127.50 wk. wholly exempt.	Face value of check plus two times check amount up to a maximum of $400 on NSF or $750 on "no account" (Demand prescribed by law). GEN.OB.1.1-104	Legal: 16% Judgment: 9%	Bond: No License: No Fee: No Buffalo: $5,000 Bond - $50 fee NYC: License - $150 - 2 yr. fee
OH	Federal Garnishment Restrictions* Garnishment limited to once a month per employee.	The greater of $200 or three times the amount of check and attorney fees (no maximum)	Legal: 10% Judgment: 10%	Bond: No License: No Fee: No
OK	State law: 75% of earnings exempted, more if hardship established. All	N/A	Legal: 6% Judgment: 4% over U.S. Treasury Bill Rate of previous year. (1996 =	Bond: No License: No Fee: No

			9.55% 1997 = 9.15%)	
OR	75% of disposable earnings or 40 x fed. min. hourly wage.	Can recover reasonable attorney fees & statutory damages of three times the amount of the NSF check plus $500 if demand letter is sent to debtor 30 days before suit is filed.	Statutory + Judgment: 9% simple interest per annum (Unless specified by contract)	Bond: No License: Registration only Fee: Established by director Exemption for out-of-state collectors: Contact state authorities. Out-of-state agencies may be exempt if [1] collecting for out-of-state client; [2] the debt was incurred by an Oregonian outside the state; and [3] the state where the collection agency is headquartered has a registration program comparable to Oregon's law.
PA	100% of wages, certain pensions, retirement accounts & Keogh plan under certain circumstances, and $300.	After demand and judgment triple damages in amount equal to $100 or 3 times the check amount whichever is greater up to $500.	Legal: 6% Judgment: 6%	Bond: No License: No Fee: No
RI	Federal Garnishment Restrictions*	Amount of check, $25 fee & treble damage up to $1,000	Legal: 12% Judgment: 12%	Bond: No License: No Fee: No
SC	100%	Reasonable court costs amount of check & damages up to $500 or 3x check amount whichever is smaller	Legal: 8.75% Judgment: 14%	Bond: No License: Yes - all business Fee: No Exemption for out-of-state collectors: License required for in-state agency only.
SD	20% of the individual's disposable	N/A	Legal: 12% Judgment: 10%	Bond: No License: No Fee: No

	earnings for a 60 day period			
TN	Federal Garnishment Restrictions* Add $2.50 per wk. for dependent child under 16.	Treble damages up to $500 + 10% interest & reasonable service charges, atty's fees, & court costs.	Legal: 10% Judgment: 10% (or contract rate) (varies with type of transaction)	Bond: $15,000 1-4 employees $20,000 5-9 employees $25,000 10 or more License: Yes Fee: $600 - Original $350 - Renewal $25 - Each Solicitor Exemption for out-of-state collectors: Contact state licensing authority. Out-of-state agencies may be exempt if they [1] maintain office in another state; [2] resides in a state that provides reciprocity; and [3] comply with provisions of licensing.
TX	100% of wages	N/A	Legal: 6% with agreement can charge up to 18%. w/o agreement - statutory interest of 6% begins to run 30th day after becoming due Judgment: 10%	Bond: Yes License: No Fee: No Always consult counsel to charge interest - Texas has very onerous usury laws & penalties.
UT	$142.50 of disposable earnings for wages paid weekly.	Certified statutory bad check notice must be sent. Amount due, interest, court costs, reasonable attorney's fees, plus $15 bad check fee.	Legal: 7.35% Judgment: Contract rate or Federal Judgment Rate	Bond: $10,000 License: Yes Fee: Varies by city and county.

VA	Federal Garnishment Restrictions*	Lesser of $250 or three times check amount	Legal: 8% Judgment: 9% or contract rate whichever is higher	Bond:$5,000 License: Depends on Locality Fee: No
VT	75% of earning above minimum wage or what is necessary to live.	Court costs, amount of check, attorney's fees, damage of $50. (Notices required)	Legal: 12% Judgment: 12%	Bond: No License: No Fee: No
WA	Greater of 75% or $64 wk. (40 x state min. hourly wage).	Lesser of check amount or 12% interest, collection costs up to $40. If taken to court, reasonable attorney's fees, 3 x value, or up to $300. Now have 6 years to enforce a bad check.	Legal: 12% Judgment: 12%	Bond: $6,000 general, $4,000 specialty License: Yes Fee: $100 - Investigation $100 - Original $100 - Renewable $50 - Branch Office Exemption for out-of-state collectors: Contact state authorities. Out-of-state agencies may qualify for lesser licensing fees. Out-of-state collectors are no longer required to have resident office and in-state trust accounts if they don't have in-state client. Bond is not required if held in home state.
WV	See West Va code 38-5A-3-Employees withhold 20% of disposable income or 30x the minimum hourly rate, whichever is less. Other exemptions apply.	Amount due, service charge up to $10. If check is under $500 = misdemeanor. Over $500 = felony.	Legal: 6% Judgment: 10%	COLLECTION AGENCY BOND & LICENSE Bond: $5,000 License: Yes - Franchise Reg. Cert. Fee: $15 Annual Exemption for out-of-state collectors: Contact state authorities. Some out-of-state agencies may be exempt if they are only

				collecting for out-of-state clients.
WI	80% of net pay.	Amount of check plus actual damages + exemplary damages up to three times value of check. Limited to $300.	Legal: 5% Judgment: 12%	Bond: $15,000 min. License: Yes Fee: $1,000 - Investigation $200 - Annual Exemption for out-of-state collectors: Out-of-state agencies do not need to be licensed if [1] collecting by interstate means (phone, fax, mail); and [2] collecting for an out-of-state client.
WY	Federal Garnishment Restrictions* for consumer credit sale, lease or loan. Up to 65% for child support arrearage.	Double the face amount plus damages equal to collection cost and reasonable attorney fees.	Legal: 7% Judgment: contract rate or 10% judgment rate	Bond: $10,000 License: Yes Fee: $200 - Original $100 - Renewal $100 - Branch Exemption for out-of-state collectors: Out-of-state agencies may bypass licensing if they are not [1] soliciting clients in WY; or [2] collecting for WY creditors.

*Federal Restriction on garnishment
Federal Laws Title 15, Chapter 41, Subchapter II
Sec. 1673: Restriction on garnishment

(a) Maximum allowable garnishment

Except as provided in subsection (b) of this section and in section 1675 of this title, the maximum part of the aggregate disposable earnings of an individual for any work week which is subjected to garnishment may not exceed

(1) 25 per cent of disposable earnings for that week, or

(2) the amount by which disposable earnings for that week exceed thirty times the Federal minimum hourly wage prescribed by section 206(a)(1) of title 29 in effect at the time the earnings are payable, whichever is less.

In the case of earnings for any pay period other than a week, the Secretary of Labor shall by regulation prescribe a multiple of the Federal minimum hourly wage equivalent in effect to that set forth in paragraph (2).

(b) Exceptions

(1) The restrictions of subsection (a) of this section do not apply in the case of

(A) any order for the support of any person issued by a court of competent jurisdiction or in accordance with an administrative procedure, which is established by State law, which affords substantial due process, and which is subject to judicial review.

(B) any order of any court of the United States having jurisdiction over cases under chapter 13 of title 11.

(C) any debt due for any State or Federal tax.

(2) The maximum part of the aggregate disposable earnings of an individual for any workweek which is subject to garnishment to enforce any order for the support of any person shall not exceed -

(A) where such individual is supporting his spouse or dependent child (other than a spouse or child with respect to whose support such order is used), 50 per cent of such individual's disposable earnings for that week; and

(B) where such individual is not supporting such a spouse or dependent child described in clause (A), 60 per cent of such individual's disposable earnings for that week; except that, with respect to the disposable earnings of any individual for any workweek, the 50 per cent specified in clause (A) shall be deemed to be 55 per cent and the 60 per cent specified in clause (B) shall be deemed to be 65 per cent, if and to the extent that such earnings are subject to garnishment to enforce a support order with respect to a period which is prior to the twelve-week period which ends with the beginning of such workweek.

(c) Execution or enforcement of garnishment order or process prohibited

No court of the United States or any State, and no State (or officer or agency thereof), may make, execute, or enforce any order or process in violation of this section

Up 2. Sec. 1674: Restriction on discharge from employment by reason of garnishment

(a) Termination of employment :

No employer may discharge any employee by reason of the fact that his earnings have been subjected to garnishment for any one indebtedness.

(b) Penalties :

Whoever willfully violates subsection (a) of this section shall be fined not more than $1,000, or imprisoned not more than one year, or both

Up 3. Sec. 1675. - Exemption for State-regulated garnishments

The Secretary of Labor may by regulation exempt from the provisions of section 1673(a) and (b)(2) of this title garnishments issued under the laws of any State if he determines that the laws of that State provide restrictions on garnishment which are substantially similar to those provided in section 1673(a) and (b)(2) of this title

Internet links for supplemental information on state laws:

State	Link
AL	http://www.legislature.state.al.us/CodeofAlabama/1975/coatoc.htm
AR	http://www.arkleg.state.ar.us/NXT/gateway.dll?f=templates&fn=default.htm&vid=blr:code
AK	http://www.legis.state.ak.us/folhome.htm
AZ	http://www.azleg.state.az.us/ArizonaRevisedStatutes.asp?Title=47
CA	http://www.leginfo.ca.gov/calaw.html
CO	http://198.187.128.12/colorado/lpext.dll?f=templates&fn=fs-main.htm&2.0
CT	http://www.cga.state.ct.us/2003/pub/Title42a.htm
DE	http://www.delcode.state.de.us/
DC	http://www.dccouncil.washington.dc.us/
FL	http://www.flsenate.gov/Statutes/index.cfm
GA	http://www.legis.state.ga.us/cgi-bin/gl_codes_detail.pl?code=1-1-1
HI	http://www.capitol.hawaii.gov/hrscurrent/
IA	http://www.legis.state.ia.us/
ID	http://www3.state.id.us/idstat/TOC/idstTOC.html
IL	http://www.legis.state.il.us/legislation/ilcs/chapterlist.html
IN	http://www.in.gov/legislative/ic/code/
KS	http://www.accesskansas.org/government/
KY	http://www.lrc.state.ky.us/home.htm
LA	http://www.legis.state.la.us/
ME	http://www.state.me.us/
MD	http://www.lawlib.state.md.us/
MA	http://www.lawlib.state.ma.us/index.htm
MI	http://www.mileg.org/mileg.asp?page=ChapterIndex
MN	http://www.leg.state.mn.us/leg/statutes.asp
MS	http://www.mscode.com/

MO	http://www.moga.state.mo.us/homestat.asp
MT	http://www.state.mt.us/
NC	http://www.ncleg.net/gascripts/Statutes/StatutesTOC.pl
ND	http://www.state.nd.us/lr/information/statutes/cent-code.html
NE	http://statutes.unicam.state.ne.us/
NH	http://www.lawdog.com/states/nh/sta9.htm
NJ	http://www.njleg.state.nj.us/
NM	http://legis.state.nm.us/
NV	http://www.leg.state.nv.us/
NY	http://assembly.state.ny.us/
OH	http://www.legislature.state.oh.us/
OK	http://www.lsb.state.ok.us/
OR	http://www.leg.state.or.us/ors/home.htm
PA	http://www.legis.state.pa.us/
RI	http://www.rilin.state.ri.us/Statutes/Statutes.html
SC	http://www.lpitr.state.sc.us/code/statmast.htm
SD	http://legis.state.sd.us/index.cfm
TN	http://www.legislature.state.tn.us/
TX	http://www.capitol.state.tx.us/statutes/statutes.html
UT	http://www.le.state.ut.us/~code/code.htm
VA	http://legis.state.va.us/
VT	http://vermont.gov/
WA	http://www.leg.wa.gov/rcw/index.cfm
WI	http://www.legis.state.wi.us/
WV	http://www.legis.state.wv.us/
WY	http://legisweb.state.wy.us/

APPENDIX 7: SAMPLE LETTERS

Requesting the Removal of Inaccurate Information

This is a sample letter requesting the removal of inaccurate information from a credit report. With this letter, always include any copies of proof you may have (i.e., cancelled checks showing timely payments, paid off accounts, loans) that demonstrate that indeed the information in incorrect. It never hurts to include the consequences that have resulted from this wrongful information as well. The credit agencies give the most immediate attention to seriously wronged consumers. Remember the agencies are bombarded with 10,000 letters every day. Keep a copy for your files and send the letter registered mail.

Your Name
123 Your Street Address
Your City, ST 01234
(Current address for the last 5 years)
SSN XXX-XX-XXXX
DOB: 1/1/00

Credit Bureau
Credit Bureau Address
Some City, Any State 56789

Date:

To Whom it May Concern:

Dear Credit Bureau:

This letter is a formal complaint that you are reporting inaccurate credit information on my credit report.

I am very distressed that you have included the information noted below in my credit profile due to its damaging effects on my good credit standing. As you no doubt are aware, credit reporting laws ensure that bureaus report only accurate credit information. No doubt the inclusion of this inaccurate information is a mistake on either your or the reporting creditor's part. Because of the mistakes on my credit report, I have been wrongfully denied credit recently for a <insert credit type for which you were denied here>, which was highly embarrassing and has negatively impacted my lifestyle.

(Optional) With the proof I'm attaching to this letter, I'm sure you'll agree that the inaccurate information is harmful to me and, thus, needs to be removed ASAP.

The following information, therefore, needs to be verified and deleted from the report as soon as possible:

CREDITOR AGENCY, acct. XXXX-XXX-XXXX-XXXX

Sincerely,

Your Signature
Your Name

enclosure

Requesting the Removal of Inaccurate Information #2

This is a second sample letter requesting the removal of inaccurate information from a credit report. With this letter, always include any copies of proof you may have (i.e., cancelled checks showing timely payments, paid off accounts, loans) that demonstrate that indeed the information in incorrect. It never hurts to include the consequences that have resulted from this wrongful information as well. The credit agencies give the most immediate attention to seriously wronged consumers. Remember the agencies are bombarded with 10,000 letters every day. Keep a copy for your files and send the letter registered mail.

Your Name
123 Your Street Address
Your City, ST 01234
(Current address for the last 5 years)
SSN XXX-XX-XXXX
DOB: 1/1/00

Credit Bureau
Credit Bureau Address
Some City, Any State 56789

Date:

To Whom it May Concern:

I've just reviewed my credit report and noticed there are several inaccurate items on my report as follows:

Chase VISA Acct: XXXXX-XXXXX-XXXX-XXX:
This account is listed as being 30 days late. I have never been late on this account.

Sears Acct: XXXXX-XXXXX-XXXX-XXX:
This account is listed as being 30 days late. I have never been late on this account.

Universal Acct: XXXXX-XXXXX-XXXX-XXX:
This account is listed as being 30 days late. I have never been late on this account.

In addition, there are a number of credit accounts that have been inactive for more than seven years. As you know, the FCRA states that all credit older than seven years should be removed from my report. Therefore, the following accounts should be removed:

Diner's Club Acct: XXXXX-XXXXX-XXXX-XXX
GE Consumer Card Acct: XXXXX-XXXXX-XXXX-XXX
Macy's Acct: XXXXX-XXXXX-XXXX-XXX

I have enclosed a copy of my driver's license as proof of identity.

Sincerely,

Your Signature
Your Name

enclosure

Getting the Credit Bureau to Update Bankruptcy Accounts

Many times, accounts that are included in a bankruptcy are not updated to reflect it on your credit report, lowering your credit score even more than it already is. This is a sample letter requesting the update of those accounts to show "Included in Bankruptcy." Keep a copy for your files and send the letter registered mail.

Your Name
123 Your Street Address
Your City, ST 01234
(Current address for the last 5 years)
SSN XXX-XX-XXXX
DOB: 1/1/00

Credit Bureau
Credit Bureau Address
Some City, Any State 56789

RE:
CREDITOR AGENCY   Account XXXXX-XXXXXXXXXXX
CREDITOR AGENCY   Account YYYYY-XXXXXXXXXXX
CREDITOR AGENCY   Account ZZZZZ-ZZZZZZZZ

Date:

To Whom it May Concern:

Dear Credit Bureau:

This letter is a formal complaint that you are reporting inaccurate credit information on my credit report. The above referenced accounts were included in my bankruptcy and are instead showing as <chargeoffs> <pastdue> <late>. The incorrect listings are lowering my credit score unnecessarily, and it is also preventing me from purchasing a home. I am enclosing a copy of my bankruptcy discharge papers as proof of the date of my discharge.

Please correct your records to display the proper listings.

Sincerely,

Your Signature
Your Name

enclosure

Follow-Up After Initial Contact with the Bureau Contact

Use this letter if your initial attempts to gain a response from the credit reporting agency prove fruitless. In this letter, and all succeeding correspondence with the credit reporting agency, you need to get increasingly threatening. Keep a copy for your files and send the letter registered mail.

Your Name
123 Your Street Address
Your City, ST 01234
SSN

Credit Bureau
Credit Bureau Address
Some City, Any State 56789

Date:

RE: Dispute Letter of <Date you sent in first or previous requests>

Dear Credit Bureau:

This letter is formal notice that you have failed to respond to my dispute letter of <date>. I sent the initial letter registered mail and have enclosed a copy of the return receipt that you signed on <date>.

As you are well aware, federal law requires you to respond within 30 days. It has now been over that period since your receipt of my letter. As you no doubt are aware, failure to comply with federal regulations by credit reporting agencies is a serious violation of the Fair Credit Reporting Act and may be investigated by the FTC. Obviously, I am maintaining detailed records of all my correspondence with you.

I am aware that you may have misplaced my letters or have failed to respond to my letter because of an oversight due to the high volume of the requests you receive daily. If this is the case, I'm sure you'll want to handle this matter as soon as possible. For this purpose, I have included a copy of my original request, the dated receipt of your reception of the original letter, and a copy of the proof verifying the incorrectness of the credit item you have mistakenly placed on my records.

The following information, therefore, needs to be verified and deleted from my credit report as soon as possible:

CREDITOR AGENCY, acct. XXXX-XXXX-XXXX-XXXX

Sincerely,

Your Signature
Your Name

enclosure

Requesting the Removal of Inquiries

Prepare letters to each inquiring creditor asking them to remove their inquiry. The Fair Credit Reporting Act allows only authorized inquiries to appear on the consumer credit report. You must challenge whether the inquiring creditor had proper authorization to pull your credit file. Keep a copy for your files and send the letter registered mail.

Your Name
123 Your Street Address
Your City, ST 01234

Credit Bureau
Credit Bureau Address
Some City, Any State 56789

Date:

Re: Unauthorized Credit Inquiry

Dear American BestGuess,

I recently received a copy of my credit report. The credit report showed a credit inquiry by your company that I do not recall authorizing. I understand that you shouldn't be allowed to put an inquiry on my file unless I have authorized it. Please have this inquiry removed from my credit file because it is making it very difficult for me to acquire credit.

I have sent this letter certified mail because I need your prompt response to this issue. Please be so kind as to forward me documentation that you have had the unauthorized inquiry removed.

If you find that I am remiss, and you do have my authorization to inquire into my credit report, then please send me proof of this.

Thanking you in advance,

Your Name

Credit Bureau Verification Procedure Request

This letter should be sent to the credit bureaus if they come back with a "verified" response when you dispute a negative mark. Credit bureaus will not take the time or trouble to send you this information unless you ask, but it is your right to know it under the FCRA. Many times you can use this information as ammunition for your credit disputes. Keep a copy for your files and send the letter registered mail.

Your Name
Address1
Address2
City, State Zip

Company
Address1
Address2
City, State Zip

Date

To Whom It May Concern:

This letter is a formal request for the description of the procedures used to determine the accuracy and completeness of the disputed information, including the business name, address, and telephone number of any furnisher of information contacted in connection with this reinvestigation, in compliance with the Fair Credit Reporting Act, Section 611, part B, subsection (iii)

§ 611. Procedure in case of disputed accuracy [15 U.S.C. § 1681i]
(6)
(B) Contents. As part of, or in addition to, the notice under subparagraph (A), a consumer reporting agency shall provide to a consumer in writing before the expiration of the 5-day period referred to in subparagraph (A)
(i) a statement that the reinvestigation is completed;
(ii) a consumer report that is based upon the consumer's file as that file is revised as a result of the reinvestigation;
(iii) a notice that, if requested by the consumer, a description of the procedure used to determine the accuracy and completeness of the information shall be provided to the consumer by the agency, including the business name and address of any furnisher of information contacted in connection with such information and the telephone number of such furnisher, if reasonably available;

I am disappointed that you have failed to maintain reasonable procedures to assure complete accuracy in the information you publish, and insist you comply with the law by providing the requested information within the 15 days allowed.

As a matter of convenience to you and to expedite my request, I am resubmitting my request to correct my credit report.

Name of Creditor/Agency, Account #_____

<List your reasons for disputing this negative mark here, inaccurate account information, dates wrong, etc.>

As already stated, the listed item is inaccurate and incomplete, and is a very serious error in reporting.

Sincerely,

Signature
Your Name
Your SSN

An Agreement to Compromise Debt

NEVER settle a debt with a creditor without getting it in writing from them. Here is a letter you can send them to sign. Be sure to insert your terms for the debt within, and don't pay it until you received an original copy with a signature on it. Keep a copy for your files and send the letter registered mail.

Max Creditor, referred to as CREDITOR and Jane Doe, referred to as DEBTOR, agree to compromise the indebtedness as between them. CREDITOR, hereby agrees to compromise the indebtedness due the CREDITOR on the following terms and conditions:

The CREDITOR and the DEBTOR agree that the present debt due is $1436.18 (one thousand four hundred thirty six & 18/100 dollars). The parties agree that the CREDITOR shall accept the sum of $1,000 (one thousand & no/100 dollars) as full payment on the debt. The acceptance of the payment will serve as a complete discharge of all monies due. The payment shall be made in cash.

This compromise is expressly conditioned upon the payment being received by <date>. If the DEBTOR fails to pay the compromised amount by <date>, the original amount owed by the DEBTOR will be reinstated in full, and immediately due.

Max Creditor hereby declares that he is authorized to act as an agent of the credit agency.

This Agreement shall be binding upon and inure to the benefit of the parties, their successors, and assignees.

Dated:

Signature:

Max Creditor
CREDITOR

Signature:

Jane Doe
DEBTOR

Acceptance of Verbal Offer (Debt Settlement)

If you have worked out a settlement with a credit card company or collection agency, before you send them any money, you need to confirm the offer in writing and get a company representative's signature on it. This letter is best combined with the "Agreement to settle a debt" letter. Keep a copy for your files and send the letter registered mail.

Dear Creditor,
Re: Account Number_____

This letter is to confirm the settlement offer made between myself and your customer service representative _____ phone number
_____ made on _____, 20__.

I really appreciate the fact that your company is willing to work with me on this matter; I wanted to make an honest attempt to settle this debt.

The amount your customer service representative and I agreed to settle this debt in full is $_____. In addition, any references to late payment or charge off regarding this account are to be removed from my credit file.

If these terms are acceptable to your company, please sign the attached letter of agreement and return a copy to me. Upon receipt of this **signed acknowledged** agreement, I will express you a money order in the amount stated above.

Yours truly,

Your name
Enclosed attachments

Counter Offer (Debt Settlement)

If you want to counter an offer made to you by a creditor, verbal or otherwise, this is the way to go. You should pair this letter with the "Agreement to Settle a Debt" letter, also included in this appendix. Keep a copy for your files and send the letter registered mail.

Dear Creditor,
Re: Account Number_____

This letter is to make a **counter offer** to the settlement offer made between myself and your customer service representative _____ phone number _____ made on _____, 20__.

I really appreciate the fact that your company is willing to work with me on this matter; I want to make an honest attempt to settle this debt.

The amount I would like to propose as the payment in full for this debt is $_____. In addition, this settlement would require any references to late payment or charge off regarding this account to be removed from my credit file.

Unfortunately, I have several other companies with which to conduct negotiations over debt, and a limited amount of funds. I will most likely be able to make payments to those companies who are willing to meet my terms. I do not have enough money to pay everyone. Time is of the essence; I have already reached agreeable settlements with a couple of my creditors and I doubt if I will have any funds remaining after the end of this calendar month.

<optional clause>
My credit rating is the most important item in this settlement agreement to me, I may be willing to offer more money to regain a perfect credit rating as reported to the credit bureaus.

If these terms are acceptable to your company, please sign the attached letter of agreement and return a copy to me. Upon receipt of this **signed acknowledged** agreement, I will express you a money order in the amount stated above.

Yours truly,

Your name

Unsolicited Offer

If you want to make a creditor a written offer without discussing it first, here is the way to go. You should pair this letter with the "Agreement to Settle a Debt" letter, also included in this appendix. Keep a copy for your files and send the letter registered mail.

Dear Creditor,
Re: Account Number_____

After a long period of difficult times with my personal finances, I am finally in a position where I would like to take care of the debt whose account number is above. I really appreciate in advance all efforts your company is willing to make to help us resolve this issue; I want to make an honest attempt to settle this debt.

The amount I would like to propose as the payment in full for this debt is $_____. In addition, this settlement would require any references to late payment or charge off regarding this account to be removed from my credit file.

Unfortunately, I have several other companies with which to conduct negotiations over debt, and a limited amount of funds. I will most likely be able to make payments to those companies who are willing to meet my terms. I do not have enough money to pay everyone. Time is of the essence; I have already reached agreeable settlements with a couple of my creditors and I doubt if I will have any funds remaining after the end of this calendar month.

<optional clause>
My credit rating is the most important item in this settlement agreement to me, I may be willing to offer more money to regain a perfect credit rating as reported to the credit bureaus.

If these terms are acceptable to your company, please sign the attached letter of agreement and return a copy to me. Upon receipt of this signed acknowledged agreement, I will express you a money order in the amount stated above.

Yours truly,

Your name

Settle With Your Credit Card Companies

If you are having trouble making your credit card payments, you may want to contact them and ask them if they can work out an alternate payment plan for you, reduce the interest rate or even the debt. But you will have to explain to them the circumstances you are in to convince them. Keep a copy for your files and send the letter registered mail.

Company
Address
City, State Zip

Date:

RE: Account XXXXX-XXXX-XXXXX

Dear Sir/Madame:

I am currently undergoing some financial difficulties and I fear I will no longer be able to make my monthly obligations to you. I don't want to declare bankruptcy, and I feel a moral obligation to try and work out something with you so I will not have to default on this debt. I would like to work out an alternate payment plan with you if possible.

I would like to propose that you close my account, waive the interest payments and accept a new balance of 50% of what I currently owe. I can make a monthly payment of <state payment, should be between $50-$100>.

Here are the circumstances in which I find myself: <Write the reasons for your trouble. Make sure that circumstances included here sound like they were beyond your control, not that you spent too much money and now can't pay it. Any medical hardships, divorce, thefts, accidents are especially good here.>

I'm sure you will agree that the situation I described above has forced me to this point. Please feel free to have one of your representatives call me and work out a final plan. If you feel you can't work with me, I will be forced to default on this account and pay creditors who can work with me. Thanks for your time.

Sincerely,
Your Name

Cease and Desist to a Collection Agency

Under the Fair Debt Collection Act, you have the right to ask the collection agencies to stop contacting you-and they must comply with this request. Here is a letter you might use as a guide. Keep a copy for your files and send the letter registered mail.

Your Name
123 Your Street Address
Your City, ST 01234

Cheatem Collections
123 Fagetaboutit Ave
Chicago, IL 00001

Date

RE: Account XXXX-XXXX-XXXX-XXXX

Dear Sir or Madam:

I request that you CEASE and DESIST in your efforts to collect on the above referenced account (see letter attached). It is my personal policy not to deal with collection agencies and I will only deal with the original creditor of this account.

You are hereby instructed to cease collection efforts immediately or face legal sanctions under applicable federal and state law.

GIVE THIS LETTER THE IMMEDIATE ATTENTION IT DESERVES.

Cordially,

Your Signature
Your Name

Debt Validation

Under the Federal Debt Collection Practices Act, you are allowed to challenge the validity of a debt that a collection agency states you owe to them. Use this letter and the following form to make the agency verify that the debt is actually yours and owed by you. Keep a copy for your files and send the letter registered mail.

Your Name
123 Your Street Address
Your City, ST 01234

ABC Collections
123 NotOnYourLife Ave
Chicago, IL

Date

Re: Acct # XXXX-XXXX-XXXX-XXXX

To Whom It May Concern:

I recently pulled a copy of my credit report and noticed that there was a collection from your agency on my credit report. I was never notified of this collection. This is not a refusal to pay, but a notice that your claim is disputed.

Under the FDCPA, I have the right to request validation of the debt you say I owe you. I am requesting proof that I am indeed the party you are asking to pay this debt, and there is some contractual obligation which is binding on me to pay this debt.

You should also be aware that reporting such invalidated information to major credit bureaus might constitute defamation of character, as the negative marks on my credit report harm my credit and prevent me from enjoying all the benefits of good credit. In addition, until you provide me with proper validation of this debt, you are not allowed to pursue any collection activities, including reporting this information on my credit report. I'm sure your legal staff will agree that non-compliance with this request could put your company in serious legal trouble with the FTC and other state or federal agencies.

I also noticed that you are not licensed to in my state of Arizona, and under Arizona State law, all collection agencies must be licensed to collect from any Arizona resident. I am planning to contact my state attorney general to notify him of your illegal activities. I also think the Federal Trade Commission and the Better Business Bureaus would be interested in your actions against me.

Please attach copies of:

1. Agreement with your client that grants you the authority to collect on this alleged debt
2. Agreement that bears the signature of the alleged debtor wherein he agreed to pay the creditor.
3. The complete payment history on this account so I have proof that the amount is correct.

Best regards,

Your Signature
Your Name

Debt Validation Follow Up Letter to a Collection Agency

If you do not hear back from the collection agency within the 30 days of sending your "Debt Validation" letter, you can send them this letter. Keep a copy for your files and send the letter registered mail.

Your Name
123 Your Street Address
Your City, ST 01234

ABC Collections
123 NotOnYourLife Ave
Chicago, IL

Date:

Re: Acct # XXXX-XXXX-XXXX-XXXX

To Whom It May Concern:

I have previously sent you a request to validate my debt, account number XXX-XXX-XXX on February 15, 2002.

Under the Fair Debt Collections Practices Act (FDCPA), I have the right to request validation of the debt you say I owe you, and it is your responsibility to provide me with proper documentation should you continue with your collection activities. I have received no reply from you, though I did receive confirmation via mail that you did receive my letter on February 20, 2002, and my dispute with the 3 credit bureaus over this collection came back as "verified." According to an opinion letter written by the FTC and posted on their website, reporting this collection is considered collection activity.

You are now in violation of the FCPDA, and are now subject to fines of $1,000, which I may collect from you by filing a claim in small claims court. I intend to follow through with the suit if I do not hear back from you within 15 days.

You should also be aware that reporting such invalidated information to major credit bureaus might constitute defamation of character, as the negative marks on my credit report harm my credit and prevent me from enjoying all the benefits of good credit. I'm sure your legal staff will agree that non-compliance with this request could put your company in serious legal trouble with the FTC and other state or federal agencies.

Jane Doe

After the Collection Agency Fails to Validate Your Debt/ The Letter to Send to the Credit Bureaus

Assuming you have contacted the collection agency using our debt validation methods, and they have failed to send you adequate proof of your legal obligation to pay a debt, this is the letter you need to write to the credit bureaus. Keep a copy for your files and send the letter registered mail.

Company
Address1
Address2
City, State Zip

Date

RE: Account XXXXX-XXXX-XXXXX

Dear Sir/Madame:

I am writing to dispute the account referenced above. I have disputed this account information as inaccurate with you, and you have come back to me and stated you were able to verify this debt. How is this possible? Under the laws of the FDCPA, I have contacted the collection agency myself and have been unable to get them to verify that this is indeed my debt.

I enclose copies of my requests to the collection agency, asking them to validate my debts, and the receipts showing that I sent these letter certified signature request. This debt is not mine and I was given no evidence of my obligation to pay this debt to this collection agency.

The FCRA requires you to verify the validity of the item within 30 days. If the validity cannot be verified, you are obligated by law to remove the item. There is a clear case of unverified debt here, and I urge you to remove this item before I am forced to take legal action.

In the event that you can not verify the item pursuant to the FCRA, and you continue to list the disputed item on my credit report I will find it necessary to sue you for actual damages and declaratory relief under the FCRA. According to this regulation, I may sue you in any qualified state or federal court, including small claims court in my area.

While I prefer not to litigate, I will use the courts as needed to enforce my rights under the FCRA.

I look forward to an uneventful resolution of this matter.

Sincerely,

Signature
Your Name
Your Address
City, State Zip

enclosures

Getting the Original Creditor to Verify Debt

Debt validation does not work with the original creditor, only with collection agencies. The only way you can get an original creditor to budge on responding to you via snail mail (so you can send it certified) is to tell them you will sue them for defamation if they can't prove that you were actually late or even that you are on the account.

This letter is perfect for those people who are trying to get "Authorized User" accounts off of their credit reports. The court case cited in the below letter is included on the CD under Court Cases. Keep a copy for your files and send the letter registered mail.

Company
Address1
Address2
City, State Zip

Date

RE: Account XXXXX-XXXX-XXXXX

Dear Sir/Madame:

I am writing to dispute the account referenced above. I have disputed this account information as inaccurate with the credit bureaus <insert names of credit bureaus here>, and you have been able to verify this debt. How is this possible? I was <not late> <this is not my account> <I am only an authorized user>.

In the event that you can not verify the item pursuant to the FCRA, and you continue to list the disputed item on my credit report I will find it necessary to sue you for actual defamation damages and declaratory relief under the FCRA. According to this regulation, I may sue you in any qualified state or federal court, including small claims court in my area. You have severely limited my ability to <purchase a home> <get a job> <get a credit card>.

In light of the recent court case opinion No. 00-15946 CV-99-00290-D.C. by the US Court of Appeals 9th Circuit, Nelson Vs. Chase Manhattan, the court ruled that the creditor has the responsibility to investigate and make sure that correct information is being reported to the bureaus, and that the consumer has a right to sue under the FCRA, should his or her rights be violated.

While I prefer not to litigate, I will use the courts as needed to enforce my rights under the FCRA.

I look forward to an uneventful resolution of this matter.

Sincerely,

Signature
Your Name
Your Address
City, State Zip

Enclosures <you can enclose a copy of the court case referenced above>

Asking ChexSystems to Remove a Listing

ChexSystems is the "credit bureau" for checking accounts; it maintains a database of individuals who have written a number of bad checks. If you get on their list, you won't be able to open a checking account anywhere in the United States. Keep a copy for your files and send the letter registered mail.

Your Name
123 Your Street Address
Your City, ST 01234
SSN

ChexSystems
Customer Relations
12005 Ford Road Suite 600
Dallas, TX 75234

Date:

To Whom It May Concern:

My bank has informed me that there is negative information reported by Glendale Federal Bank included in the file ChexSystems maintains under my Social Security Number. Upon ordering a copy of the report, I see an entry from this bank listing a "debit card revoked" in March 1997.

I do not recall having a debit card from this bank in 1997.

Please validate this information with Glendale Federal Bank and provide me with copies of any documentation associated with this "debit card" bearing my signature. In the absence of any such documentation bearing my signature, I ask that this information be immediately deleted from the file you maintain under my Social Security Number.

Sincerely,

Your Signature
Your Name

Notice of Intent to File a Lawsuit

If the credit bureaus don't respond to your requests to verify listings in the period specified by law, or have not removed negative listings despite the proof you have provided, you have every right to sue them. They are not a government agency. You can even sue them in small claims court. Keep a copy for your files and send the letter registered mail.

Your Name
123 Your Street Address
Your City, ST 01234

Equifax
1550 Peachtree Street
Atlanta, GA 30309

Date:

Re: Acct # XXXX-XXXX-XXXX-XXXX

To Whom It May Concern:

Enclosed is a copy of the lawsuit that I filed against you in <your court> on <date>. Currently, the Pretrial Conference is scheduled for <date> at <time> in courtroom #XX. The case number is <insert case #>.

The reason the lawsuit was filed was due to a completely inadequate response from your company. When someone is the victim of identity theft, it is simply a nightmare trying to get false information removed from a credit file. I have contacted all of the false creditors listed on my credit file. I have challenged all of the false listings on my credit file. Nothing ever happened to fix the situation.

Over 90 days ago, I wrote to each of the creditors in question and demanded proof that I am their customer. I asked for proof of the alleged debt, including specifically the alleged contract or other instrument bearing my signature. So far, none of them has been able to provide such proof to me. I have sent follow-up letters to each of them and there still is no proof. I have attempted phone contact, but I simply get transferred around and nothing ever gets accomplished.

I have fully investigated my rights in this matter. Under the principals of estoppel, if no proof is provided to me within 30 days, I may presume that no proof of the alleged debt, nor therefore any such debt, in fact exists. I have copies of the certified letters and dates prepared to bring to court on <date> at <time>. Also, under the Fair Credit Reporting Act, these disputed items may not appear on my credit report if they cannot be supported by evidence.

Under the Fair Credit Reporting Act, if the debt can't be verified within 30 days, then it must be removed. Your letters to me claim to have 'verified' the debt, but this is in fact not true under law. Simply contacting the alleged creditor and asking them to match up numbers in their database is not sufficient verification for identity theft. Of course, the information matches up. Someone clearly used my information without my authorization.

Now I am suing Equifax for being such a pain in the posterior to me. I have provided more than sufficient evidence to get these false accounts removed. You may contact me before <date> at <time> at <your phone number> or at my address listed at the top of this letter. This matter can be settled simply by your agreement to remove the false information from my credit file.

I require a response, on point, in writing, hand signed, and in a timely manner. If I get another pointless letter from you saying that it has already been 'verified' then there will be no more opportunity for negotiation. This will proceed in court until I have successfully proven to a judge that this false information must be removed from my credit file. I will also be aggressively pursuing the full judgment that I get against Equifax for violation of the Fair Credit Reporting Act and Defamation.

I have already won a similar lawsuit against TransUnion. Enclosed is a copy of that settlement. I will agree to a similar settlement with Equifax if you contact me before <date> at <time>. If you accept the same terms as TransUnion did, then I will dismiss my lawsuit against Equifax and you will not need to appear in <your county and state>.

The items to be removed from my credit report are listed as follows:

(list accounts and account numbers)

Sincerely,

Your Signature
Your Name

Request for Credit Report If You Were Denied Credit

By law, if you were denied credit, you have a right to see your credit report within 60 days of the turn down. You may send a copy of this letter to all three bureaus.

A Credit Bureau
Credit Bureaus Address 1
Bureau City, ST 12345

6/21/2001

Dear Credit Bureau,

I was recently turned down for a <select one - credit card, mortgage, auto loan. Under the FCRA, I am entitled to a free copy of my credit report. I am enclosing a copy of the turn down letter. Please send me a copy of my credit report.

My full name is Your Name.
My birth date is 01-01-1950.
My Social Security number is 123-45-6789.
My current address is 123 Your Street Address, Your City, ST 01234.
I formerly lived at 456 Old Street Address, Old City, ST 34567.

Enclosed, also please find a photocopy of my driving license, showing my current address, and a photocopy of my Social Security card.

Please send the credit report as soon as you can. Thank you.

Sincerely,

Your Name
123 Your Street Address
Your City, ST 01234

Enclosures

Request for Credit File from an "Alternate" Credit Bureau

As we saw in Chapter 3, there are many other data repositories which contain your personal information. Many of these data repositories are classified as credit bureaus per the FCRA, and as such are required to give you a one free copy of your personal information file per year. We are going to use Innovis as the example here, but you can use it for any of the companies listed in Chapter 3. Why do you want to see your file? To remove damaging information from it, just as you would want to correct your Experian, Equifax, or TransUnion files.

_____, 2001

Innovis Data Solutions
P.O. Box 219297
Houston, Texas 77218-9297

Dear Sirs:

This is a request for my Innovis credit file which you are maintaining in your credit databases.

As you know or, at least should know, the federal Fair Credit Reporting Act ("FRCA"), specifically 15 USC 1681, et seq., requires that upon request, a consumer reporting agency must disclose to an individual his or her credit file upon receipt of appropriate information proving the identity of that individual. For purposes of this statute, "consumer reporting agency" is defined in relevant part as "any person which, for monetary fees, due, or on a cooperative nonprofit basis, regularly engages in whole or in part in the practice of assembling or evaluating consumer credit information or other information on consumers for the purpose of furnishing consumer reports to third parties . . .", and a credit "file" is defined as "all information on [a] consumer recorded and maintained by a consumer reporting agency regardless of how the information is stored."

It is well known within the lending industry that you are a credit bureau, and as a matter of fact, many high-profile industry players are reporting credit information to you on a regular basis. As such, Innovis is unconditionally obligated under both of these statutory authorities to disclose to me the complete contents of all files which Innovis maintains on me. The failure and/or refusal of Innovis to disclose this information makes available to me a number of remedies, including $1,000 in fines as mandated by the FCRA.

Under the new FACTA regulations, you are also required to give me my information free of charge one time each year.

In light of the above, I hereby demand that Innovis immediately send to me any and all credit files and/or information which it is maintaining on me.

Very truly yours,

xxxxxxxxxxx
SSN: 123-45-6789
1 E. Main
Anytown, USA 00000

Request for Credit Report If You Are Buying One

If you would like to order your credit report, you can do so online or send them a check in the mail. Don't forget to check Chapter 3 to see if your state allows you to order one free.

A Credit Bureau
Credit Bureaus Address 1
Bureau City, ST 12345

6/21/2001

Dear Credit Bureau,

Please send me a copy of my credit report.

My full name is Your Name.
My birth date is 01-01-1950.
My Social Security number is 123-45-6789.
My current address is 123 Your Street Address, Your City, ST 01234.
I formerly lived at 456 Old Street Address, Old City, ST 34567.

Enclosed, also please find a check for $8.50, a photocopy of my driving license, showing my current address, and a photocopy of my Social Security card.

Please send the credit report as soon as you can. Thank you.

Sincerely,

Your Name
123 Your Street Address
Your City, ST 01234

Enclosures

Remove My Name from Mailing List

Want to get rid of all your junk mail? This is the letter to send!

Refer to Chapter 16 to find all the addresses to send this letter to remove your name from mailing lists.

Your Name
123 Your Street Address
Your City, ST 01234
SSN

Mail Preference Service
Direct Marketing Association
P.O. Box 9008
Farmingdale, NY 11735

Date:

To Whom It May Concern:

Please remove my name from your mailing list. According to state and federal laws, this means you will not be able to send me any mail unless I ask for it.

Sincerely,

Your Signature
Your Name

Contact Your Credit Card Companies

If you are having trouble making your credit card payments, you may want to contact them and ask them if they can work out an alternate payment plan for you, reduce the interest rate or even the debt. But you will have to explain to them the circumstances you are in to convince them.

Company
Address
City, State Zip

Date

RE: Account XXXXX-XXXX-XXXXX

Dear Sir/Madame:

I am currently undergoing some financial difficulties and I fear I will no longer be able to make my monthly obligations to you. I don't want to declare bankruptcy, and I feel a moral obligation to try and work out something with you so I will not have to default on this debt. I would like to work out an alternate payment plan with you if possible.

I would like to propose that you close my account, waive the interest payments and accept a new balance of 50% of what I currently owe. I can make a monthly payment of <state payment, should be between $50-$100>.

Here are the circumstances in which I find myself. <Write the reasons for your trouble. Make sure that circumstances included here sound like they were beyond your control, not that you spent too much money and now can't pay it. Any medical hardships, divorce, thefts, accidents are especially good here.>

I'm sure you will agree that the situation I described above has forced me to this point. Please feel free to have one of your representatives call me and work out a final plan. If you feel you can't work with me, I will be forced to default on this account and pay creditors who can work with me.

Thanks for your time,
Your name

APPENDIX 8 – SAMPLE LEGAL DOCUMENTS

Motion to Vacate

This document tells the court why a judgment against you should be vacated (or dismissed). First, you need to identify the case by name and court reference number and all the persons involved in the judgment. Next, explain your reasons for bringing the motion. State your "procedural defenses," that is, the good reason(s) why you did not respond to the summons and complaint on time or appear at a "show cause" hearing.

IN THE SUPERIOR COURT OF THE STATE OF <YOUR STATE>
IN AND FOR THE COUNTY OF <YOUR COUNTY>

<The Original Plaintiff> Plaintiff,

      vs.

<YOU>,

      Defendant.

No. <COURT REFERENCE NUMBER>

MOTION AND DECLARATION TO VACATE JUDGMENT

NOW COMES the Plaintiff, Pro Se and prays this Honorable Court to Deny the Defendant's Motion to Dismiss and Motion for Sanction for the following reasons:

1. Relief requested. The defendant(s) move(s) the court for an order vacating the judgment entered in this action until the motion can be heard.

2. Statement of facts and issues. This motion is based on the following grounds: <Enter your reasons: you weren't properly served, the judgment was entered even though you filed the right paperwork>

Dated:

      _____

      Defendant(s) (Signature)

      Defendant(s) Name (Print)

      Address

Telephone Number

DECLARATION

I, <my name>, declare as follows:

1. I am the defendant in this unlawful detainer action.

2. I request that the judgment entered in this action be vacated for the following reasons:

< Give your reasons: A) the collection agency never responded to my request for validation, therefore never giving any proof that the debt was mine under the FDCPA. B) The amount of the debt exceeded the state's usury interest limits>

I certify under penalty of perjury under the laws of the state of <YOUR STATE> that the foregoing statement is true.

Signed in [CITY], [STATE] on [DATE].

_____

Signature

Print or Type Name

Basis of Lawsuit

When a company refuses to validate your debt, and furthermore decides to contact you after you have sent them notice of your request for validation, they are in clear violation of the FDCPA. You are within your rights to sue them for damages in small claims court for these violations. To do so, you need to file a Basis of Lawsuit document, which will clearly explain to the court and the judge what you are suing for. The more clearly you state your case, the better chances you have of winning, should the case go to court. You need to include all copies of the documentation included here.

<Court Name>
<YOUR NAME>
Plaintiff
v.
<Evil Collection Agency X>
Defendant

Statement of facts

PLAINTIFF, <your name>, is an individual living in the State of <Your State>.

DEFENDANT, <Evil Collection Agency X>, is a <corporation, LLC or whatever> formed under the laws of the State of <STATE the business is incorporated in>.

COUNTS <Provide detail and documentation as in the following sample.>

I
Defendant sent a collection notice to Plaintiff on or about January 1, 2001. (Exhibit A)

II
As is Plaintiff's lawful right in accordance with the Fair Debt Collection Practices Act (FDCPA), Plaintiff sent via United States Postal Service Certified Return Receipt, a letter requesting formal debt validation. This letter was sent on January 10, 2002 and signed for by Defendant's office on January 18th, 2002, well within the 30-day period expressly provided by the FDCPA. (Exhibit B validation letter sent to Defendant)(Exhibit C proof of delivery to defendant)

III
Defendant failed to respond with any type of requested validation.

IV

On February 18th, 2002, in a good faith effort to allow Defendant ample opportunity to validate the alleged debts, sent a second letter via Certified mail with return receipt requested, which was signed for by the defendant on February 23rd, 2002. (Exhibit D Letter sent to Defendant) (Exhibit E proof of delivery to defendant)

V

Defendant again failed to respond.

VI

On February 18th, 2002, Plaintiff received a collection notice, this notice informing Plaintiff that this item will be placed on Plaintiff's credit reports, again violating the Plaintiff's rights under the FDCPA.

VII

On February 19th, 2001, Plaintiff contacted the Defendant via telephone, to inform the Defendant of the possible legal ramifications. Defendant then demanded payment of the debt from the Plaintiff, another violation of the FDCPA Section 809 (b), continuance of debt collection before validation of debt.

VIII

On or around February 20th, 2002, this account was reported to Experian in violation of the FDCPA, the FCRA, and an FTC staff opinion letter which clearly state that a collection agency may not report an account to the credit reporting agencies during the pendency of its verification of the account to the debtor, if the debtor has so requested.

IX

On or around March 5th, 2002., this account was reported to TransUnion in violation of the FDCPA, the FCRA, and an FTC staff opinion letter which clearly states that a collection agency may not report an account to the credit reporting agencies during the pendency of its verification of the account to the debtor, if the debtor has so requested.

X

On or around March 5th, 2002, this account was reported to Equifax in violation of the FDCPA, the FCRA, and an FTC staff opinion letter which clearly states that a collection agency may not report an account to the credit reporting agencies during the pendency of its verification of the account to the debtor, if the debtor has so requested.

XI

On March 9th, 2002, Plaintiff received a printout of the original creditors terms of service (TOS) as well as a printout of what appeared to be the last statement from the original creditor. The plaintiff specifically asked for the original contract bearing the plaintiff's signature, as well as the Defendant's right to collect on this debt.

XII

Because of the Defendant's blatant disregard for the Plaintiff's rights as allowed by the FDCPA and FCRA, the Plaintiff has been denied $8,000 in credit with Plaintiff's current creditor. (Exhibit E and F). The Defendant has also hampered the Plaintiff's ability to obtain a mortgage.

XII

These actions on the part of Defendant demonstrate a willful disregard for federal law and constitute a blatant attempt to injure or ruin the credit rating of Plaintiff since Defendant has demonstrated an inability to validate the alleged debt and subsequently attempted to coerce payment.

Wherefore PLAINTIFF prays for the following relief:

<State the relief you are seeking. Be sure to include actual, statutory and punitive damages, as in the following sample.>
Plaintiff requests judgment in the amount of $1,000 plus accrued court costs plus permanent removal of all Defendant's collection account trade lines from Plaintiff's files with the four national credit reporting agencies (Equifax, Experian, TransUnion and Innovis).

PLAINTIFF further prays for the following relief:

- For award of court costs and incurred herein.
- For prejudgment and post judgment interest.
- For such other and further relief deemed just by the court

APPENDIX 9 – FTC OPINION LETTERS

The Cass-Lefevre letter

Opinion letter #1: Regarding whether or not a collection agency can report your listing to a CRA if they have not validated the debt.

UNITED STATES OF AMERICA
FEDERAL TRADE COMMISSION
WASHINGTON, D.C. 20580

Federal Trade Commission

December 23, 1997

Robert G. Cass
Compliance Counsel
Commercial Financial Services, Inc.
2448 E. 81st Street, Suite 5500
Tulsa, OK 74137-4248

Dear Mr. Cass:

Mr. Medine has asked me to reply to your letter of October 28, 1997, concerning the circumstances under which a debt collector may report a "charged-off debt" to a consumer reporting agency under the enclosed Fair Debt Collection Practices Act. In that letter, you pose four questions, which I set out below with our answers.

I. "Is it permissible under the FDCPA for a debt collector to report charged-off debts to a consumer reporting agency during the term of the 30-day validation period detailed in Section 1692g?" Yes. As stated in the Commission's Staff Commentary on the FDCPA (copy enclosed), a debt collector may accurately report a debt to a consumer reporting agency within the thirty day validation period (p. 50103). We do not regard the action of reporting a debt to a consumer reporting agency as inconsistent with the consumer's dispute or verification rights under § 1692g.

II. "Is it permissible under the FDCPA for a debt collector to report, or continue to report, a consumer's charged-off debt to a consumer reporting agency after the debt collector has received, but not responded to, a consumer's written dispute during the 30-day validation period detailed in § 1692g?" As you know, Section 1692g(b) requires the debt collector to cease collection of the debt at issue if a written dispute is received within the 30-day validation period until verification is obtained. Because we believe that reporting a charged-off debt to a consumer reporting agency, particularly at this stage of the collection process, constitutes "collection activity" on the part of the collector, our answer to your question is No. Although the FDCPA is unclear on this point, we believe the reality is that debt collectors use the reporting mechanism as a tool to persuade consumers to pay, just like dunning letters and telephone calls. Of course, if a dispute is received after a debt has been reported to a consumer reporting agency, the debt collector is obligated by Section 1692e(8) to inform the consumer reporting agency of the dispute.

III. "Is it permissible under the FDCPA to cease collection of a debt rather than respond to a written dispute from a consumer received during the 30-day validation period?" Yes. There is nothing in the FDCPA that requires a debt collector to continue collecting a debt after a written dispute is received. Further, there is nothing in the FDCPA that requires a response to a written dispute if the debt collector chooses to abandon its collection effort with respect to the debt at issue. See Smith v. Transworld Systems, Inc., 953 F.2d 1025, 1032 (6th Cir. 1992).

IV. "Would the following action by a debt collector constitute continued collection activity under § 1692g(b): reporting a charged-off consumer debt to a consumer reporting agency as disputed in accordance with § 1692e(8), when the debt collector became aware of the dispute when the consumer sent a written dispute to the debt collector during the 30-day validation period, and no verification of the debt has been provided by the debt collector?" Yes. As stated in our answer to Question II, we view reporting to a consumer reporting agency as a collection activity prohibited by § 1692g(b) after a written dispute is received and no verification has been provided. Again, however, a debt collector must report a dispute received after a debt has been reported under § 1692e(8).

I hope this is responsive to your request.

Sincerely,
John F. LeFevre
Attorney

The Wollman letter

FTC Opinion Letter #2: Sending a computerized print out of a debt does not constitute debt validation.

Jeffrey S. Wollman
Vice President and Controller
Retrieval Masters Creditors Bureau, Inc.
1261 Broadway
New York, New York 10001

Dear Mr. Wollman:

This is in response to your letter of February 9, 1993 to David Medine regarding the type of verification required by Section 809(b) of the Fair Debt Collection Practices Act. You ask whether a collection agency for a medical provider will fulfill the requirements of that Section if it produces "an itemized statement of services rendered to a patient on its own computer from information provided by the medical institution . . ." in response to a request for verification of the debt. You also ask who is responsible for mailing the verification to the consumer.

The statute requires that the debt collector obtain verification of the debt and mail it to the consumer (emphasis mine). Because one of the principal purposes of this Section is to help consumers who have been misidentified by the debt collector or who dispute the amount of the debt, it is important that the verification of the identity of the consumer and the amount of the debt be obtained directly from the creditor. Mere itemization of what the debt collector already has does not accomplish this purpose. As stated above, the statute requires the debt collector, not the creditor, to mail the verification to the consumer.

Your interest in writing is appreciated. Please be aware that since this is only the opinion of Commission staff, the Commission itself is not bound by it.

Sincerely,

John F. LeFevre
Attorney
Division of Credit Practices

APPENDIX 10-BUDGET WORKSHEET

SIMPLE BUDGETING

	Jan	Feb	Mar	Apr	May	Jun	Jul	Aug	Sept	Oct	Nov	Dec
INCOME												
Pay												
Interest												
TOTAL INCOME	$0	$0	$0	$0	$0	$0	$0	$0	$0	$0	$0	$0
EXPENSES												
Savings												
Food												
Rent/ Mortgage												
Transport												
Clothes												
Bills												
Entertain												
TOTAL EXPENSES	$0	$0	$0	$0	$0	$0	$0	$0	$0	$0	$0	$0
CASH OVER/(SHORT)	$0	$0	$0	$0	$0	$0	$0	$0	$0	$0	$0	$0

INDEX

About the Author

Having survived and flourished after her own unfortunate bankruptcy, Welsh turned her personal experience into the widely respected and well-visited creditinfocenter.com website. A web designer by trade, with a background in the mortgage loan industry and an insatiable appetite for the facts, Welsh has grown her website to more than 500 pages of up-to-date credit information. *Good Credit is Sexy* was a natural extension, in a format that is easier to cozy up to in bed. Welsh designs and writes from her home in Scottsdale, Arizona.